InuYasha

犬夜叉

Ani-Manga Vol. 23

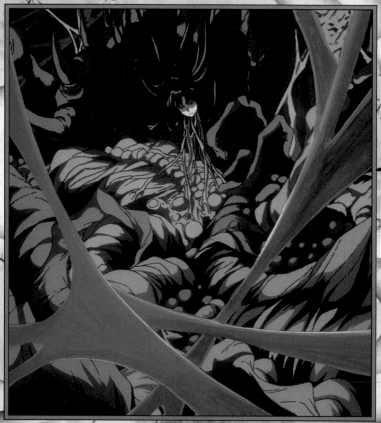

CREATED BY
RUMIKO TAKAHASHI

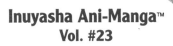

Inuyasha Ani-Manga™
Vol. #23

Created by
Rumiko Takahashi

Translation based on the VIZ anime TV series
Translation Assistance/Katy Bridges
Lettering & Editorial Assistance/John Clark
Cover Design & Graphics/Hidemi Sahara
Editor/Ian Robertson

Editor in Chief, Books/Alvin Lu
Editor in Chief, Magazines/Marc Weidenbaum
VP of Publishing Licensing/Rika Inouye
VP of Sales/Gonzalo Ferreyra
Sr. VP of Marketing/Liza Coppola
Publisher/Hyoe Narita

Printed in the U.S.A.

Published by VIZ Media, LLC
P.O. Box 77010
San Francisco, CA 94107

10 9 8 7 6 5 4 3 2 1
First printing, October 2007

www.viz.com
store.viz.com

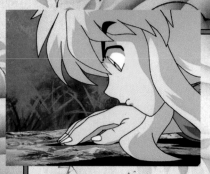

Story thus far

Kagome's mundane teenage existence was turned upside down when she was transported into a mythical version of Japan's medieval past! Kagome is the reincarnation of Lady Kikyo, a great warrior and the defender of the Shikon Jewel, or the Jewel of Four Souls. Kikyo was in love with Inuyasha, a dog-like half-demon who wishes to possess the jewel in order to transform himself into a full-fledged demon. But 50 years earlier, the evil shape-shifting Naraku tricked Kikyo and Inuyasha into betraying one another. The betrayal led to Kikyo's death and Inuyasha's imprisonment under a binding spell…and Inuyasha remained trapped by the spell until Kagome appeared in feudal Japan and unwittingly released him!

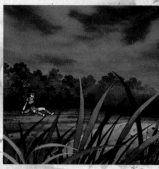

In a skirmish for its possession, the Shikon Jewel accidentally shatters and is strewn across the land. Only Kagome has the power to find the jewel shards, and only Inuyasha has the strength to defeat the demons that now hold them, so the two unlikely partners are bound together in the quest to reclaim all the pieces of the sacred jewel. To prevent Inuyasha from stealing the jewel, Kikyo's sister, Lady Kaede, puts a magical necklace around Inuyasha's neck that allows Kagome to make him "sit" on command. Inuyasha's greatest tool in the fight to recover the sacred jewel shards is his father's sword, the Tetsusaiga, but Inuyasha's half-brother Sesshomaru covets the mighty blade and has tried to steal it more than once.

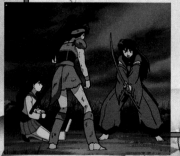

Dark Priestess Tsubaki was once Kikyo's rival to be keeper of the sacred Jewel. Now unable to forgive and consumed by her ambition to control the jewel, she uses a shard in her eye to devour demons and gain their power, and Inuyasha is next on her list! Later, Wind Sorceress Kagura plans to escape her evil master Naraku by using jewel shards ripped from Koga's legs!

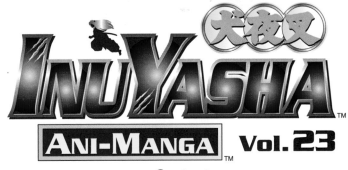

INUYASHA™

ANI-MANGA™ Vol. 23

Contents

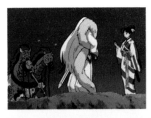
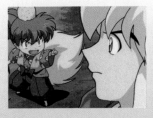
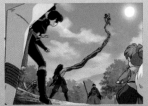

67
The Howling Wind of Betrayal

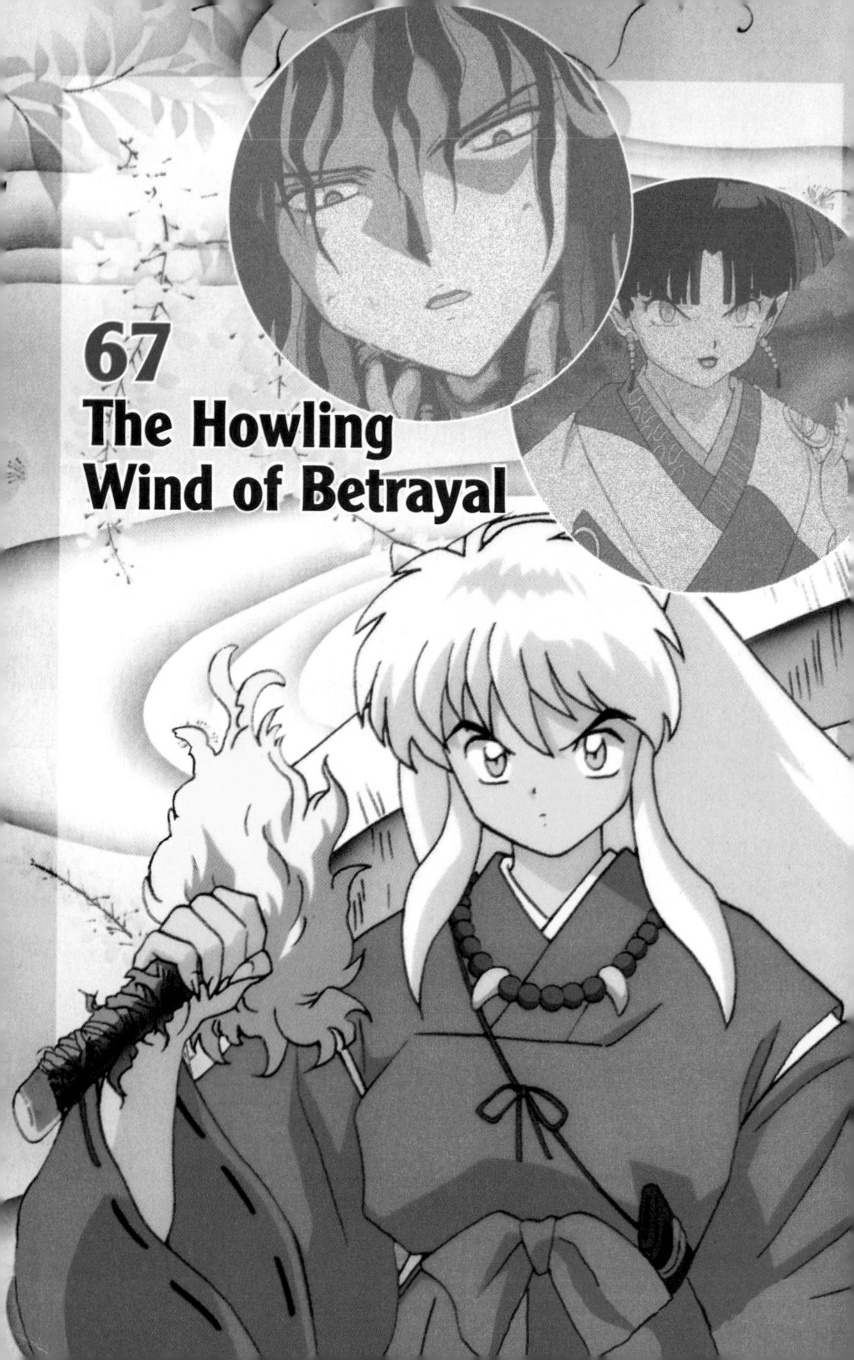

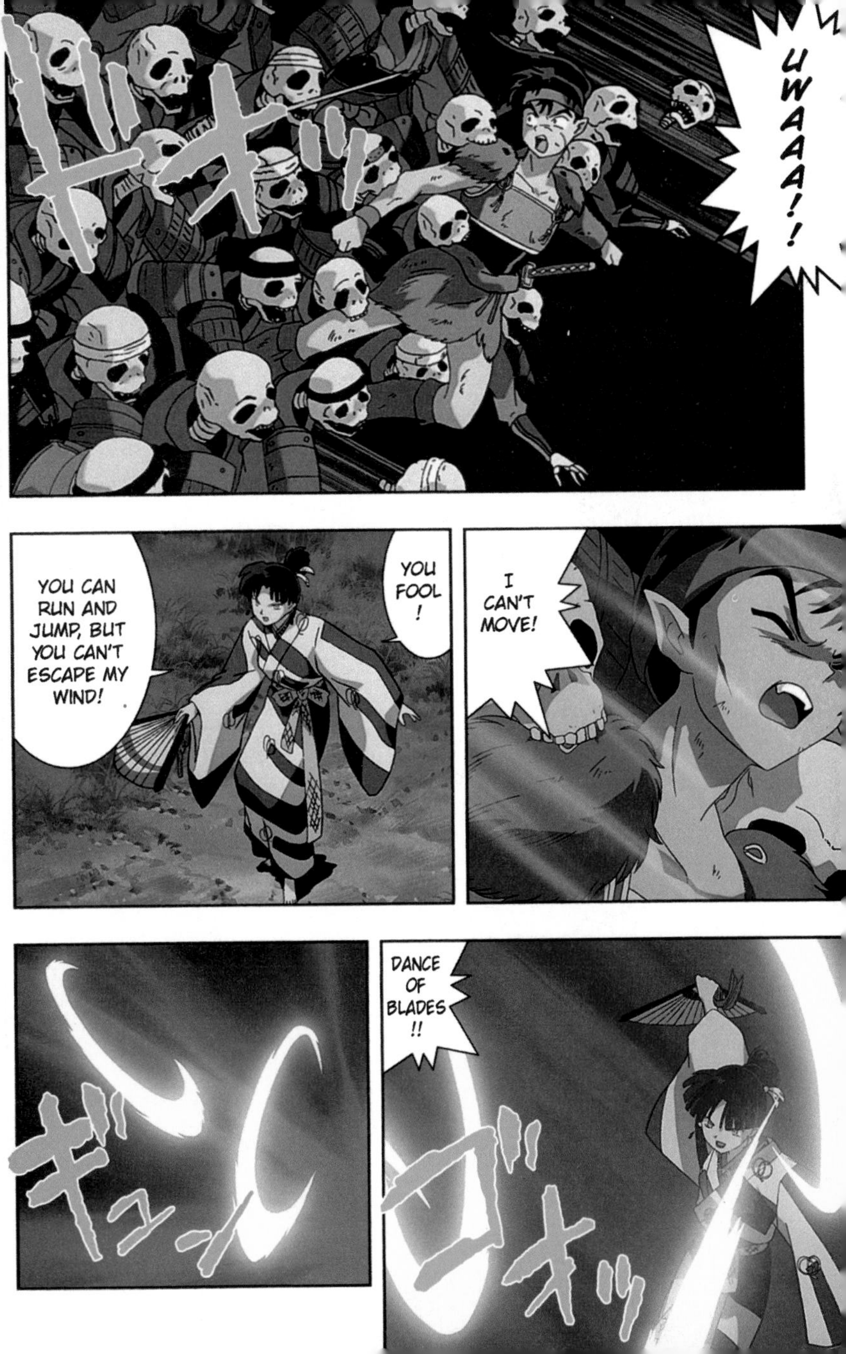

UWAAAA!!
ドオッ
I CAN'T MOVE!
YOU FOOL!
YOU CAN RUN AND JUMP, BUT YOU CAN'T ESCAPE MY WIND!
DANCE OF BLADES!!
ゴオッ
ギューン

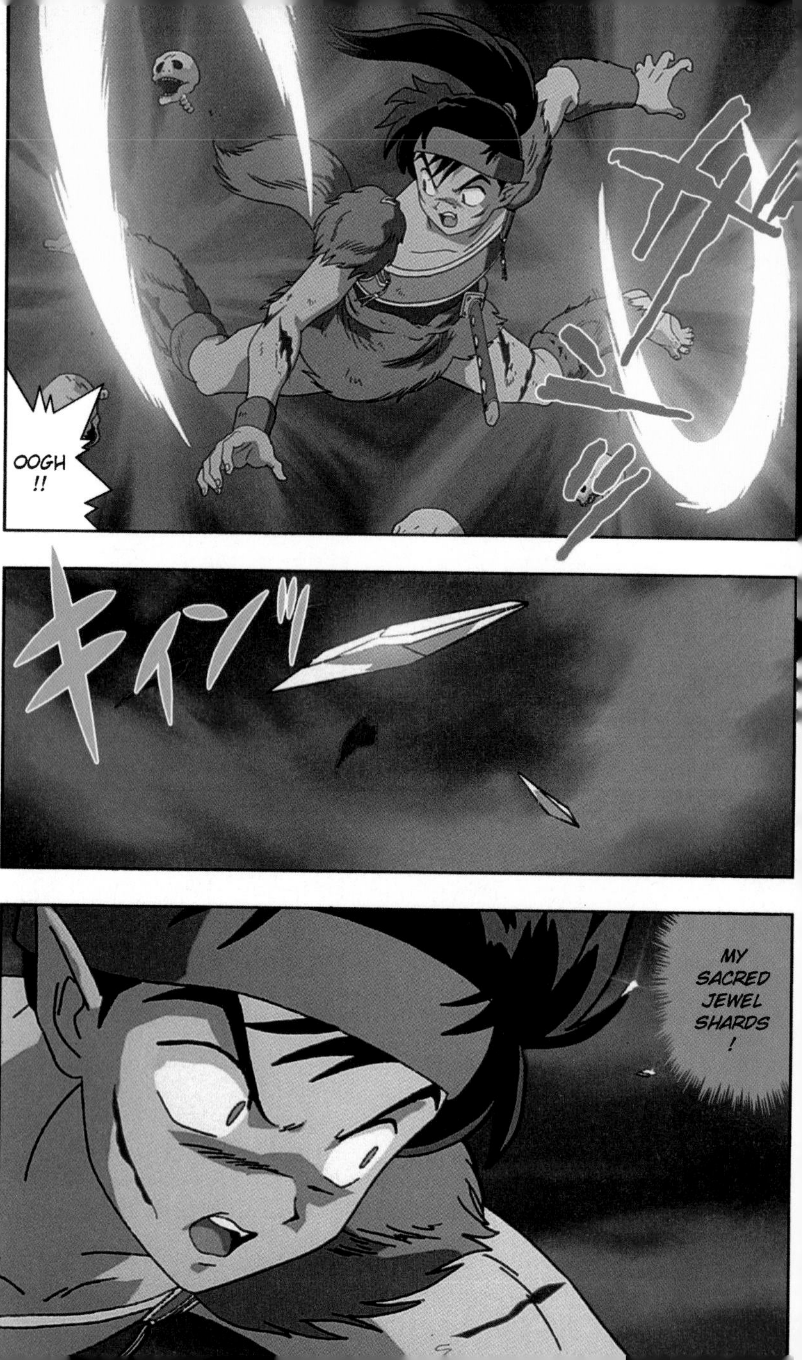
OOGH !!
MY SACRED JEWEL SHARDS !

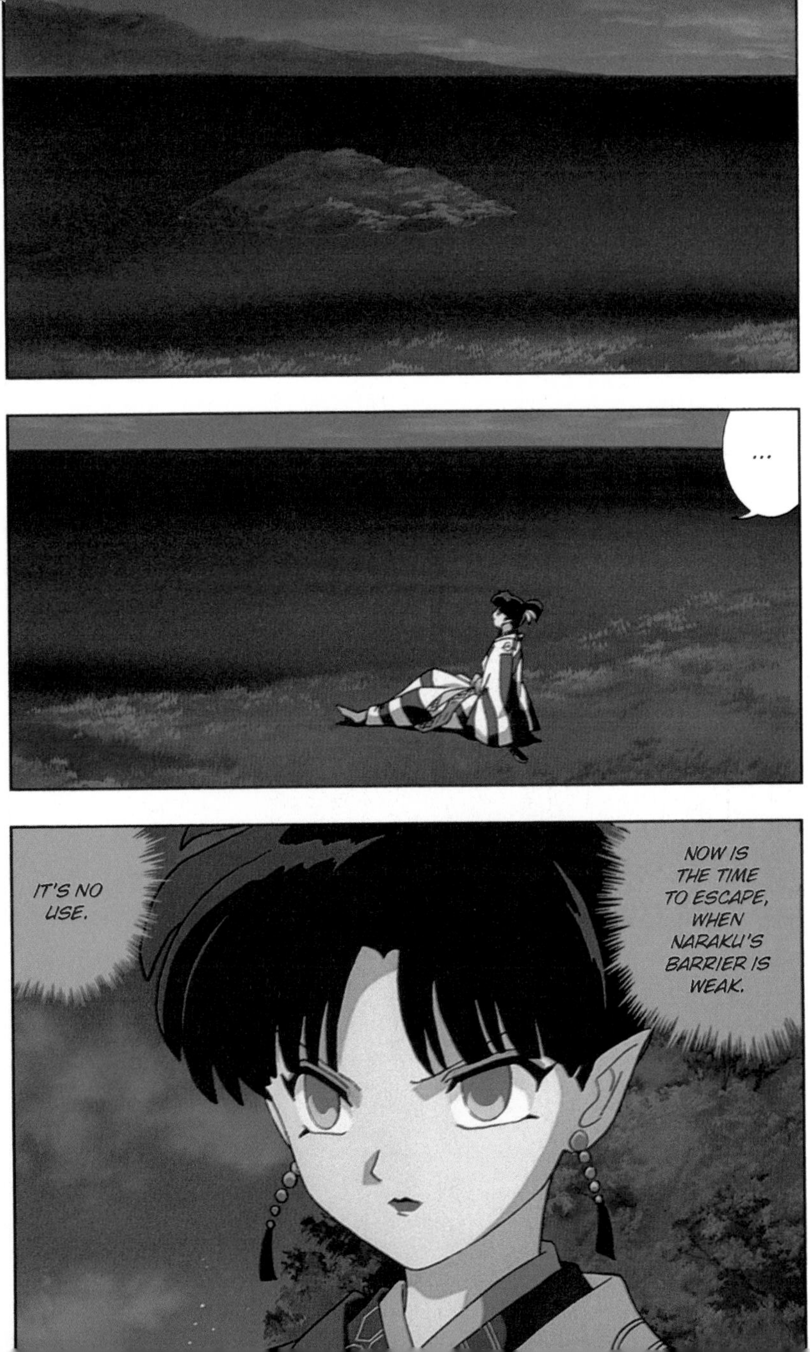
...
NOW IS THE TIME TO ESCAPE, WHEN NARAKU'S BARRIER IS WEAK.
IT'S NO USE.

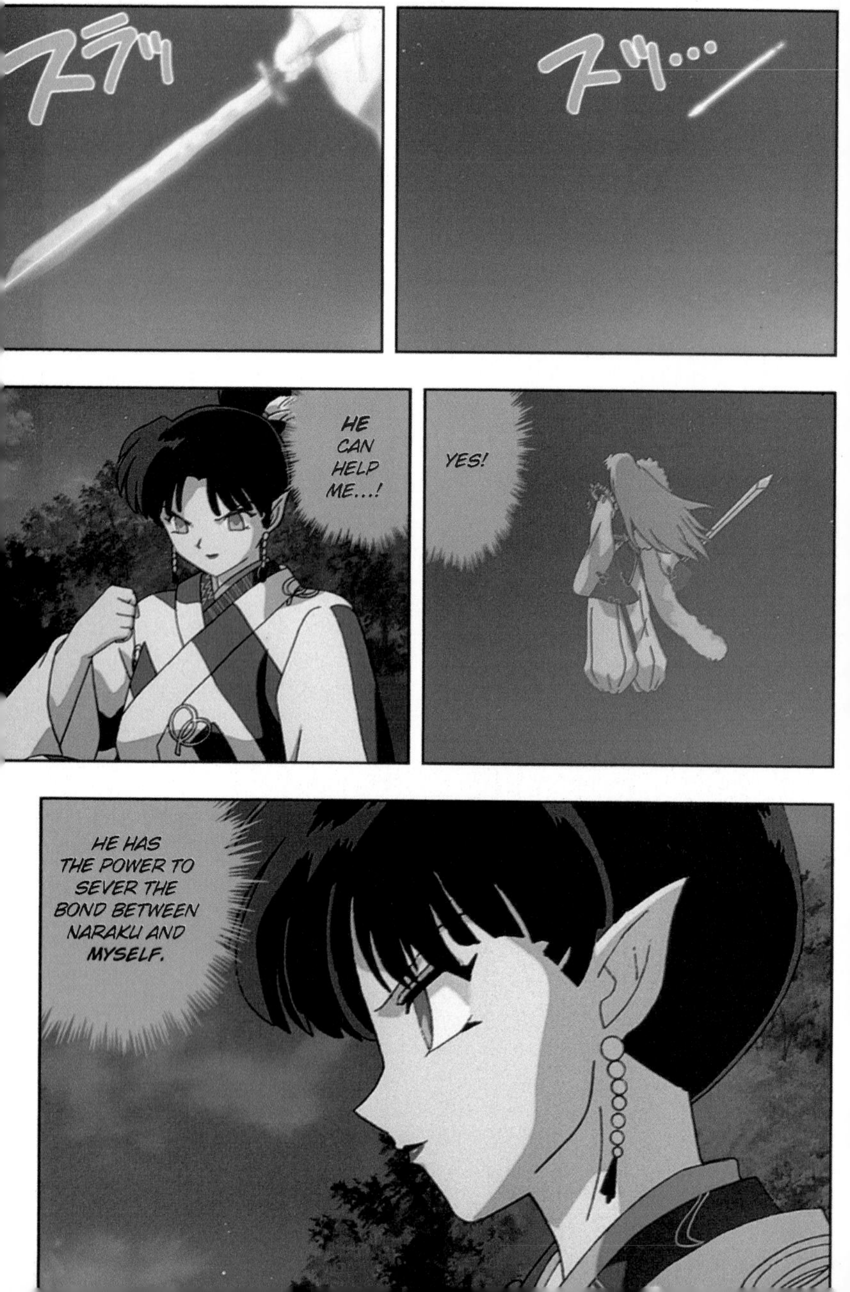
スッ…
スラッ
YES!
HE CAN HELP ME...!
HE HAS THE POWER TO SEVER THE BOND BETWEEN NARAKU AND MYSELF.

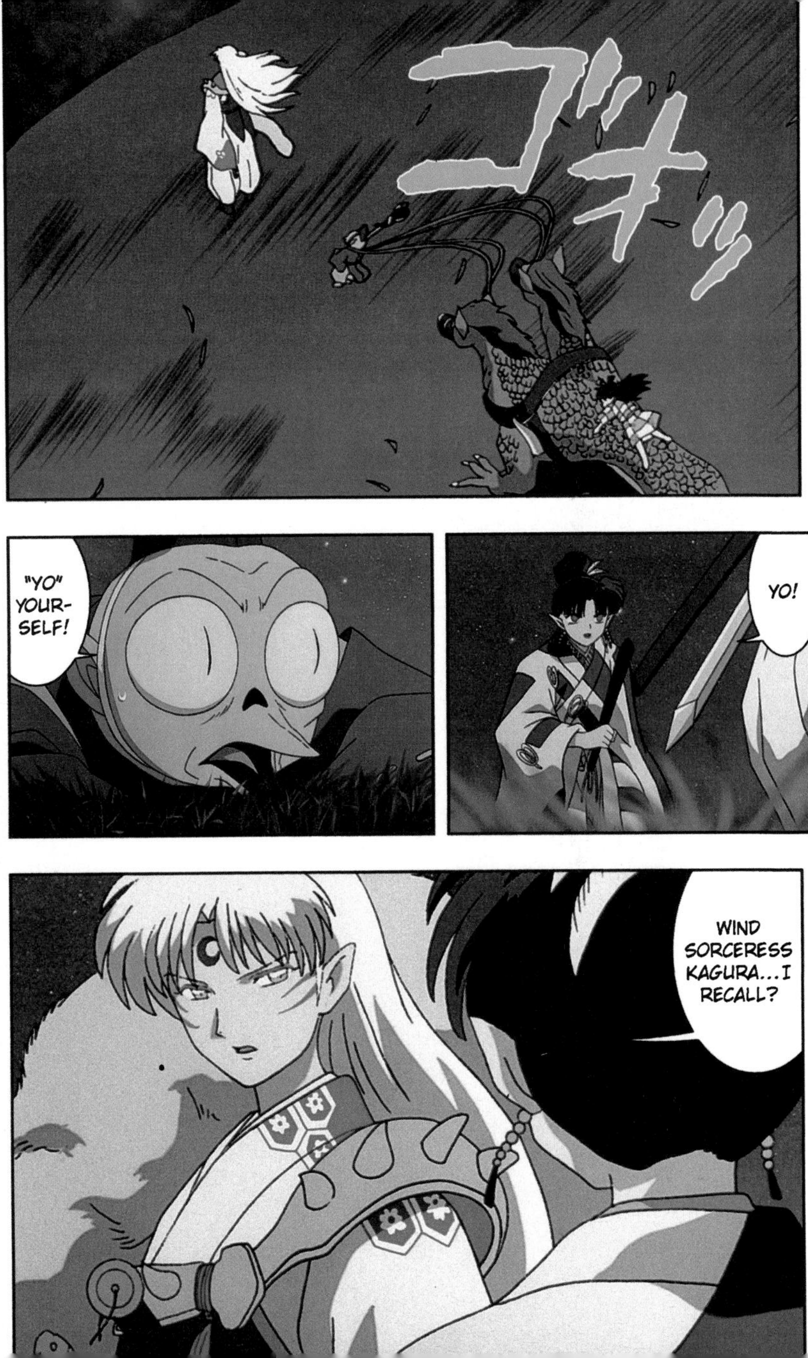
ゴキッ
YO!
"YO" YOURSELF!
WIND SORCERESS KAGURA...I RECALL?

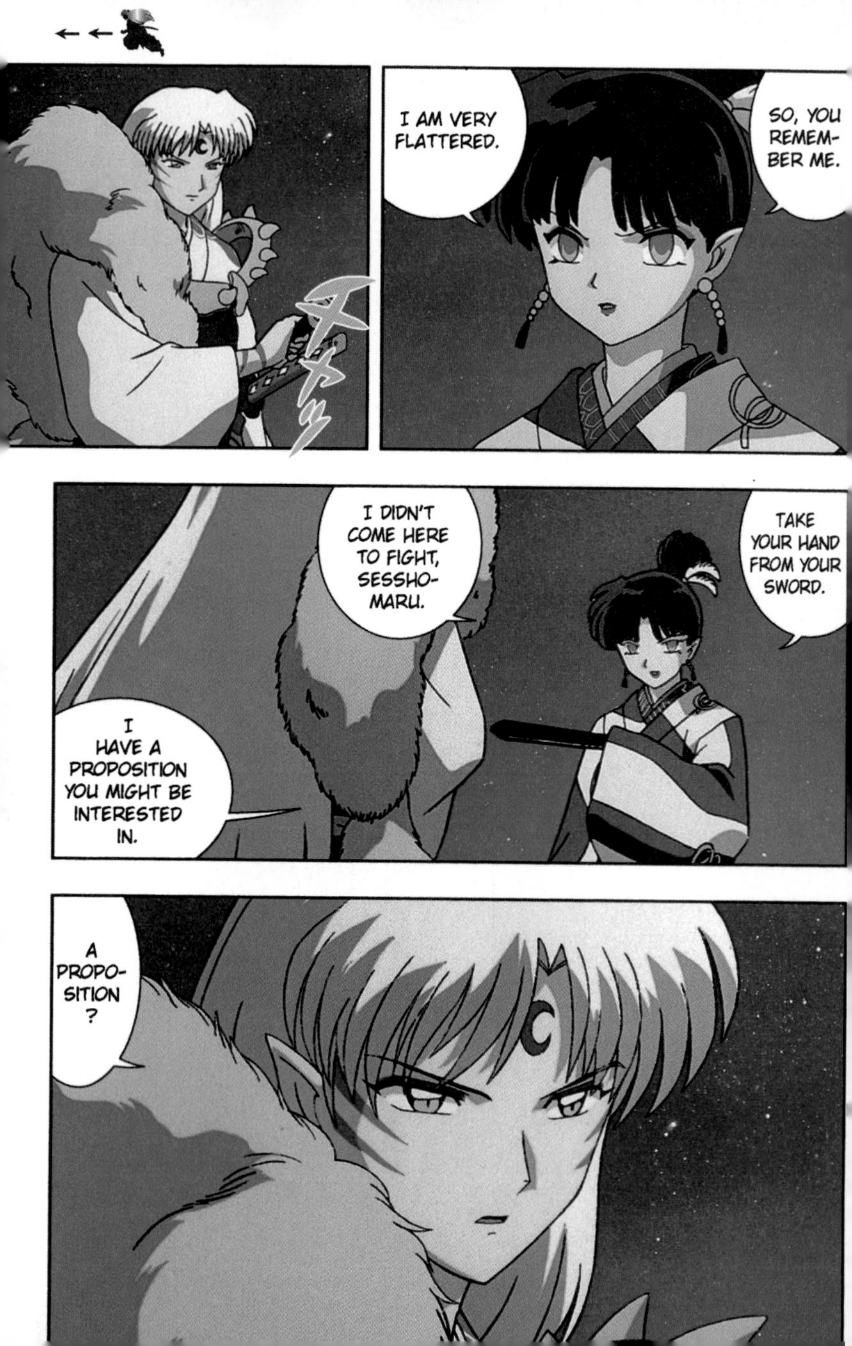
SO, YOU REMEMBER ME.
I AM VERY FLATTERED.
TAKE YOUR HAND FROM YOUR SWORD.
I DIDN'T COME HERE TO FIGHT, SESSHOMARU.
I HAVE A PROPOSITION YOU MIGHT BE INTERESTED IN.
A PROPOSITION?

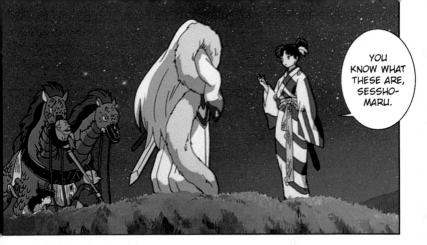

YOU KNOW WHAT THESE ARE, SESSHO-MARU.

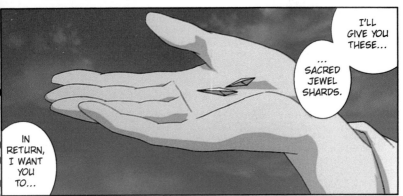

I'LL GIVE YOU THESE...

...SACRED JEWEL SHARDS.

IN RETURN, I WANT YOU TO...

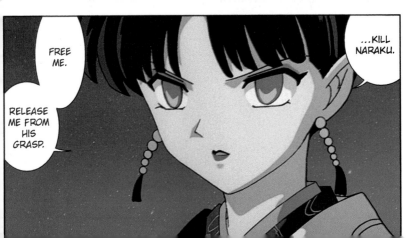

FREE ME.

RELEASE ME FROM HIS GRASP.

...KILL NARAKU.

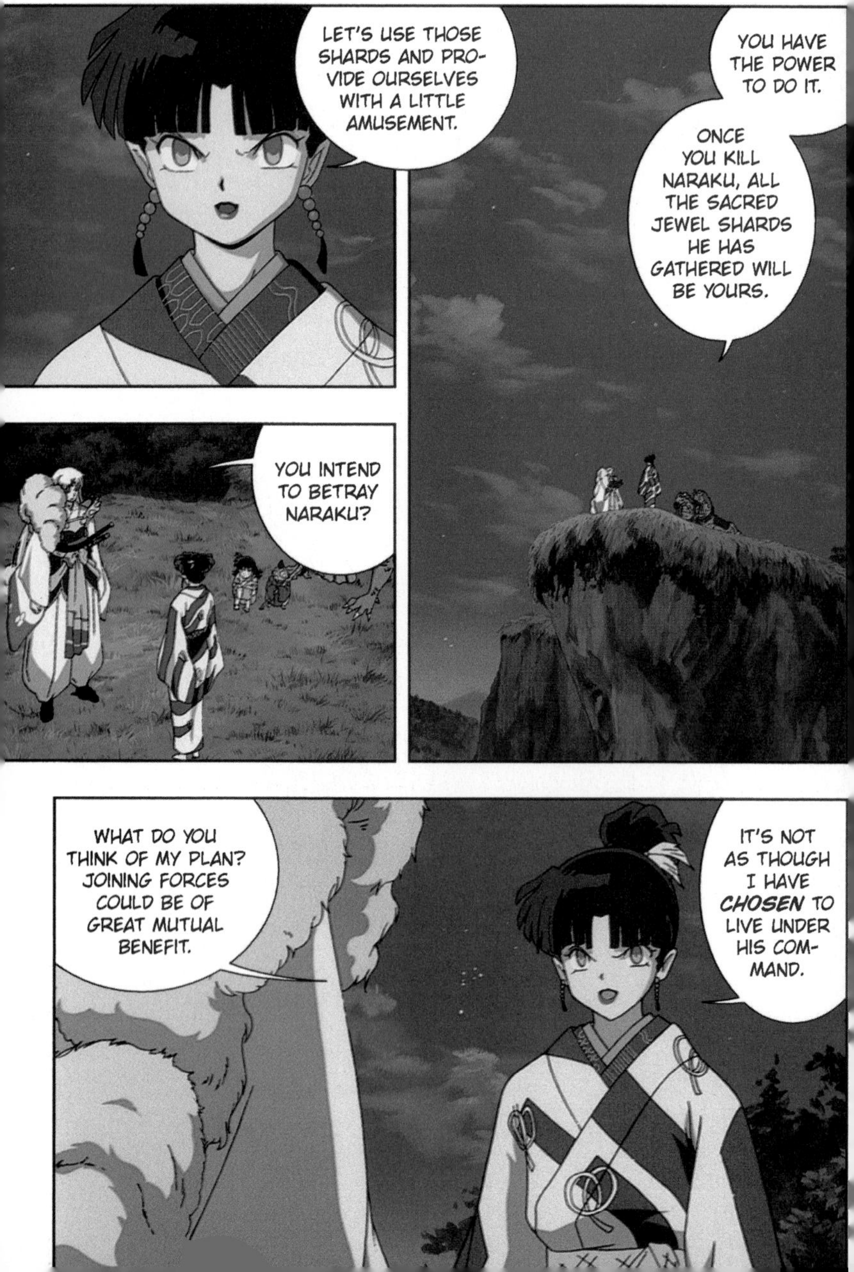
YOU HAVE THE POWER TO DO IT.
ONCE YOU KILL NARAKU, ALL THE SACRED JEWEL SHARDS HE HAS GATHERED WILL BE YOURS.
LET'S USE THOSE SHARDS AND PRO-VIDE OURSELVES WITH A LITTLE AMUSEMENT.
YOU INTEND TO BETRAY NARAKU?
IT'S NOT AS THOUGH I HAVE *CHOSEN* TO LIVE UNDER HIS COM-MAND.
WHAT DO YOU THINK OF MY PLAN? JOINING FORCES COULD BE OF GREAT MUTUAL BENEFIT.

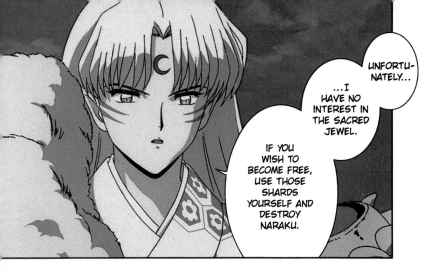

UNFORTU-NATELY...

...I HAVE NO INTEREST IN THE SACRED JEWEL.

IF YOU WISH TO BECOME FREE, USE THOSE SHARDS YOURSELF AND DESTROY NARAKU.

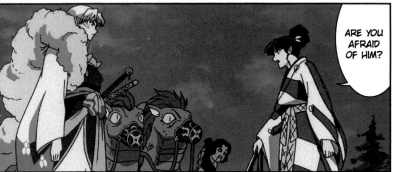

ARE YOU AFRAID OF HIM?

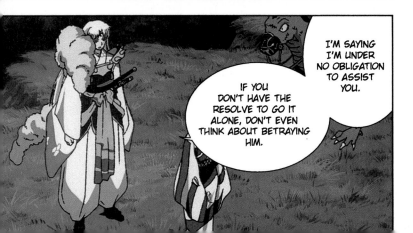

I'M SAYING I'M UNDER NO OBLIGATION TO ASSIST YOU.

IF YOU DON'T HAVE THE RESOLVE TO GO IT ALONE, DON'T EVEN THINK ABOUT BETRAYING HIM.

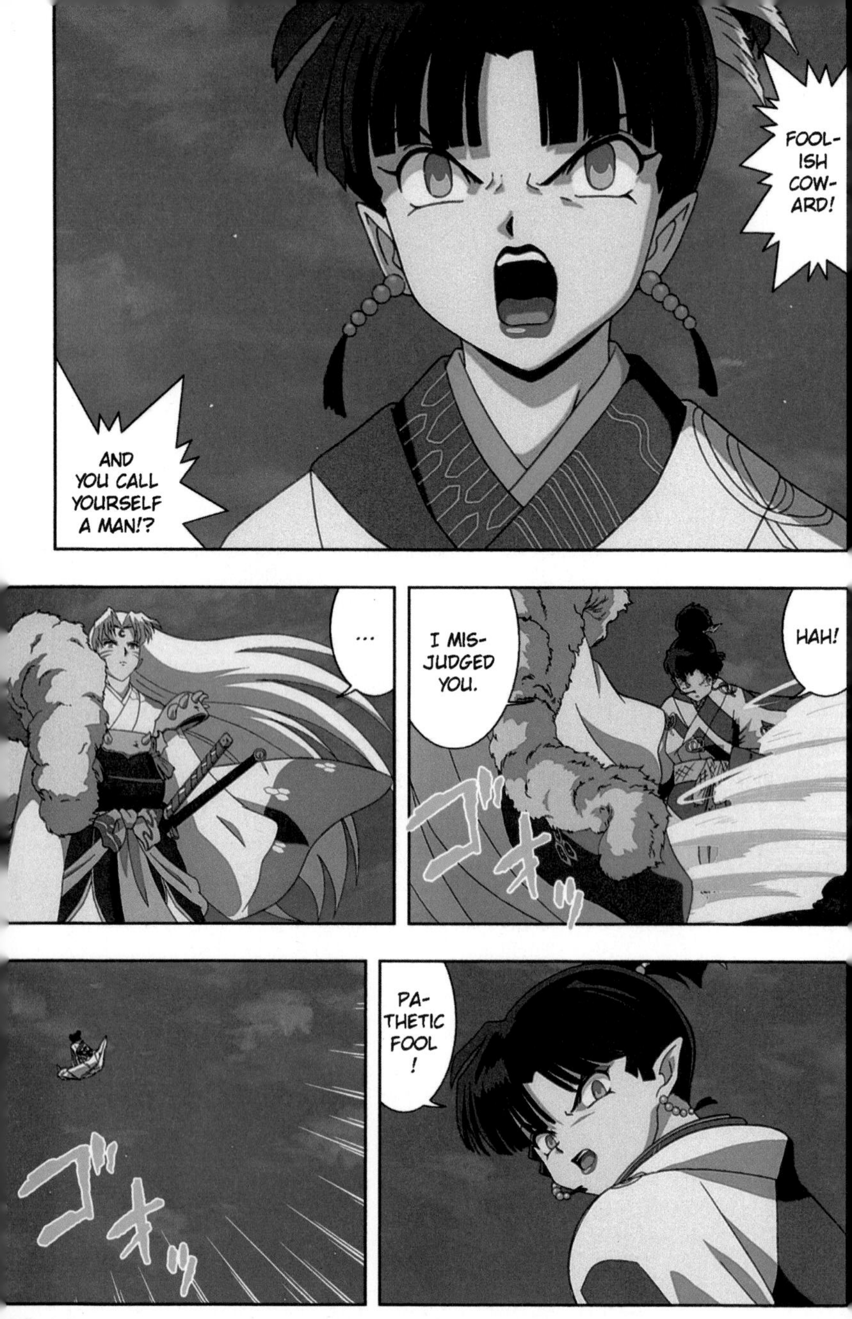
FOOL-ISH COW-ARD!
AND YOU CALL YOURSELF A MAN!?
HAH!
I MIS-JUDGED YOU.
ゴォッ
...
PA-THETIC FOOL!
ゴォッ

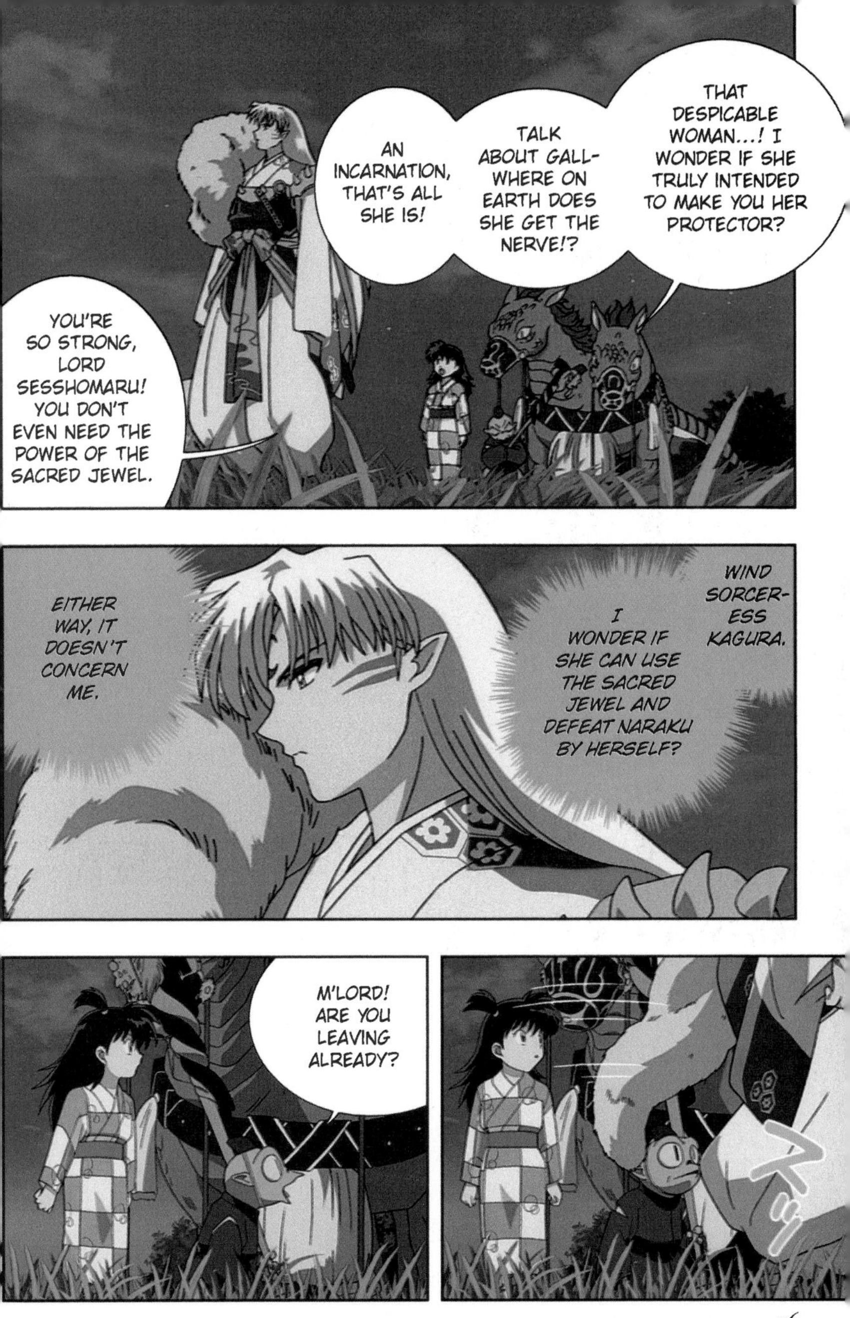
THAT DESPICABLE WOMAN...! I WONDER IF SHE TRULY INTENDED TO MAKE YOU HER PROTECTOR?
TALK ABOUT GALL-WHERE ON EARTH DOES SHE GET THE NERVE!?
AN INCARNATION, THAT'S ALL SHE IS!
YOU'RE SO STRONG, LORD SESSHOMARU! YOU DON'T EVEN NEED THE POWER OF THE SACRED JEWEL.
WIND SORCERESS KAGURA.
I WONDER IF SHE CAN USE THE SACRED JEWEL AND DEFEAT NARAKU BY HERSELF?
EITHER WAY, IT DOESN'T CONCERN ME.
スッ
M'LORD! ARE YOU LEAVING ALREADY?

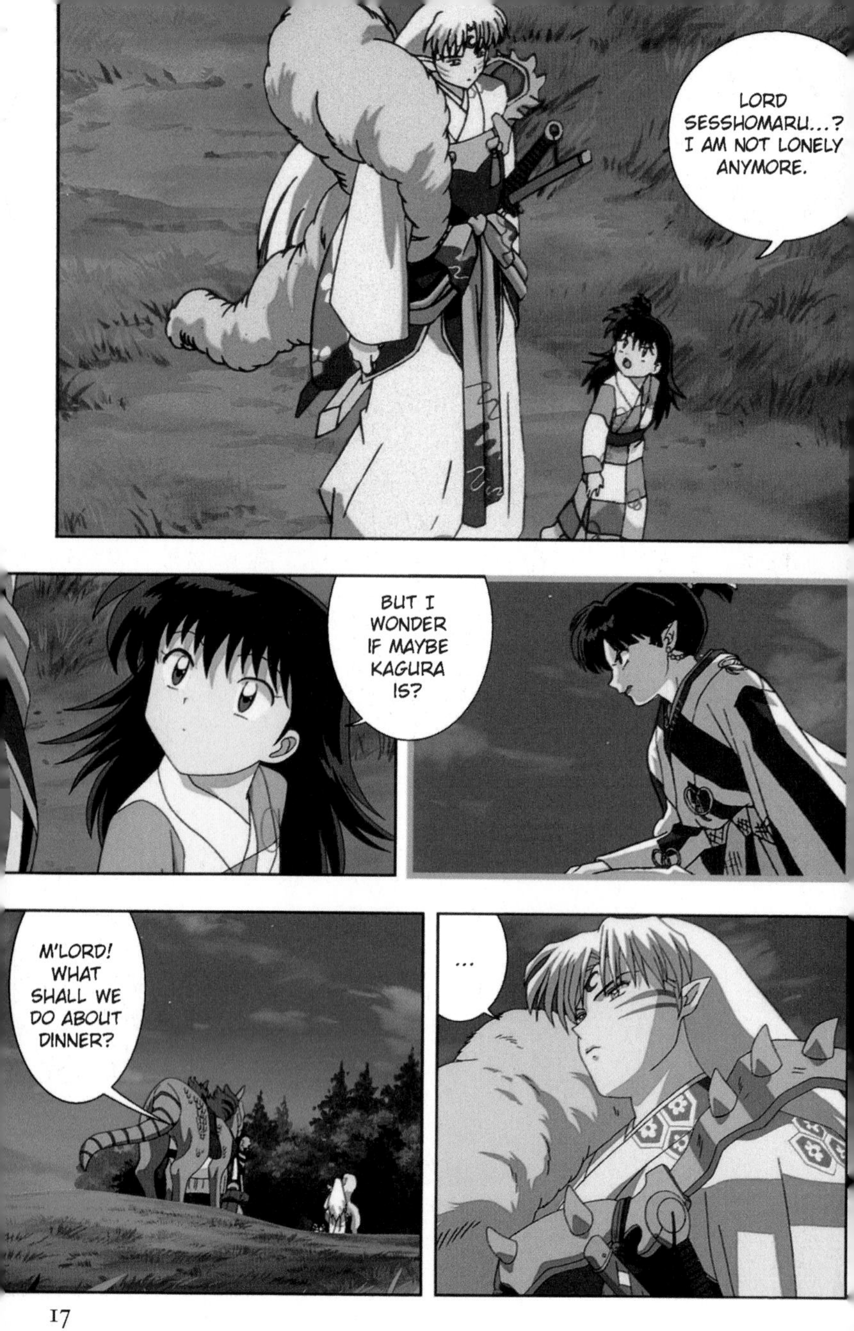
LORD SESSHOMARU...? I AM NOT LONELY ANYMORE.
BUT I WONDER IF MAYBE KAGURA IS?
...
M'LORD! WHAT SHALL WE DO ABOUT DINNER?

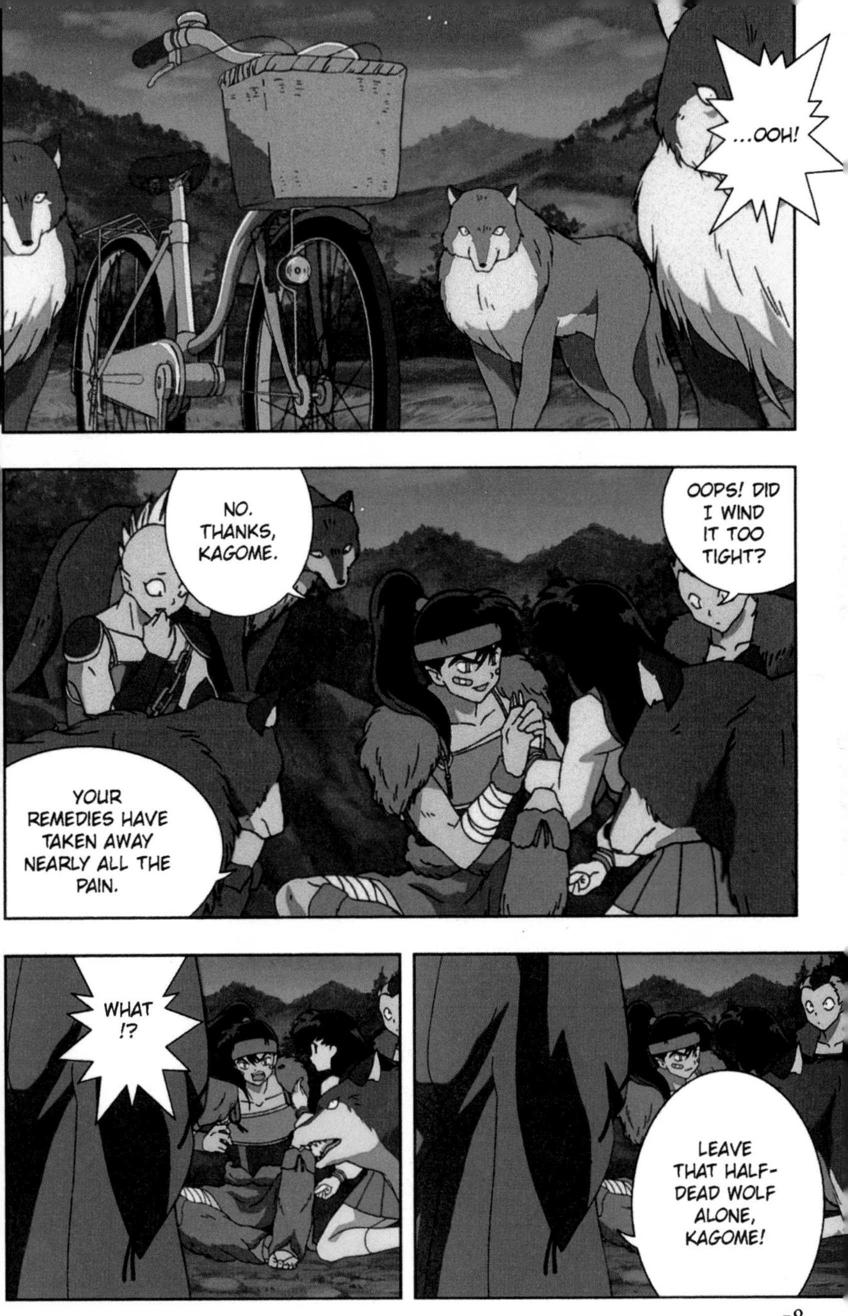
...OOH!
OOPS! DID I WIND IT TOO TIGHT?
NO. THANKS, KAGOME.
YOUR REMEDIES HAVE TAKEN AWAY NEARLY ALL THE PAIN.
LEAVE THAT HALF-DEAD WOLF ALONE, KAGOME!
WHAT !?

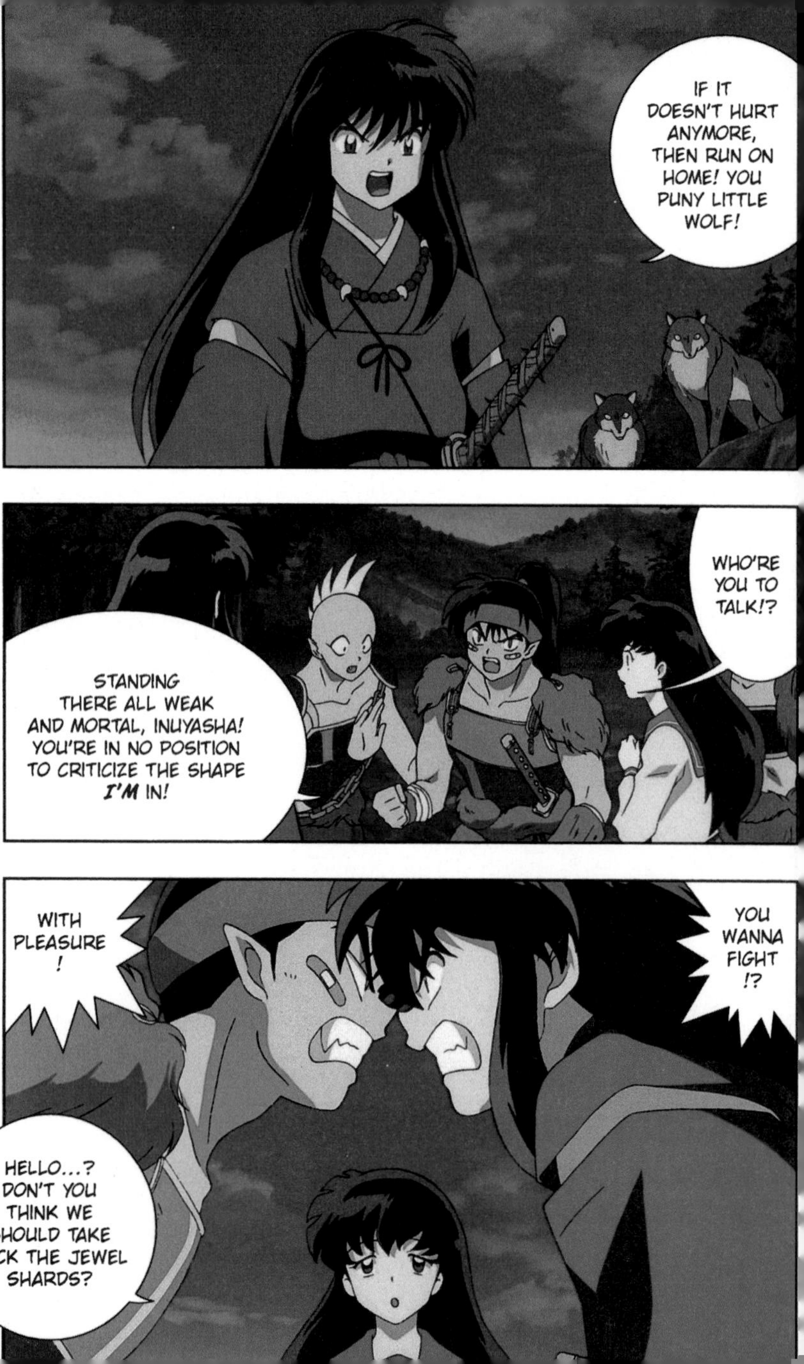
IF IT DOESN'T HURT ANYMORE, THEN RUN ON HOME! YOU PUNY LITTLE WOLF!
WHO'RE YOU TO TALK!?
STANDING THERE ALL WEAK AND MORTAL, INUYASHA! YOU'RE IN NO POSITION TO CRITICIZE THE SHAPE *I'M* IN!
YOU WANNA FIGHT!?
WITH PLEASURE!
HELLO...? DON'T YOU THINK WE SHOULD TAKE BACK THE JEWEL SHARDS?

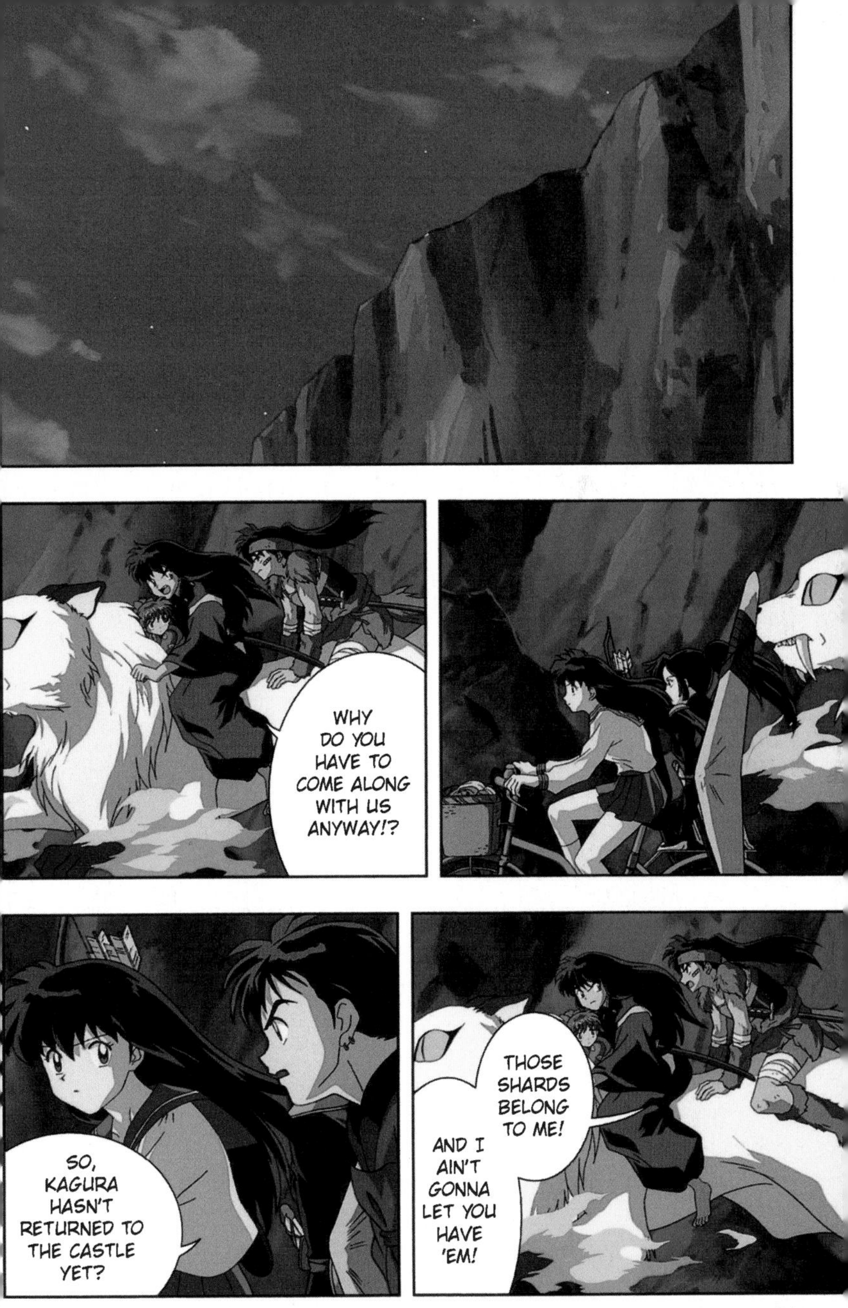
WHY DO YOU HAVE TO COME ALONG WITH US ANYWAY!?
THOSE SHARDS BELONG TO ME!
AND I AIN'T GONNA LET YOU HAVE 'EM!
SO, KAGURA HASN'T RETURNED TO THE CASTLE YET?

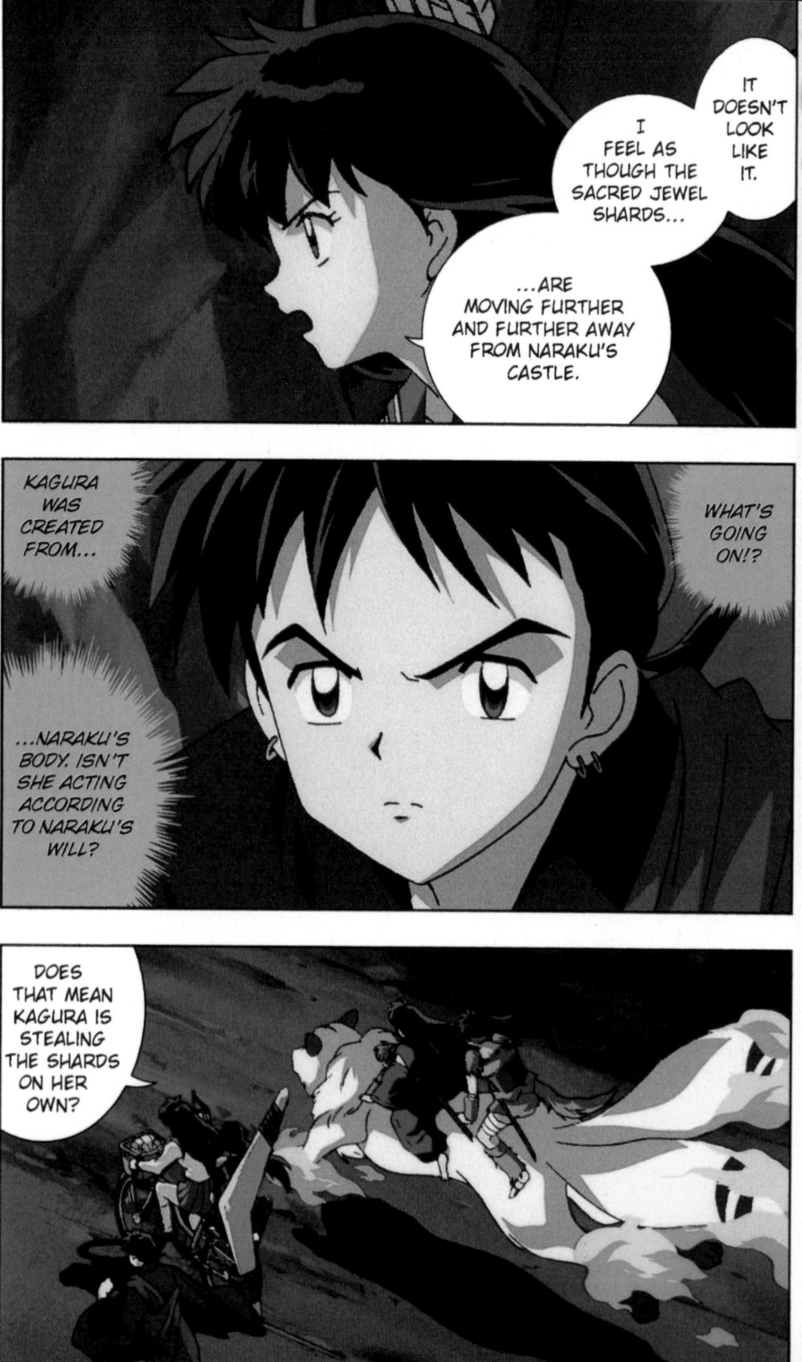
IT DOESN'T LOOK LIKE IT.
I FEEL AS THOUGH THE SACRED JEWEL SHARDS...
...ARE MOVING FURTHER AND FURTHER AWAY FROM NARAKU'S CASTLE.
WHAT'S GOING ON!?
KAGURA WAS CREATED FROM...
...NARAKU'S BODY. ISN'T SHE ACTING ACCORDING TO NARAKU'S WILL?
DOES THAT MEAN KAGURA IS STEALING THE SHARDS ON HER OWN?

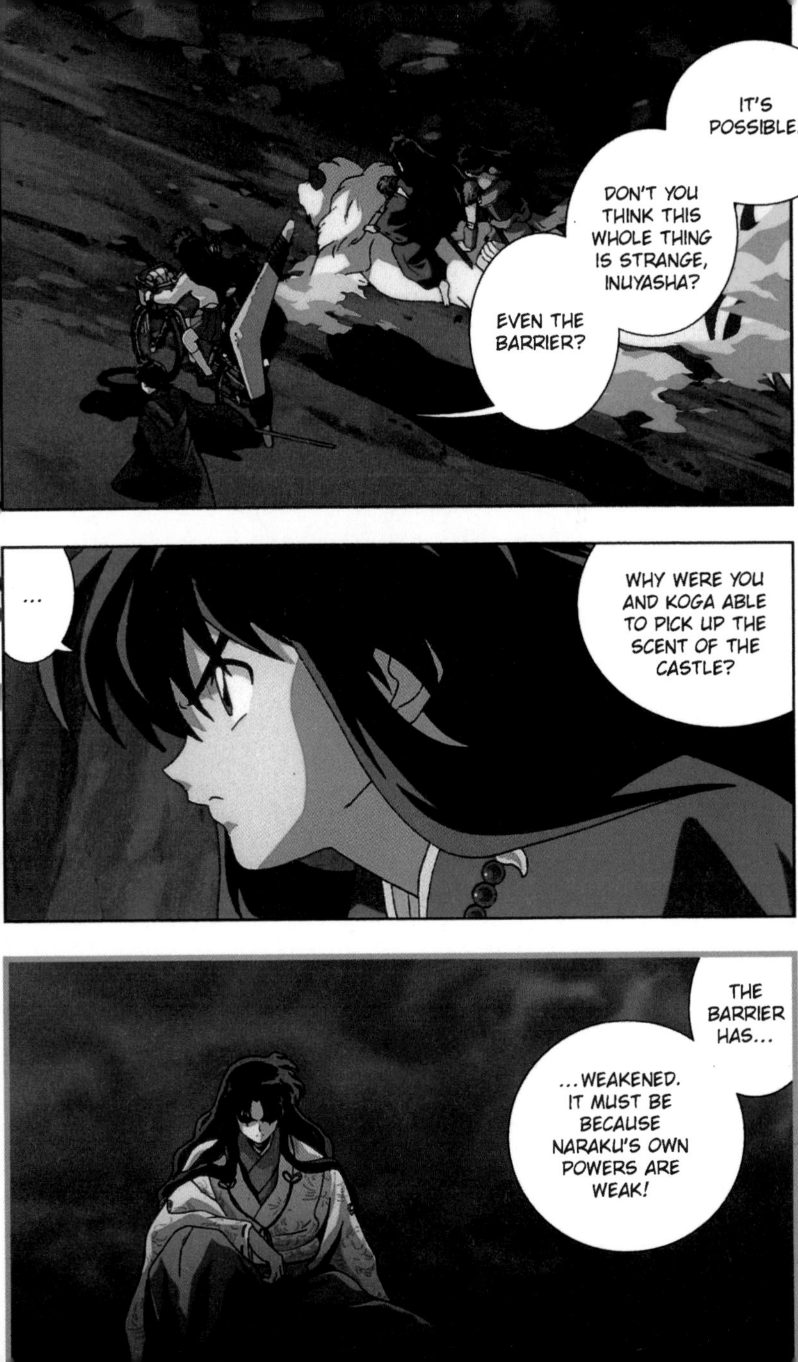
IT'S POSSIBLE.
DON'T YOU THINK THIS WHOLE THING IS STRANGE, INUYASHA?
EVEN THE BARRIER?
WHY WERE YOU AND KOGA ABLE TO PICK UP THE SCENT OF THE CASTLE?
...
THE BARRIER HAS...
...WEAKENED. IT MUST BE BECAUSE NARAKU'S OWN POWERS ARE WEAK!

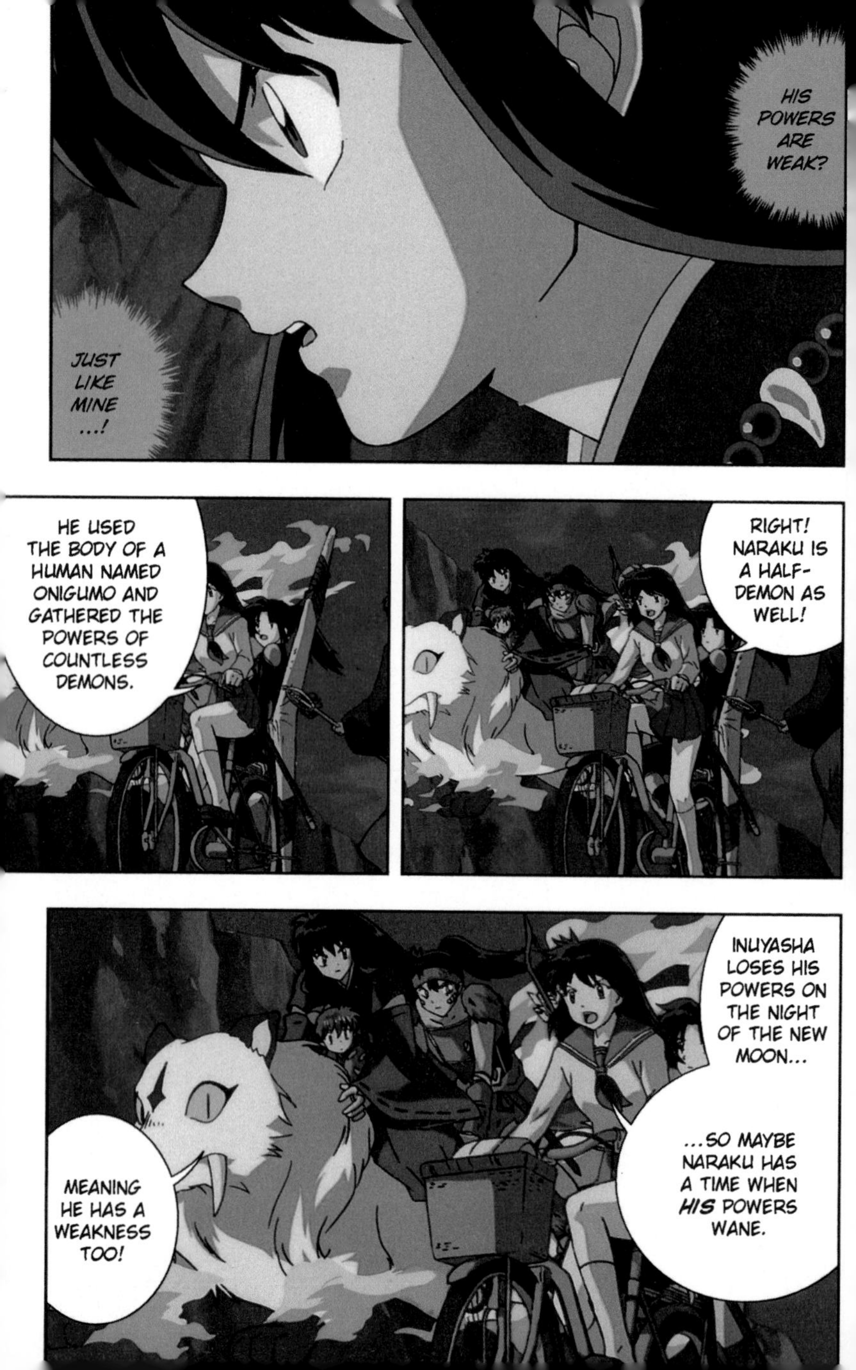
HIS POWERS ARE WEAK?
JUST LIKE MINE ...!
RIGHT! NARAKU IS A HALF-DEMON AS WELL!
HE USED THE BODY OF A HUMAN NAMED ONIGUMO AND GATHERED THE POWERS OF COUNTLESS DEMONS.
INUYASHA LOSES HIS POWERS ON THE NIGHT OF THE NEW MOON...
...SO MAYBE NARAKU HAS A TIME WHEN *HIS* POWERS WANE.
MEANING HE HAS A WEAKNESS TOO!

ドクン
ドクン…

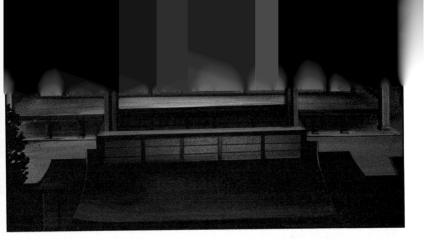

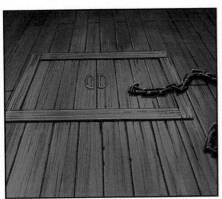

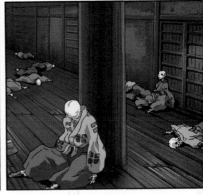

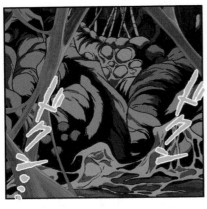

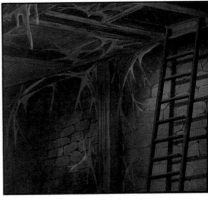

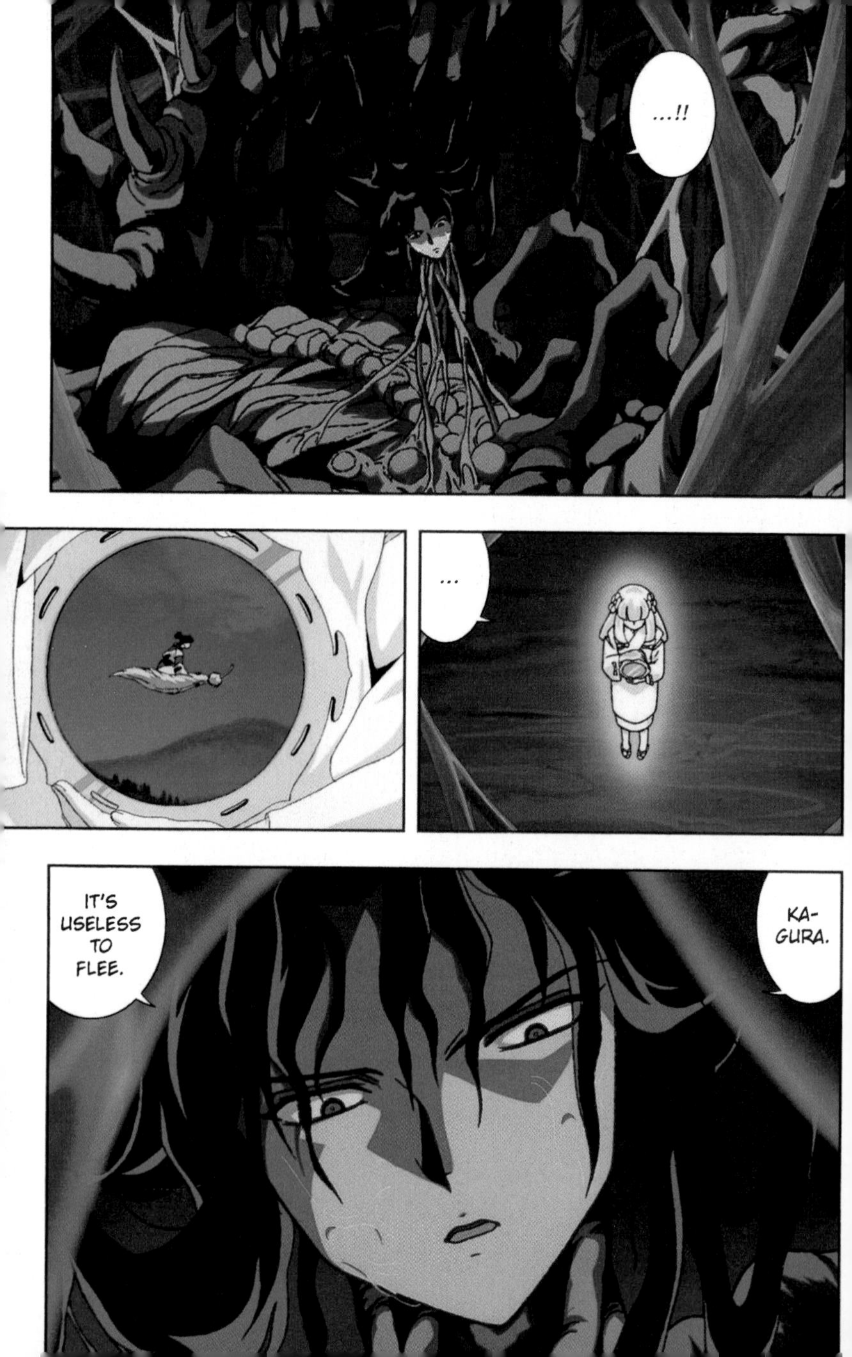
...!!
...
KA-GURA.
IT'S USELESS TO FLEE.

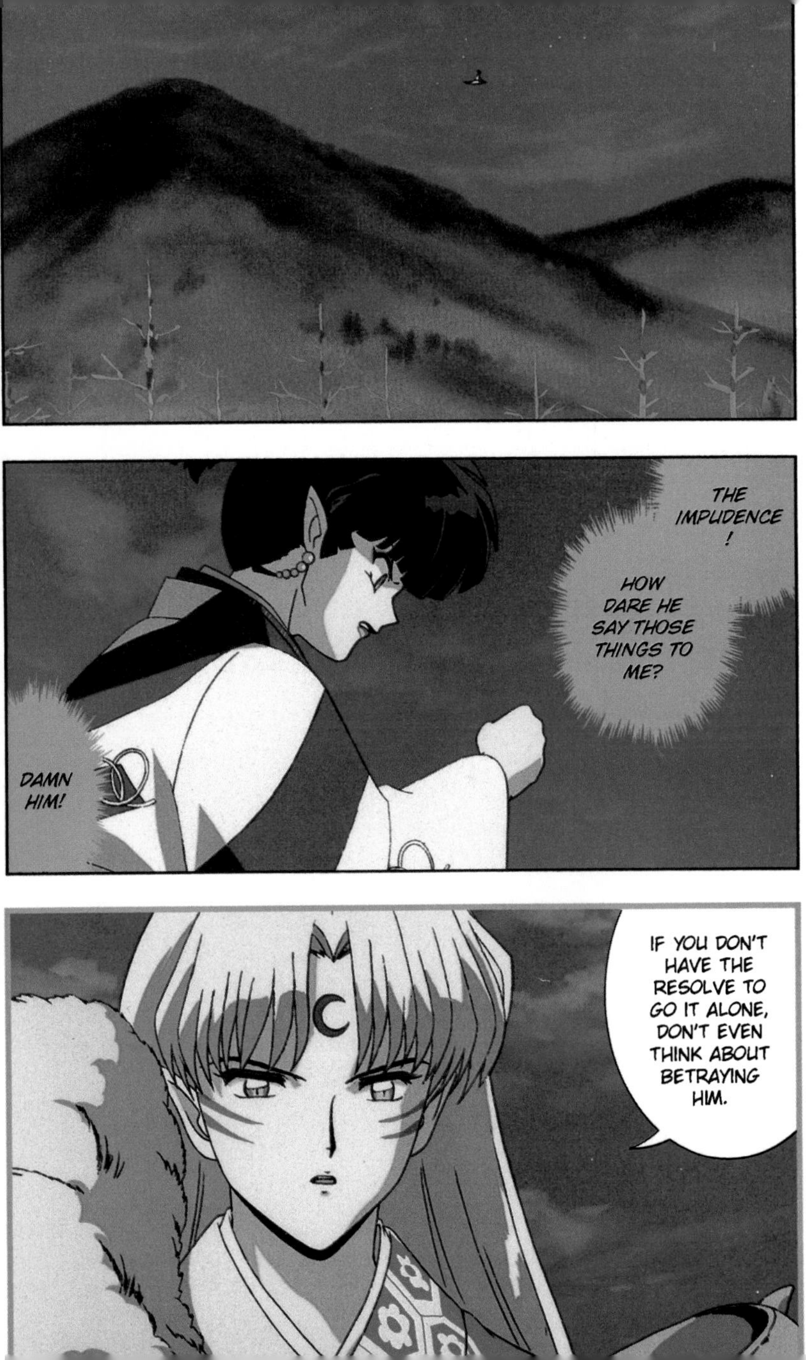
THE IMPUDENCE!
HOW DARE HE SAY THOSE THINGS TO ME?
DAMN HIM!
IF YOU DON'T HAVE THE RESOLVE TO GO IT ALONE, DON'T EVEN THINK ABOUT BETRAYING HIM.

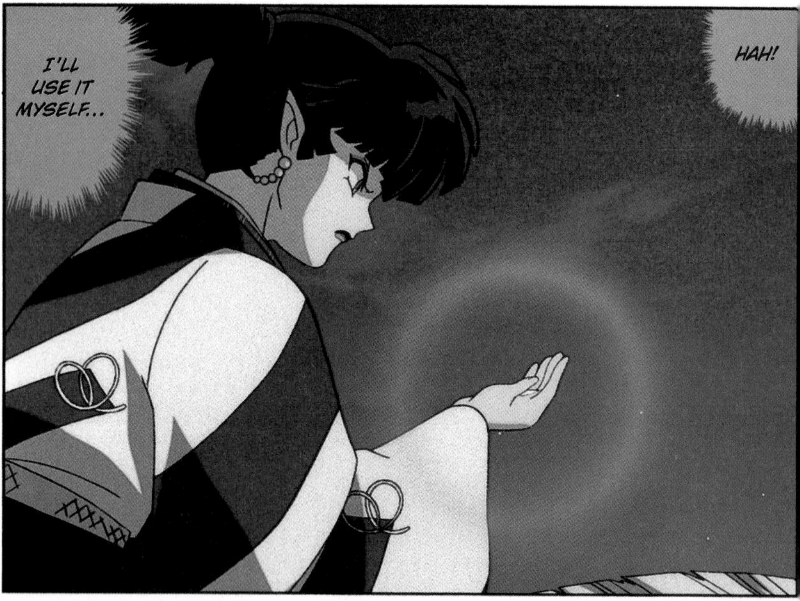
HAH!
I'LL USE IT MYSELF...

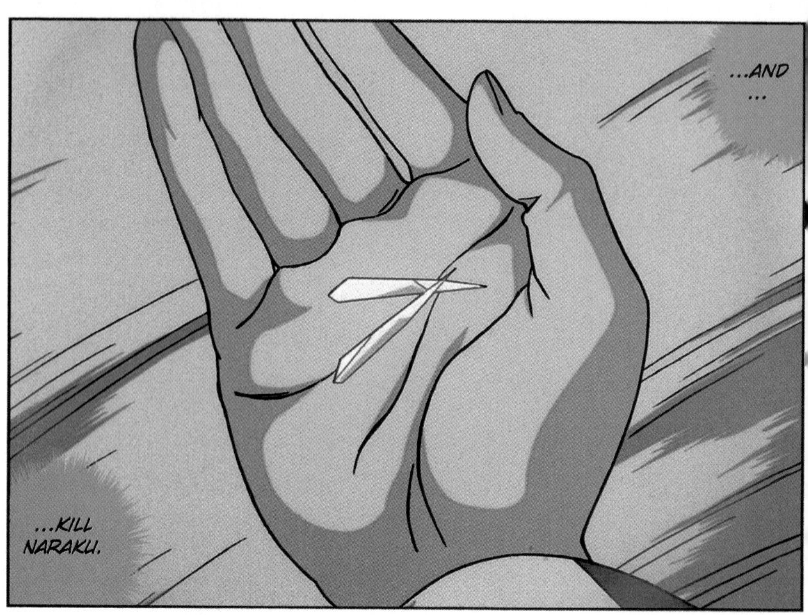
...AND ...
...KILL NARAKU.

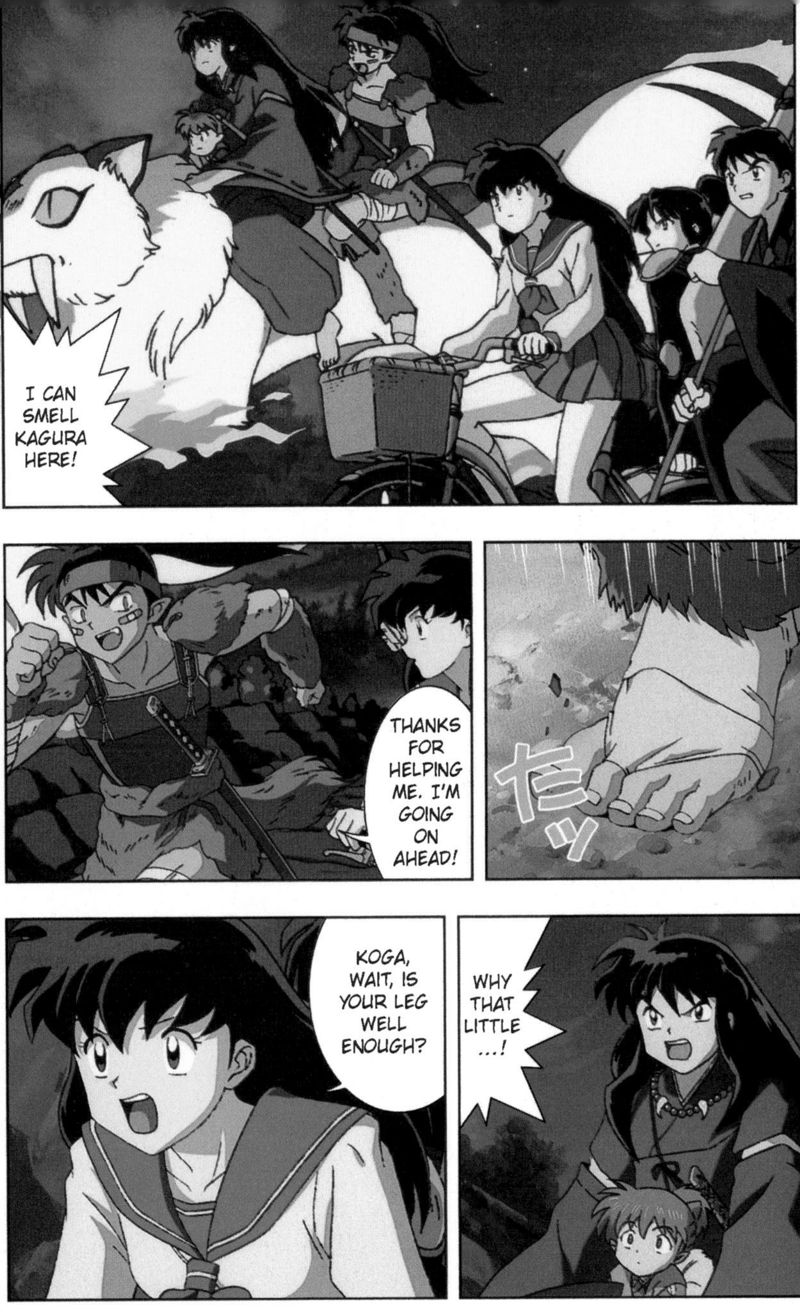
I CAN SMELL KAGURA HERE!
タッ
THANKS FOR HELPING ME. I'M GOING ON AHEAD!
WHY THAT LITTLE ...!
KOGA, WAIT, IS YOUR LEG WELL ENOUGH?

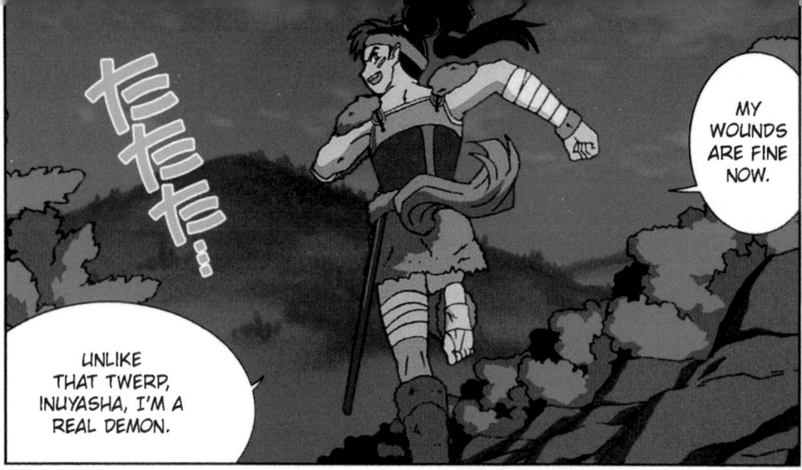
MY WOUNDS ARE FINE NOW.
たたた…
UNLIKE THAT TWERP, INUYASHA, I'M A REAL DEMON.

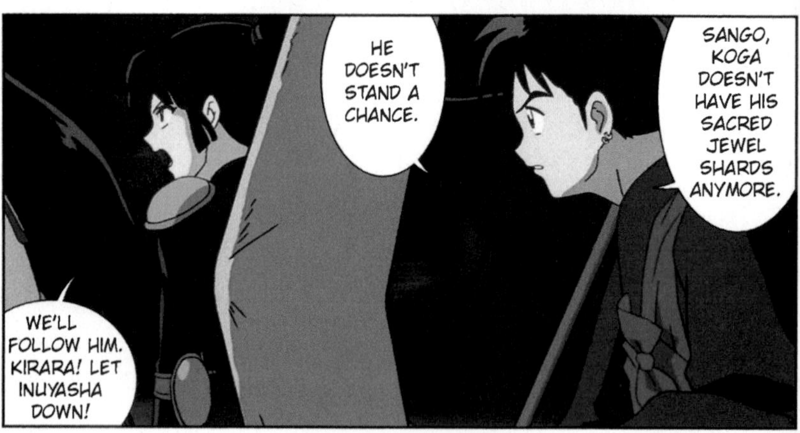
SANGO, KOGA DOESN'T HAVE HIS SACRED JEWEL SHARDS ANYMORE.
HE DOESN'T STAND A CHANCE.
WE'LL FOLLOW HIM. KIRARA! LET INUYASHA DOWN!

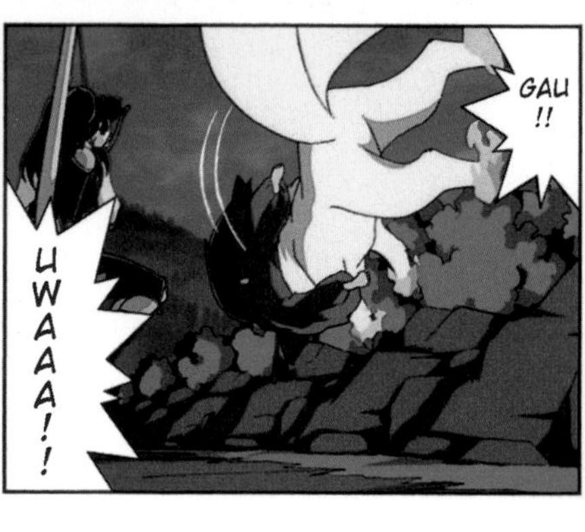
GAU !!
UWAAAA!!

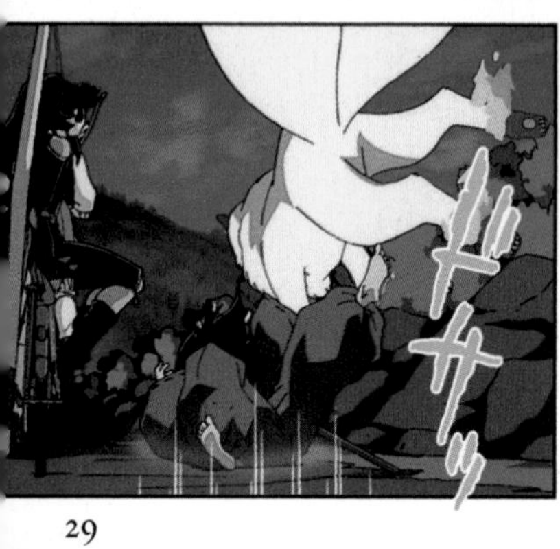
ドサッ

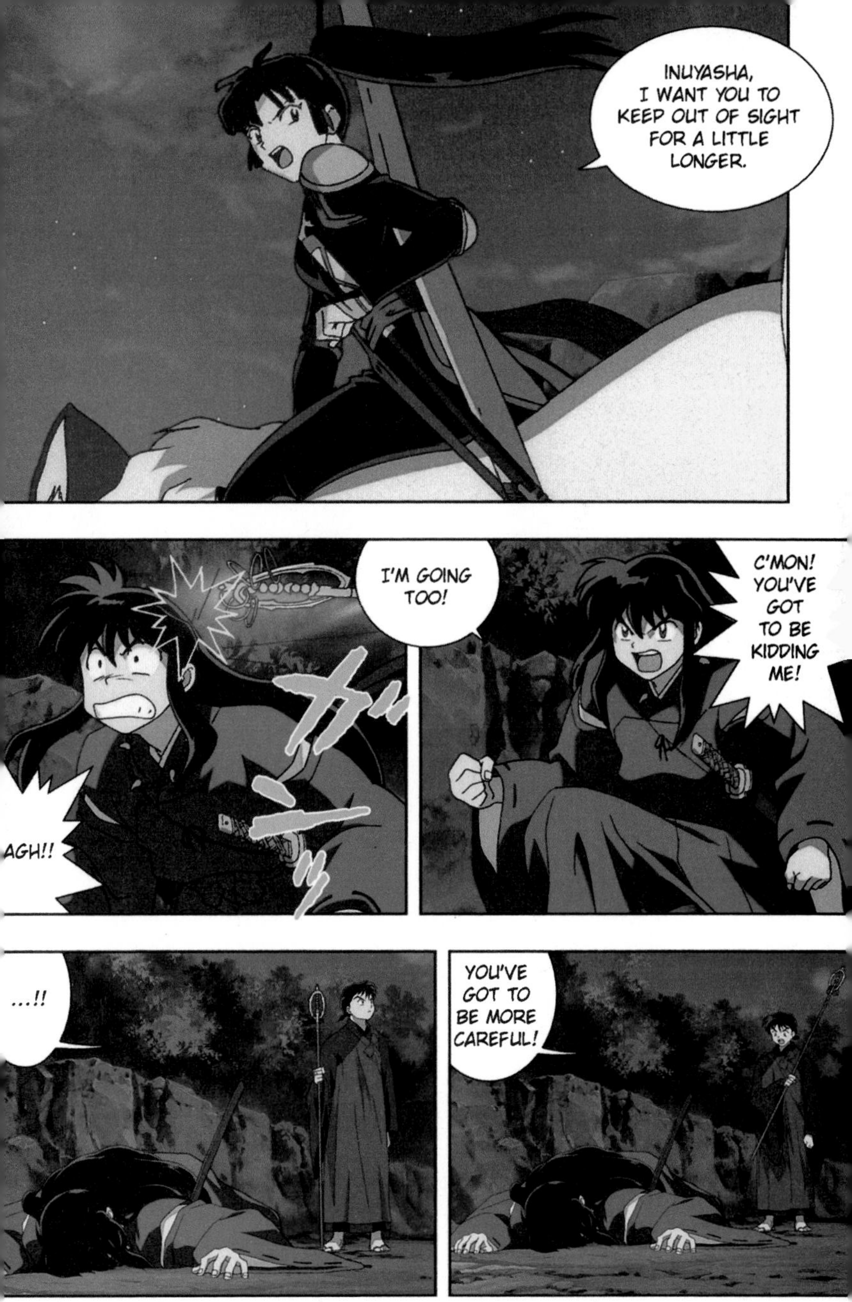
INUYASHA, I WANT YOU TO KEEP OUT OF SIGHT FOR A LITTLE LONGER.
C'MON! YOU'VE GOT TO BE KIDDING ME!
I'M GOING TOO!
AGH!!
YOU'VE GOT TO BE MORE CAREFUL!
...!!

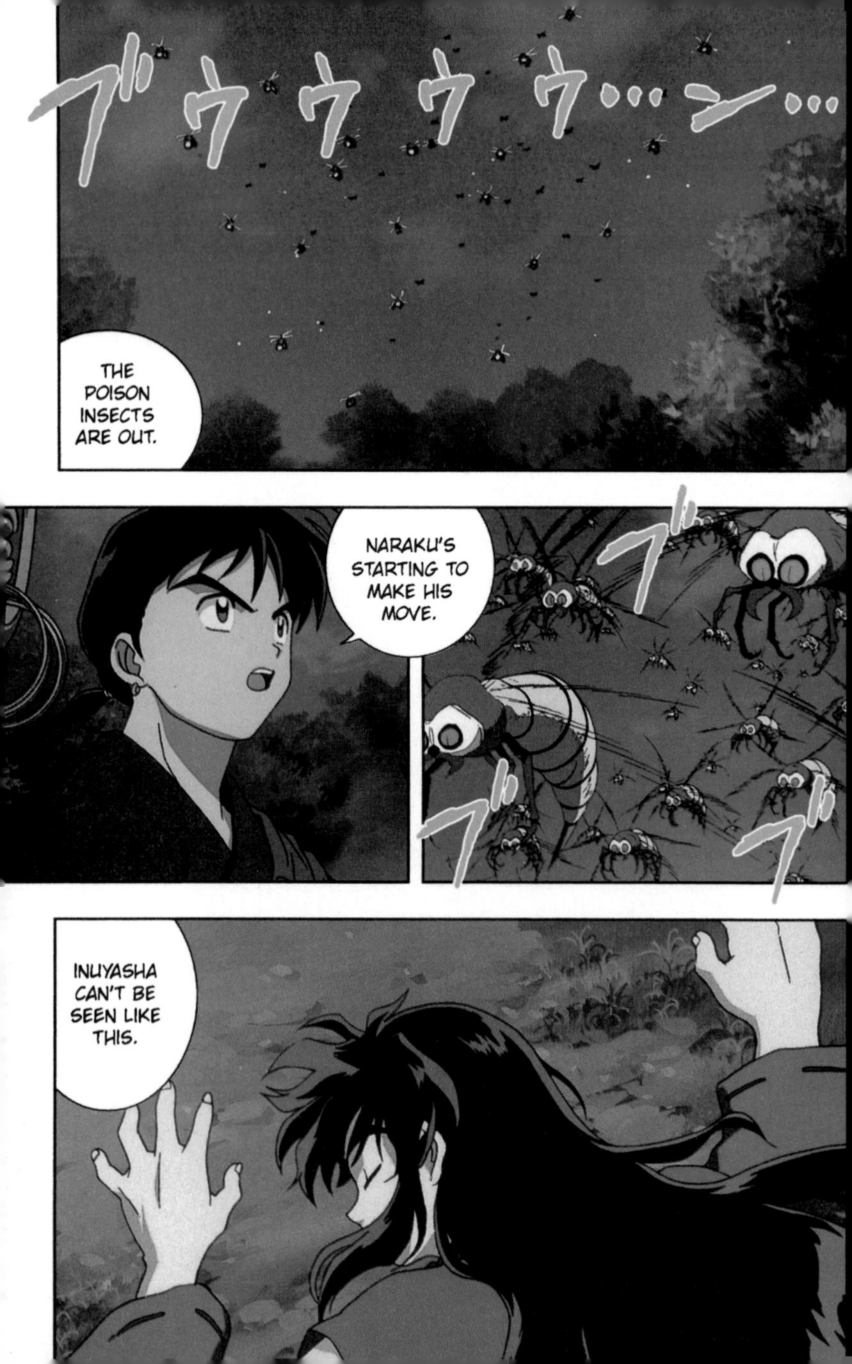
ブウウウウ…ン…
THE POISON INSECTS ARE OUT.
ブ
ブ
ブ
NARAKU'S STARTING TO MAKE HIS MOVE.
INUYASHA CAN'T BE SEEN LIKE THIS.

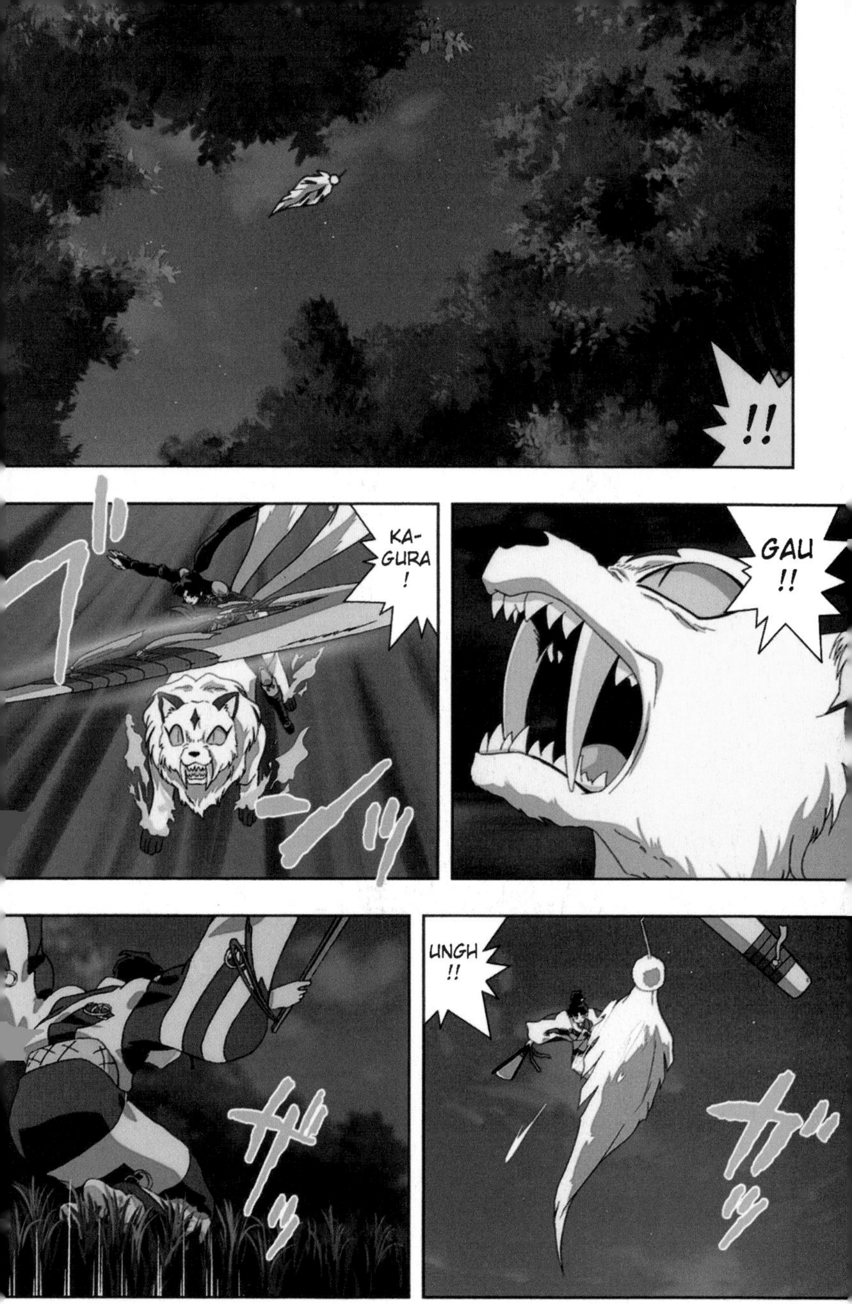
!!
GAU !!
KA-GURA !
UNGH !!

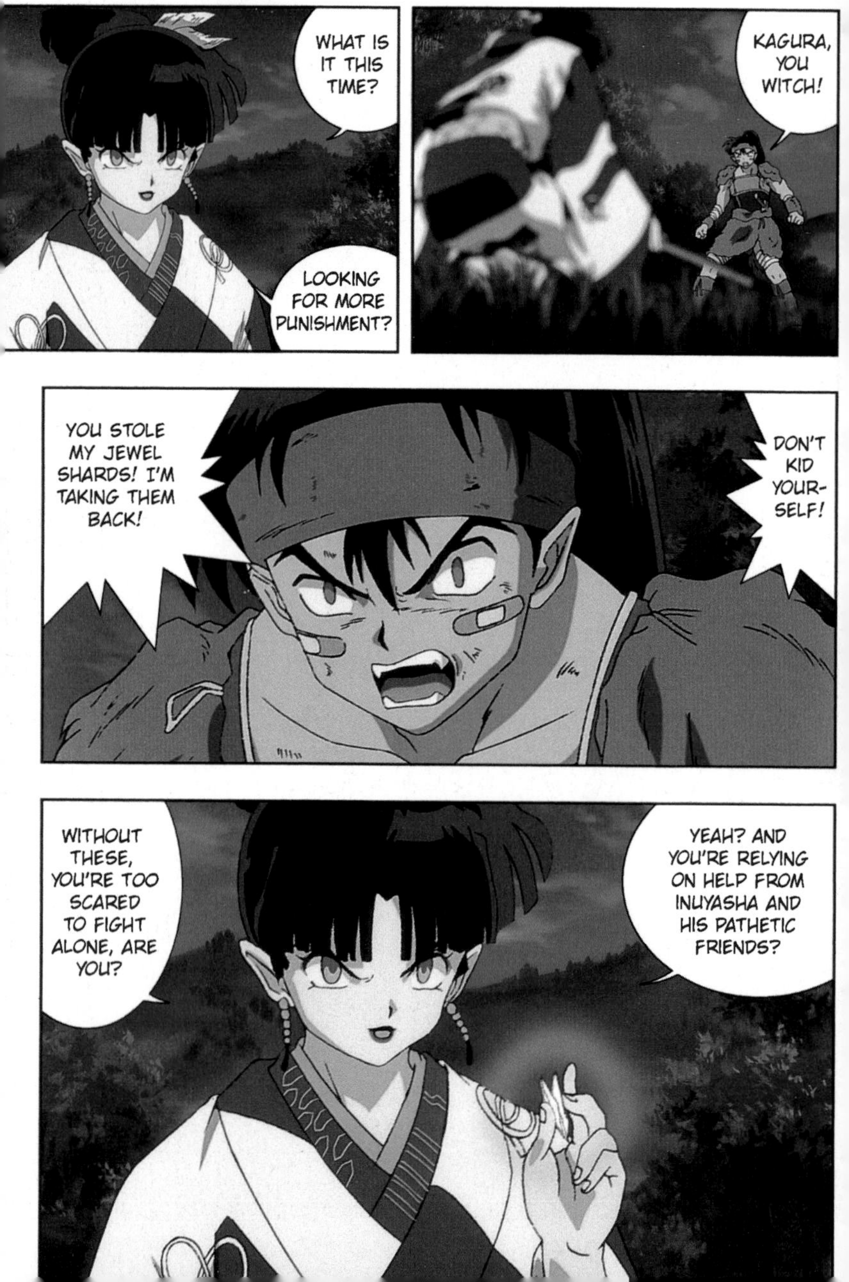
KAGURA, YOU WITCH!
WHAT IS IT THIS TIME?
LOOKING FOR MORE PUNISHMENT?
DON'T KID YOURSELF!
YOU STOLE MY JEWEL SHARDS! I'M TAKING THEM BACK!
YEAH? AND YOU'RE RELYING ON HELP FROM INUYASHA AND HIS PATHETIC FRIENDS?
WITHOUT THESE, YOU'RE TOO SCARED TO FIGHT ALONE, ARE YOU?

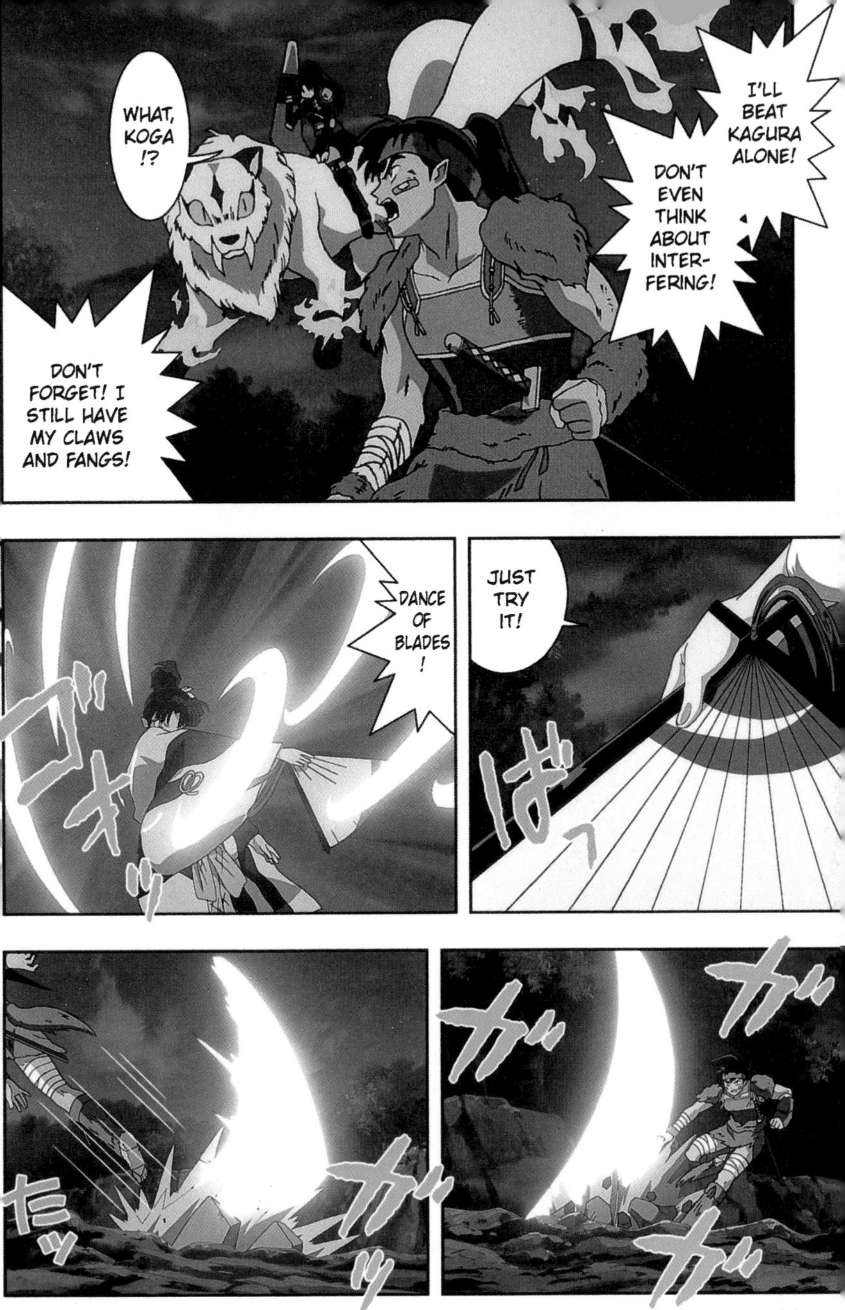

I'LL BEAT KAGURA ALONE!
DON'T EVEN THINK ABOUT INTER-FERING!
WHAT, KOGA !?
DON'T FORGET! I STILL HAVE MY CLAWS AND FANGS!
JUST TRY IT!
DANCE OF BLADES !

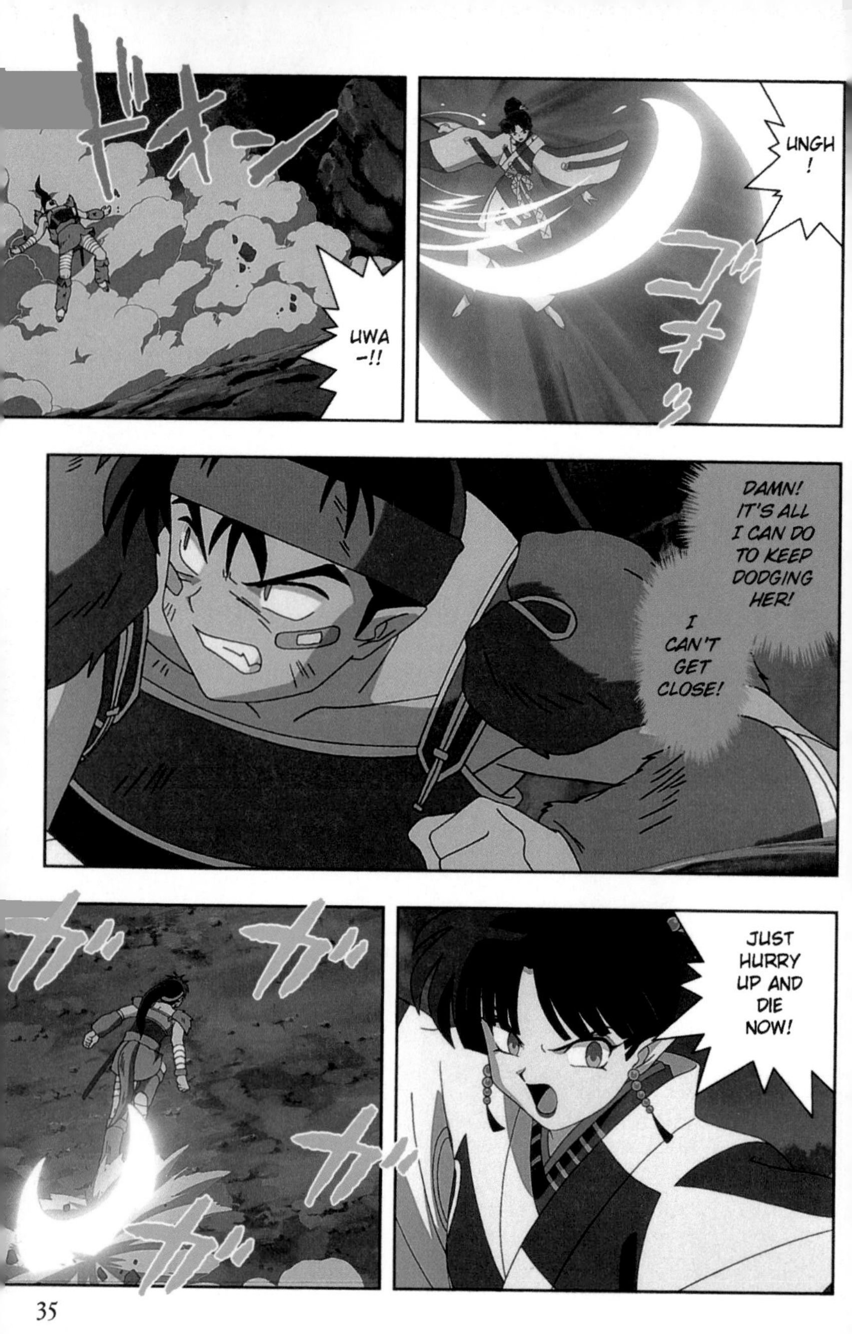
UNGH!
UWA—!!
DAMN! IT'S ALL I CAN DO TO KEEP DODGING HER!
I CAN'T GET CLOSE!
JUST HURRY UP AND DIE NOW!

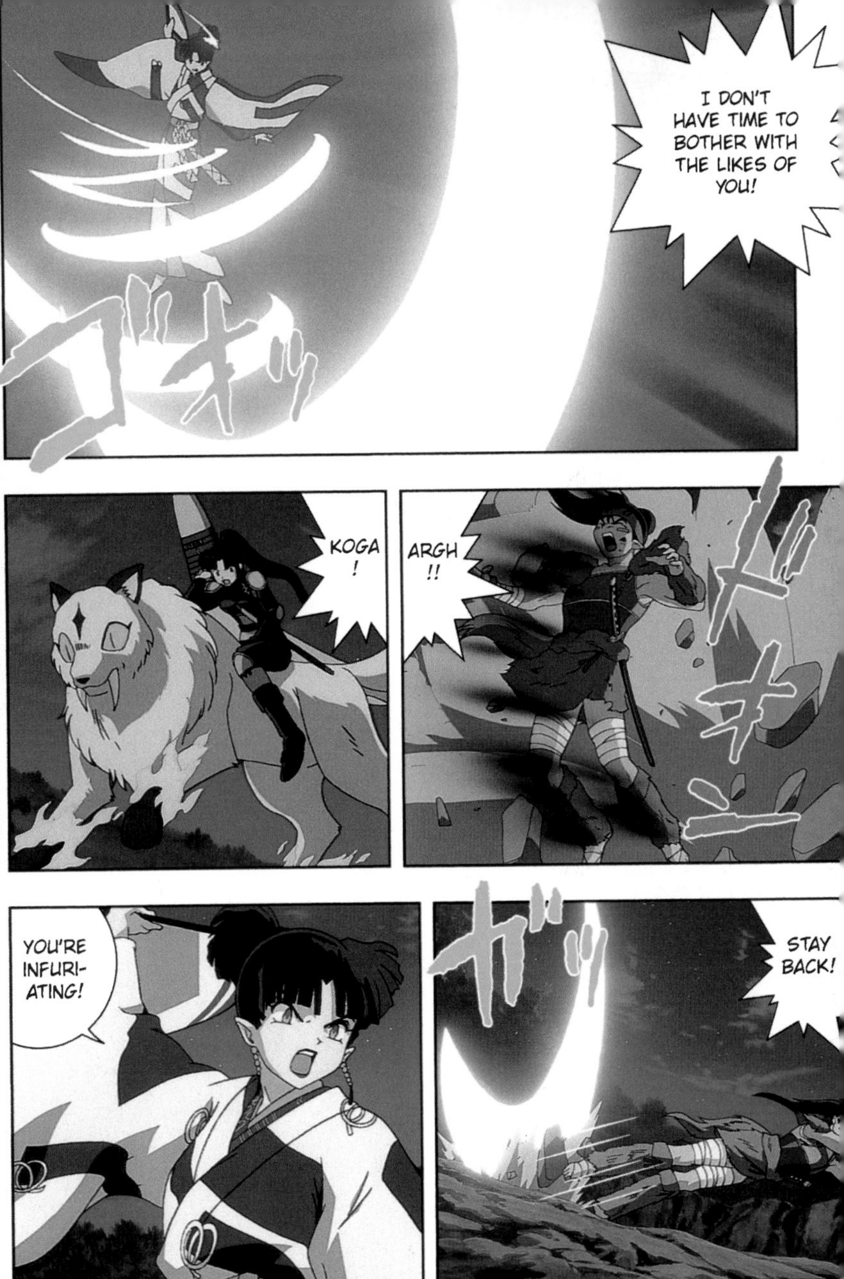
I DON'T HAVE TIME TO BOTHER WITH THE LIKES OF YOU!
ARGH !!
KOGA !
STAY BACK!
YOU'RE INFURI-ATING!

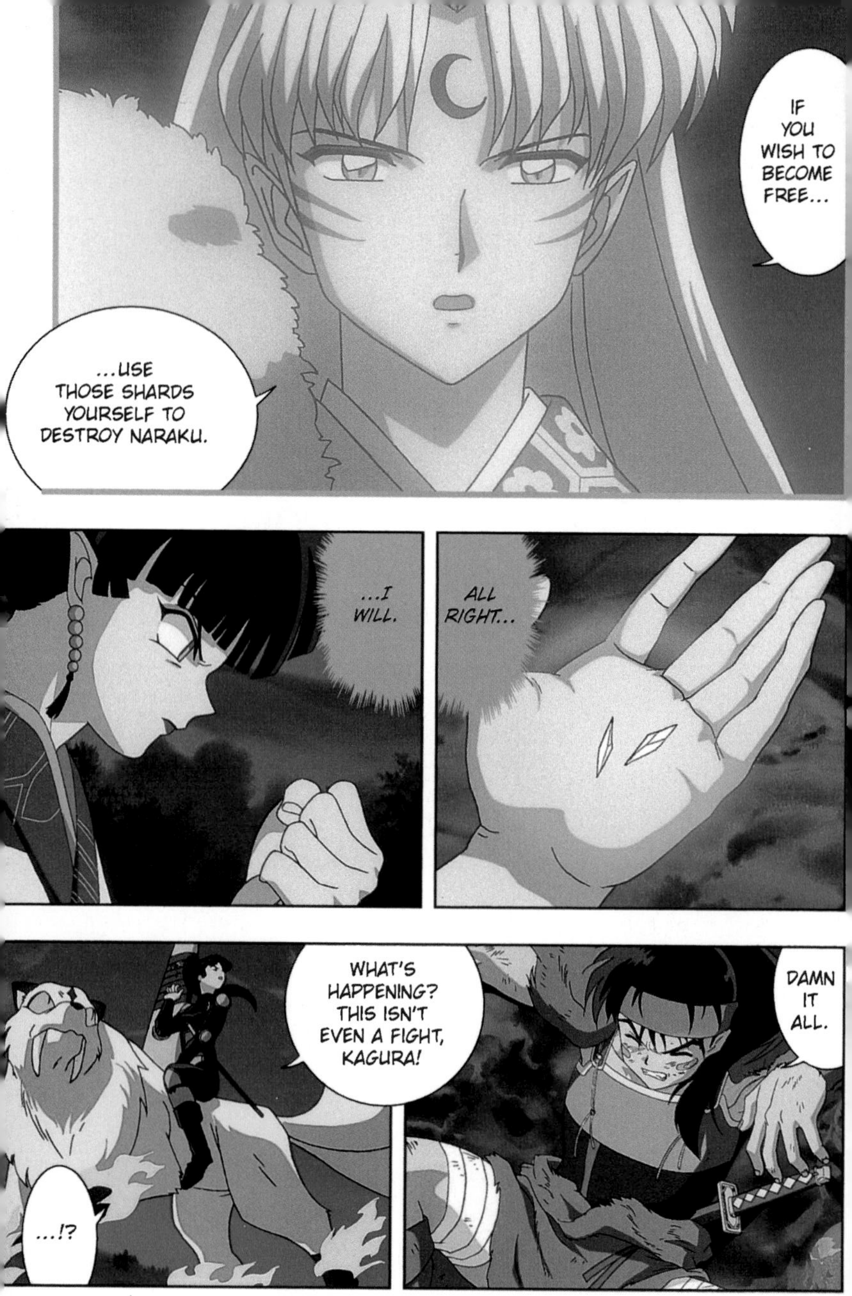
IF YOU WISH TO BECOME FREE...
...USE THOSE SHARDS YOURSELF TO DESTROY NARAKU.
ALL RIGHT...
...I WILL.
DAMN IT ALL.
WHAT'S HAPPENING? THIS ISN'T EVEN A FIGHT, KAGURA!
...!?

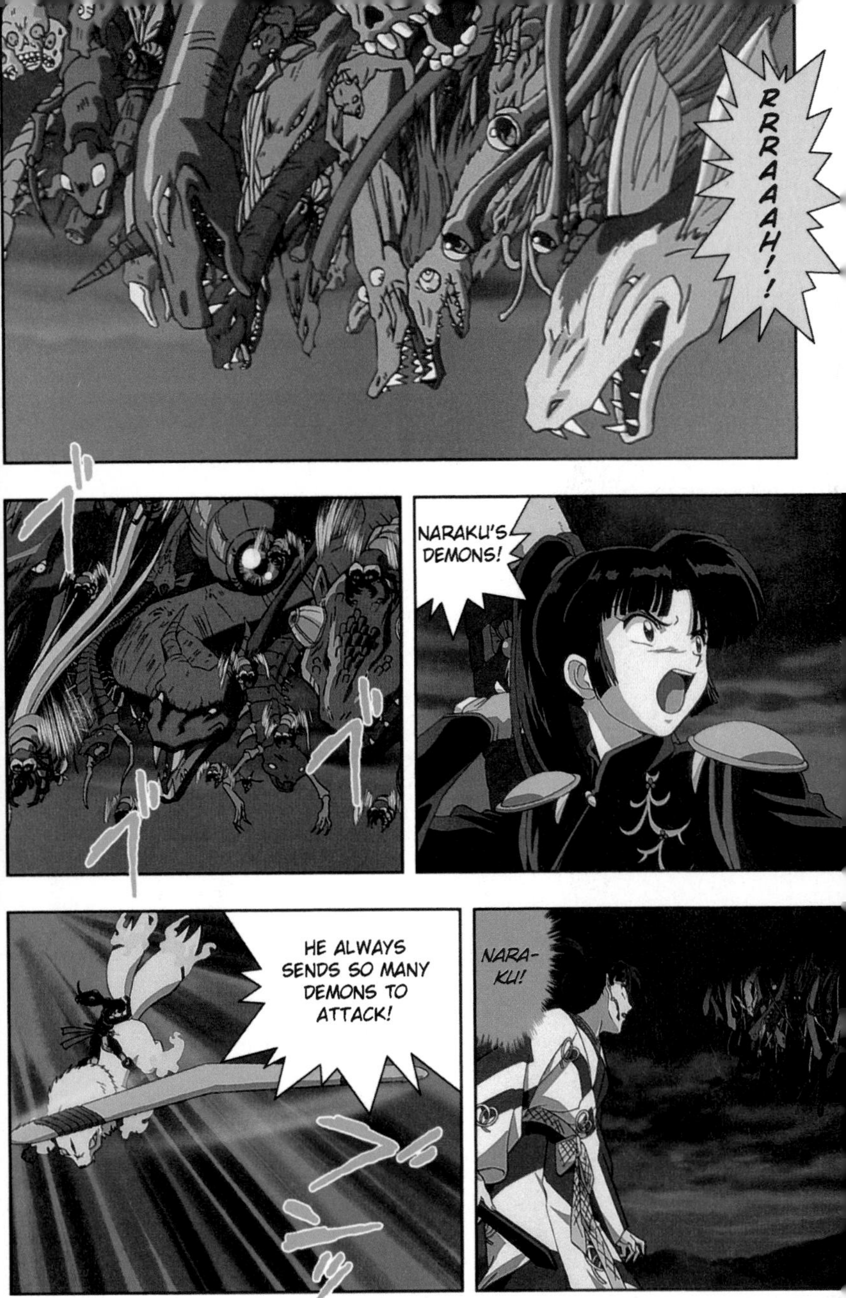
RRRAAAH!!
NARAKU'S DEMONS!
NARA-KU!
HE ALWAYS SENDS SO MANY DEMONS TO ATTACK!

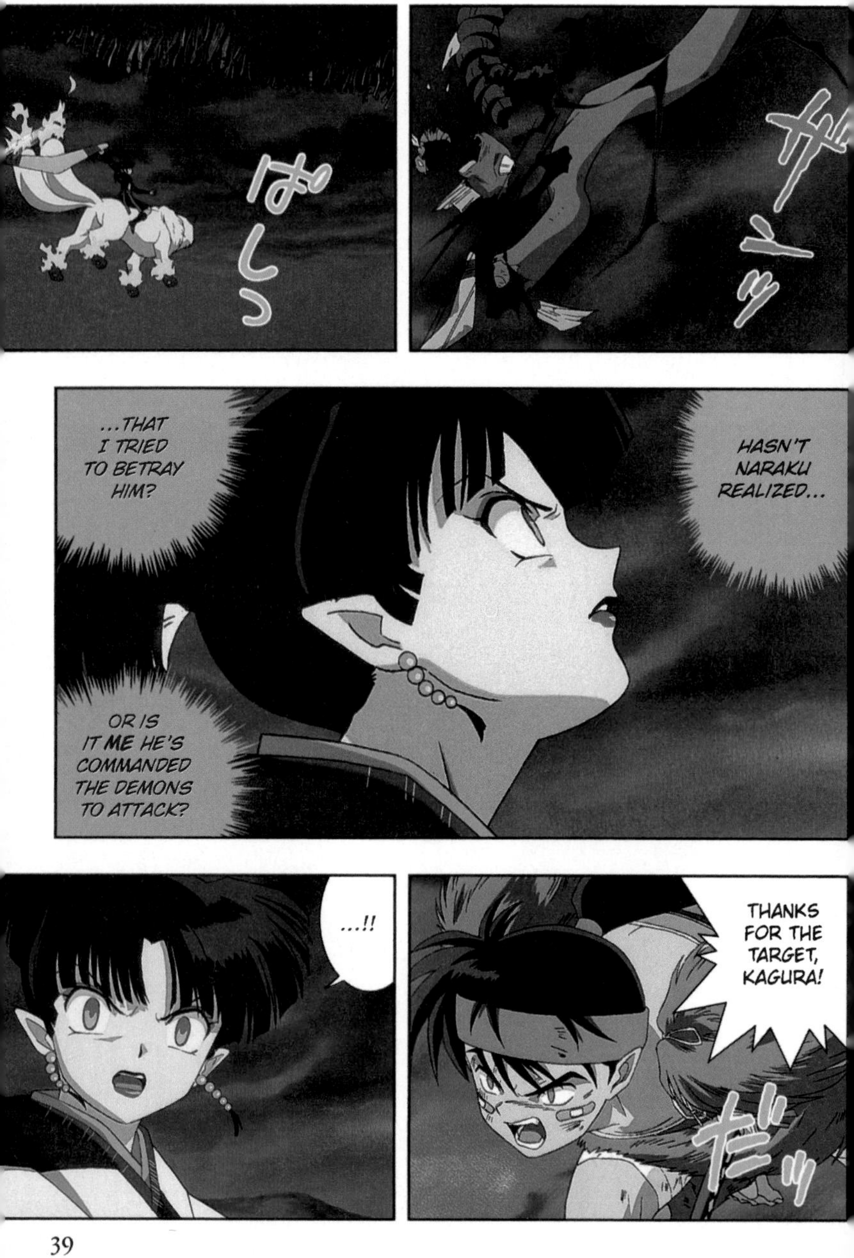
ザュッ
ぱしっ
HASN'T NARAKU REALIZED...
...THAT I TRIED TO BETRAY HIM?
OR IS IT ME HE'S COMMANDED THE DEMONS TO ATTACK?
THANKS FOR THE TARGET, KAGURA!
ダッ
...!!

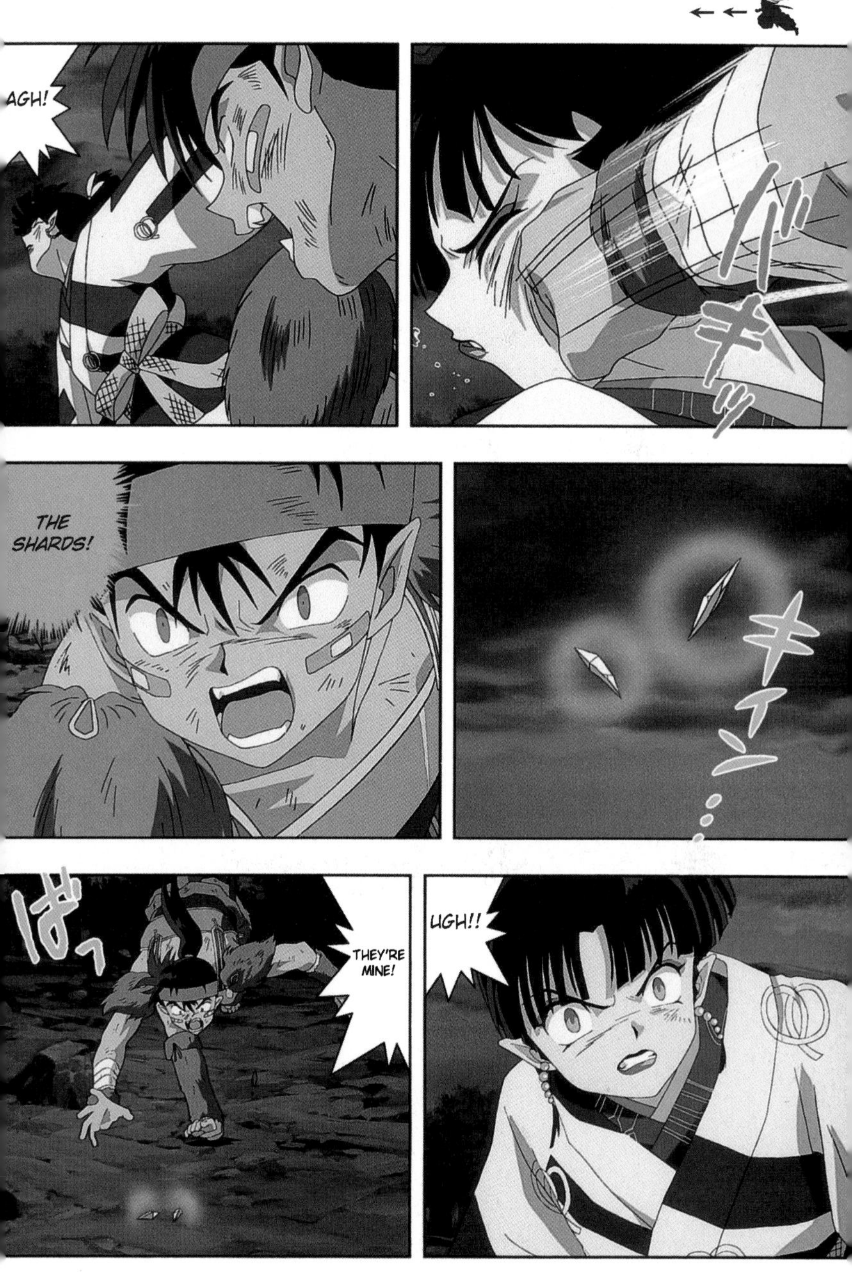

ギギッ
AGH!
キイン…
THE SHARDS!
UGH!!
THEY'RE MINE!
ぱっ

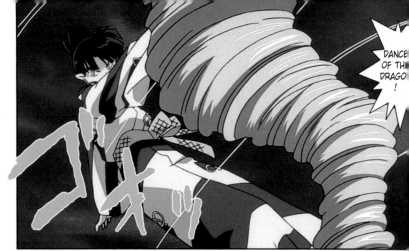

DANCE OF THE DRAGO !

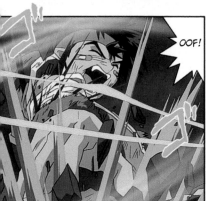

OOF!

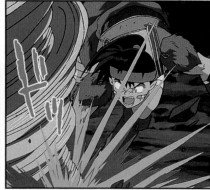

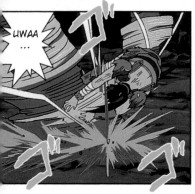

UWAA...

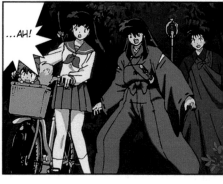

...AH!

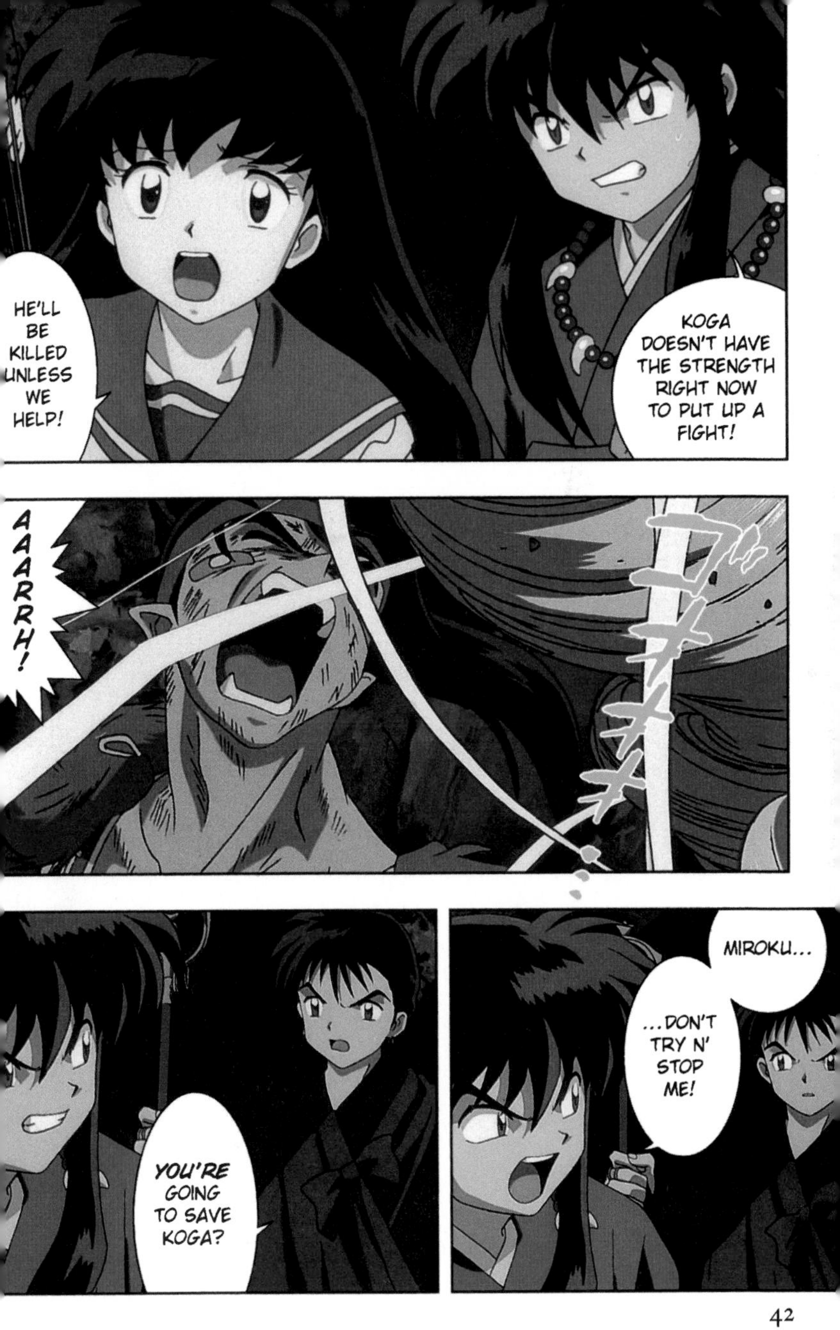
KOGA DOESN'T HAVE THE STRENGTH RIGHT NOW TO PUT UP A FIGHT!
HE'LL BE KILLED UNLESS WE HELP!
AAAARRH!
MIROKU...
...DON'T TRY N' STOP ME!
YOU'RE GOING TO SAVE KOGA?

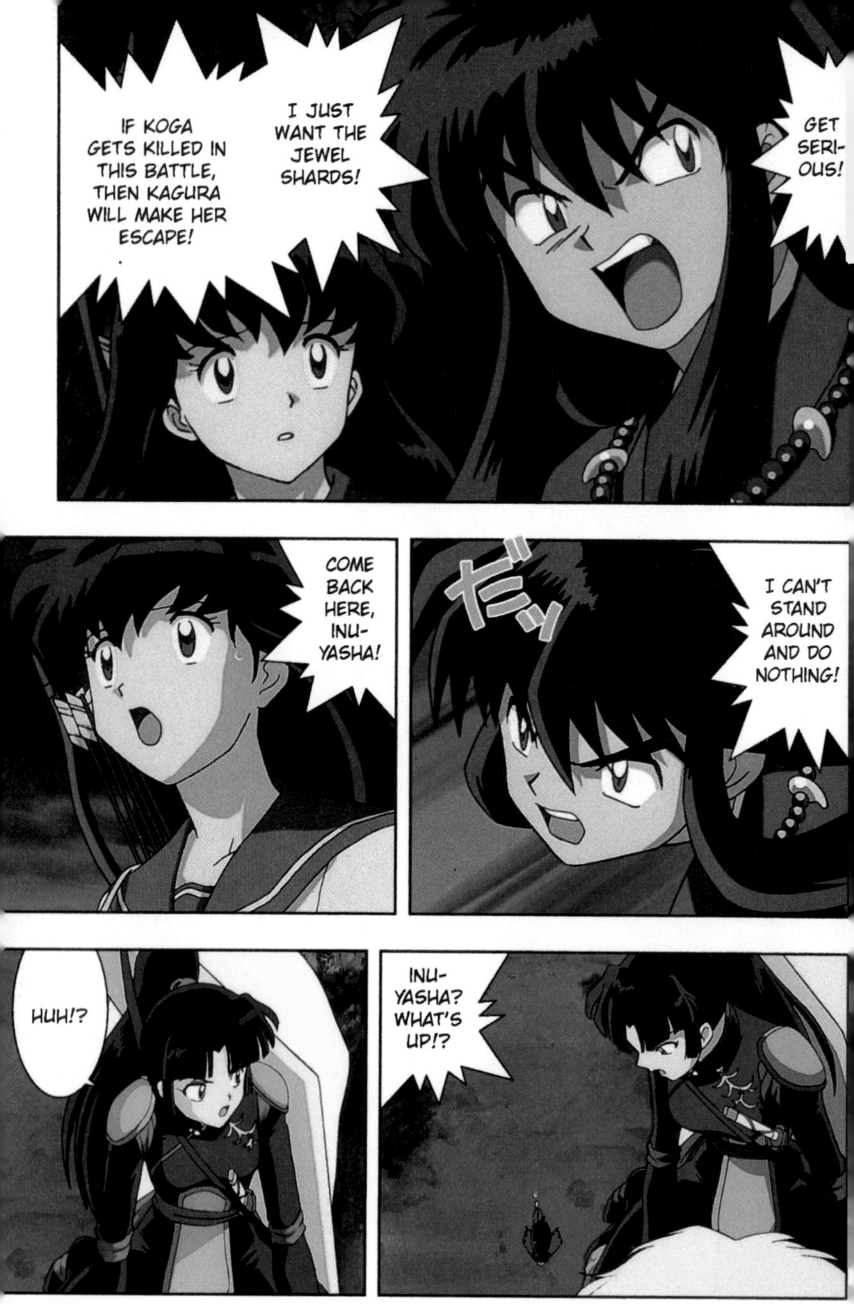
GET SERI-OUS!
I JUST WANT THE JEWEL SHARDS!
IF KOGA GETS KILLED IN THIS BATTLE, THEN KAGURA WILL MAKE HER ESCAPE!
ダッ
I CAN'T STAND AROUND AND DO NOTHING!
COME BACK HERE, INU-YASHA!
INU-YASHA? WHAT'S UP!?
HUH!?

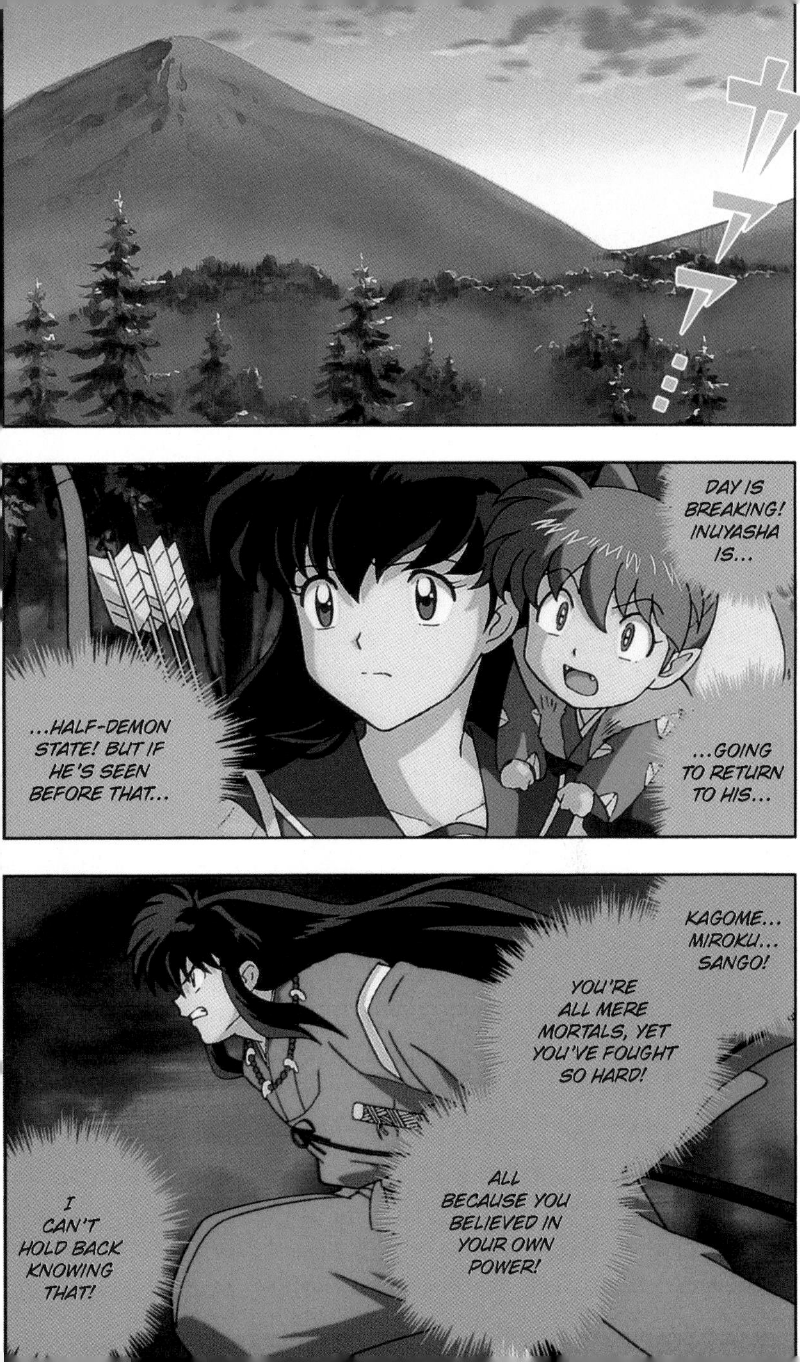
DAY IS BREAKING! INUYASHA IS...
...GOING TO RETURN TO HIS...
...HALF-DEMON STATE! BUT IF HE'S SEEN BEFORE THAT...
KAGOME... MIROKU... SANGO!
YOU'RE ALL MERE MORTALS, YET YOU'VE FOUGHT SO HARD!
ALL BECAUSE YOU BELIEVED IN YOUR OWN POWER!
I CAN'T HOLD BACK KNOWING THAT!

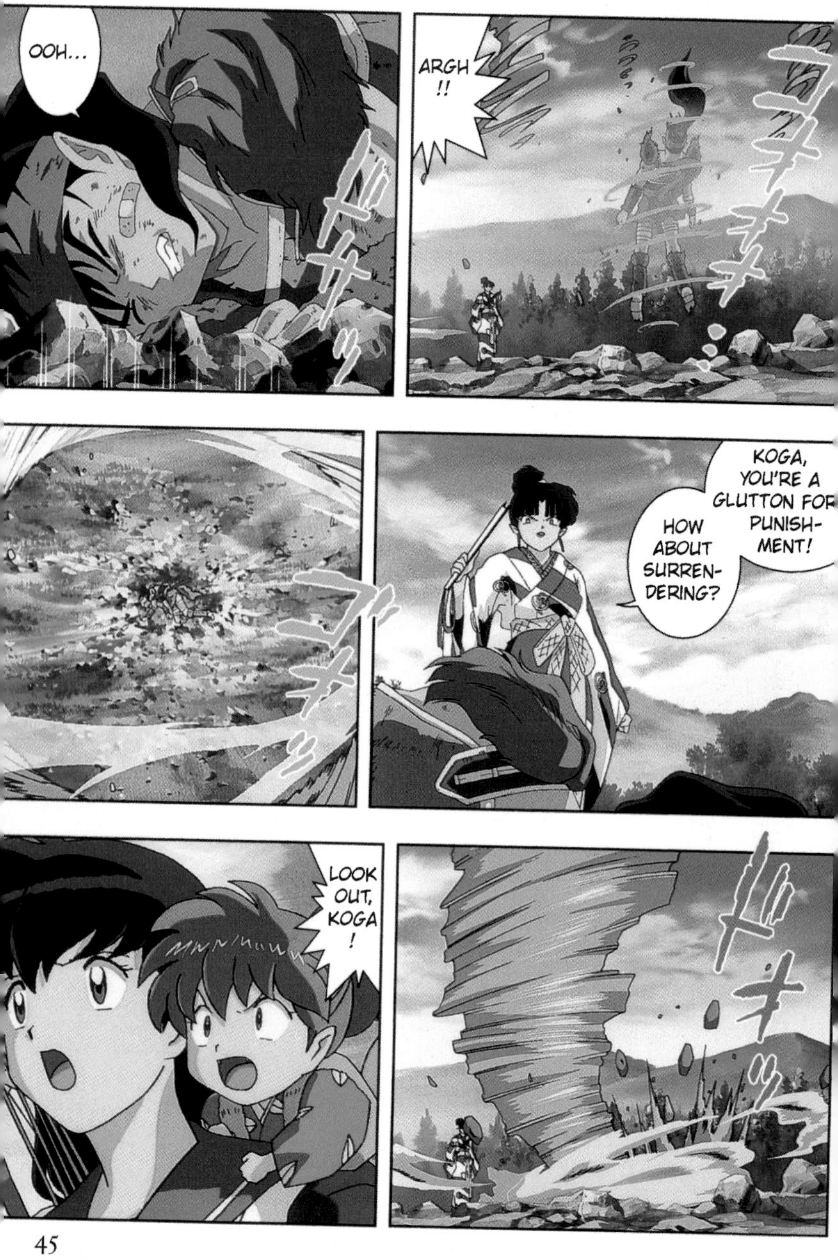
ARGH!!
OOH...
KOGA, YOU'RE A GLUTTON FOR PUNISHMENT!
HOW ABOUT SURRENDERING?
LOOK OUT, KOGA!

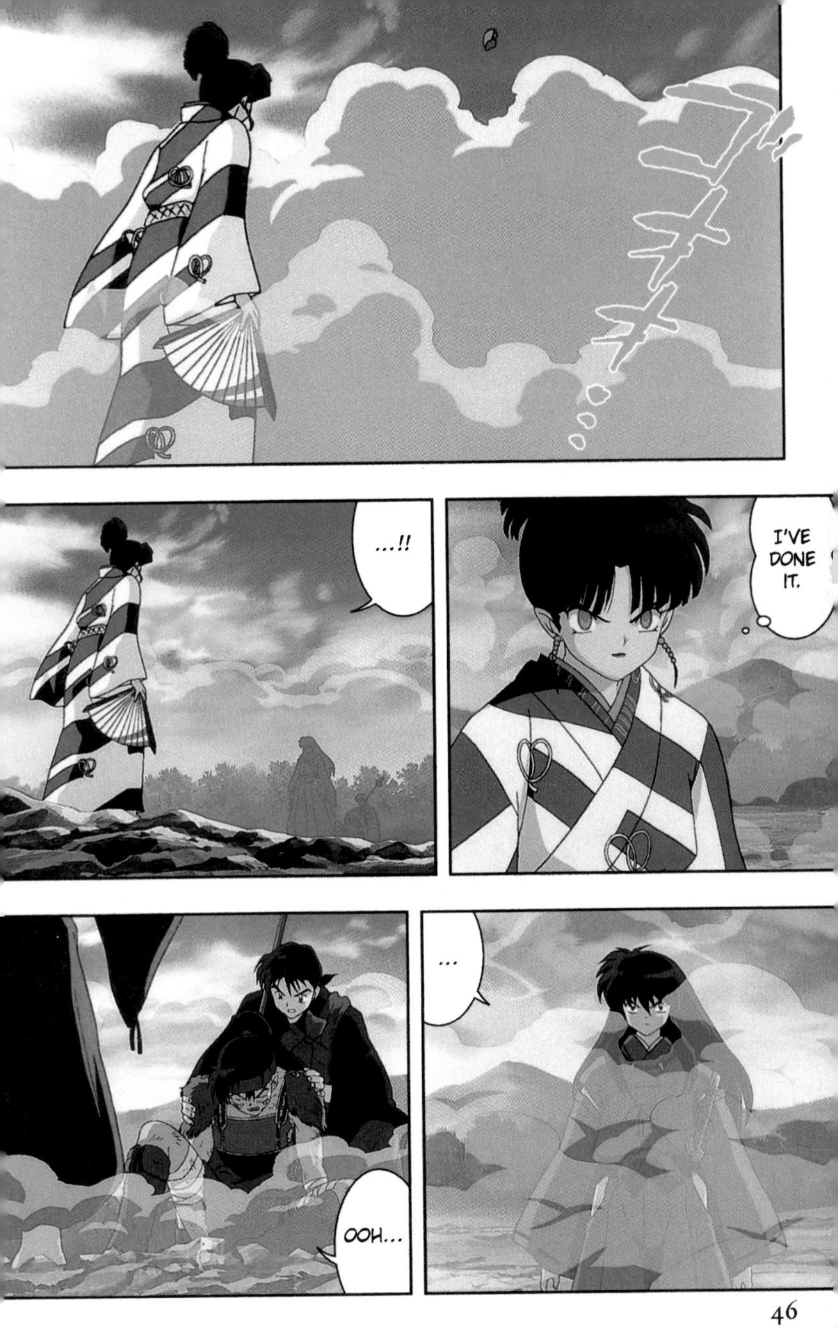
I'VE DONE IT.
...!!
...
OOH...

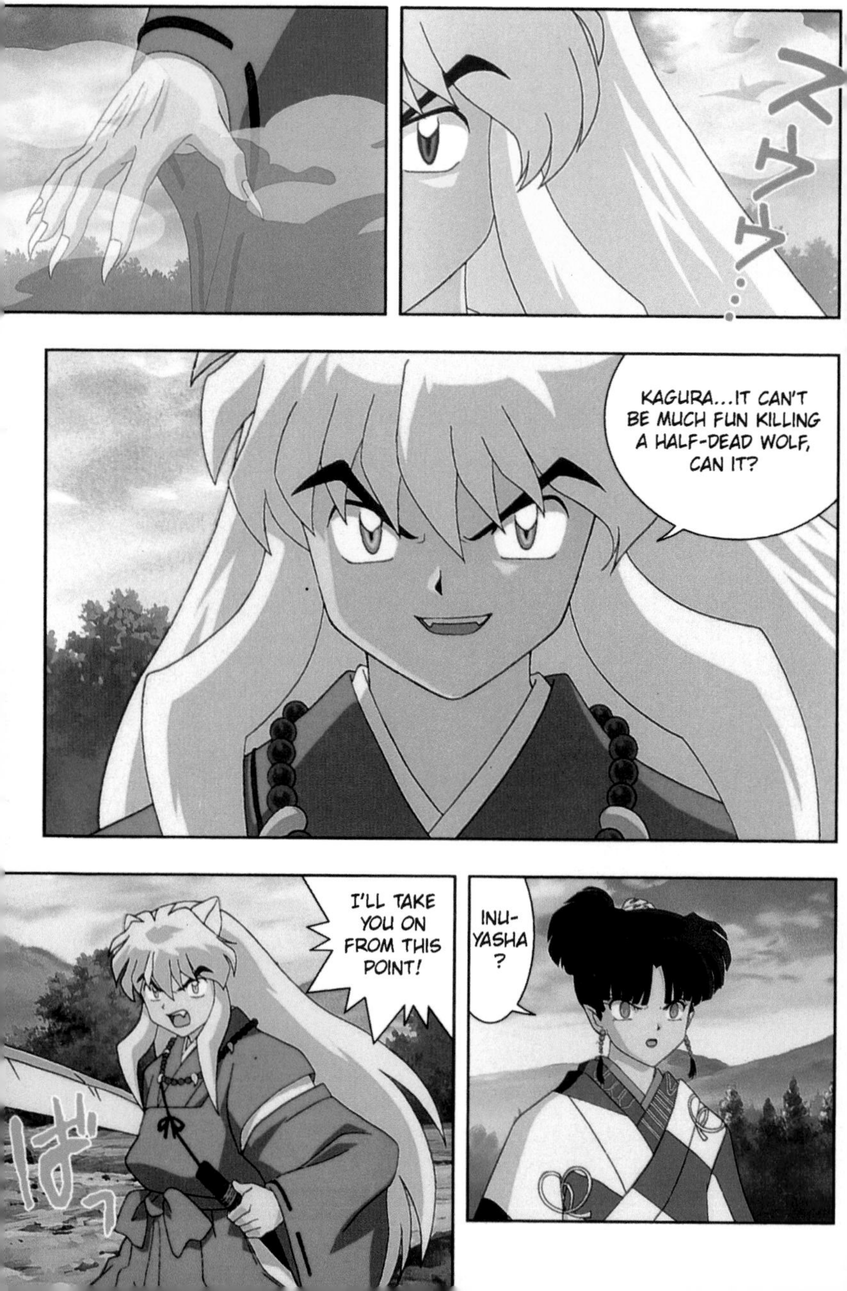
KAGURA...IT CAN'T BE MUCH FUN KILLING A HALF-DEAD WOLF, CAN IT?
INU-YASHA?
I'LL TAKE YOU ON FROM THIS POINT!

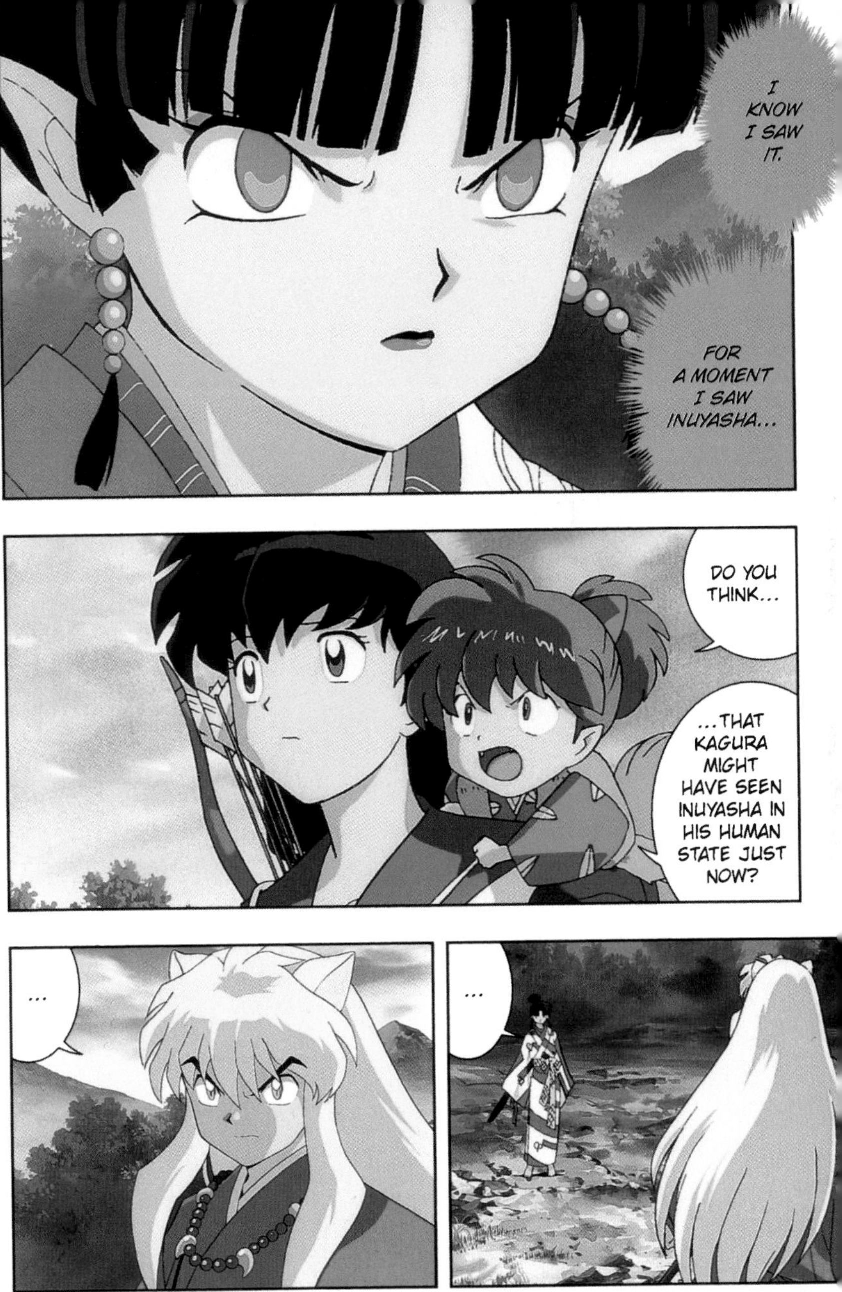
I KNOW I SAW IT.
FOR A MOMENT I SAW INUYASHA...
DO YOU THINK...
...THAT KAGURA MIGHT HAVE SEEN INUYASHA IN HIS HUMAN STATE JUST NOW?
...
...

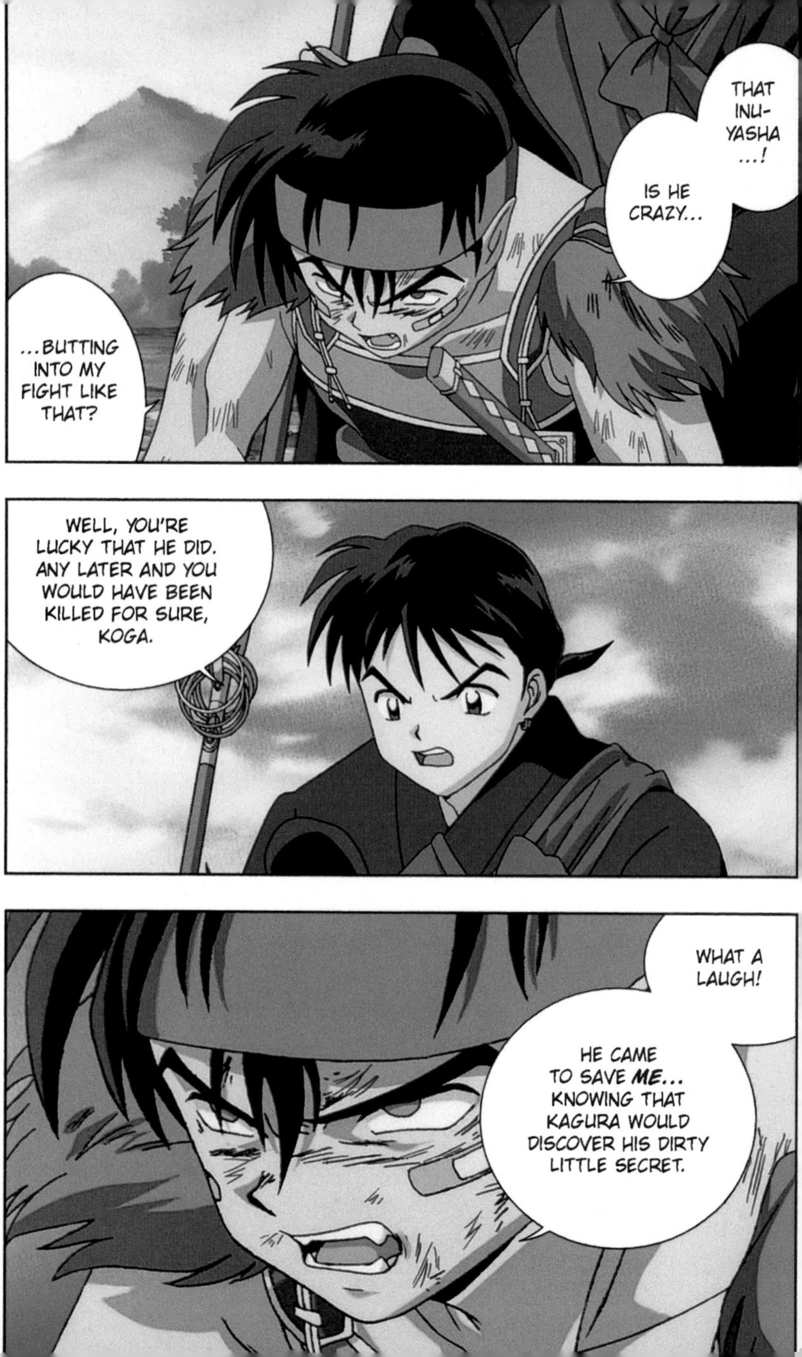
THAT INU-YASHA ...!
IS HE CRAZY...
...BUTTING INTO MY FIGHT LIKE THAT?
WELL, YOU'RE LUCKY THAT HE DID. ANY LATER AND YOU WOULD HAVE BEEN KILLED FOR SURE, KOGA.
WHAT A LAUGH!
HE CAME TO SAVE **ME...** KNOWING THAT KAGURA WOULD DISCOVER HIS DIRTY LITTLE SECRET.

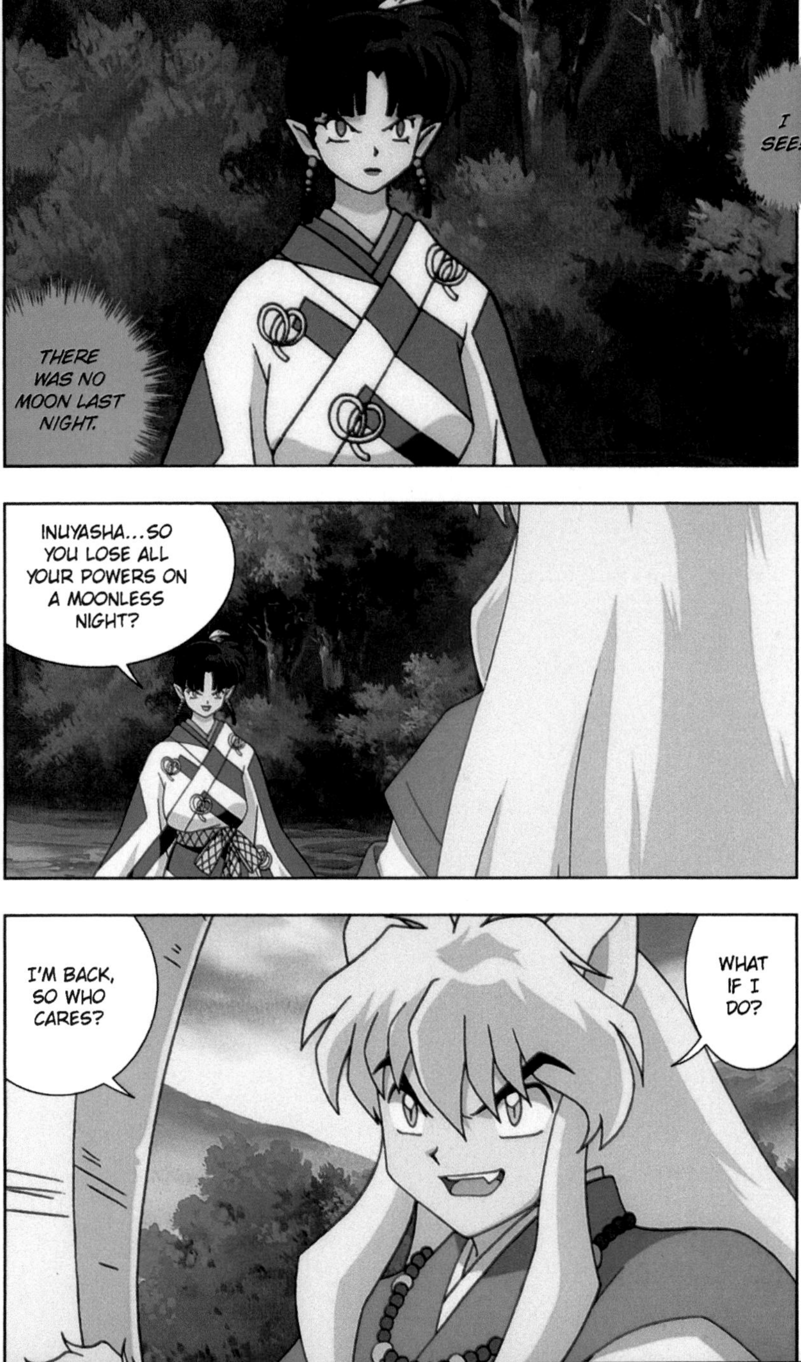
I SEE!
THERE WAS NO MOON LAST NIGHT.
INUYASHA...SO YOU LOSE ALL YOUR POWERS ON A MOONLESS NIGHT?
WHAT IF I DO?
I'M BACK, SO WHO CARES?

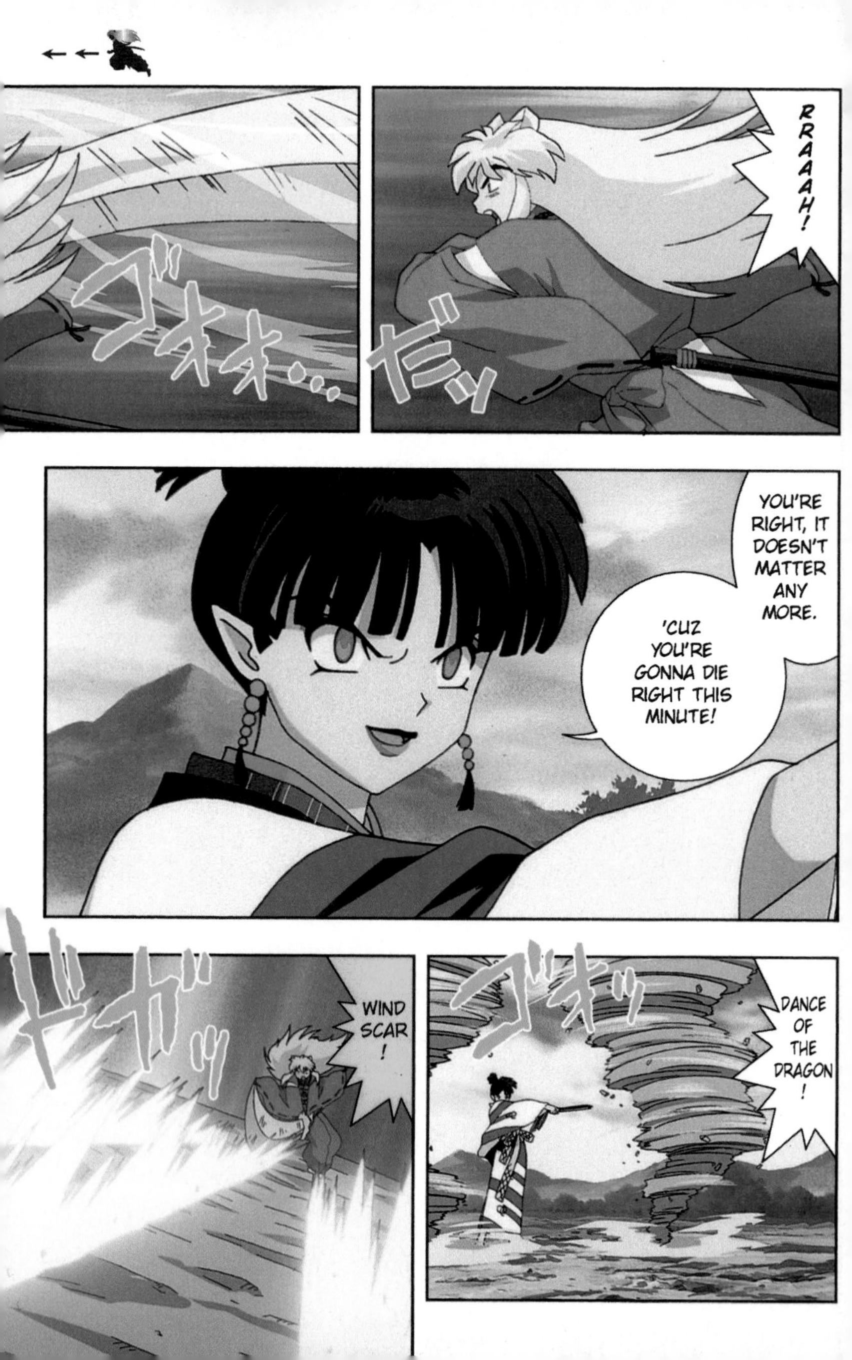
RRAAAH!
ダッ
ゴオオ…
YOU'RE RIGHT, IT DOESN'T MATTER ANY MORE.
'CUZ YOU'RE GONNA DIE RIGHT THIS MINUTE!
ゴオッ
DANCE OF THE DRAGON!
ドガッ
WIND SCAR!

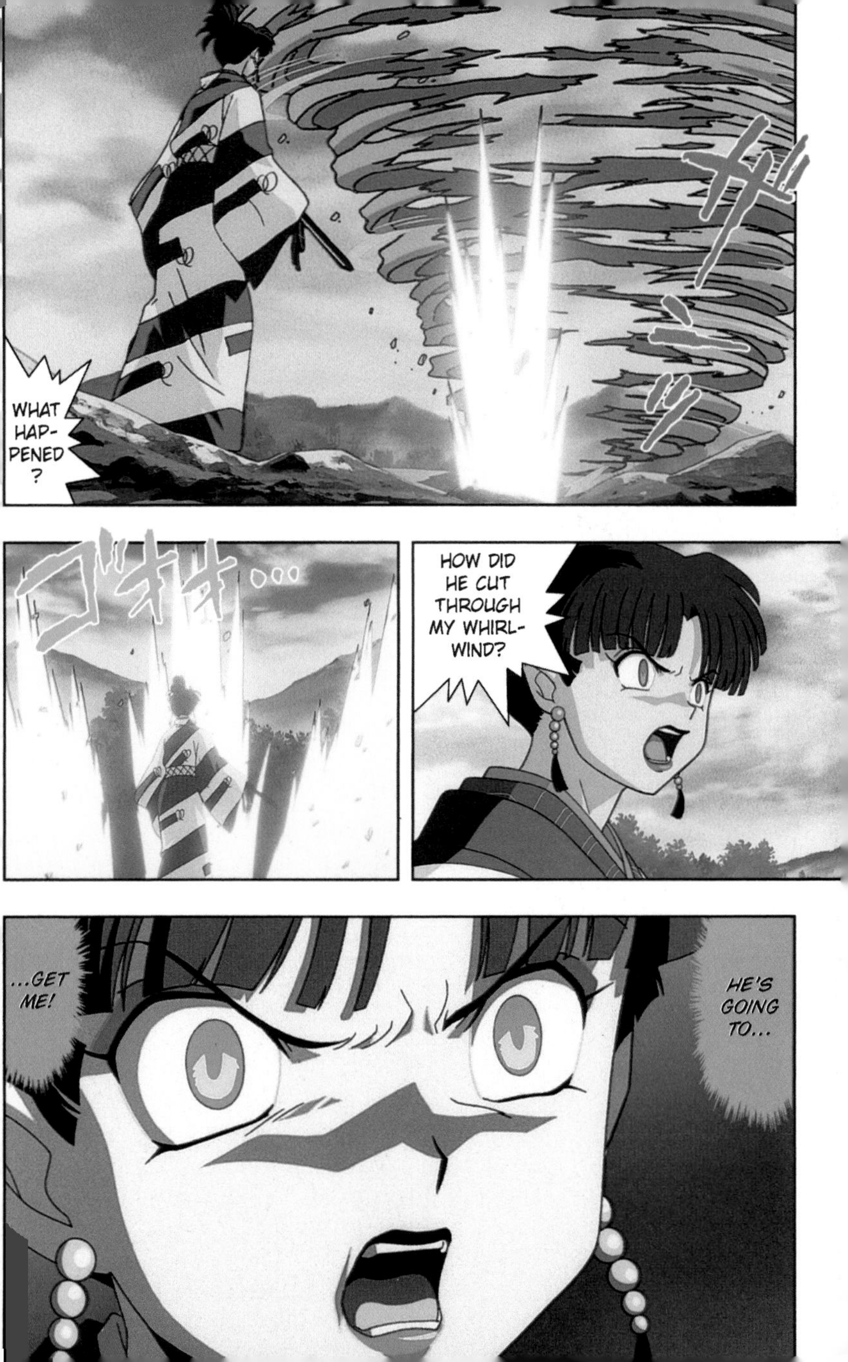
WHAT HAP-PENED?
HOW DID HE CUT THROUGH MY WHIRL-WIND?
HE'S GOING TO...
...GET ME!

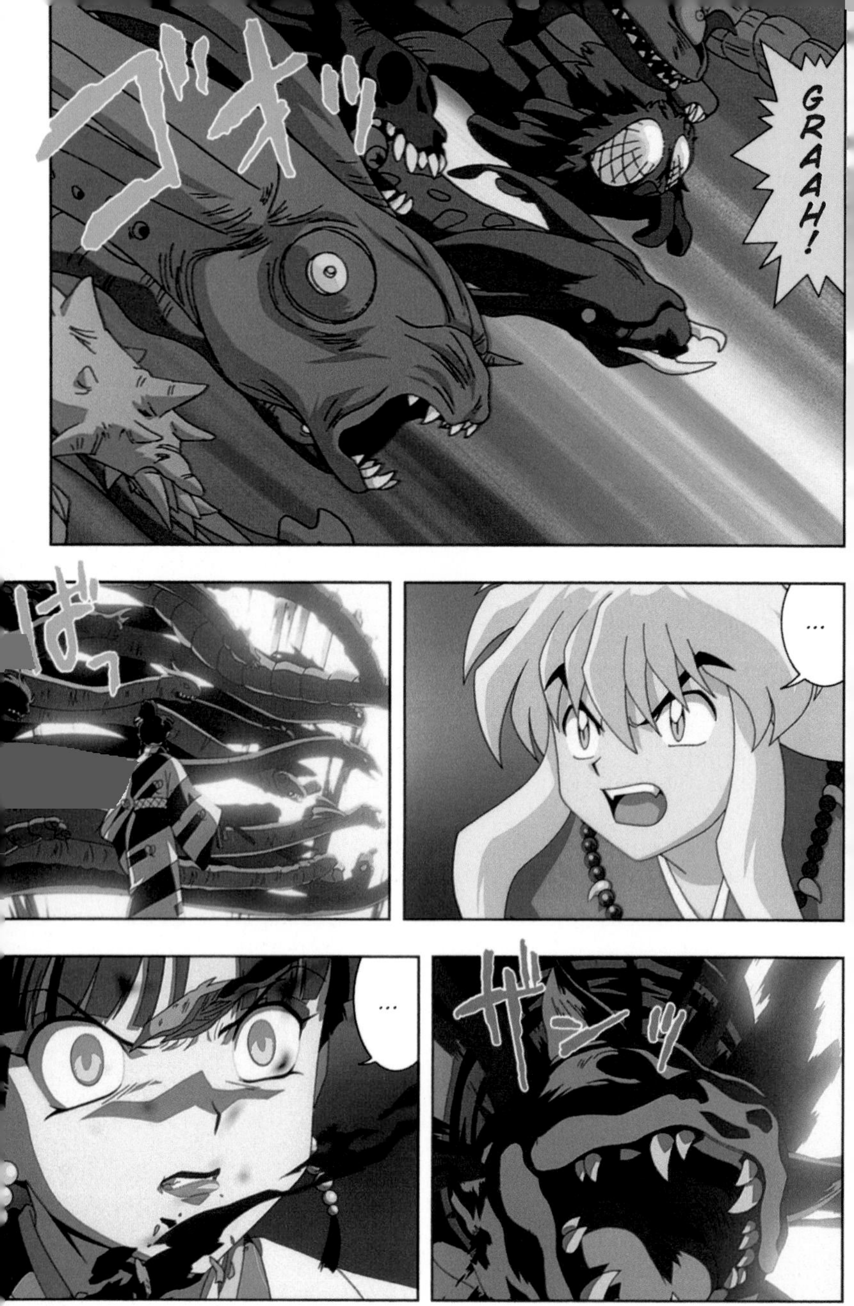
GRAAH!
ゴオッ
...
ぼっ
ザンッ
...

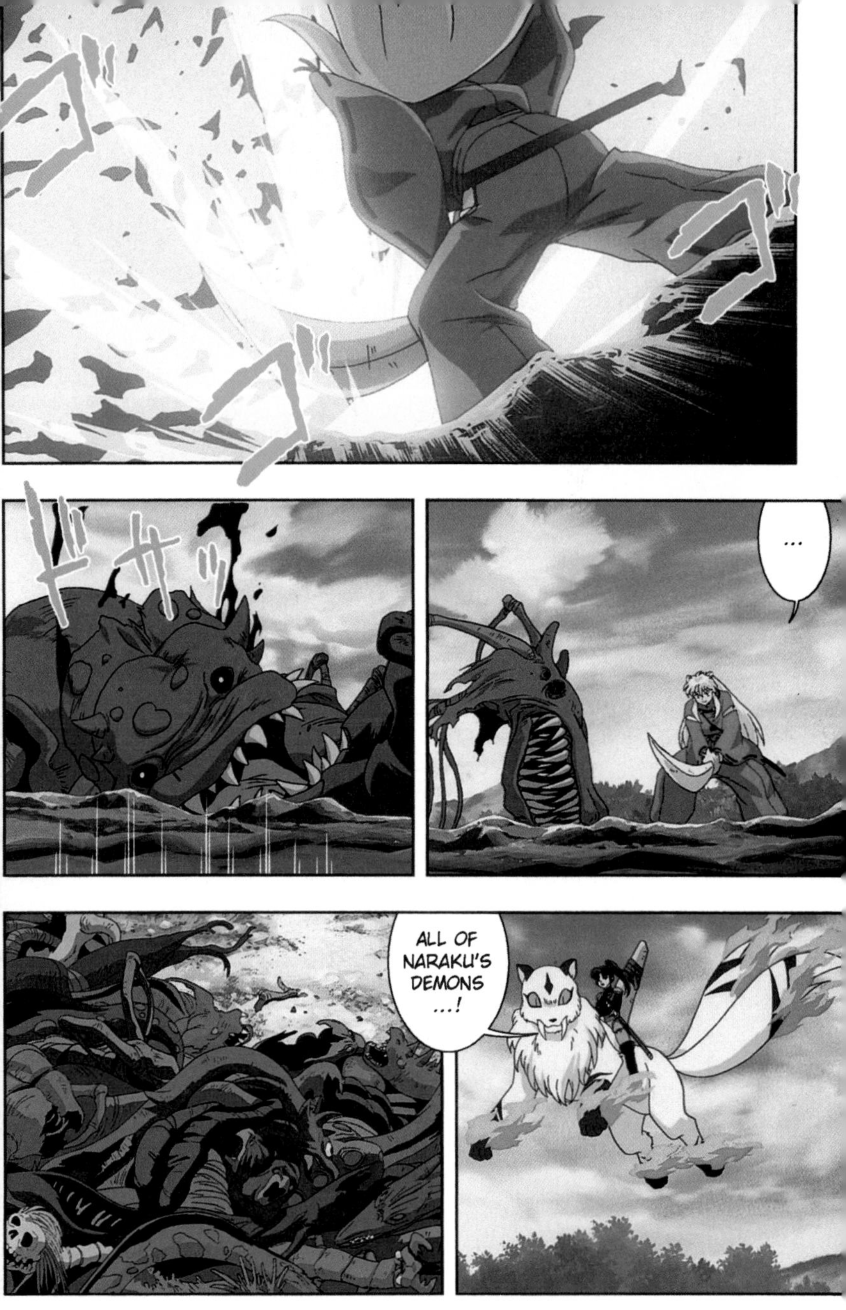
ゴゴゴ
...
ドサッ
ALL OF NARAKU'S DEMONS ...!

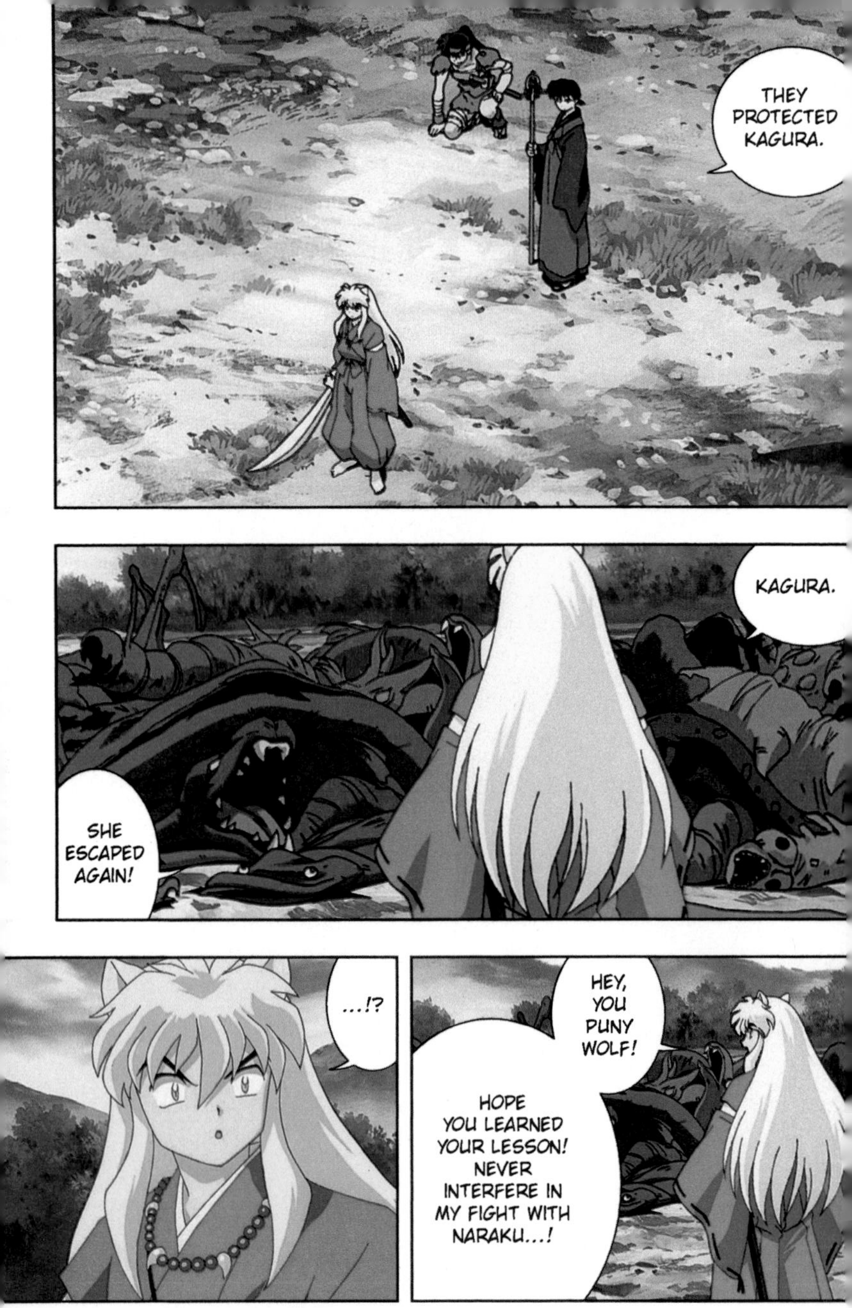
THEY PROTECTED KAGURA.
KAGURA.
SHE ESCAPED AGAIN!
HEY, YOU PUNY WOLF!
HOPE YOU LEARNED YOUR LESSON! NEVER INTERFERE IN MY FIGHT WITH NARAKU...!
...!?

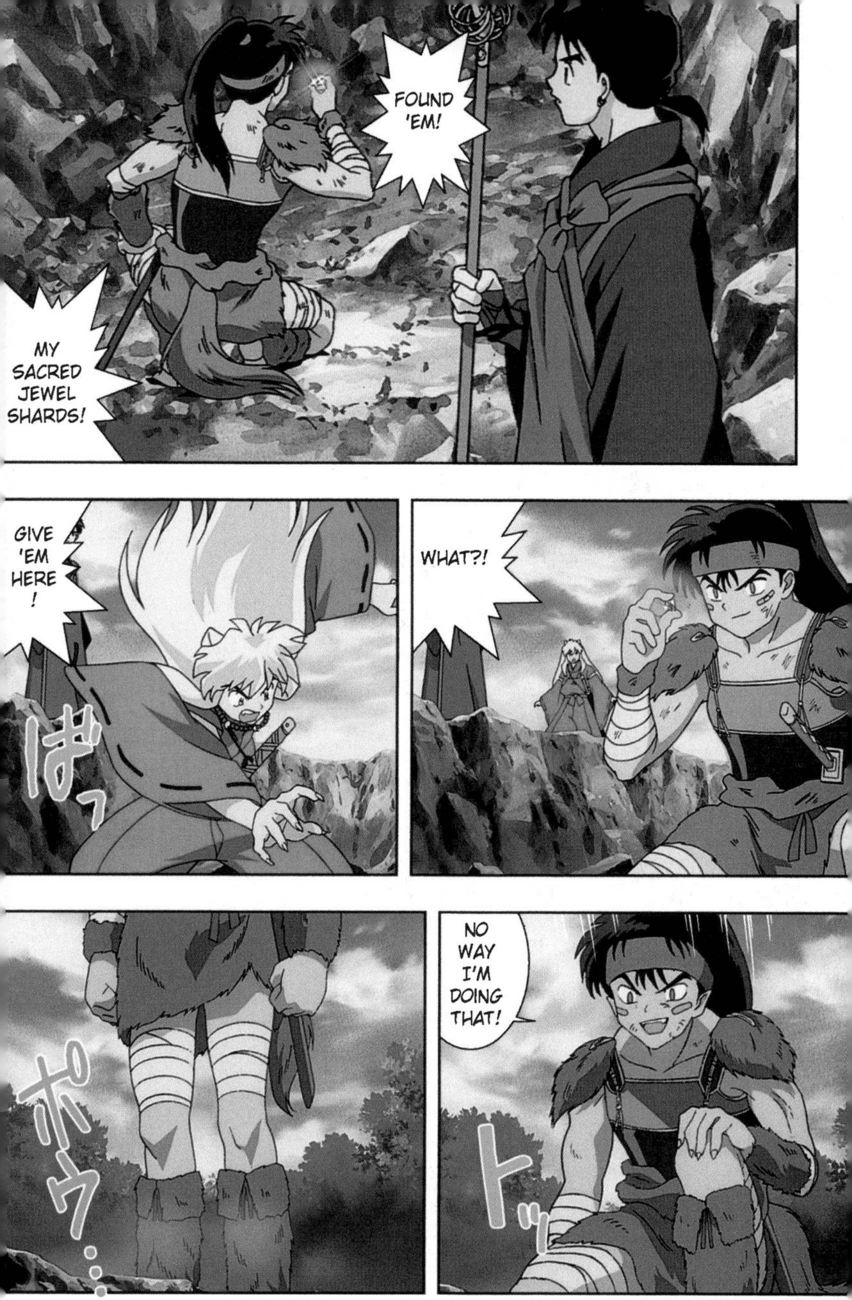
FOUND 'EM!
MY SACRED JEWEL SHARDS!
WHAT?!
GIVE 'EM HERE!
ぼっ
NO WAY I'M DOING THAT!
トッ
ポゥ…

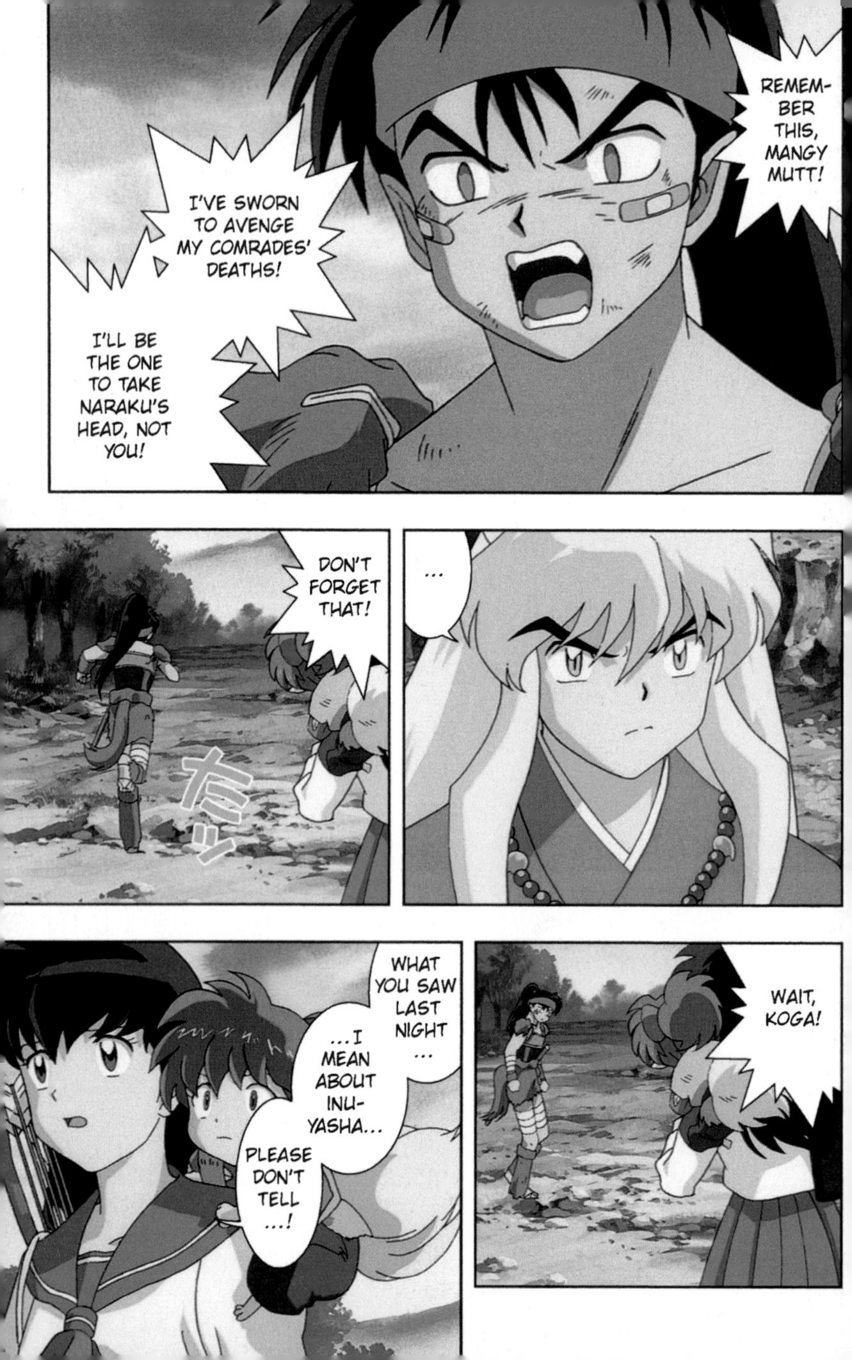
REMEMBER THIS, MANGY MUTT!
I'VE SWORN TO AVENGE MY COMRADES' DEATHS!
I'LL BE THE ONE TO TAKE NARAKU'S HEAD, NOT YOU!
...
DON'T FORGET THAT!
タッ
WAIT, KOGA!
WHAT YOU SAW LAST NIGHT ...
...I MEAN ABOUT INU-YASHA...
PLEASE DON'T TELL ...!

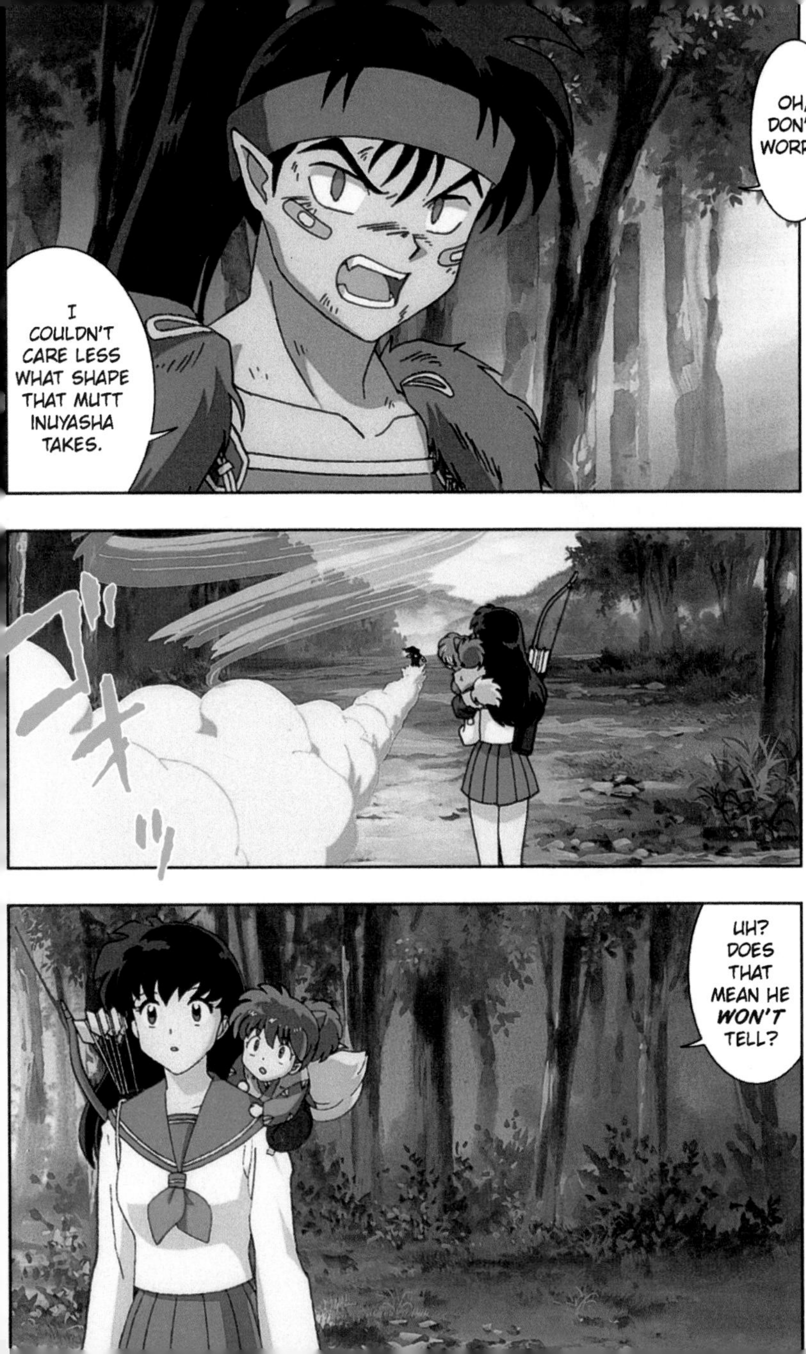
OH, DON'T WORRY.
I COULDN'T CARE LESS WHAT SHAPE THAT MUTT INUYASHA TAKES.
ゴオッ
UH? DOES THAT MEAN HE *WON'T* TELL?

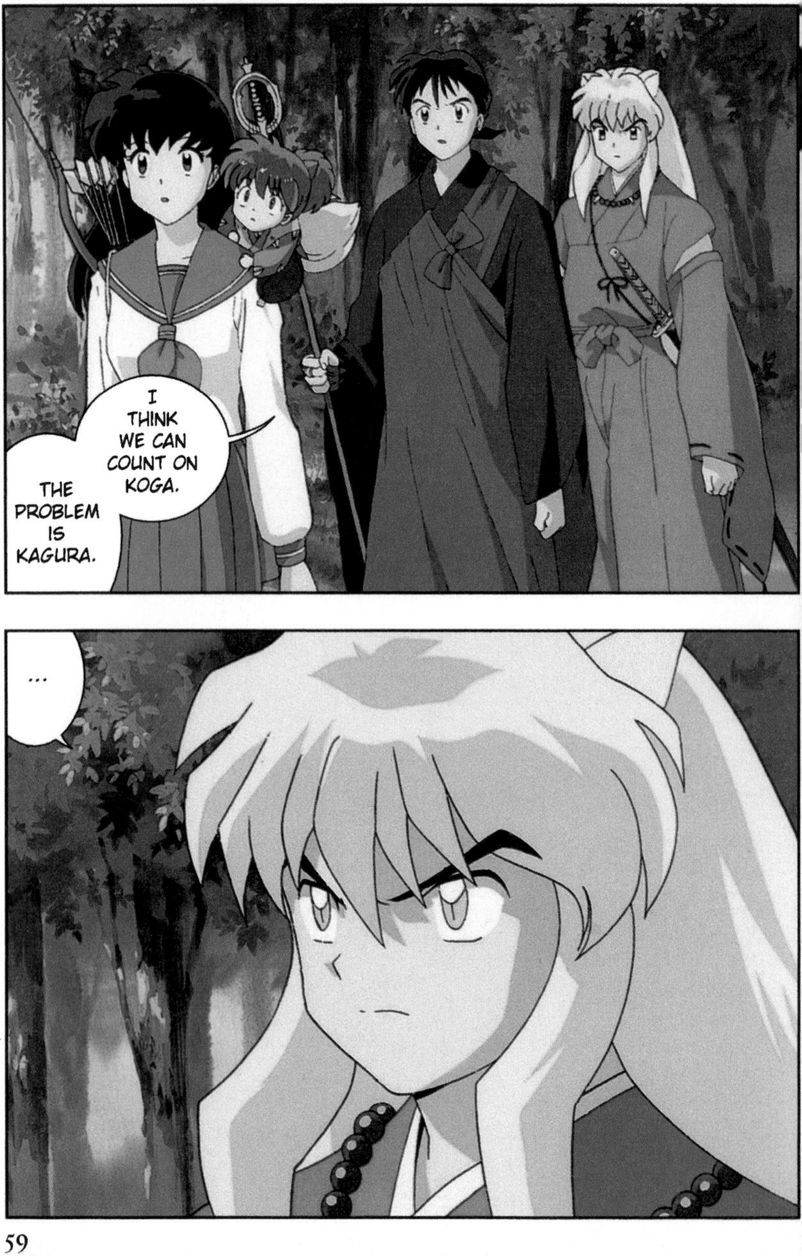
I THINK WE CAN COUNT ON KOGA.
THE PROBLEM IS KAGURA.
...

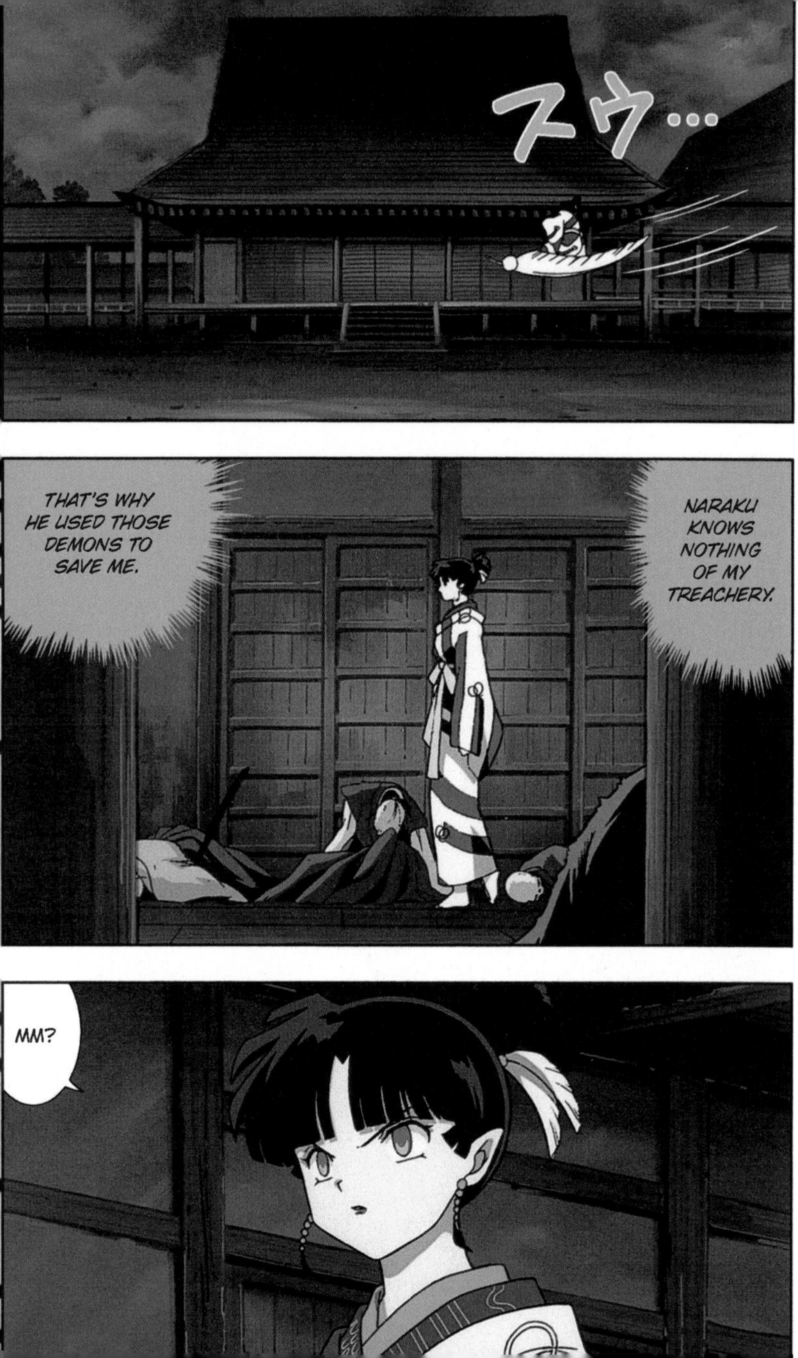
スウ…
NARAKU KNOWS NOTHING OF MY TREACHERY.
THAT'S WHY HE USED THOSE DEMONS TO SAVE ME.
MM?

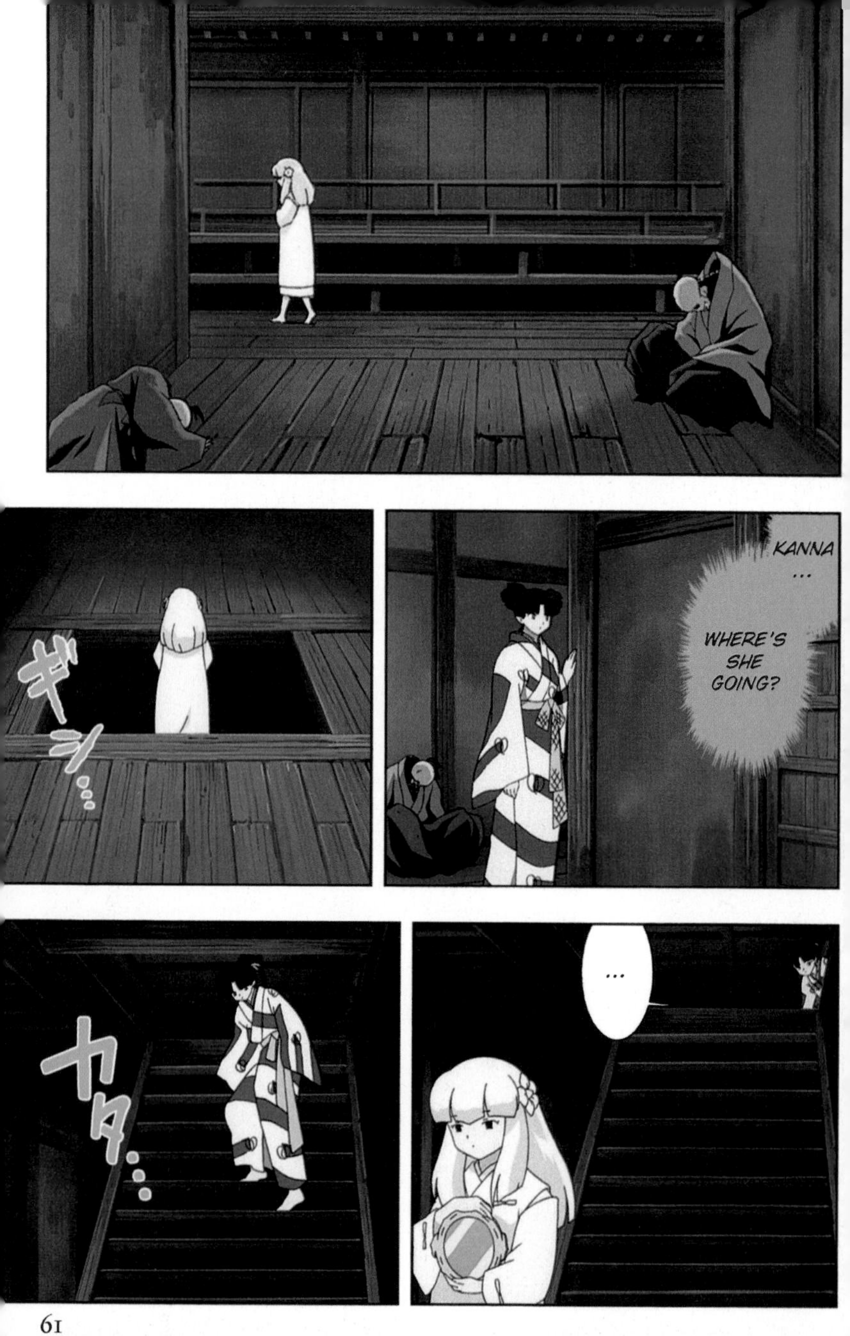
KANNA ...
WHERE'S SHE GOING?
ギシ...
...
ヤタ...

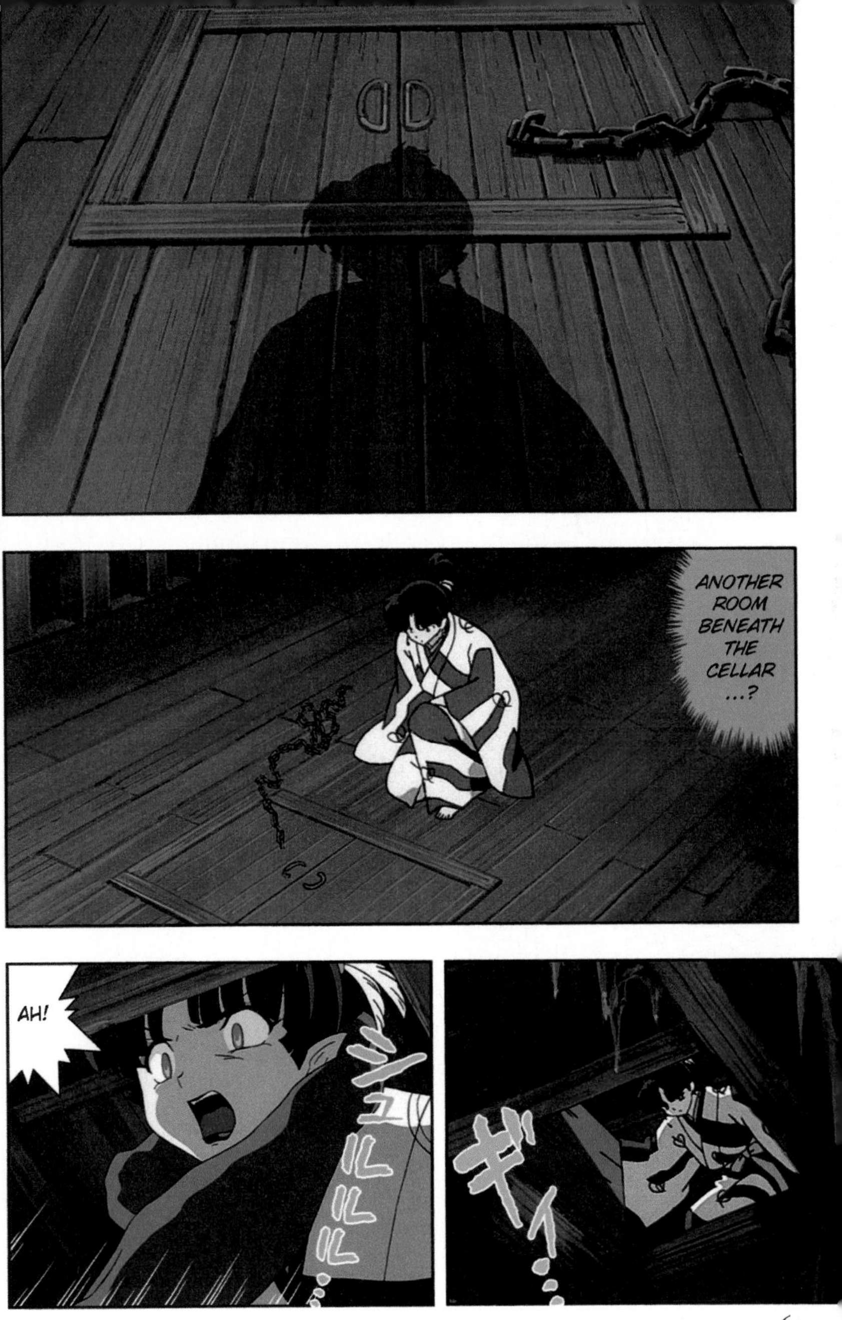
ANOTHER ROOM BENEATH THE CELLAR ...?
ギィ…
AH!
シュルルル…

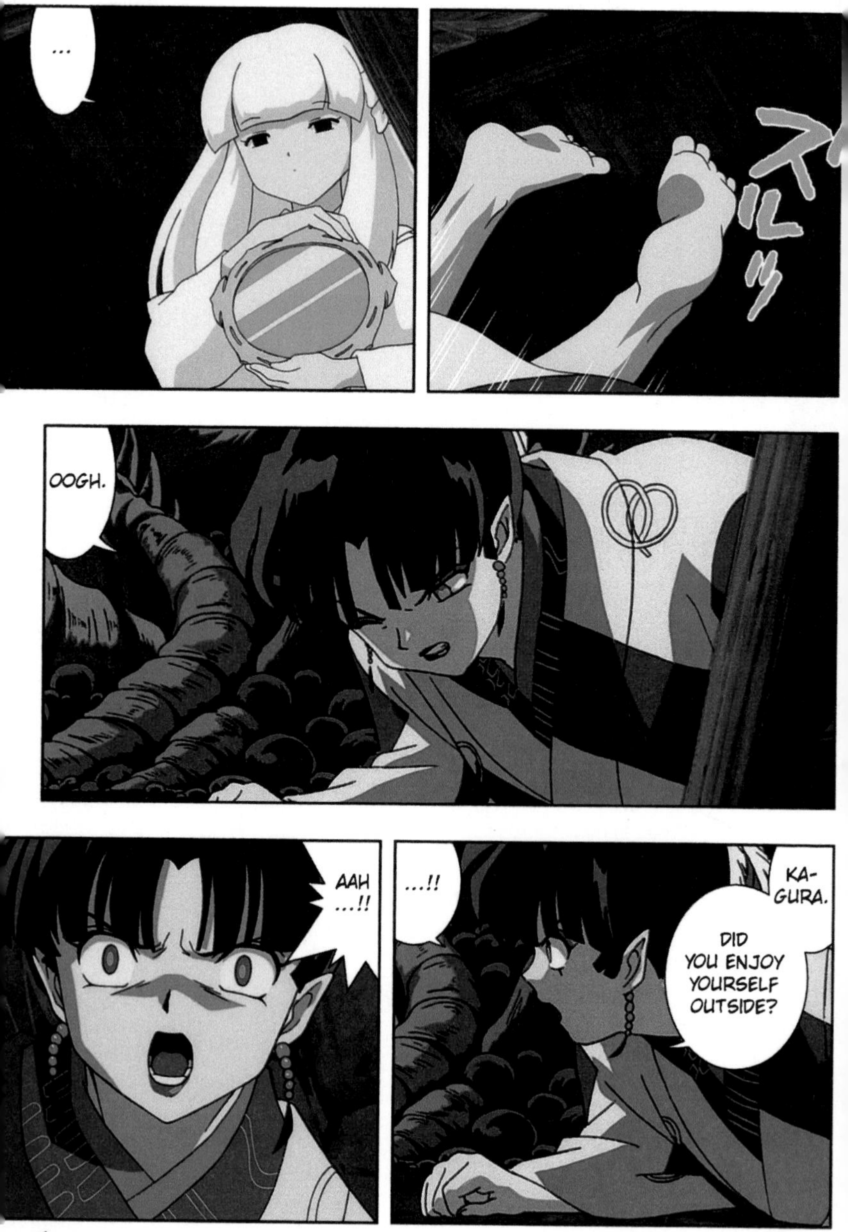

スルッ
...
OOGH.
KA-GURA.
DID YOU ENJOY YOURSELF OUTSIDE?
...!!
AAH ...!!

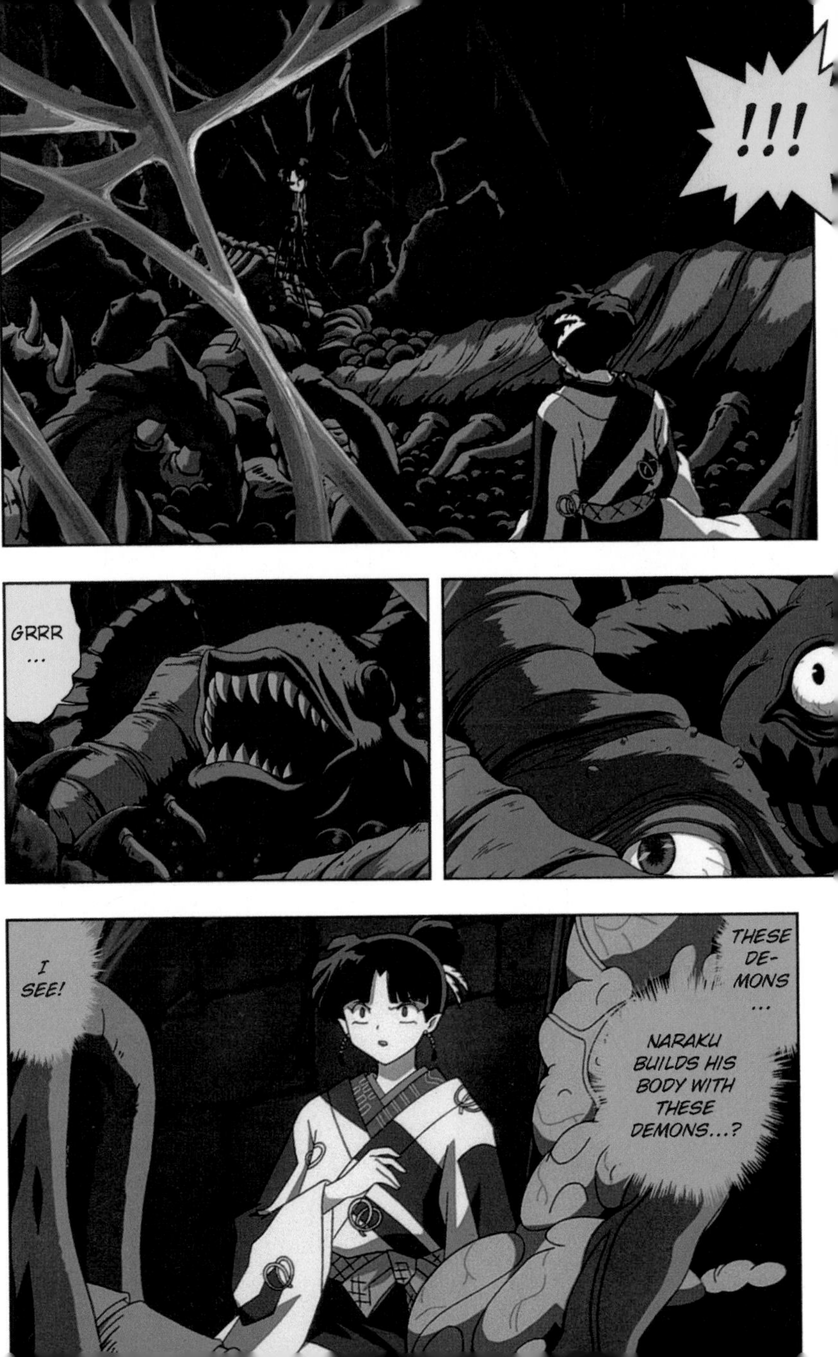
!!!
GRRR ...
THESE DE-MONS ...
NARAKU BUILDS HIS BODY WITH THESE DEMONS...?
I SEE!

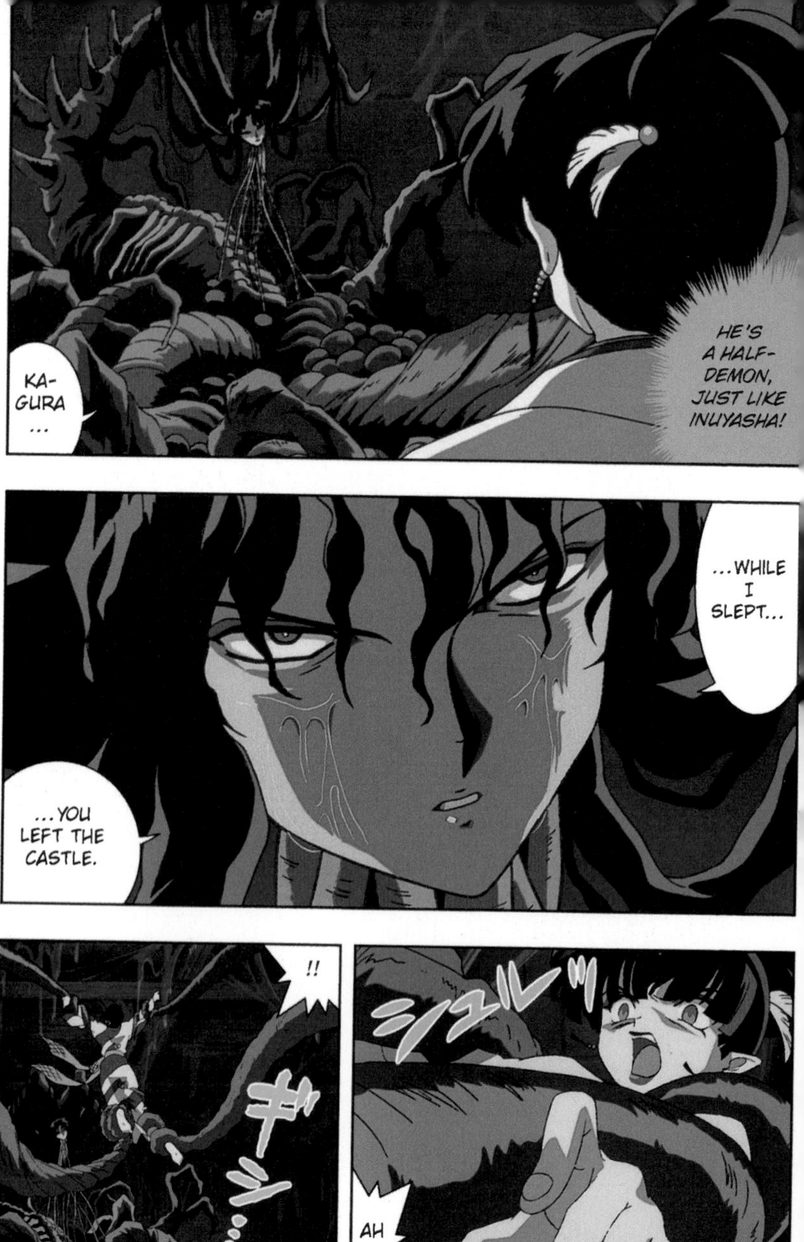
HE'S A HALF-DEMON, JUST LIKE INUYASHA!
KA-GURA...
...WHILE I SLEPT...
...YOU LEFT THE CASTLE.
シュルッ
AH!!
!!
ギシ…

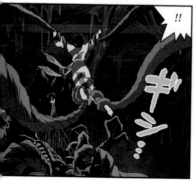

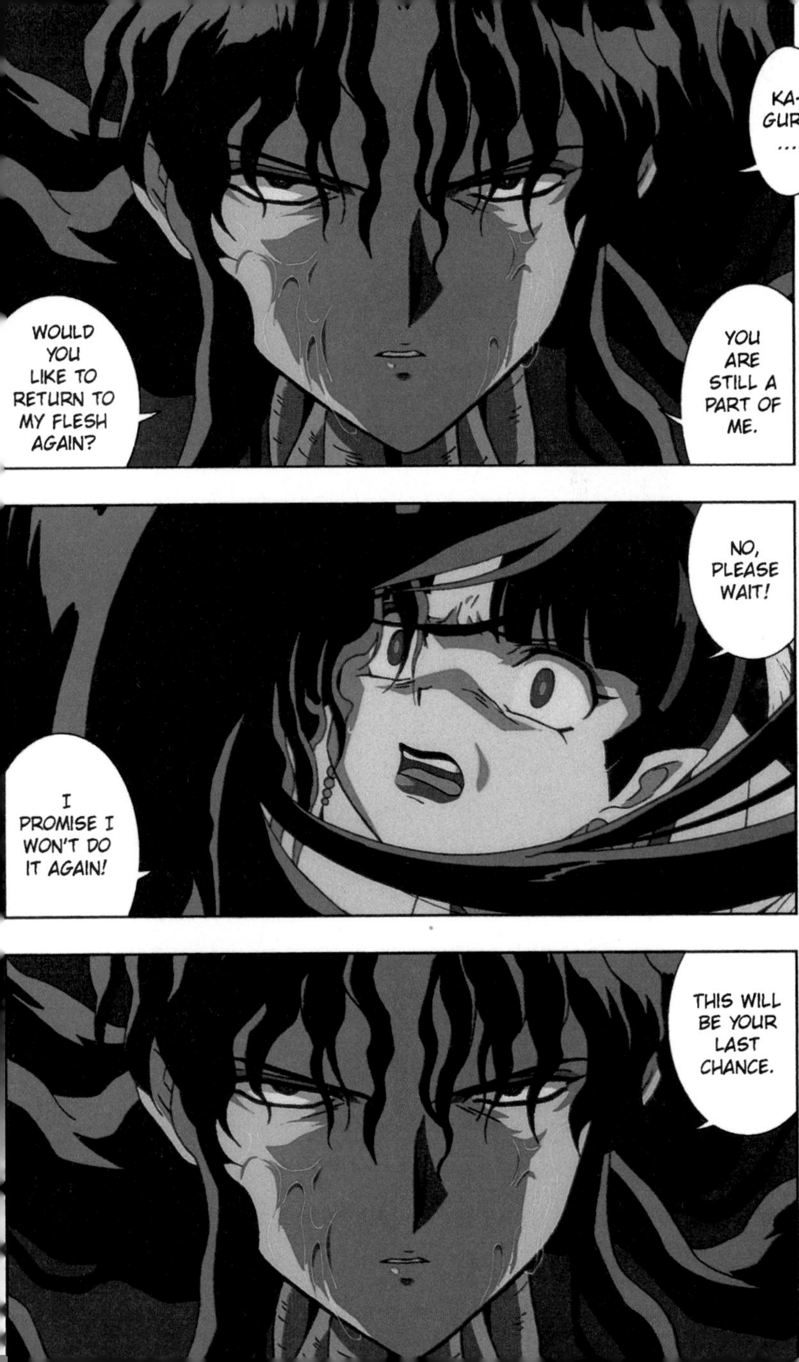
KA-GURA...
YOU ARE STILL A PART OF ME.
WOULD YOU LIKE TO RETURN TO MY FLESH AGAIN?
NO, PLEASE WAIT!
I PROMISE I WON'T DO IT AGAIN!
THIS WILL BE YOUR LAST CHANCE.

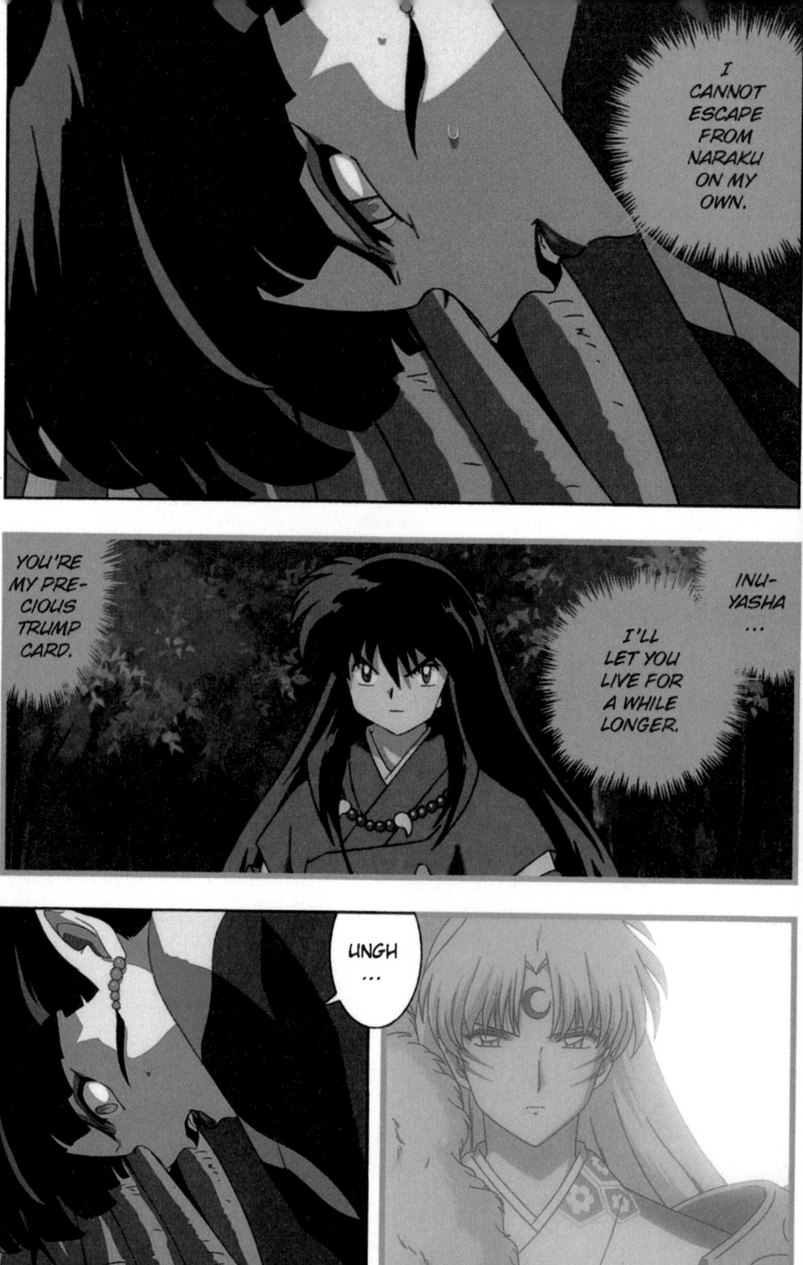
I CANNOT ESCAPE FROM NARAKU ON MY OWN.
INU-YASHA...
I'LL LET YOU LIVE FOR A WHILE LONGER.
YOU'RE MY PRE-CIOUS TRUMP CARD.
UNGH...

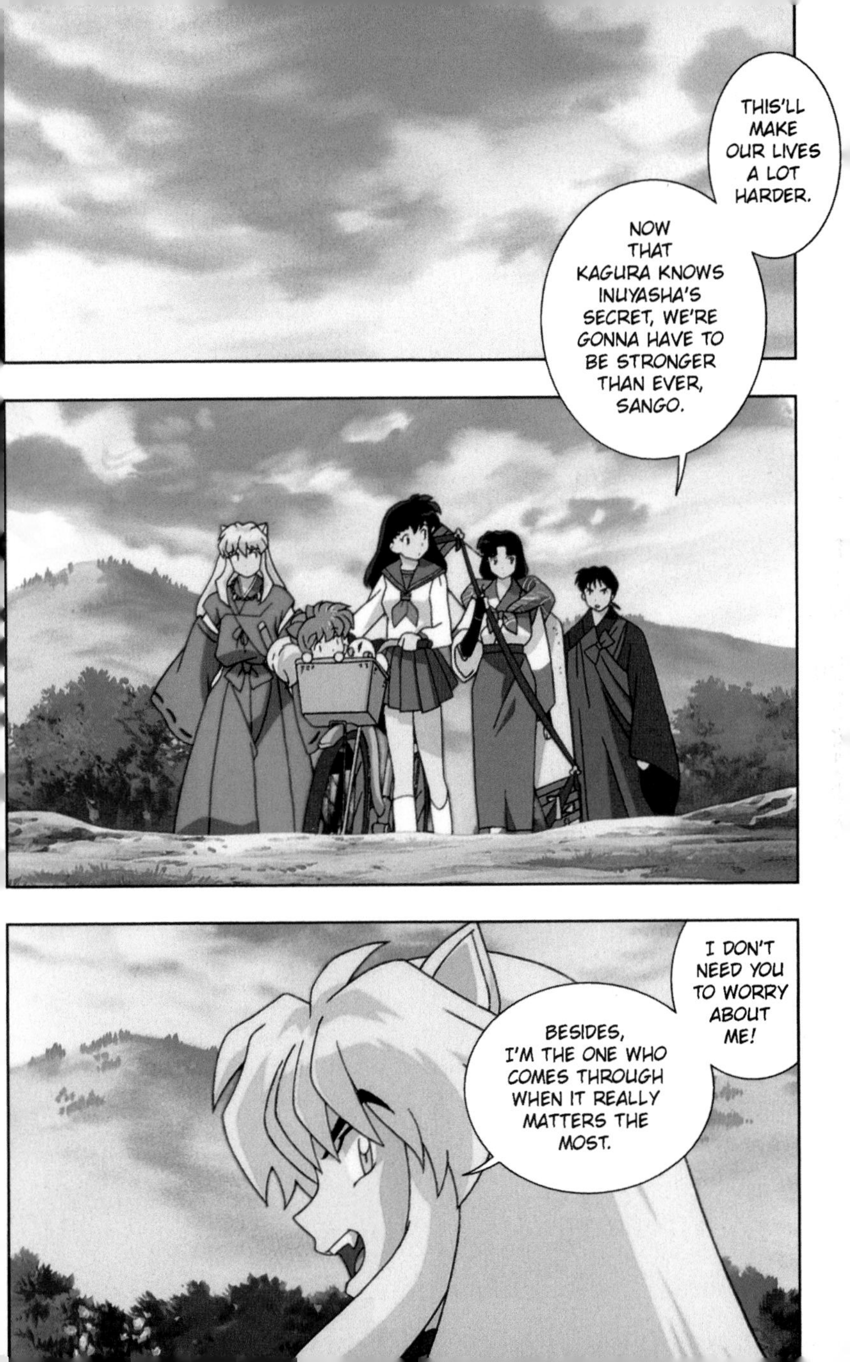
THIS'LL MAKE OUR LIVES A LOT HARDER.
NOW THAT KAGURA KNOWS INUYASHA'S SECRET, WE'RE GONNA HAVE TO BE STRONGER THAN EVER, SANGO.
I DON'T NEED YOU TO WORRY ABOUT ME!
BESIDES, I'M THE ONE WHO COMES THROUGH WHEN IT REALLY MATTERS THE MOST.

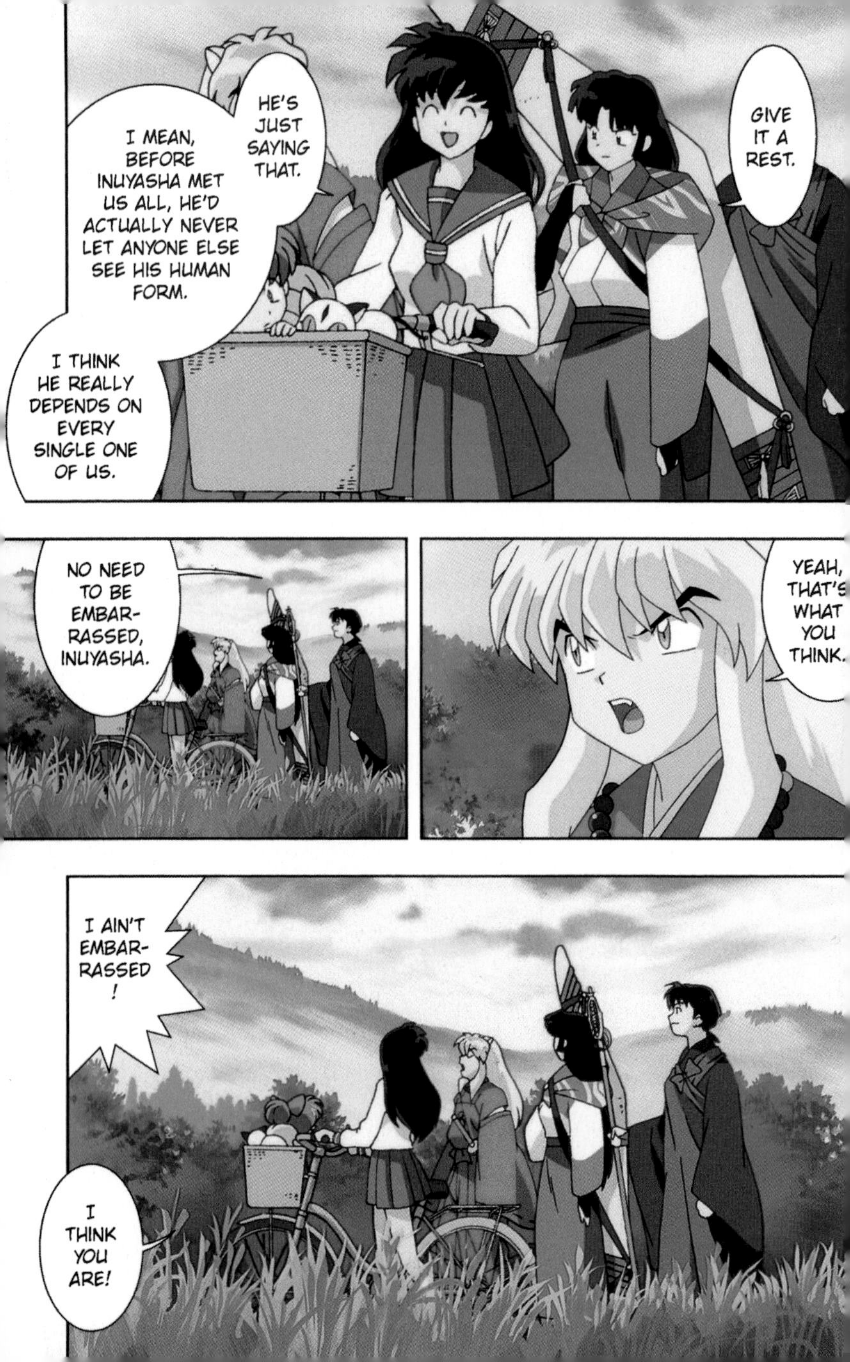
GIVE IT A REST.
HE'S JUST SAYING THAT.
I MEAN, BEFORE INUYASHA MET US ALL, HE'D ACTUALLY NEVER LET ANYONE ELSE SEE HIS HUMAN FORM.
I THINK HE REALLY DEPENDS ON EVERY SINGLE ONE OF US.
YEAH, THAT'S WHAT YOU THINK.
NO NEED TO BE EMBARRASSED, INUYASHA.
I AIN'T EMBARRASSED!
I THINK YOU ARE!

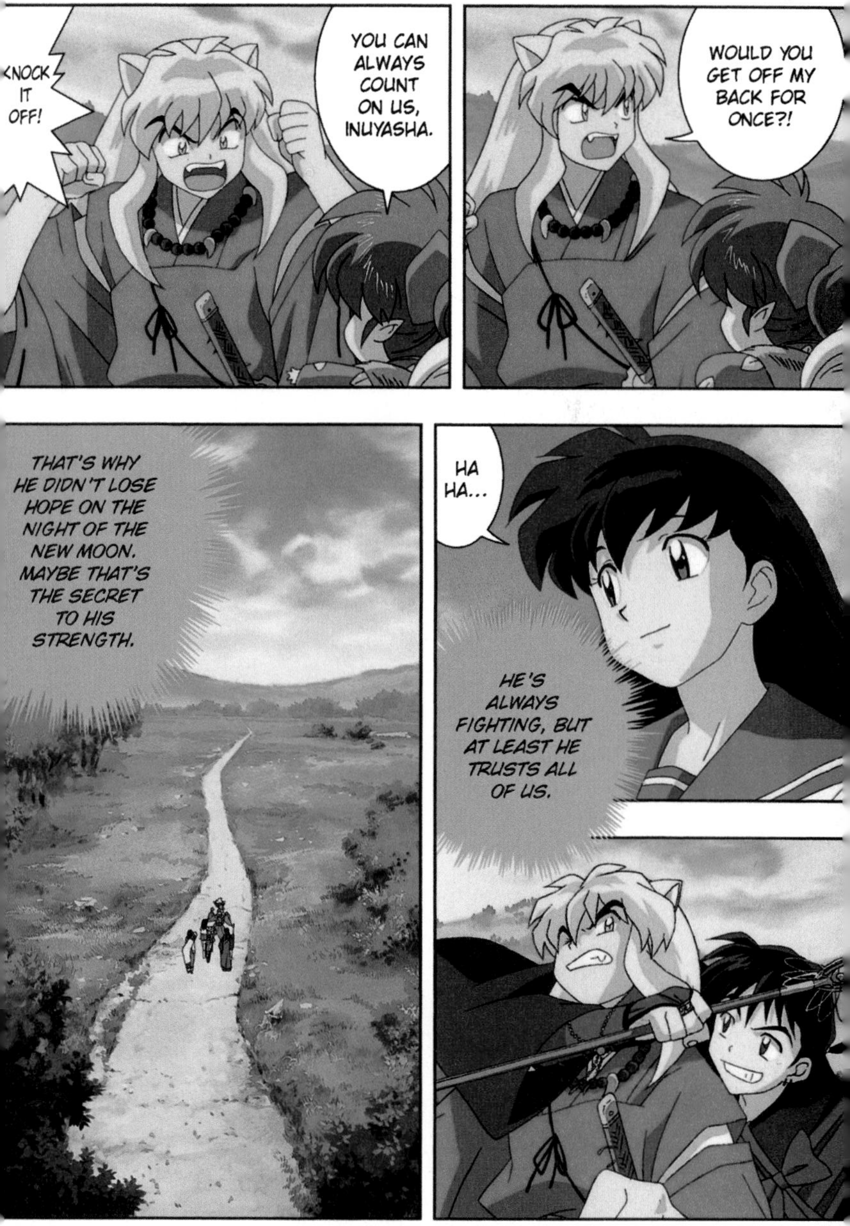
WOULD YOU GET OFF MY BACK FOR ONCE?!
YOU CAN ALWAYS COUNT ON US, INUYASHA.
KNOCK IT OFF!
HA HA...
HE'S ALWAYS FIGHTING, BUT AT LEAST HE TRUSTS ALL OF US.
THAT'S WHY HE DIDN'T LOSE HOPE ON THE NIGHT OF THE NEW MOON. MAYBE THAT'S THE SECRET TO HIS STRENGTH.

68
Shippo Gets an Angry Challenge

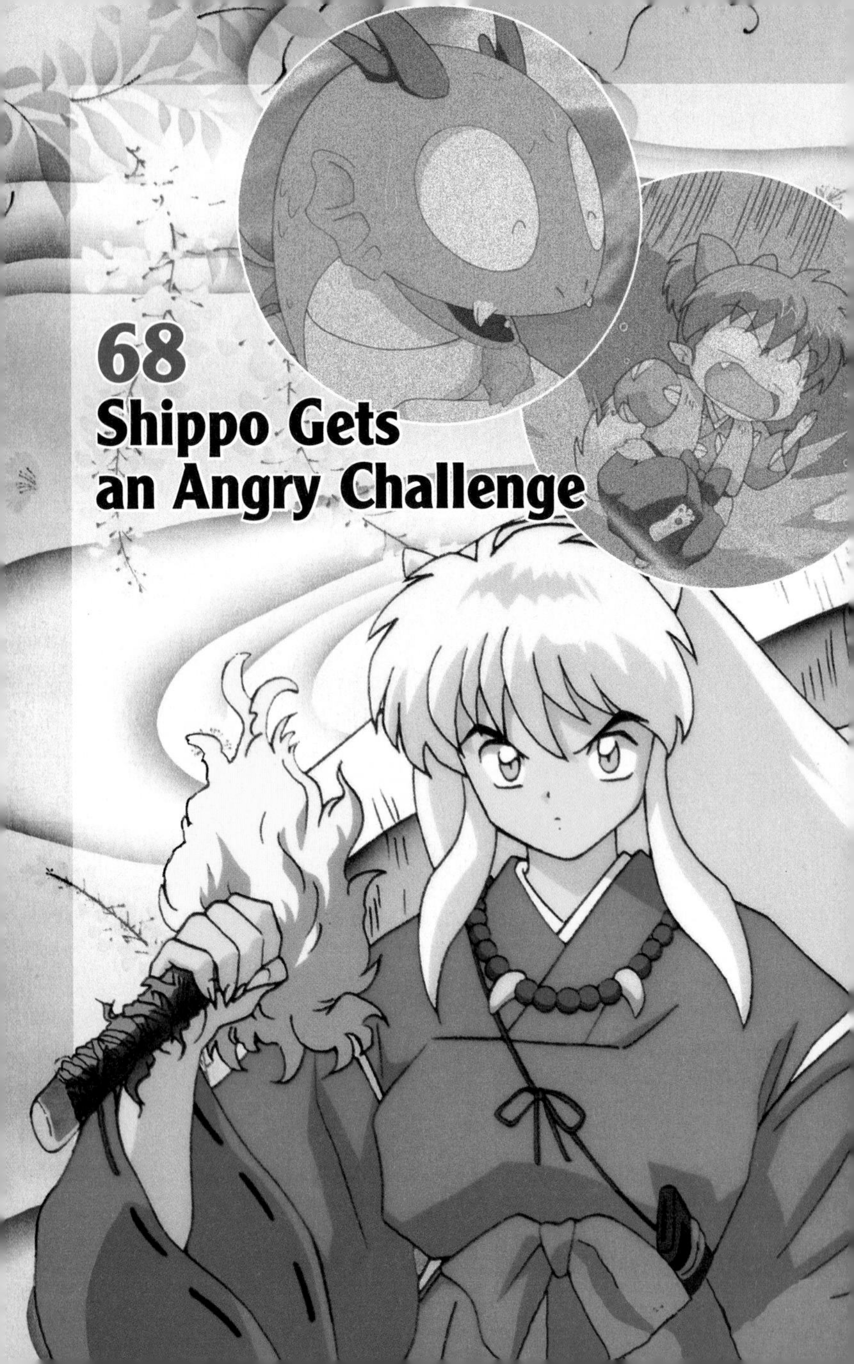

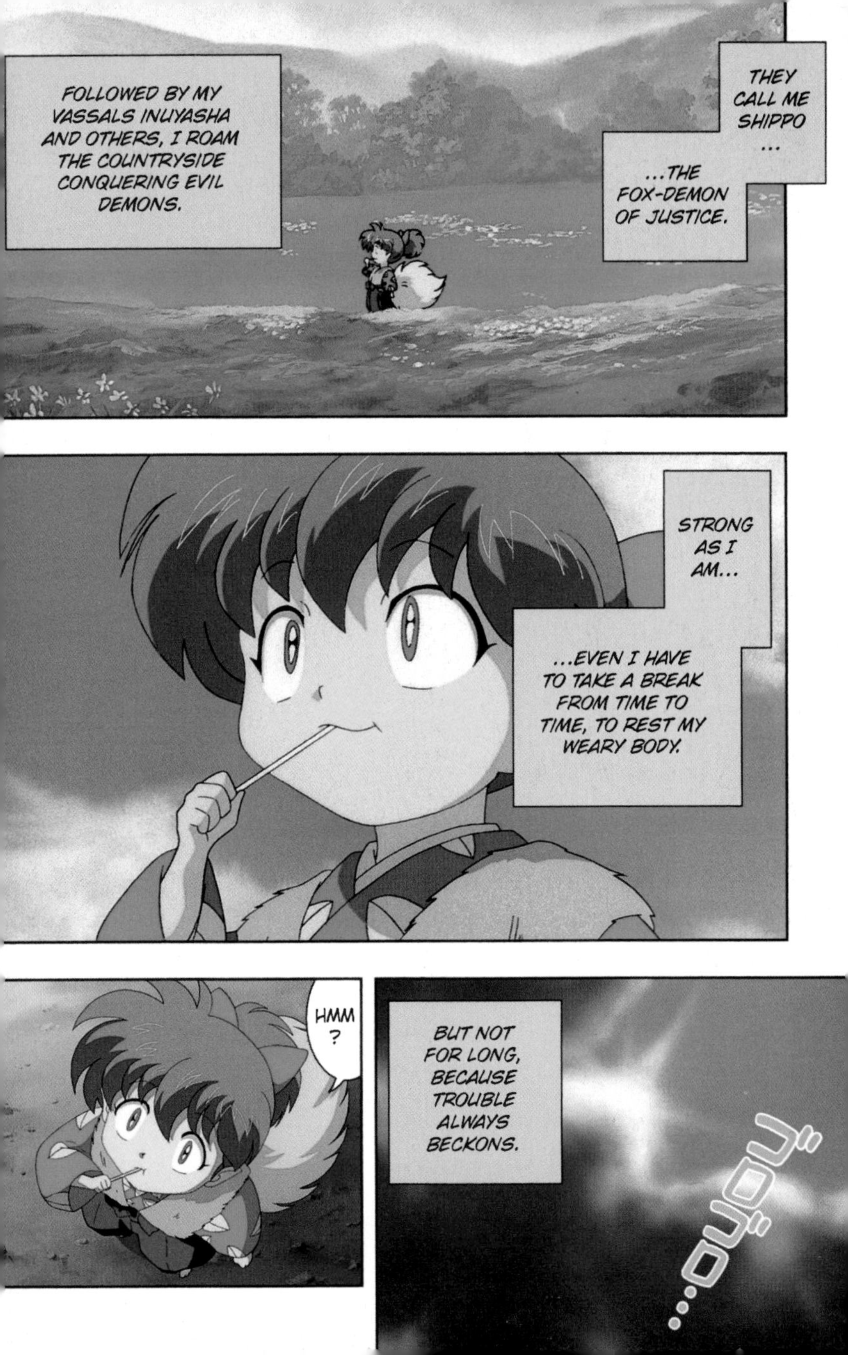
THEY CALL ME SHIPPO ...
...THE FOX-DEMON OF JUSTICE.
FOLLOWED BY MY VASSALS INUYASHA AND OTHERS, I ROAM THE COUNTRYSIDE CONQUERING EVIL DEMONS.
STRONG AS I AM...
...EVEN I HAVE TO TAKE A BREAK FROM TIME TO TIME, TO REST MY WEARY BODY.
BUT NOT FOR LONG, BECAUSE TROUBLE ALWAYS BECKONS.
ゴロゴロ…
HMM ?

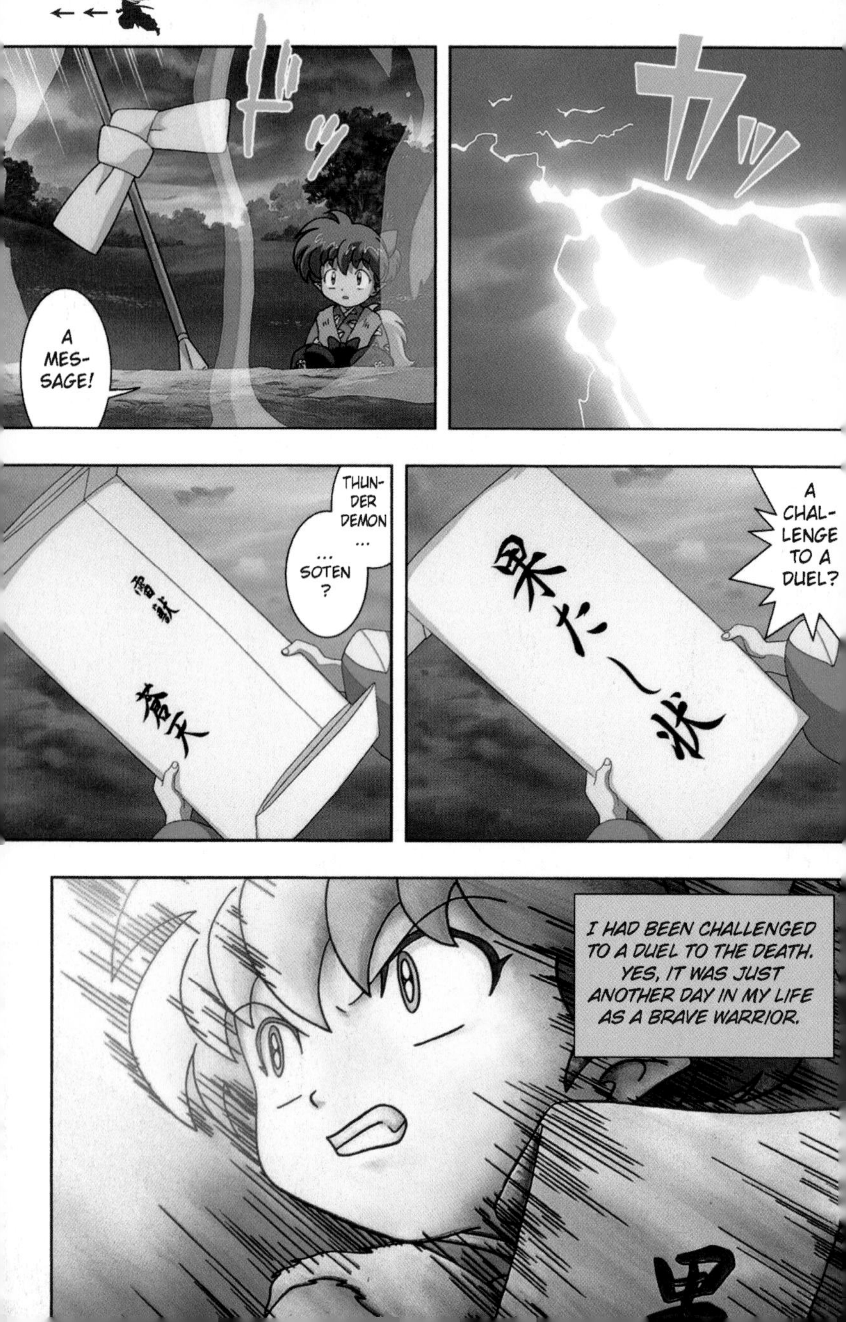
カッ
ドッ
A MESSAGE!
果たし状
A CHALLENGE TO A DUEL?
雷獣
蒼天
THUNDER DEMON ... ... SOTEN?
I HAD BEEN CHALLENGED TO A DUEL TO THE DEATH. YES, IT WAS JUST ANOTHER DAY IN MY LIFE AS A BRAVE WARRIOR.

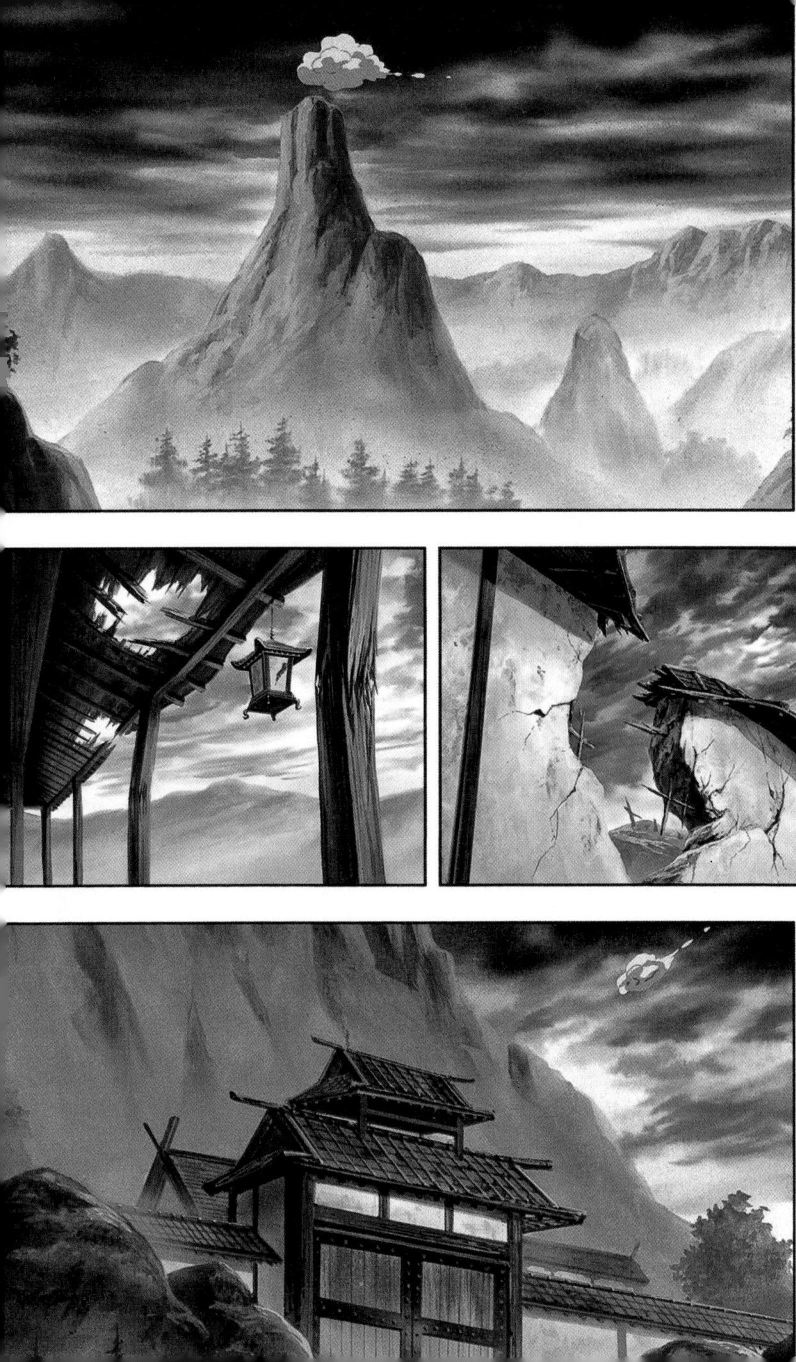

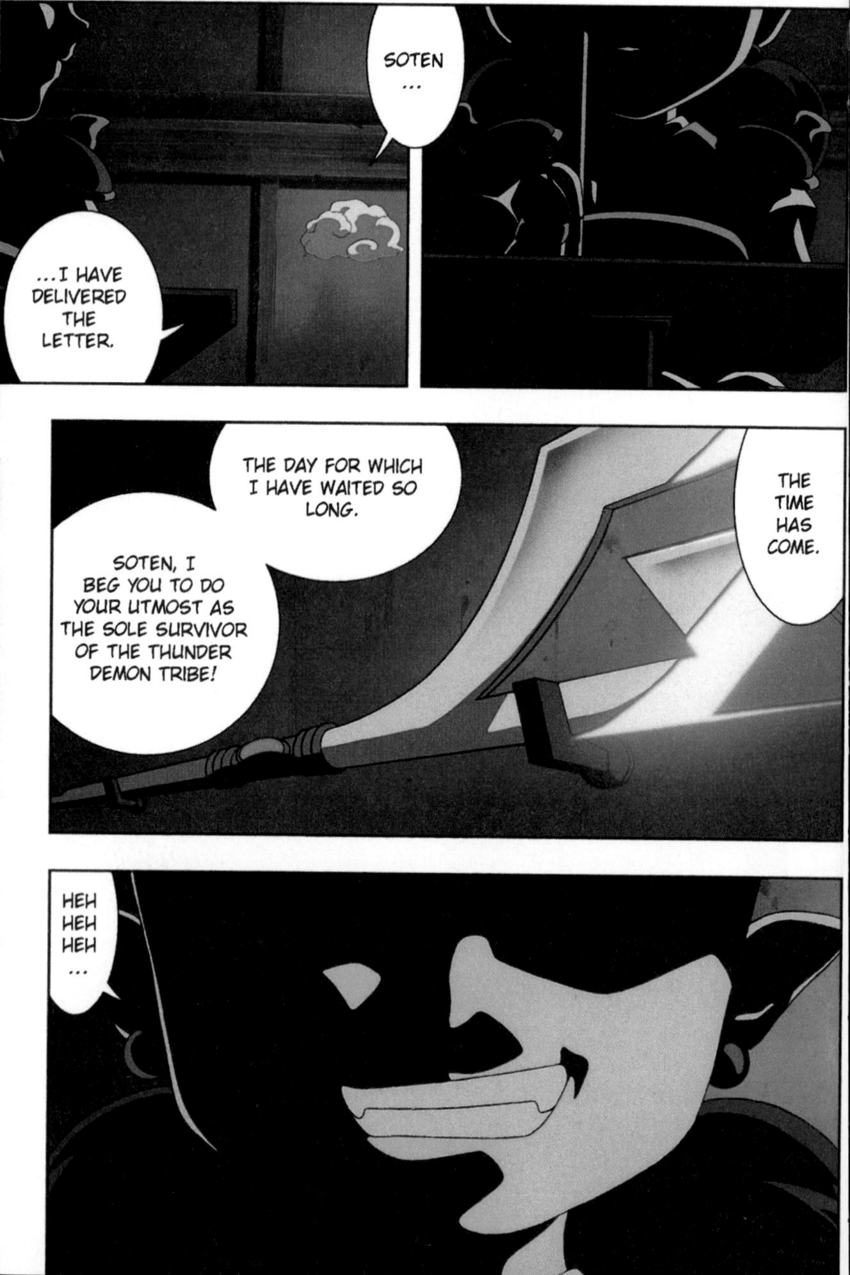
SOTEN ...
...I HAVE DELIVERED THE LETTER.
THE TIME HAS COME.
THE DAY FOR WHICH I HAVE WAITED SO LONG.
SOTEN, I BEG YOU TO DO YOUR UTMOST AS THE SOLE SURVIVOR OF THE THUNDER DEMON TRIBE!
HEH HEH HEH ...

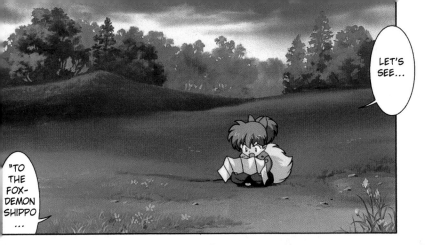

LET'S SEE...

"TO THE FOX-DEMON SHIPPO..."

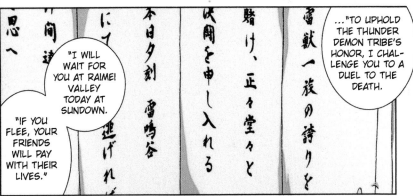

..."TO UPHOLD THE THUNDER DEMON TRIBE'S HONOR, I CHALLENGE YOU TO A DUEL TO THE DEATH.

"I WILL WAIT FOR YOU AT RAIME! VALLEY TODAY AT SUNDOWN.

"IF YOU FLEE, YOUR FRIENDS WILL PAY WITH THEIR LIVES."

雷獣一族の誇りを

賭け、正々堂々と

決闘を申し入れる

本日夕刻　雷鳴谷

にて

間達

思へ

進げれ

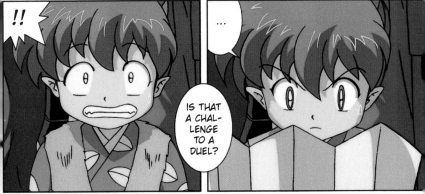

!!

...

IS THAT A CHALLENGE TO A DUEL?

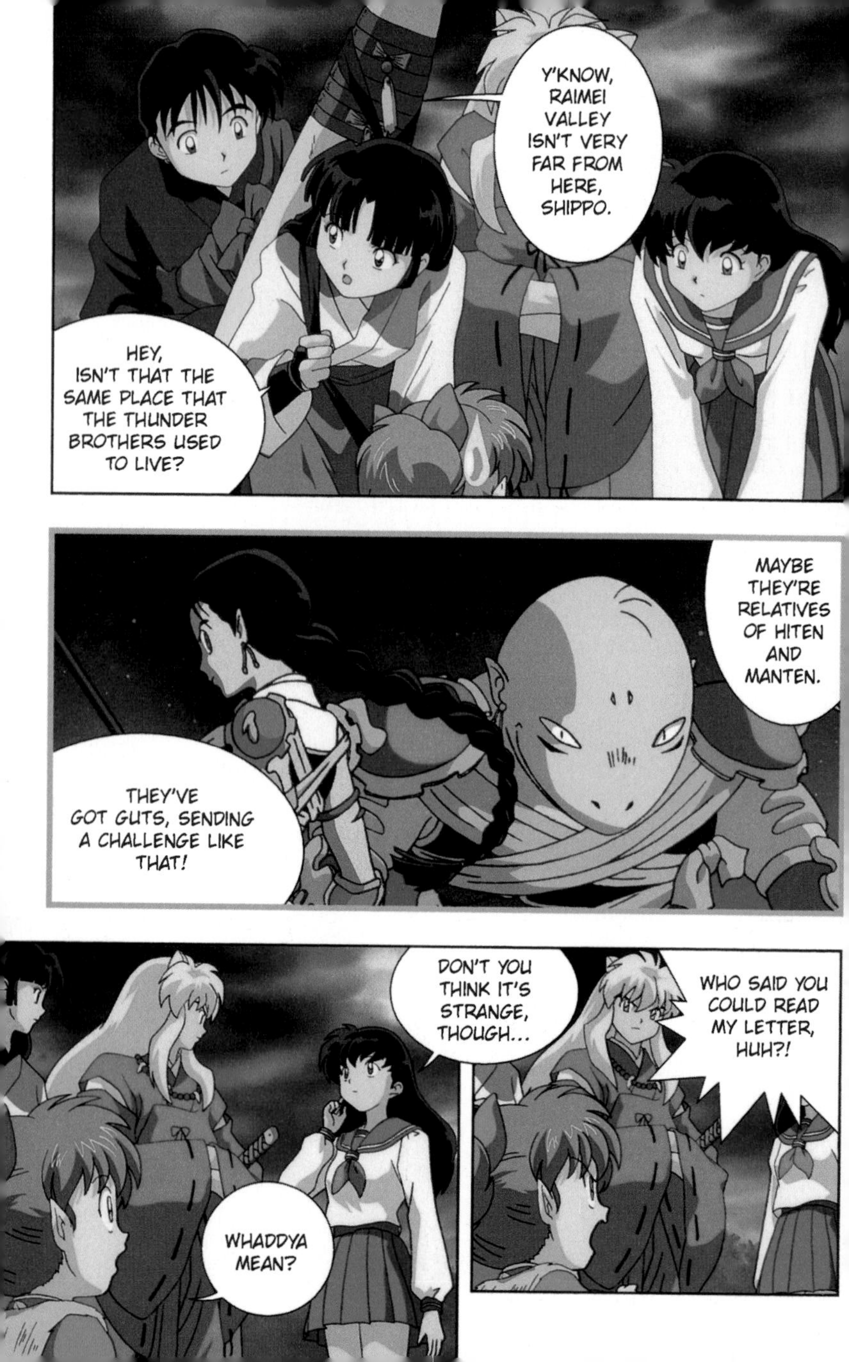
Y'KNOW, RAIMEI VALLEY ISN'T VERY FAR FROM HERE, SHIPPO.
HEY, ISN'T THAT THE SAME PLACE THAT THE THUNDER BROTHERS USED TO LIVE?
MAYBE THEY'RE RELATIVES OF HITEN AND MANTEN.
THEY'VE GOT GUTS, SENDING A CHALLENGE LIKE THAT!
WHO SAID YOU COULD READ MY LETTER, HUH?!
DON'T YOU THINK IT'S STRANGE, THOUGH...
WHADDYA MEAN?

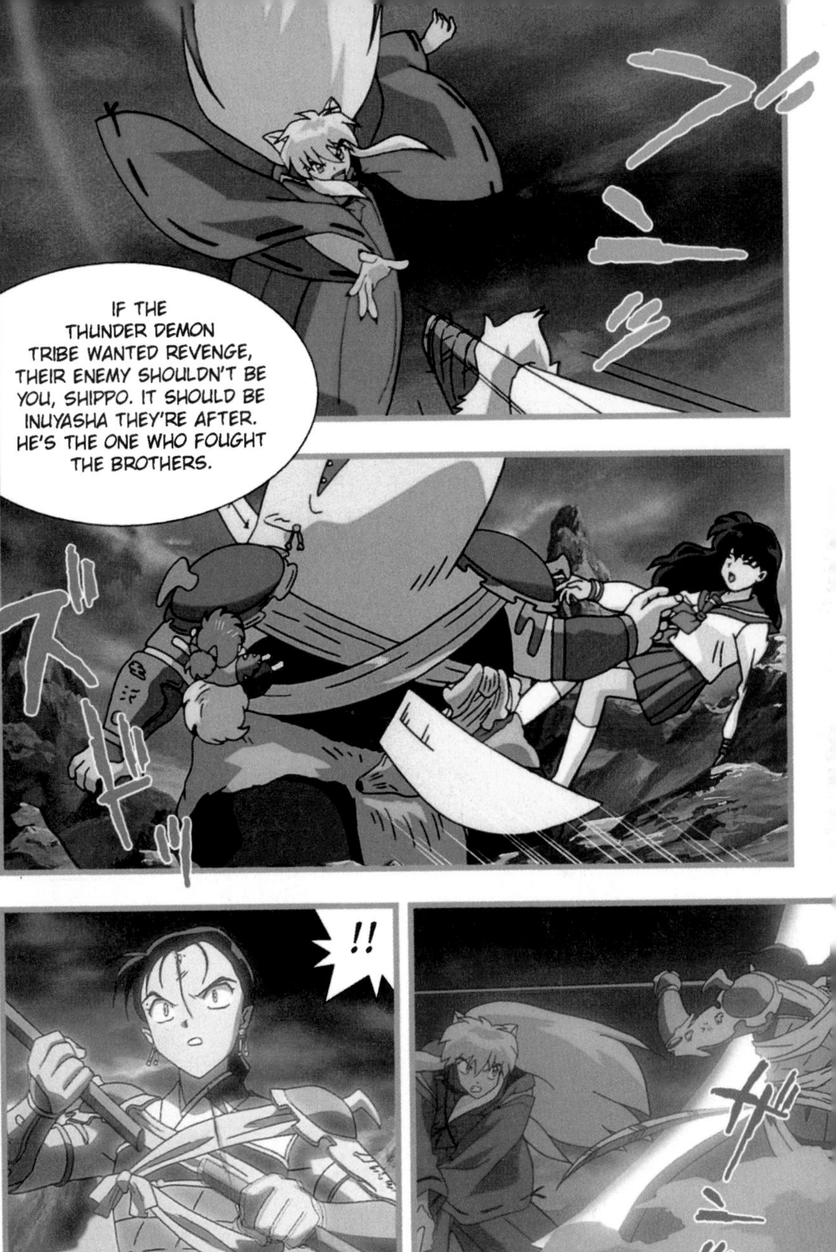
IF THE THUNDER DEMON TRIBE WANTED REVENGE, THEIR ENEMY SHOULDN'T BE YOU, SHIPPO. IT SHOULD BE INUYASHA THEY'RE AFTER. HE'S THE ONE WHO FOUGHT THE BROTHERS.
!!

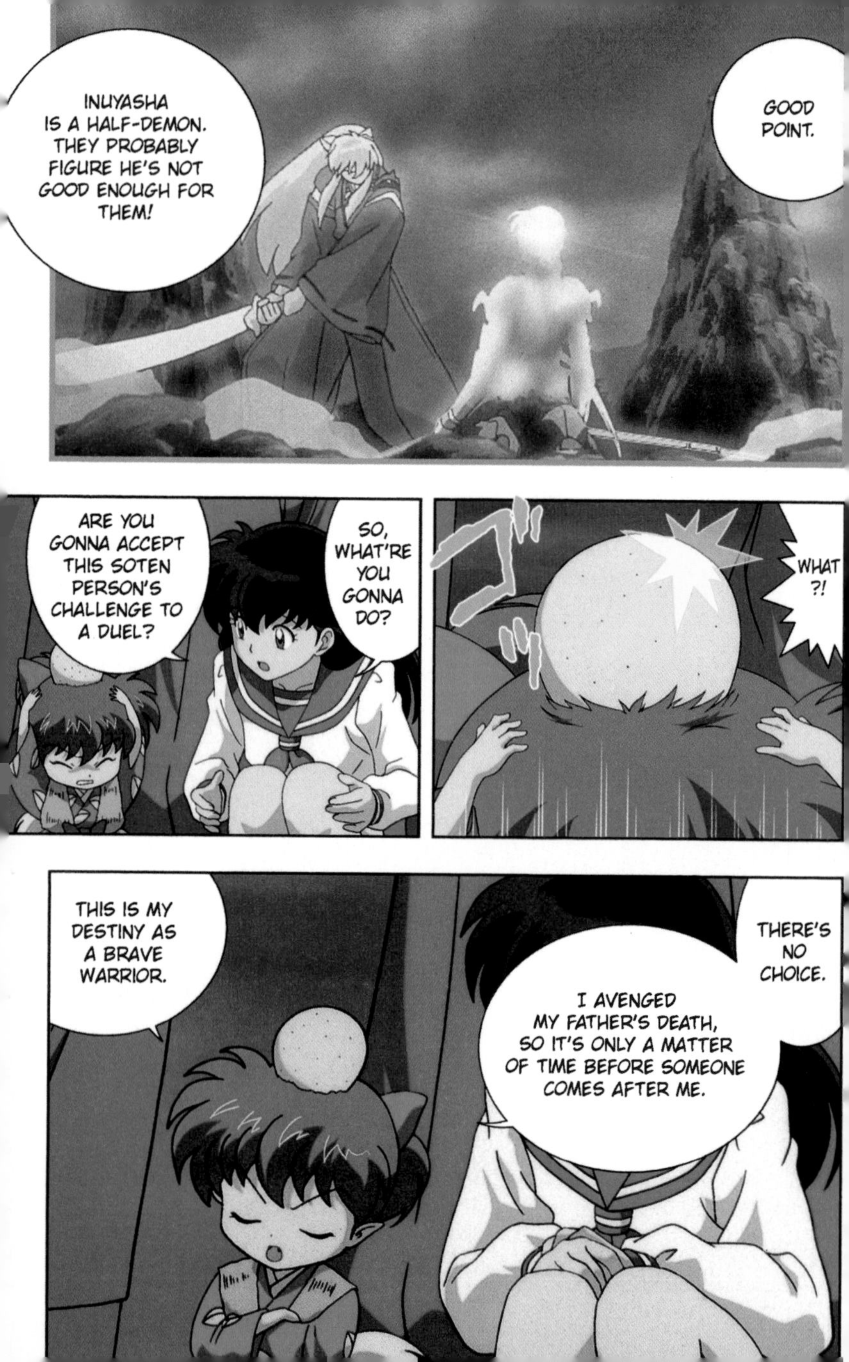
GOOD POINT.
INUYASHA IS A HALF-DEMON. THEY PROBABLY FIGURE HE'S NOT GOOD ENOUGH FOR THEM!
WHAT ?!
SO, WHAT'RE YOU GONNA DO?
ARE YOU GONNA ACCEPT THIS SOTEN PERSON'S CHALLENGE TO A DUEL?
THERE'S NO CHOICE.
I AVENGED MY FATHER'S DEATH, SO IT'S ONLY A MATTER OF TIME BEFORE SOMEONE COMES AFTER ME.
THIS IS MY DESTINY AS A BRAVE WARRIOR.

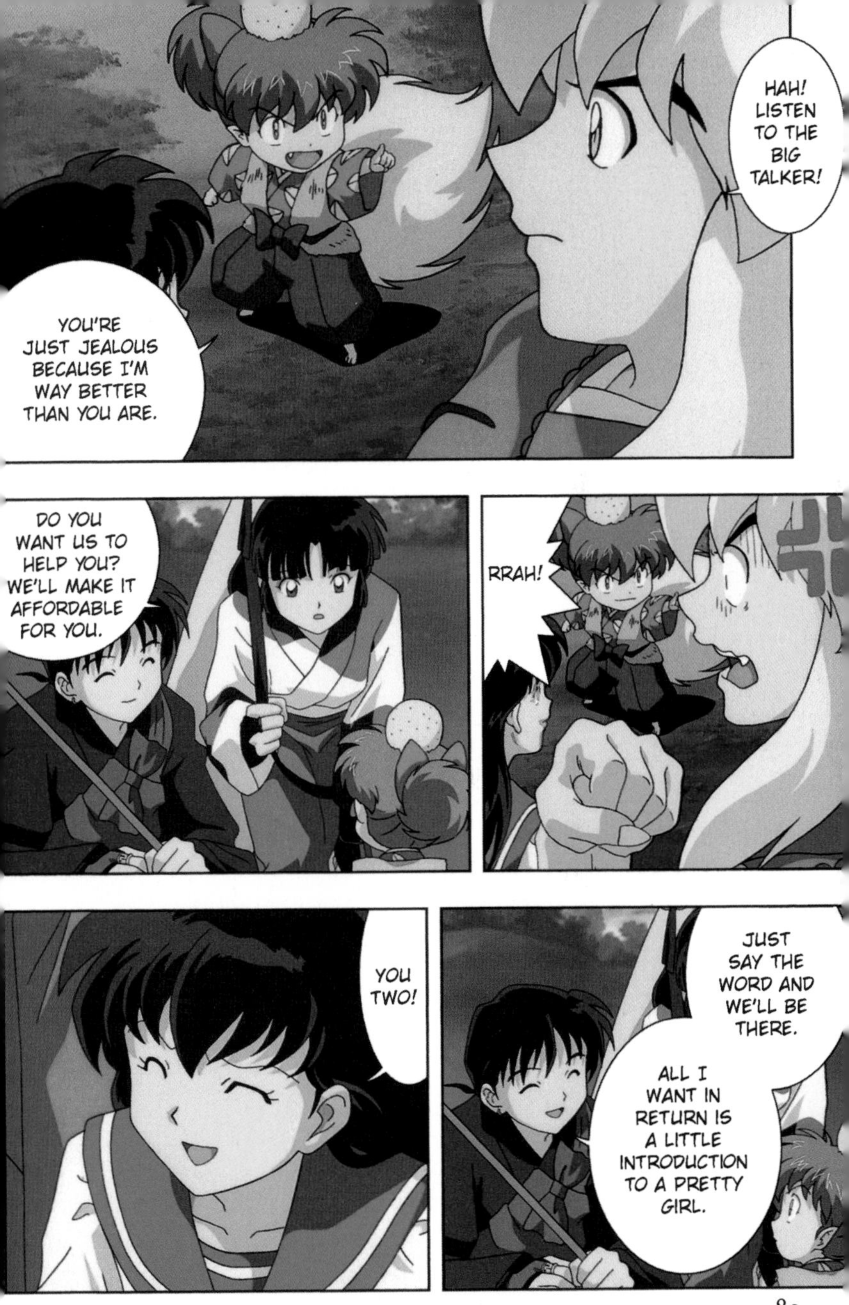
HAH! LISTEN TO THE BIG TALKER!
YOU'RE JUST JEALOUS BECAUSE I'M WAY BETTER THAN YOU ARE.
RRAH!
DO YOU WANT US TO HELP YOU? WE'LL MAKE IT AFFORDABLE FOR YOU.
JUST SAY THE WORD AND WE'LL BE THERE.
ALL I WANT IN RETURN IS A LITTLE INTRODUCTION TO A PRETTY GIRL.
YOU TWO!

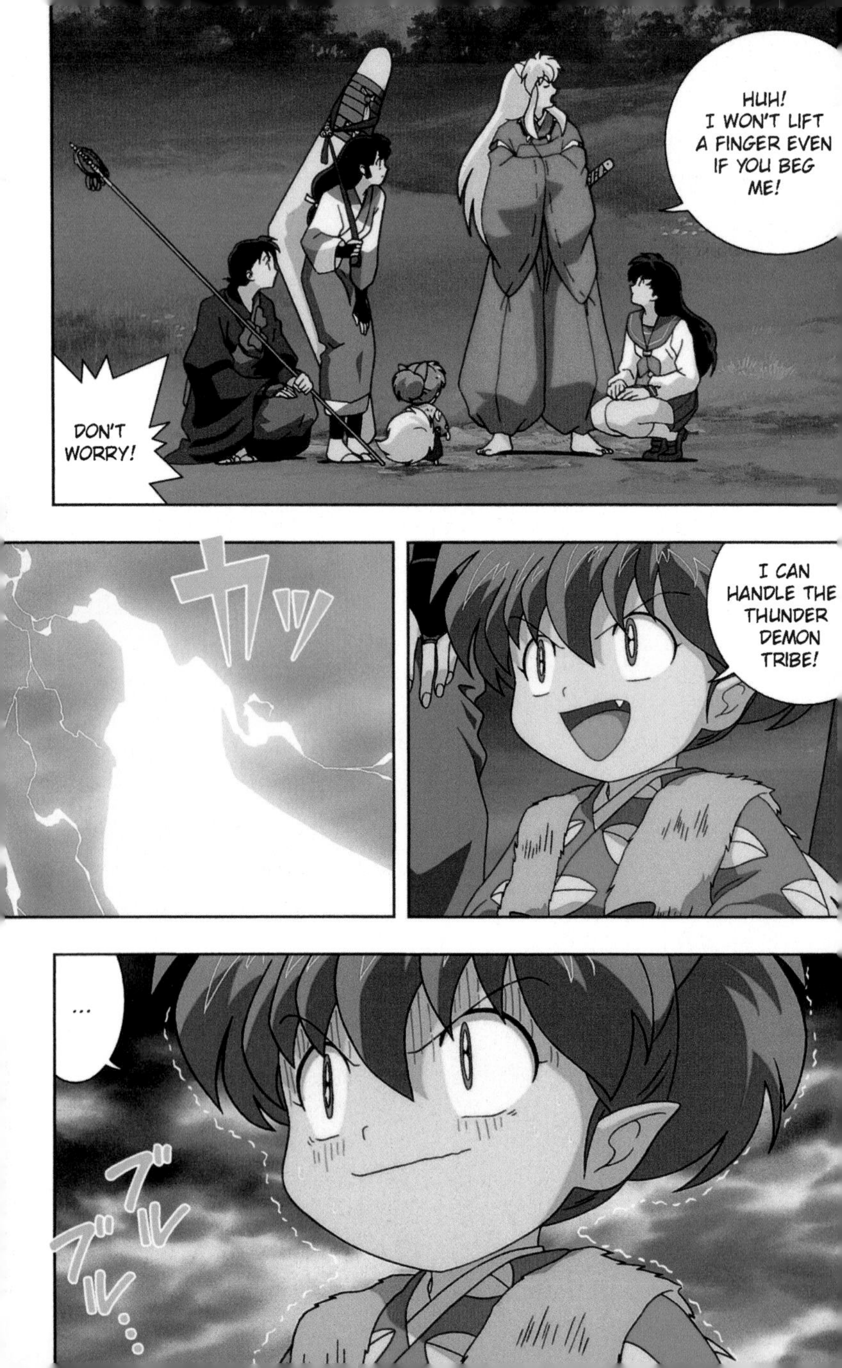
HUH! I WON'T LIFT A FINGER EVEN IF YOU BEG ME!
DON'T WORRY!
I CAN HANDLE THE THUNDER DEMON TRIBE!
カッ
...
ブルブル...

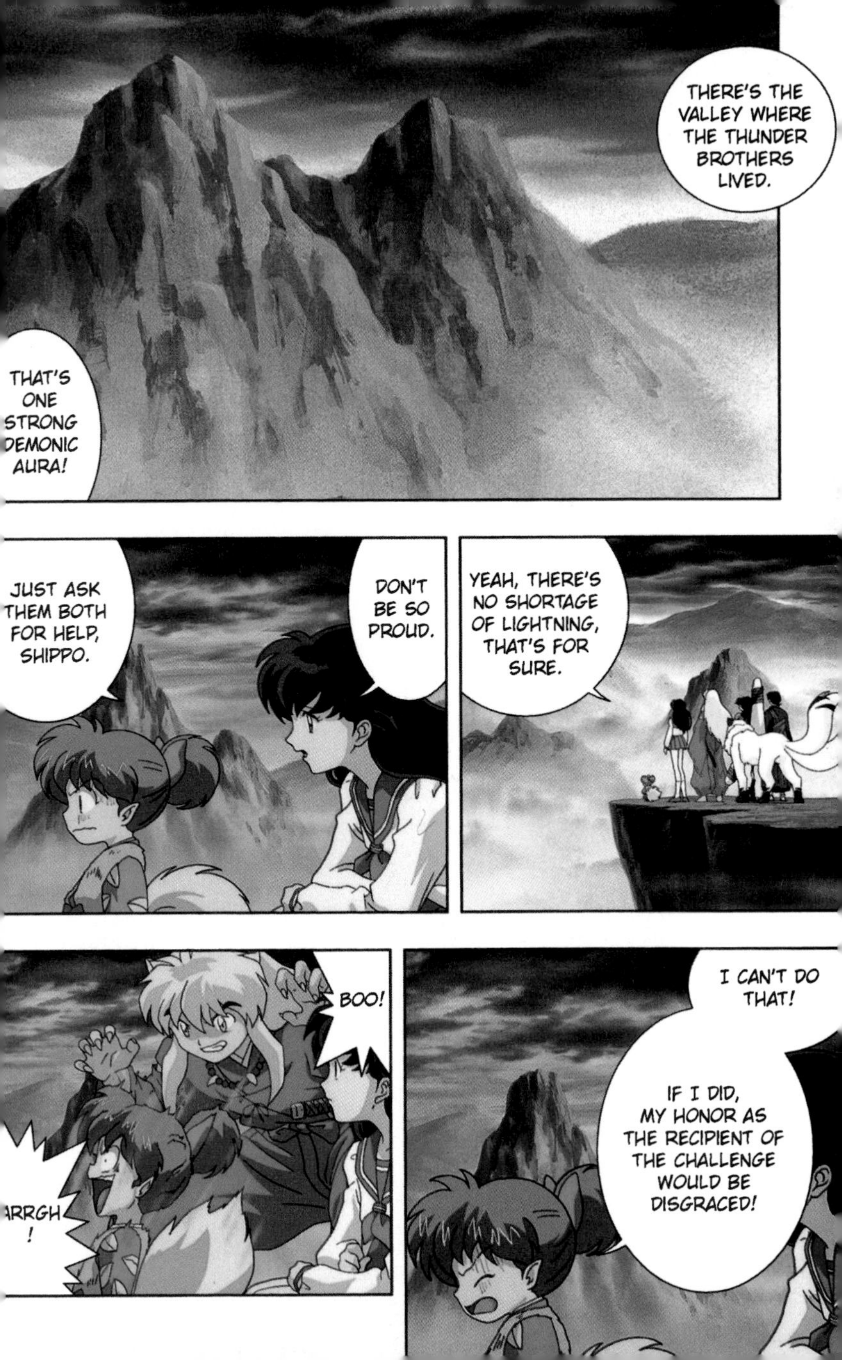
THERE'S THE VALLEY WHERE THE THUNDER BROTHERS LIVED.
THAT'S ONE STRONG DEMONIC AURA!
YEAH, THERE'S NO SHORTAGE OF LIGHTNING, THAT'S FOR SURE.
DON'T BE SO PROUD.
JUST ASK THEM BOTH FOR HELP, SHIPPO.
I CAN'T DO THAT!
IF I DID, MY HONOR AS THE RECIPIENT OF THE CHALLENGE WOULD BE DISGRACED!
BOO!
ARRGH!

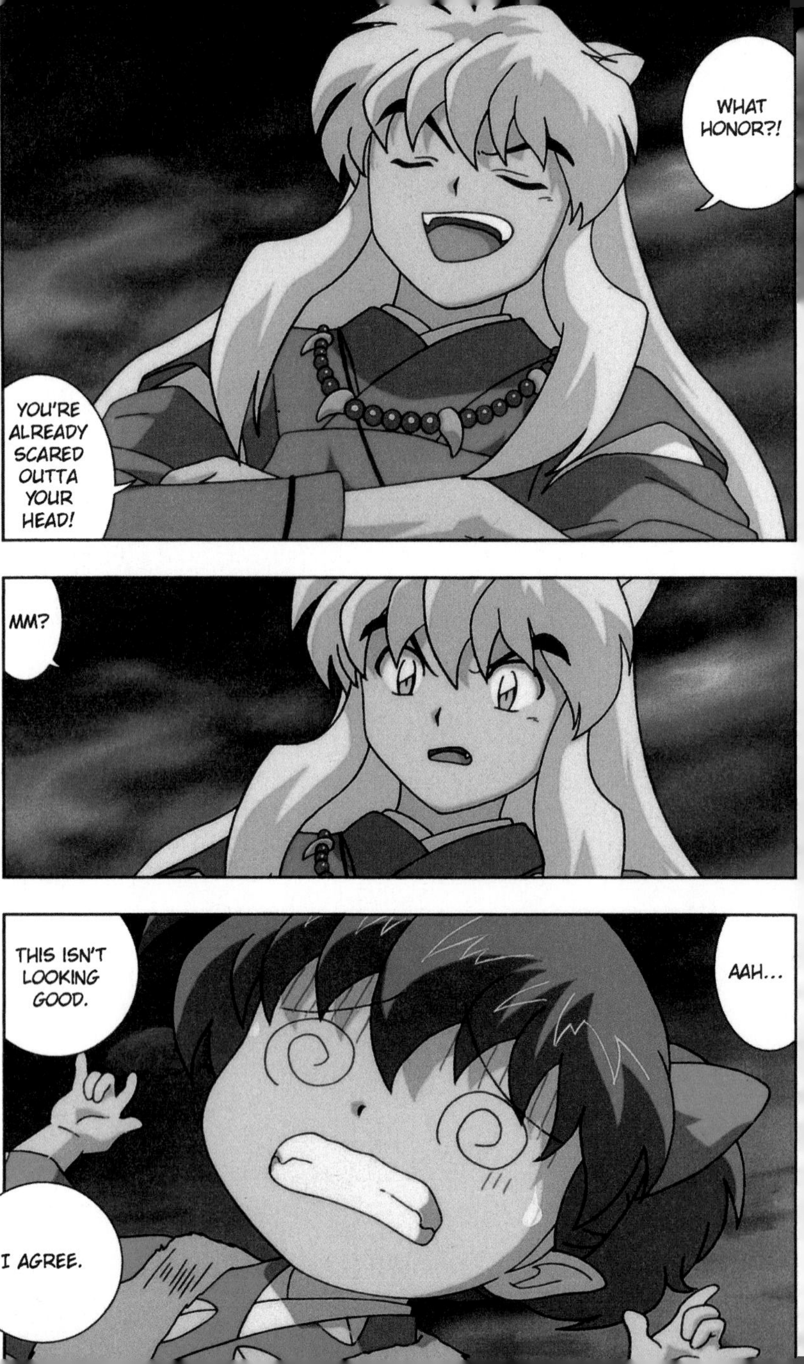
WHAT HONOR?!
YOU'RE ALREADY SCARED OUTTA YOUR HEAD!
MM?
AAH...
THIS ISN'T LOOKING GOOD.
I AGREE.

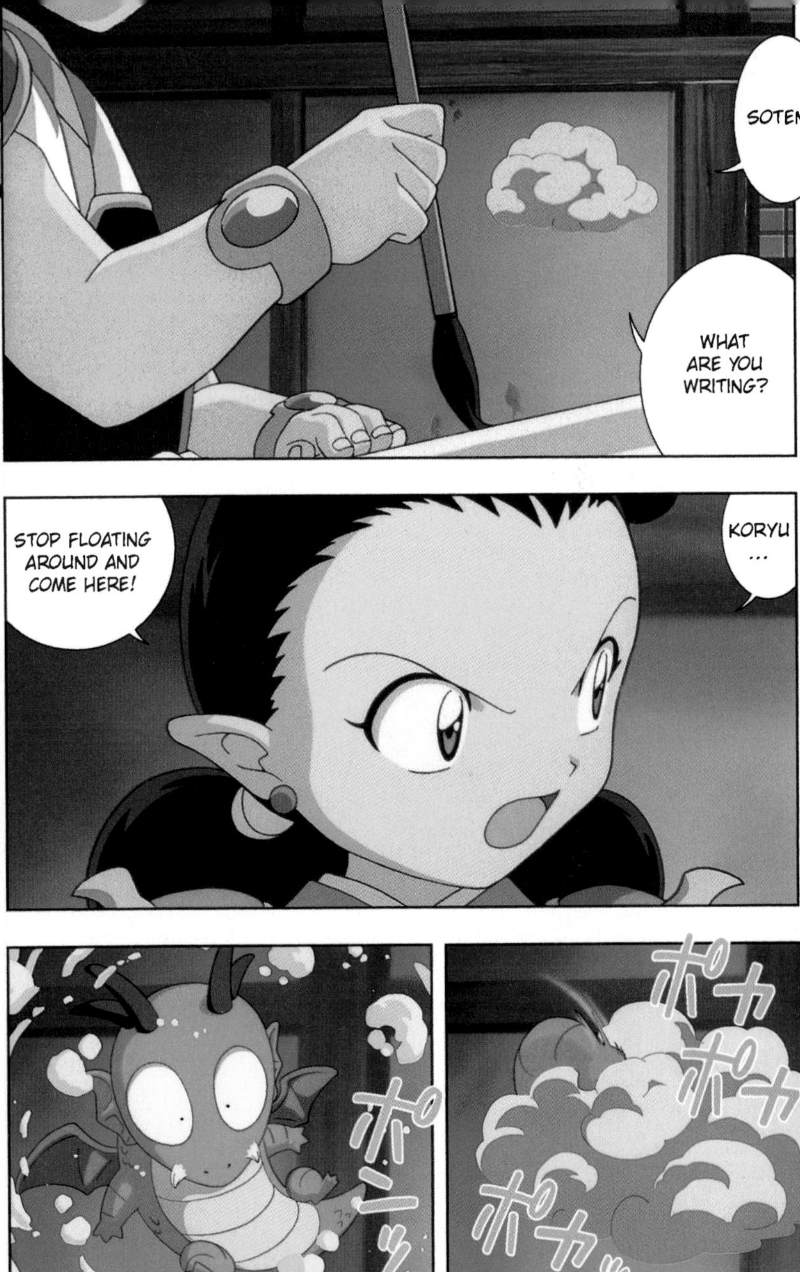
SOTEN.
WHAT ARE YOU WRITING?
KORYU ...
STOP FLOATING AROUND AND COME HERE!
ポカ
ポカ
ポカッ
ポンッ

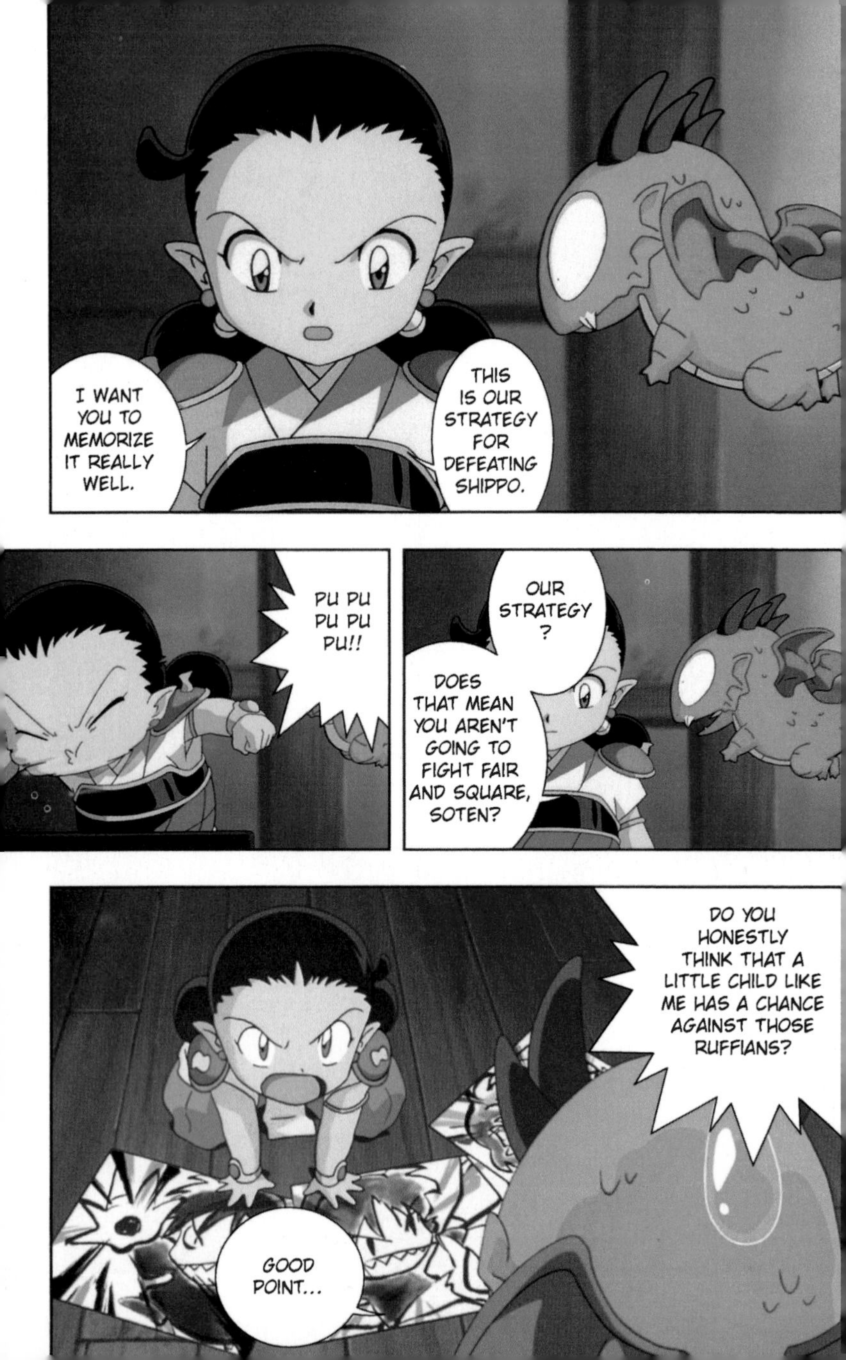
THIS IS OUR STRATEGY FOR DEFEATING SHIPPO.
I WANT YOU TO MEMORIZE IT REALLY WELL.
OUR STRATEGY?
DOES THAT MEAN YOU AREN'T GOING TO FIGHT FAIR AND SQUARE, SOTEN?
PU PU PU PU PU!!
DO YOU HONESTLY THINK THAT A LITTLE CHILD LIKE ME HAS A CHANCE AGAINST THOSE RUFFIANS?
GOOD POINT...

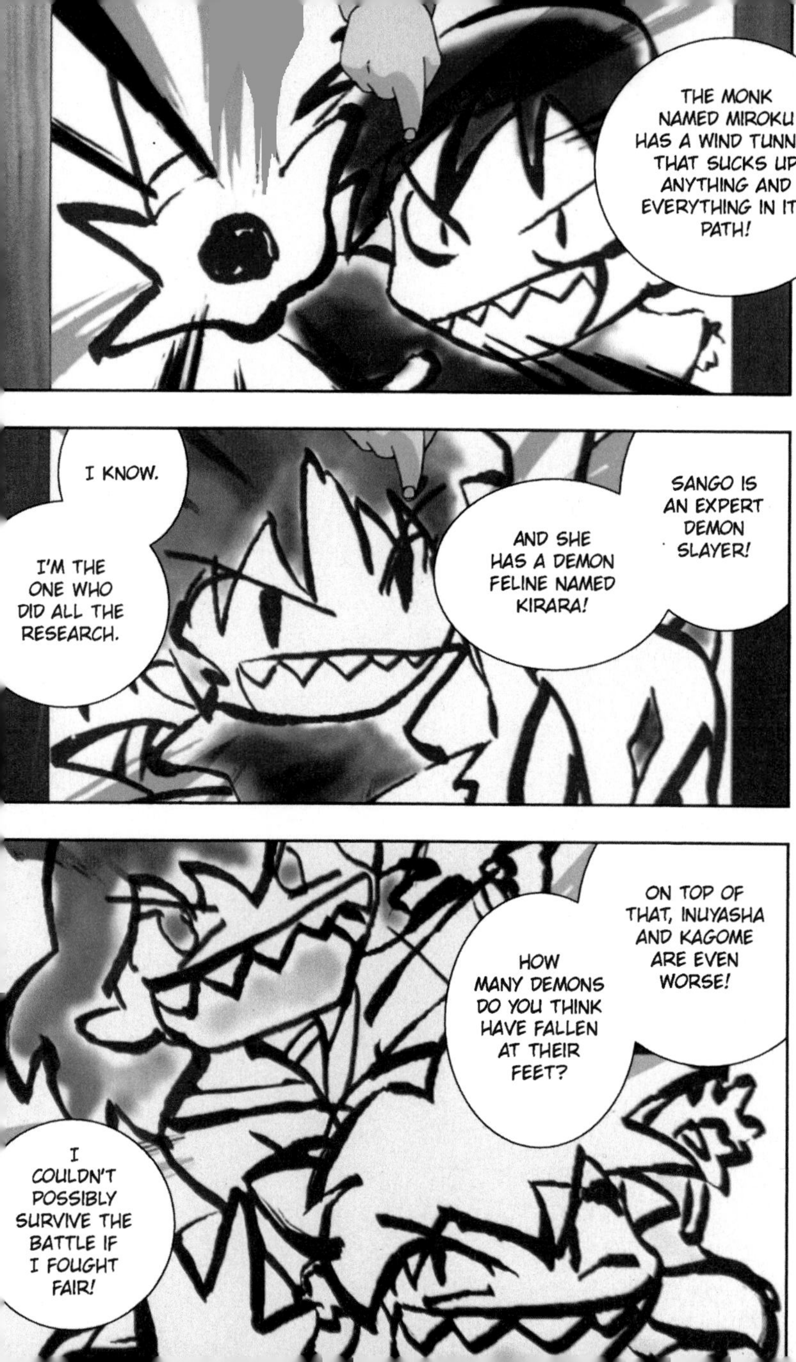
THE MONK NAMED MIROKU HAS A WIND TUNNEL THAT SUCKS UP ANYTHING AND EVERYTHING IN ITS PATH!
SANGO IS AN EXPERT DEMON SLAYER!
AND SHE HAS A DEMON FELINE NAMED KIRARA!
I KNOW.
I'M THE ONE WHO DID ALL THE RESEARCH.
ON TOP OF THAT, INUYASHA AND KAGOME ARE EVEN WORSE!
HOW MANY DEMONS DO YOU THINK HAVE FALLEN AT THEIR FEET?
I COULDN'T POSSIBLY SURVIVE THE BATTLE IF I FOUGHT FAIR!

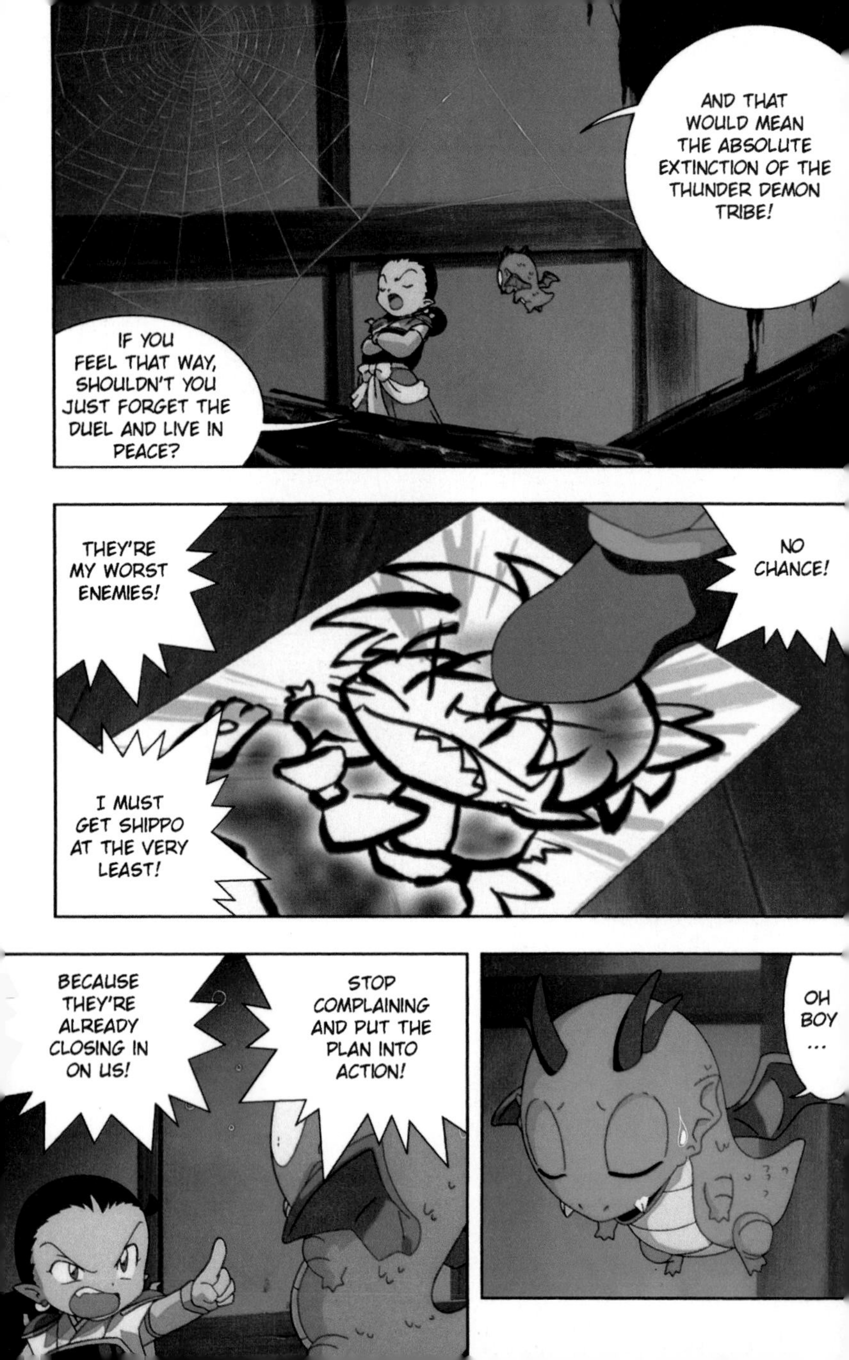
AND THAT WOULD MEAN THE ABSOLUTE EXTINCTION OF THE THUNDER DEMON TRIBE!
IF YOU FEEL THAT WAY, SHOULDN'T YOU JUST FORGET THE DUEL AND LIVE IN PEACE?
NO CHANCE!
THEY'RE MY WORST ENEMIES!
I MUST GET SHIPPO AT THE VERY LEAST!
OH BOY ...
STOP COMPLAINING AND PUT THE PLAN INTO ACTION!
BECAUSE THEY'RE ALREADY CLOSING IN ON US!

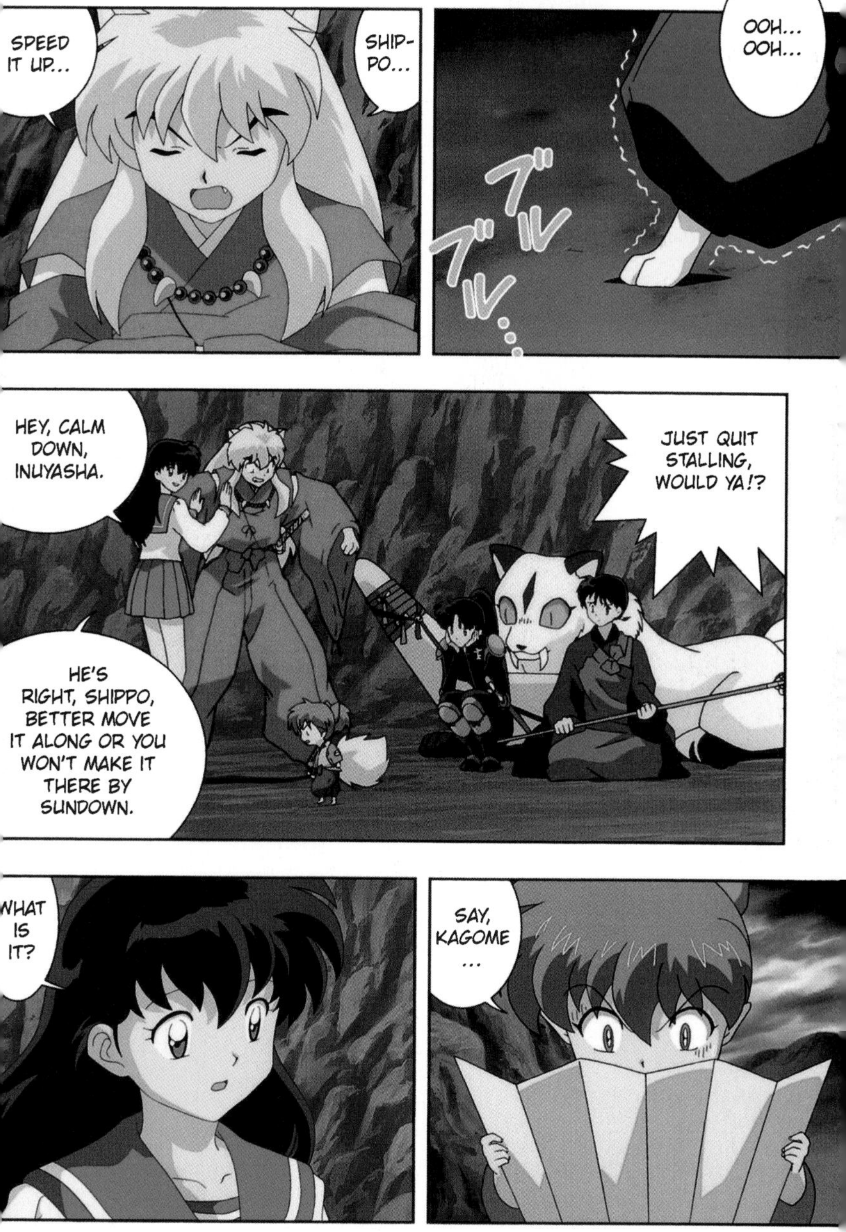
OOH... OOH...
ブルブル...
SHIP-PO...
SPEED IT UP...
JUST QUIT STALLING, WOULD YA!?
HEY, CALM DOWN, INUYASHA.
HE'S RIGHT, SHIPPO, BETTER MOVE IT ALONG OR YOU WON'T MAKE IT THERE BY SUNDOWN.
SAY, KAGOME ...
WHAT IS IT?

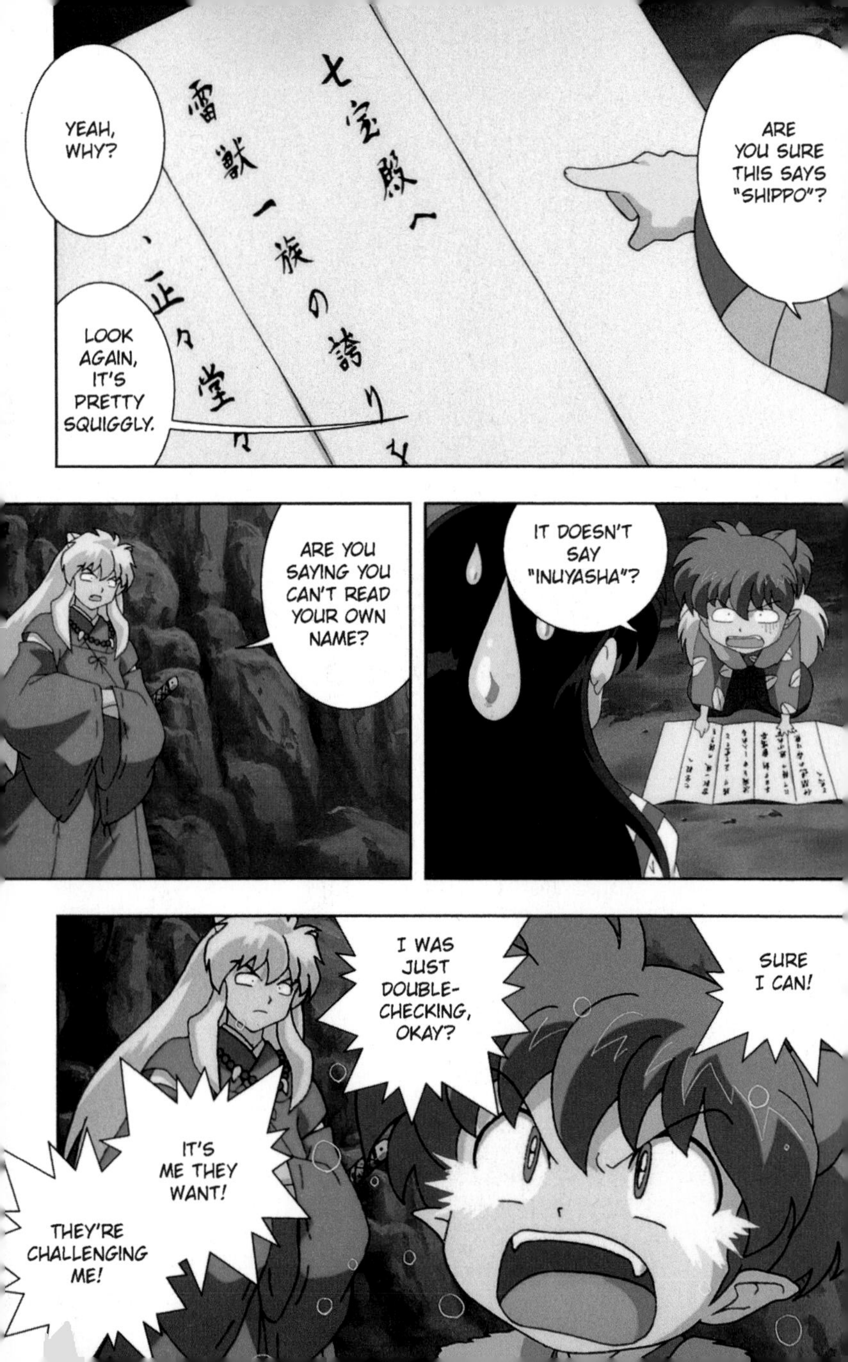
ARE YOU SURE THIS SAYS "SHIPPO"?
七宝殿へ
雷獣一族の誇り
、正々堂々
YEAH, WHY?
LOOK AGAIN, IT'S PRETTY SQUIGGLY.
IT DOESN'T SAY "INUYASHA"?
ARE YOU SAYING YOU CAN'T READ YOUR OWN NAME?
SURE I CAN!
I WAS JUST DOUBLE-CHECKING, OKAY?
IT'S ME THEY WANT!
THEY'RE CHALLENGING ME!

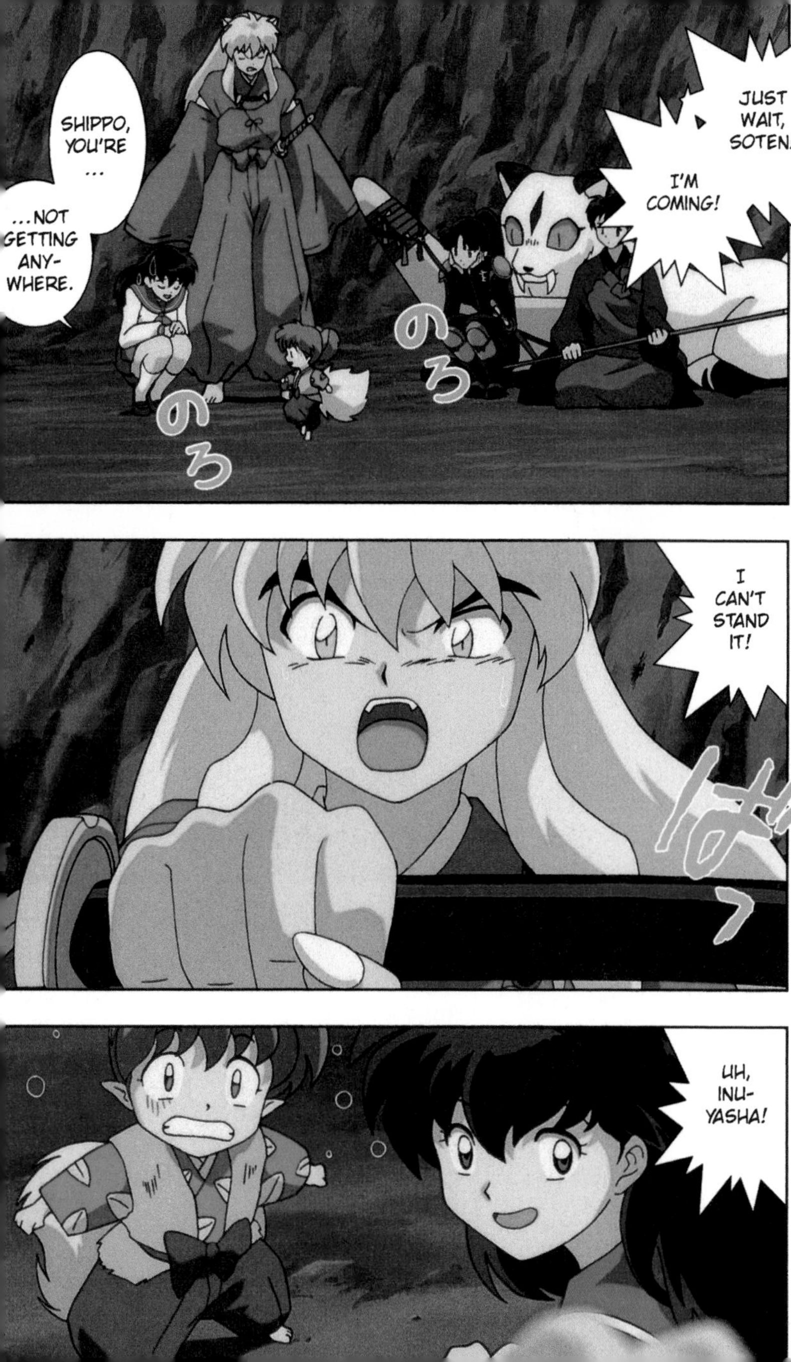
JUST WAIT, SOTEN!
I'M COMING!
SHIPPO, YOU'RE ...
...NOT GETTING ANY-WHERE.
のろ
のろ
I CAN'T STAND IT!
ばっ
UH, INU-YASHA!

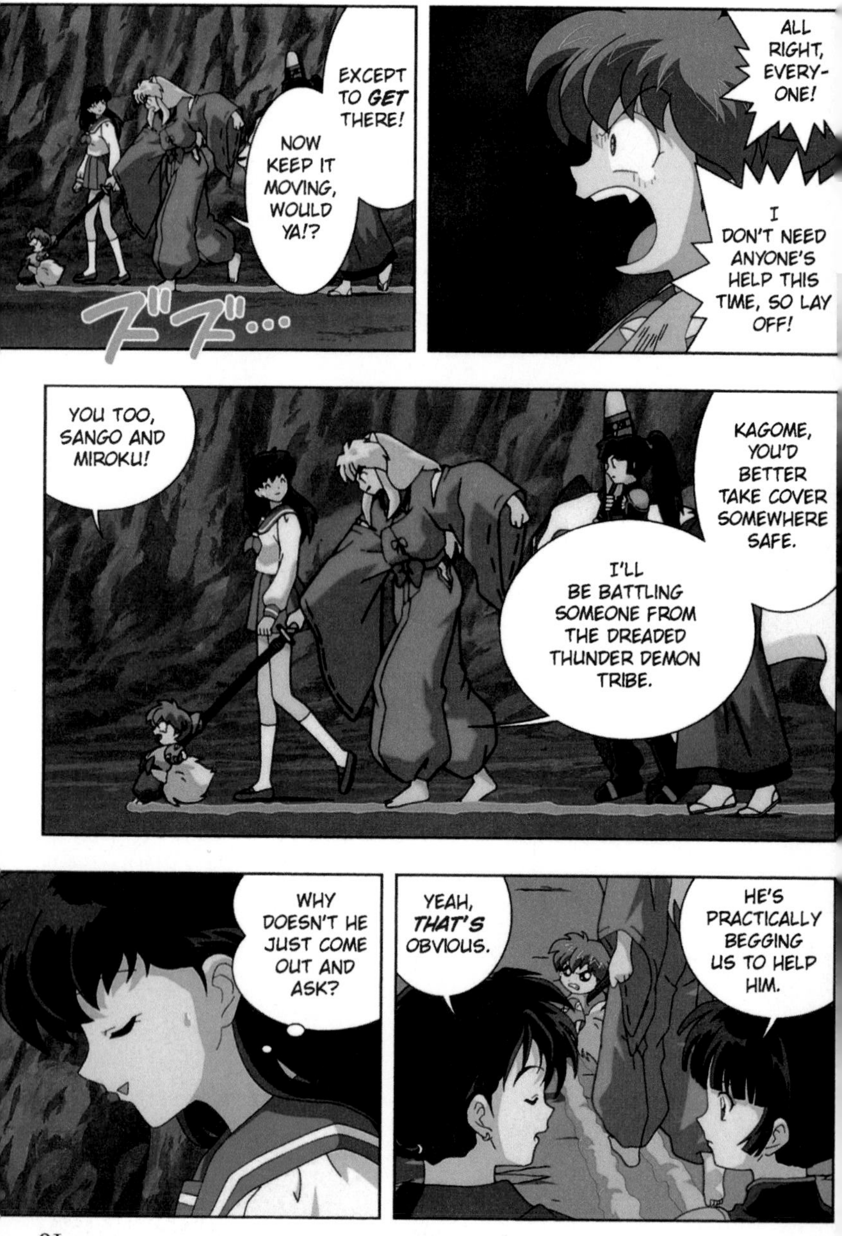
ALL RIGHT, EVERY-ONE!
I DON'T NEED ANYONE'S HELP THIS TIME, SO LAY OFF!
EXCEPT TO **GET** THERE!
NOW KEEP IT MOVING, WOULD YA!?
ブブ...
KAGOME, YOU'D BETTER TAKE COVER SOMEWHERE SAFE.
I'LL BE BATTLING SOMEONE FROM THE DREADED THUNDER DEMON TRIBE.
YOU TOO, SANGO AND MIROKU!
HE'S PRACTICALLY BEGGING US TO HELP HIM.
YEAH, ***THAT'S*** OBVIOUS.
WHY DOESN'T HE JUST COME OUT AND ASK?

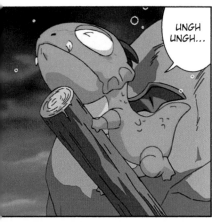

UNGH UNGH...

UNGH UNGH...

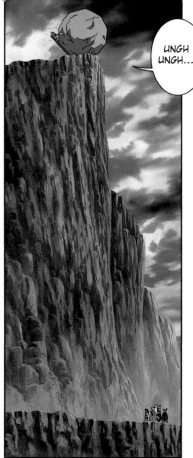

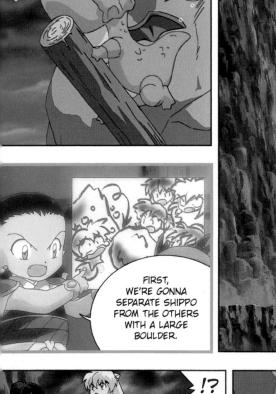

FIRST, WE'RE GONNA SEPARATE SHIPPO FROM THE OTHERS WITH A LARGE BOULDER.

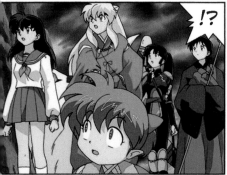

!?

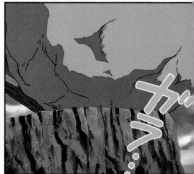

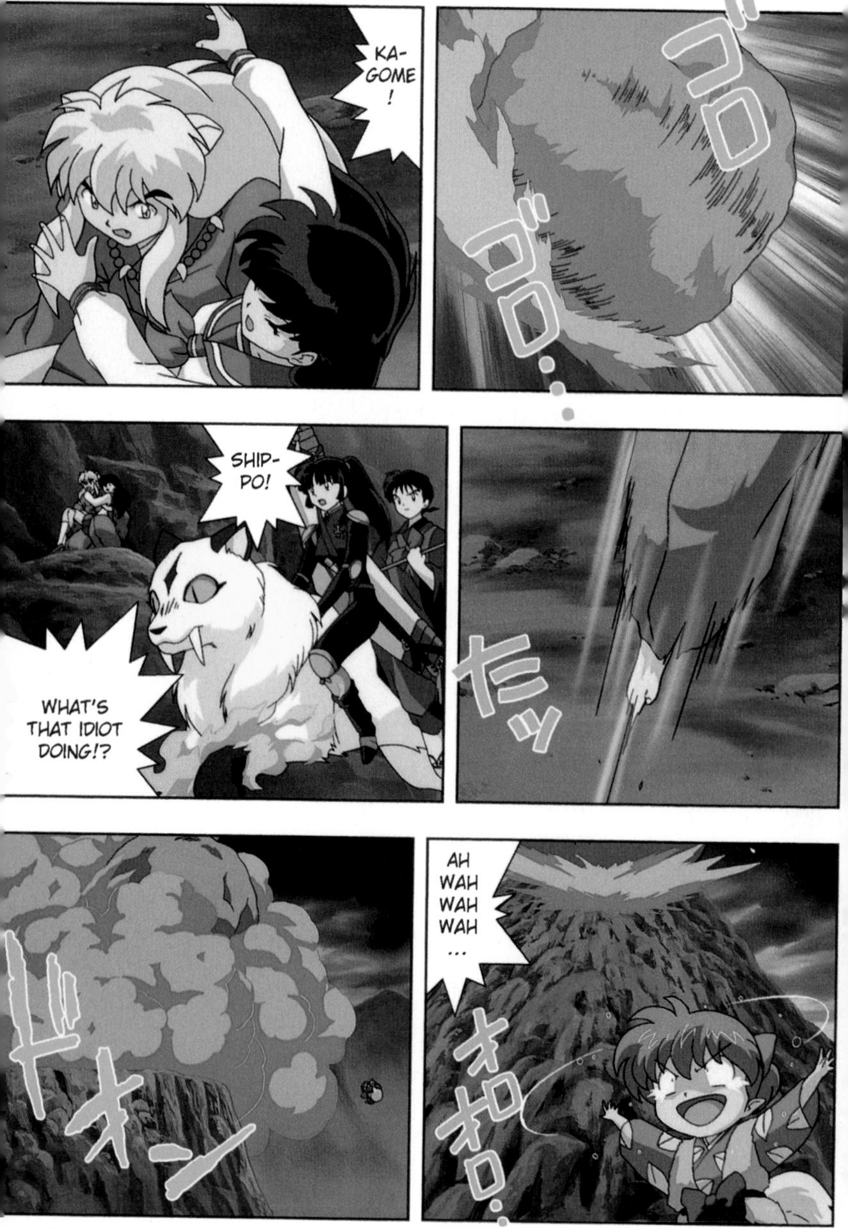

ゴロ
ゴロ…
KA-GOME!
たッ
SHIP-PO!
WHAT'S THAT IDIOT DOING!?
AH WAH WAH WAH...
オロオロ…
ドオーン

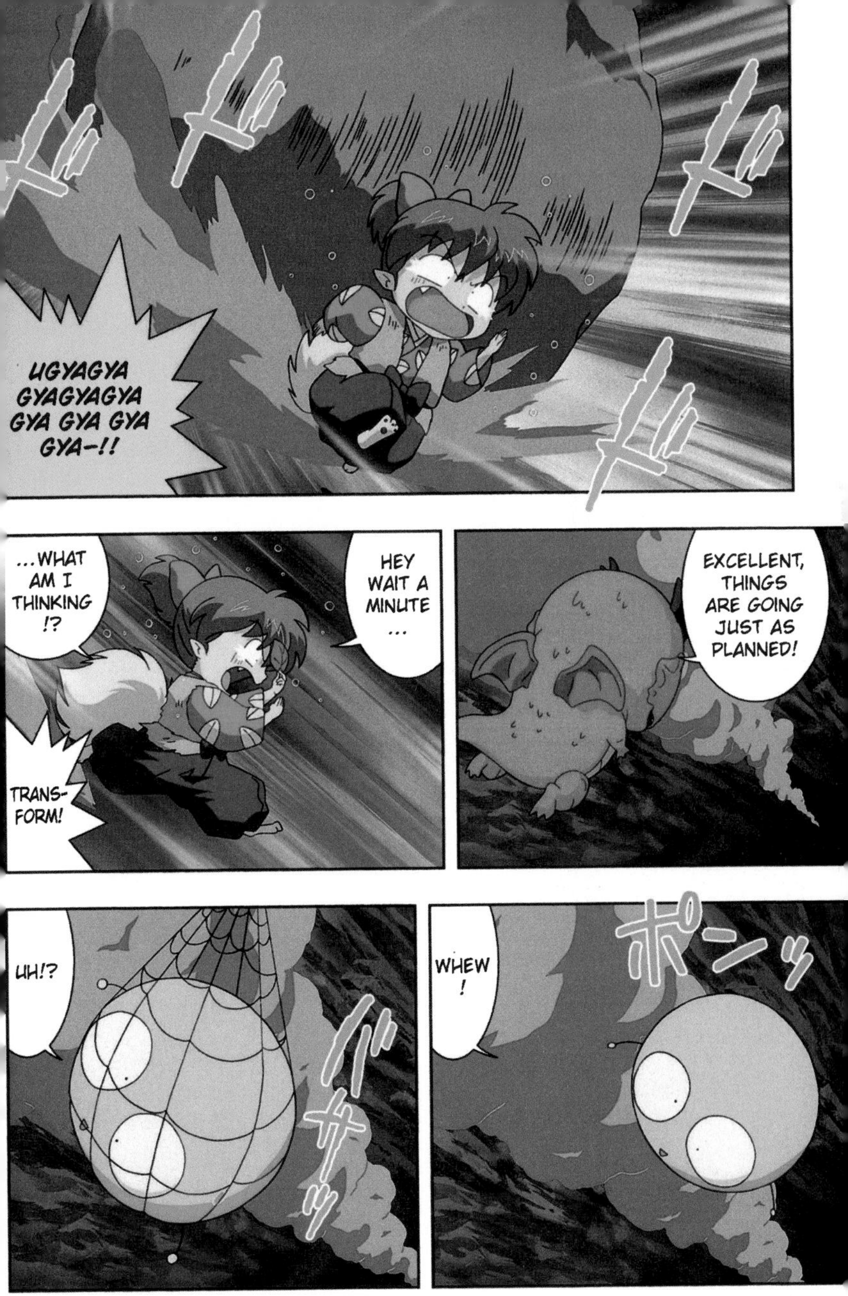
UGYAGYA GYAGYAGYA GYA GYA GYA GYA-!!
EXCELLENT, THINGS ARE GOING JUST AS PLANNED!
HEY WAIT A MINUTE ...
...WHAT AM I THINKING !?
TRANS-FORM!
ポンッ
WHEW !
UH!?

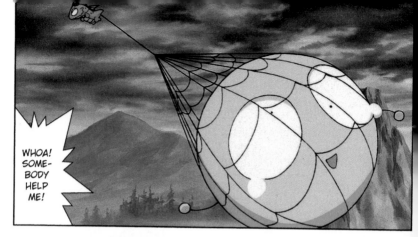

WHOA! SOMEBODY HELP ME!

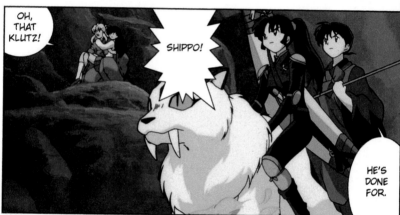

OH, THAT KLUTZ!

SHIPPO!

HE'S DONE FOR.

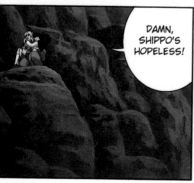

DAMN, SHIPPO'S HOPELESS!

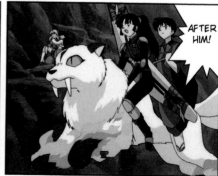

AFTER HIM!

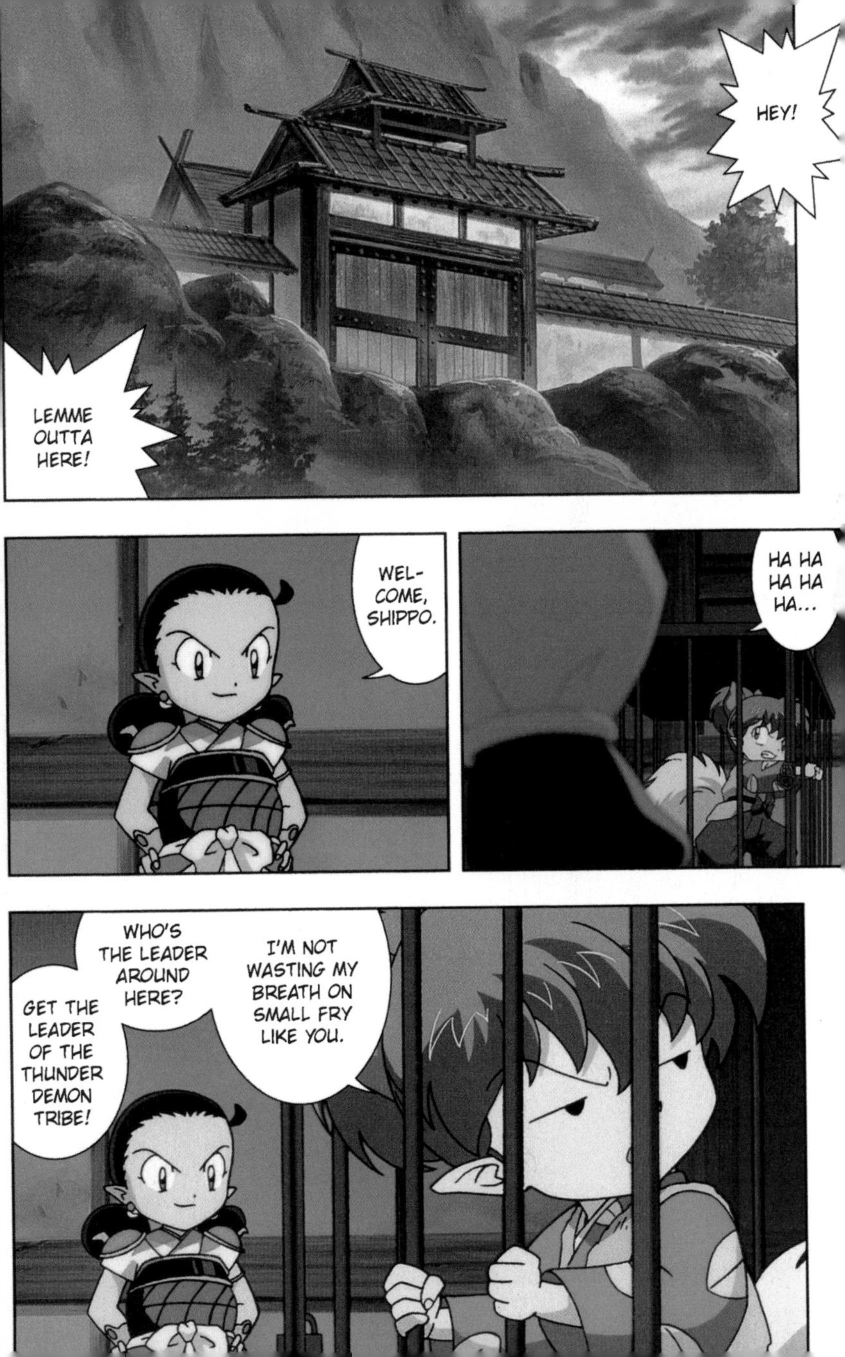
HEY!
LEMME OUTTA HERE!
HA HA HA HA HA...
WEL-COME, SHIPPO.
WHO'S THE LEADER AROUND HERE?
I'M NOT WASTING MY BREATH ON SMALL FRY LIKE YOU.
GET THE LEADER OF THE THUNDER DEMON TRIBE!

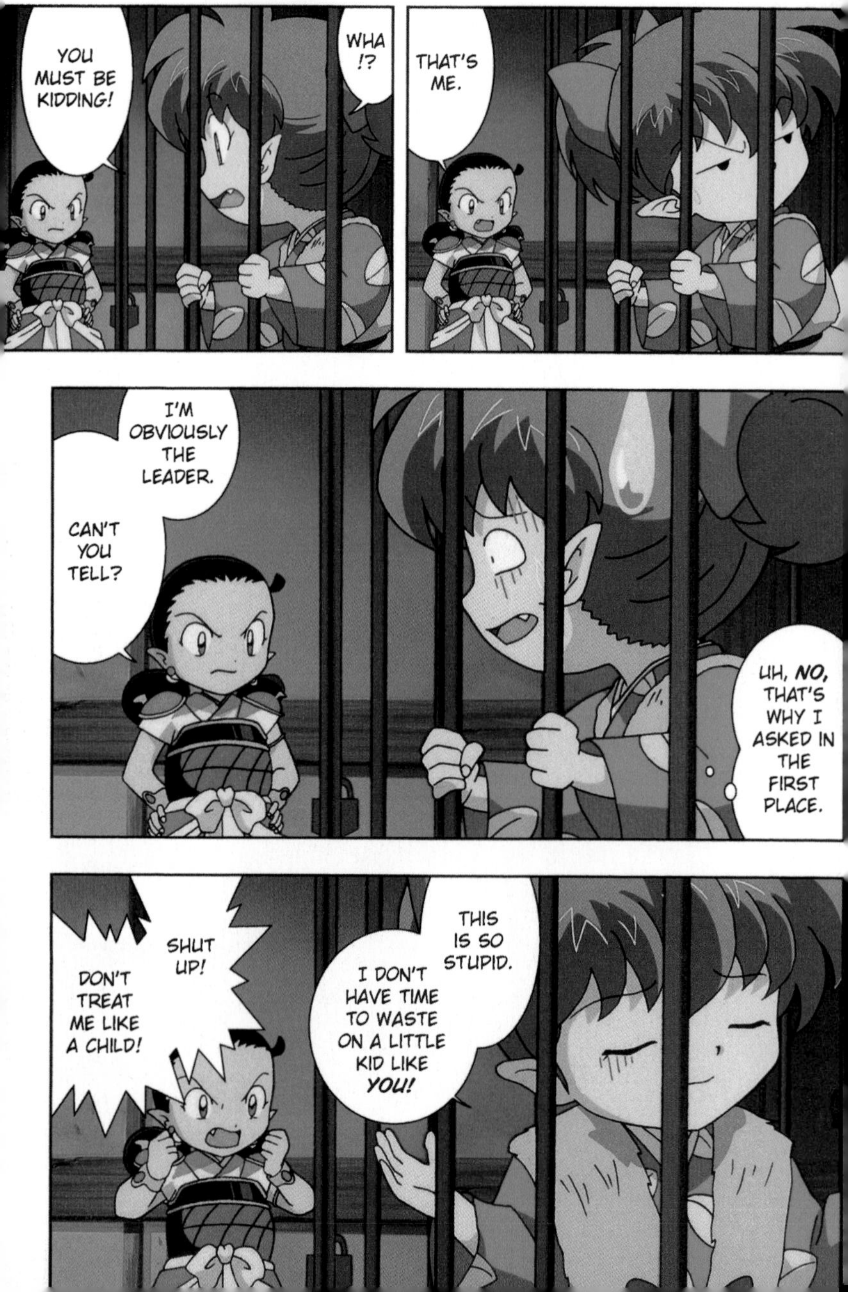

THAT'S ME.
WHA !?
YOU MUST BE KIDDING!
I'M OBVIOUSLY THE LEADER.
CAN'T YOU TELL?
UH, **NO,** THAT'S WHY I ASKED IN THE FIRST PLACE.
THIS IS SO STUPID.
I DON'T HAVE TIME TO WASTE ON A LITTLE KID LIKE ***YOU!***
SHUT UP!
DON'T TREAT ME LIKE A CHILD!

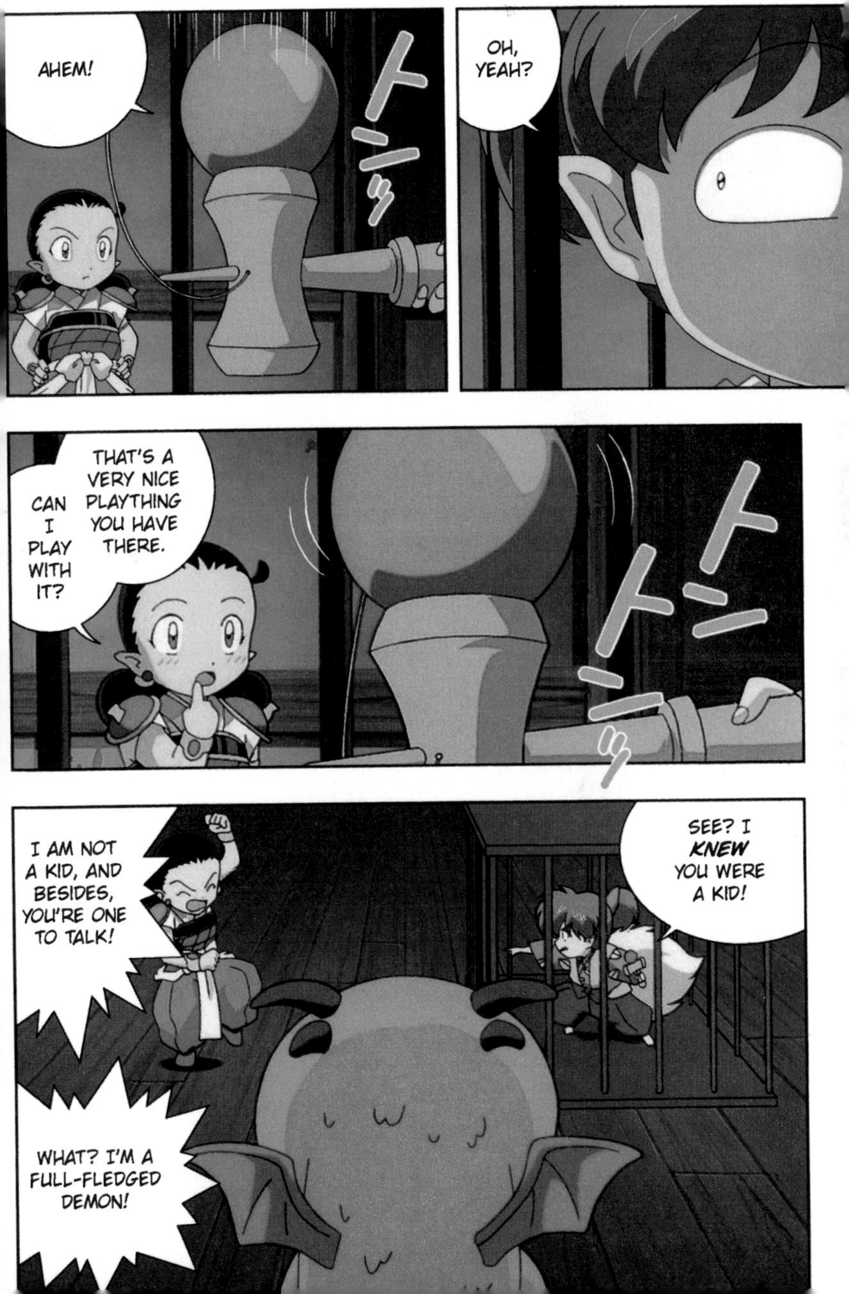
OH, YEAH?
AHEM!
トンッ
THAT'S A VERY NICE PLAYTHING YOU HAVE THERE.
CAN I PLAY WITH IT?
トントンッ
SEE? I *KNEW* YOU WERE A KID!
I AM NOT A KID, AND BESIDES, YOU'RE ONE TO TALK!
WHAT? I'M A FULL-FLEDGED DEMON!

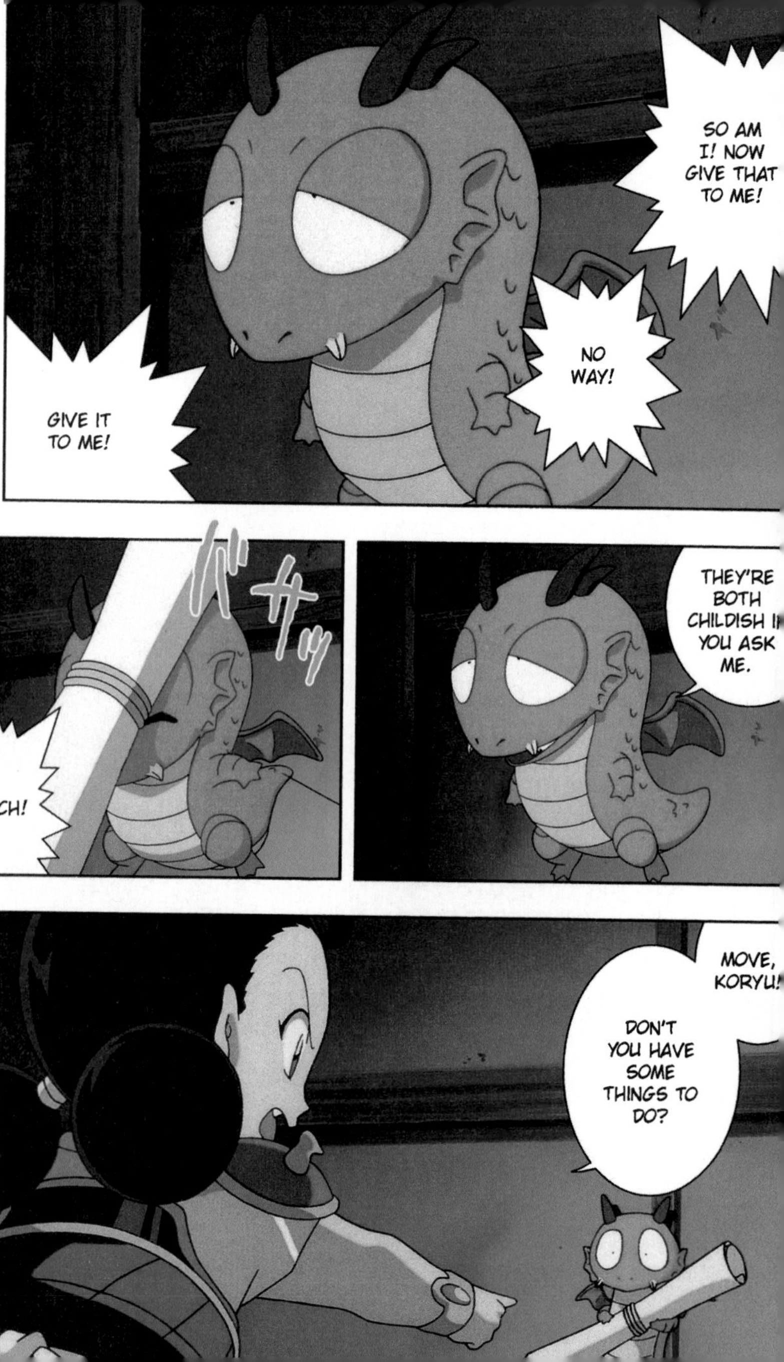
SO AM I! NOW GIVE THAT TO ME!
NO WAY!
GIVE IT TO ME!
THEY'RE BOTH CHILDISH I YOU ASK ME.
バサッ
OUCH!
MOVE, KORYU!
DON'T YOU HAVE SOME THINGS TO DO?

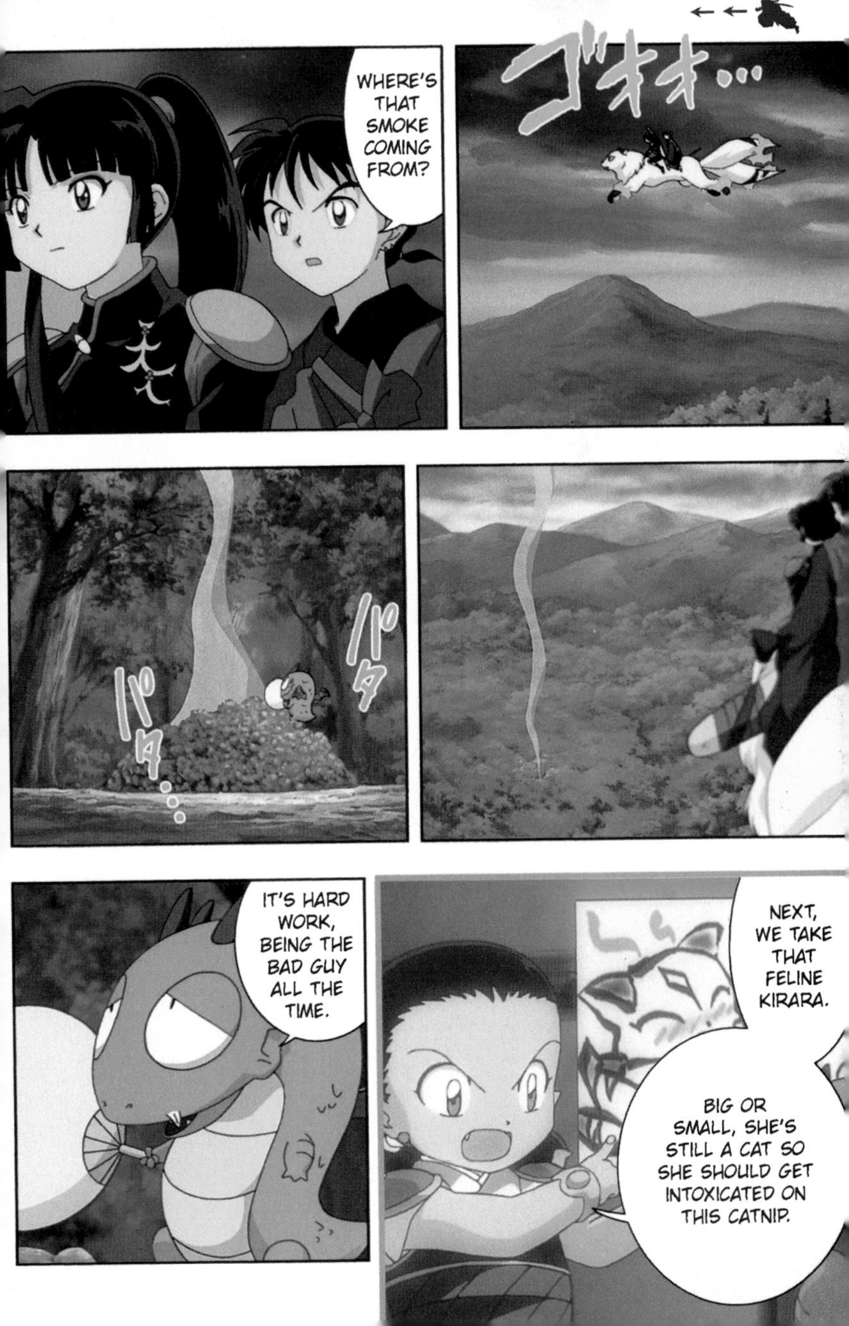
ゴオオ…
WHERE'S THAT SMOKE COMING FROM?
パタ
パタ…
NEXT, WE TAKE THAT FELINE KIRARA.
BIG OR SMALL, SHE'S STILL A CAT SO SHE SHOULD GET INTOXICATED ON THIS CATNIP.
IT'S HARD WORK, BEING THE BAD GUY ALL THE TIME.

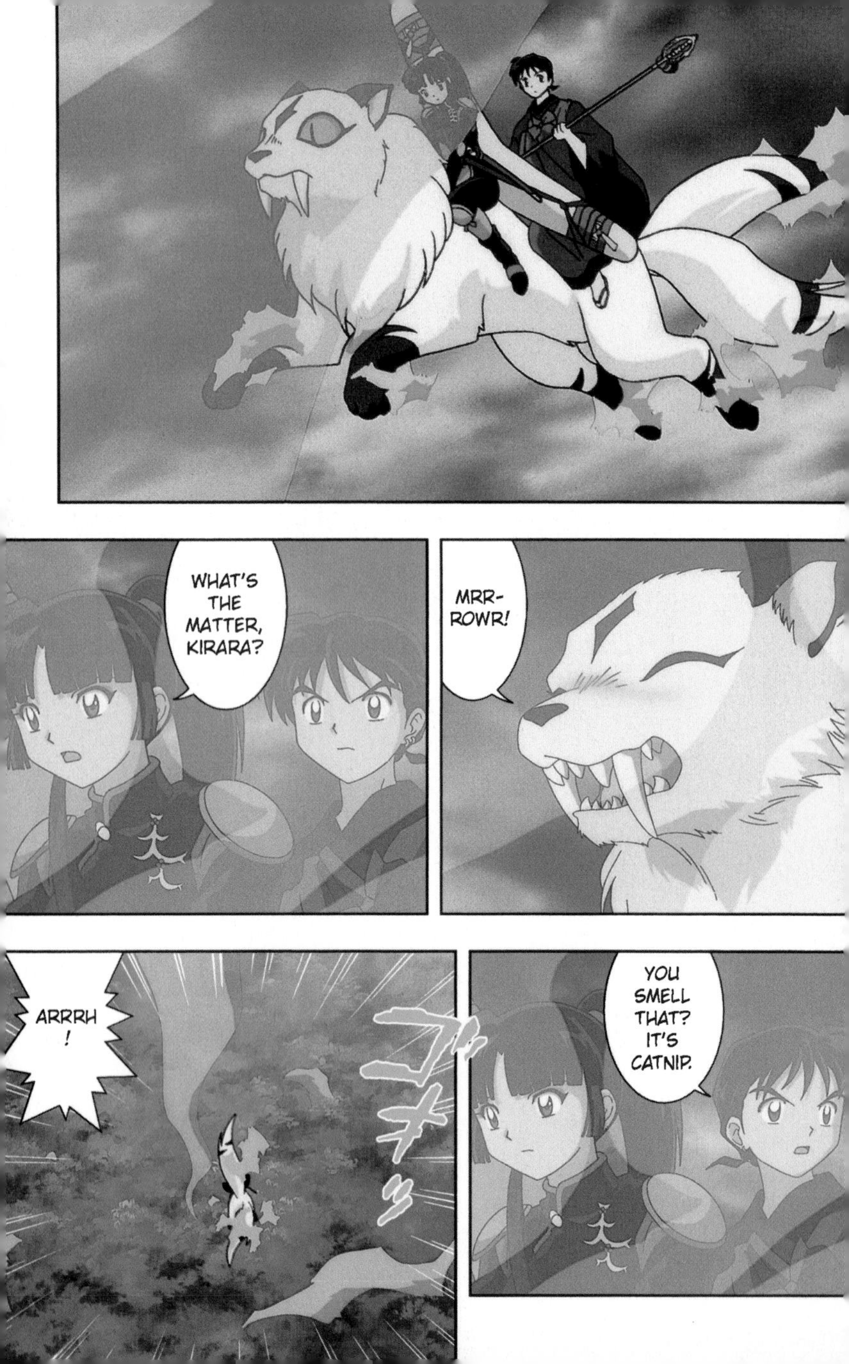
MRR-ROWR!
WHAT'S THE MATTER, KIRARA?
YOU SMELL THAT? IT'S CATNIP.
ARRRH!

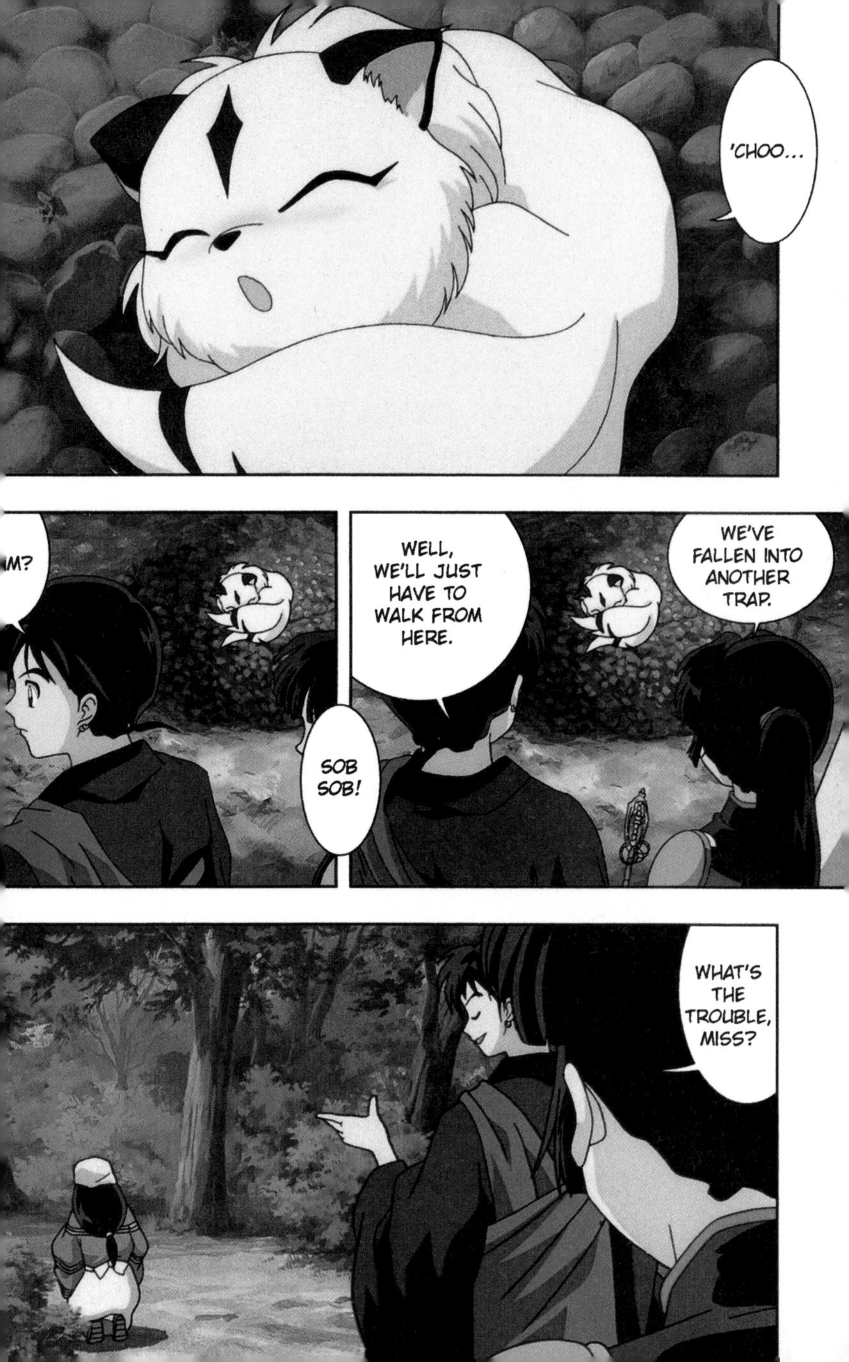
'CHOO...
WE'VE FALLEN INTO ANOTHER TRAP.
WELL, WE'LL JUST HAVE TO WALK FROM HERE.
SOB SOB!
M?
WHAT'S THE TROUBLE, MISS?

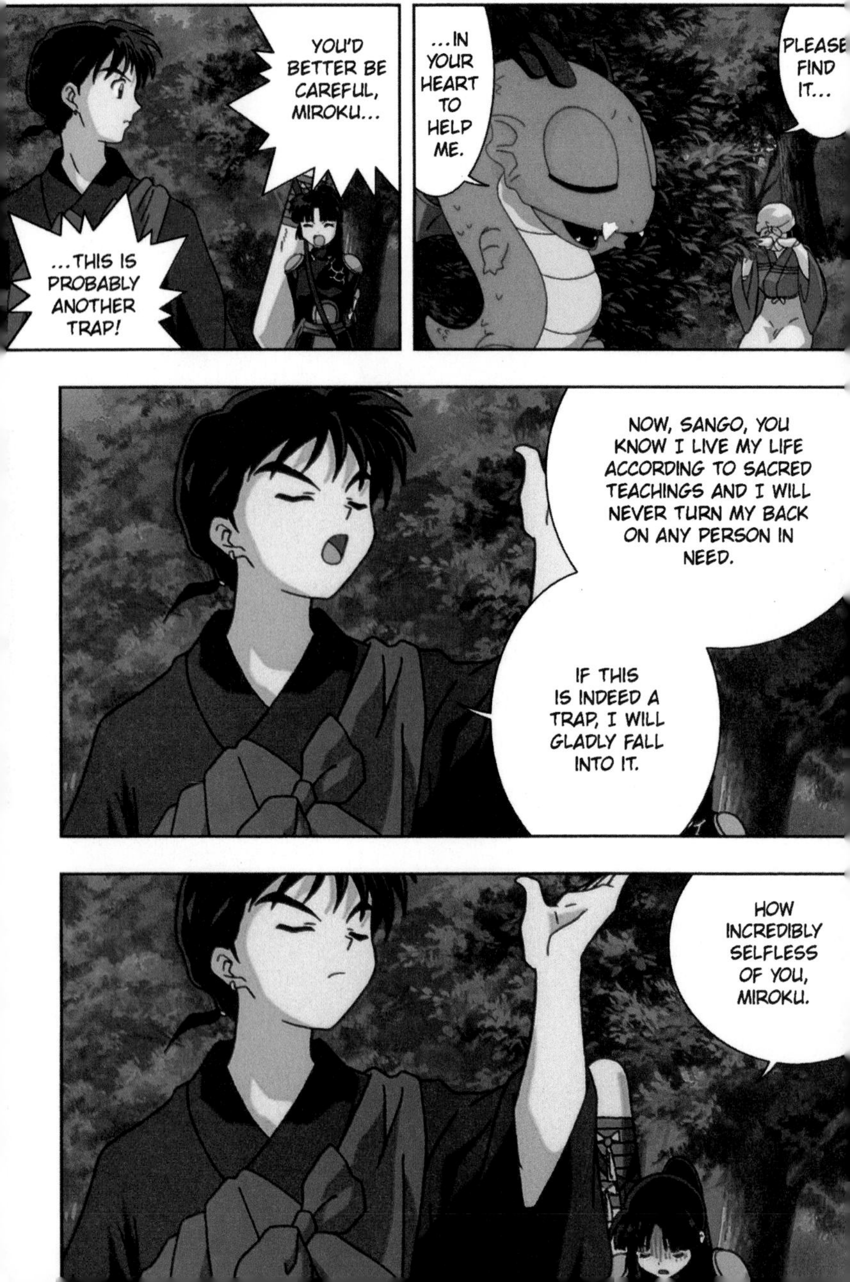
PLEASE FIND IT...
...IN YOUR HEART TO HELP ME.
YOU'D BETTER BE CAREFUL, MIROKU...
...THIS IS PROBABLY ANOTHER TRAP!
NOW, SANGO, YOU KNOW I LIVE MY LIFE ACCORDING TO SACRED TEACHINGS AND I WILL NEVER TURN MY BACK ON ANY PERSON IN NEED.
IF THIS IS INDEED A TRAP, I WILL GLADLY FALL INTO IT.
HOW INCREDIBLY SELFLESS OF YOU, MIROKU.

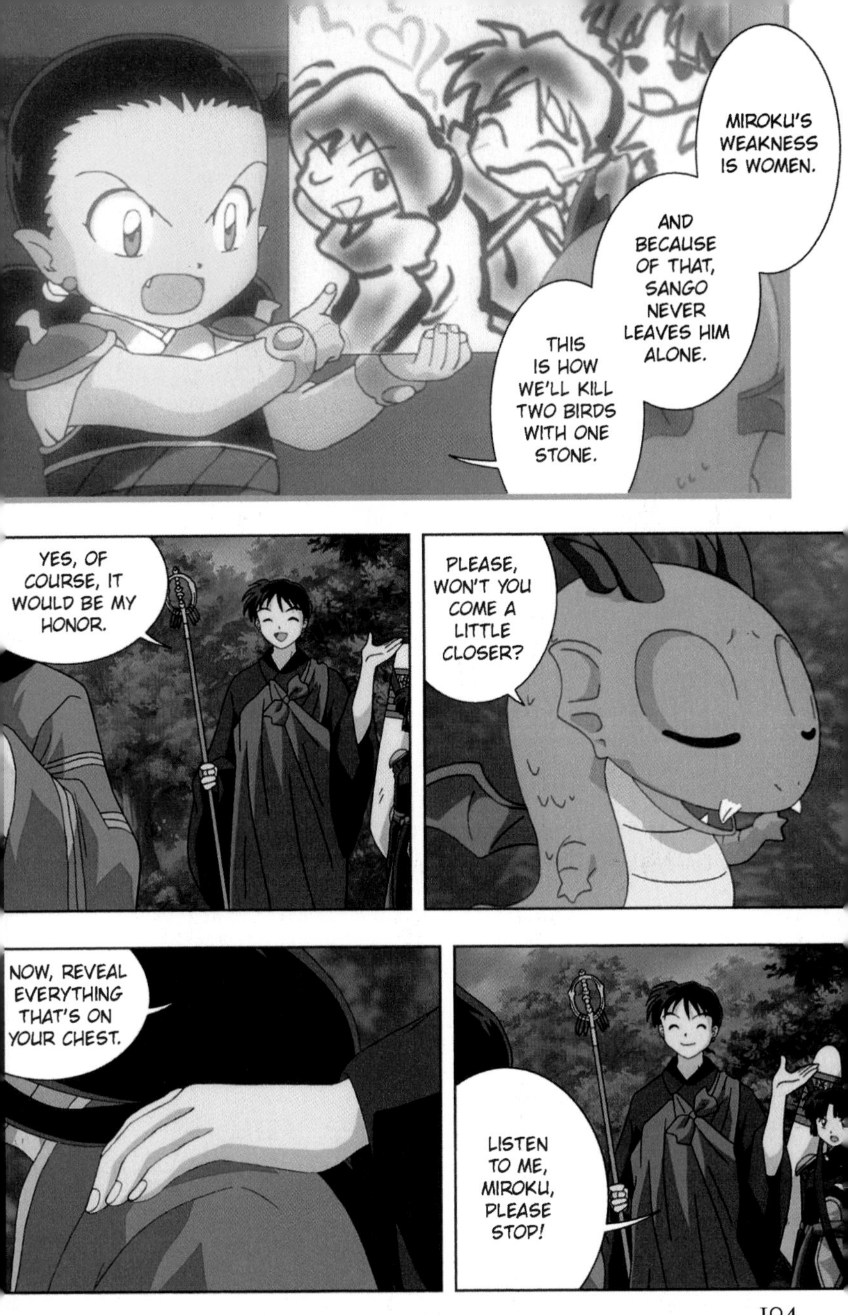
MIROKU'S WEAKNESS IS WOMEN.
AND BECAUSE OF THAT, SANGO NEVER LEAVES HIM ALONE.
THIS IS HOW WE'LL KILL TWO BIRDS WITH ONE STONE.
PLEASE, WON'T YOU COME A LITTLE CLOSER?
YES, OF COURSE, IT WOULD BE MY HONOR.
LISTEN TO ME, MIROKU, PLEASE STOP!
NOW, REVEAL EVERYTHING THAT'S ON YOUR CHEST.

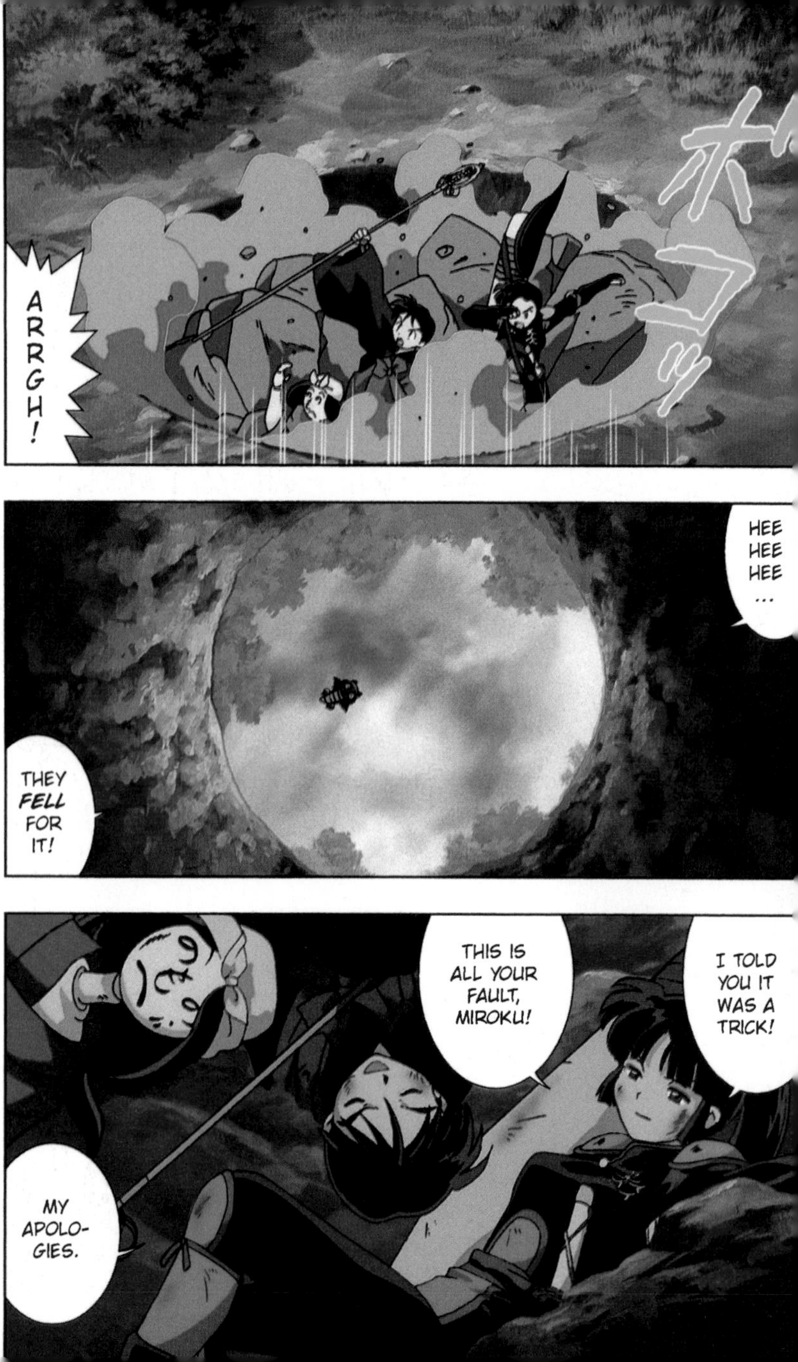
ARRGH!
HEE HEE HEE ...
THEY FELL FOR IT!
I TOLD YOU IT WAS A TRICK!
THIS IS ALL YOUR FAULT, MIROKU!
MY APOLOGIES.

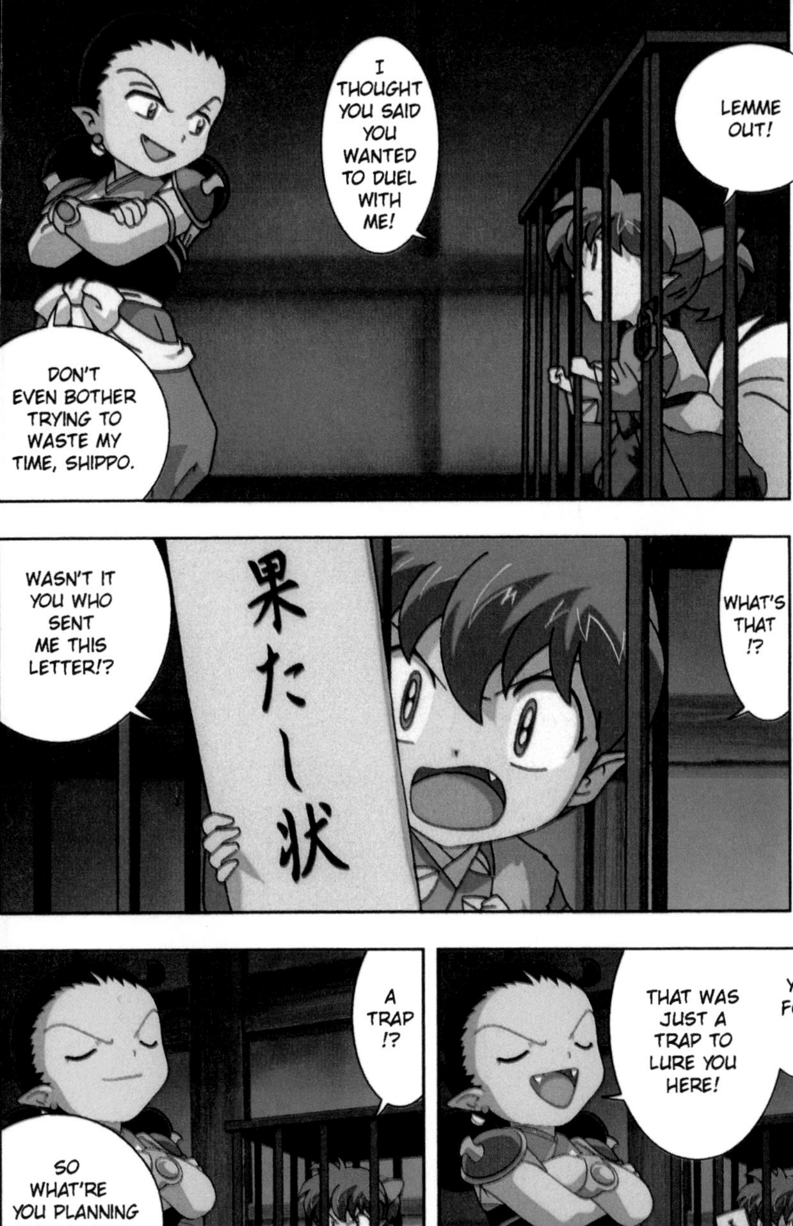
LEMME OUT!
I THOUGHT YOU SAID YOU WANTED TO DUEL WITH ME!
DON'T EVEN BOTHER TRYING TO WASTE MY TIME, SHIPPO.
WHAT'S THAT!?
果たし状
WASN'T IT YOU WHO SENT ME THIS LETTER!?
YOU FOOL!
THAT WAS JUST A TRAP TO LURE YOU HERE!
A TRAP!?
SO WHAT'RE YOU PLANNING TO DO WITH ME?

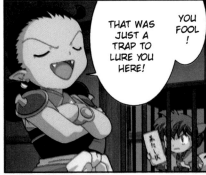

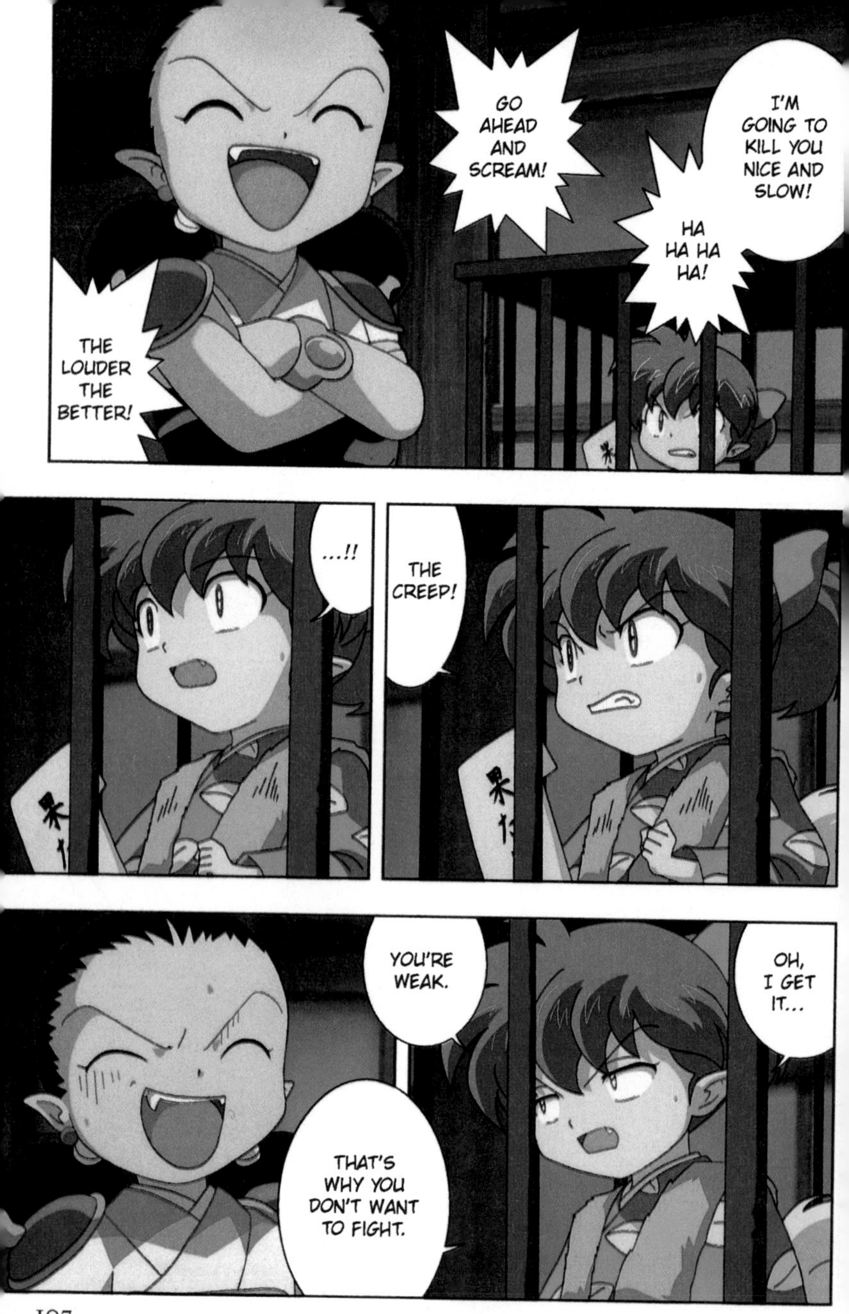
I'M GOING TO KILL YOU NICE AND SLOW!
GO AHEAD AND SCREAM!
HA HA HA HA!
THE LOUDER THE BETTER!
THE CREEP!
...!!
OH, I GET IT...
YOU'RE WEAK.
THAT'S WHY YOU DON'T WANT TO FIGHT.

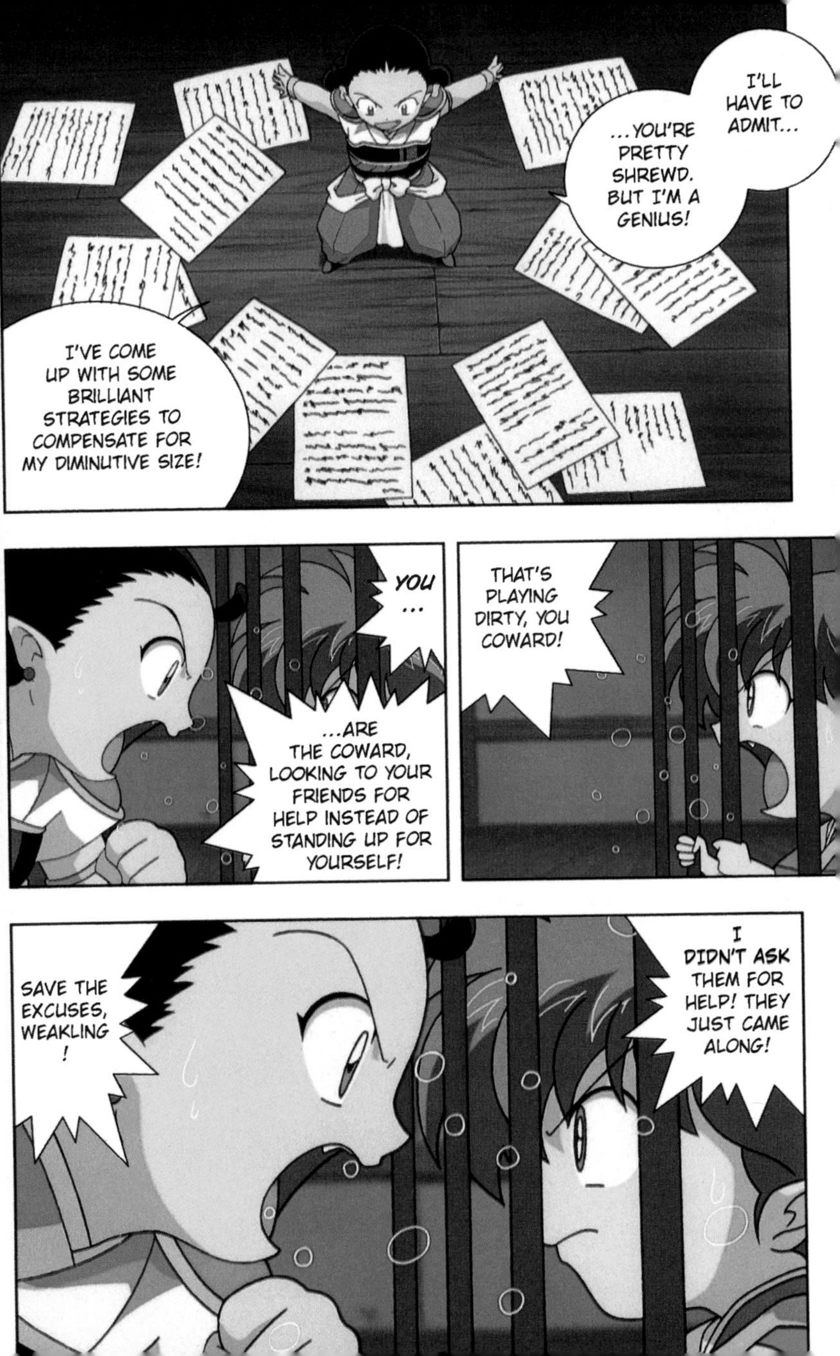
I'LL HAVE TO ADMIT...
...YOU'RE PRETTY SHREWD. BUT I'M A GENIUS!
I'VE COME UP WITH SOME BRILLIANT STRATEGIES TO COMPENSATE FOR MY DIMINUTIVE SIZE!
THAT'S PLAYING DIRTY, YOU COWARD!
YOU ...
...ARE THE COWARD, LOOKING TO YOUR FRIENDS FOR HELP INSTEAD OF STANDING UP FOR YOURSELF!
I DIDN'T ASK THEM FOR HELP! THEY JUST CAME ALONG!
SAVE THE EXCUSES, WEAKLING!

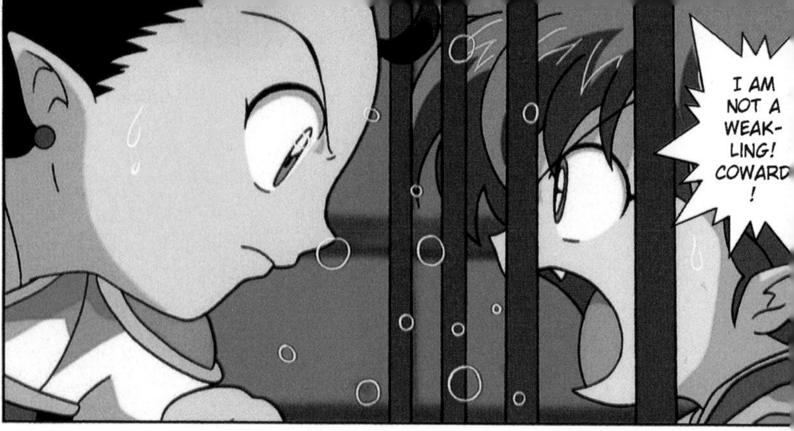
I AM NOT A WEAK-LING! COWARD!

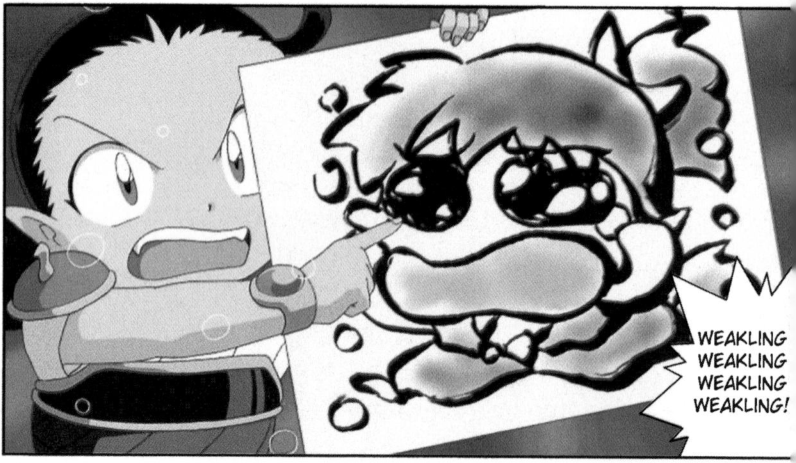
WEAKLING WEAKLING WEAKLING WEAKLING!

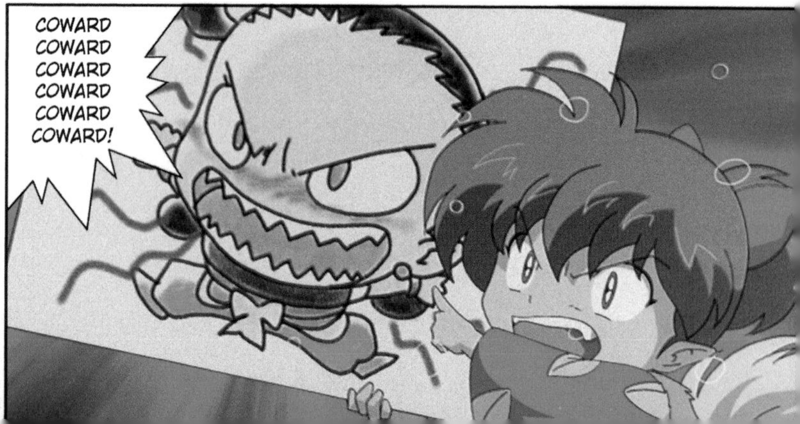
COWARD COWARD COWARD COWARD COWARD COWARD!

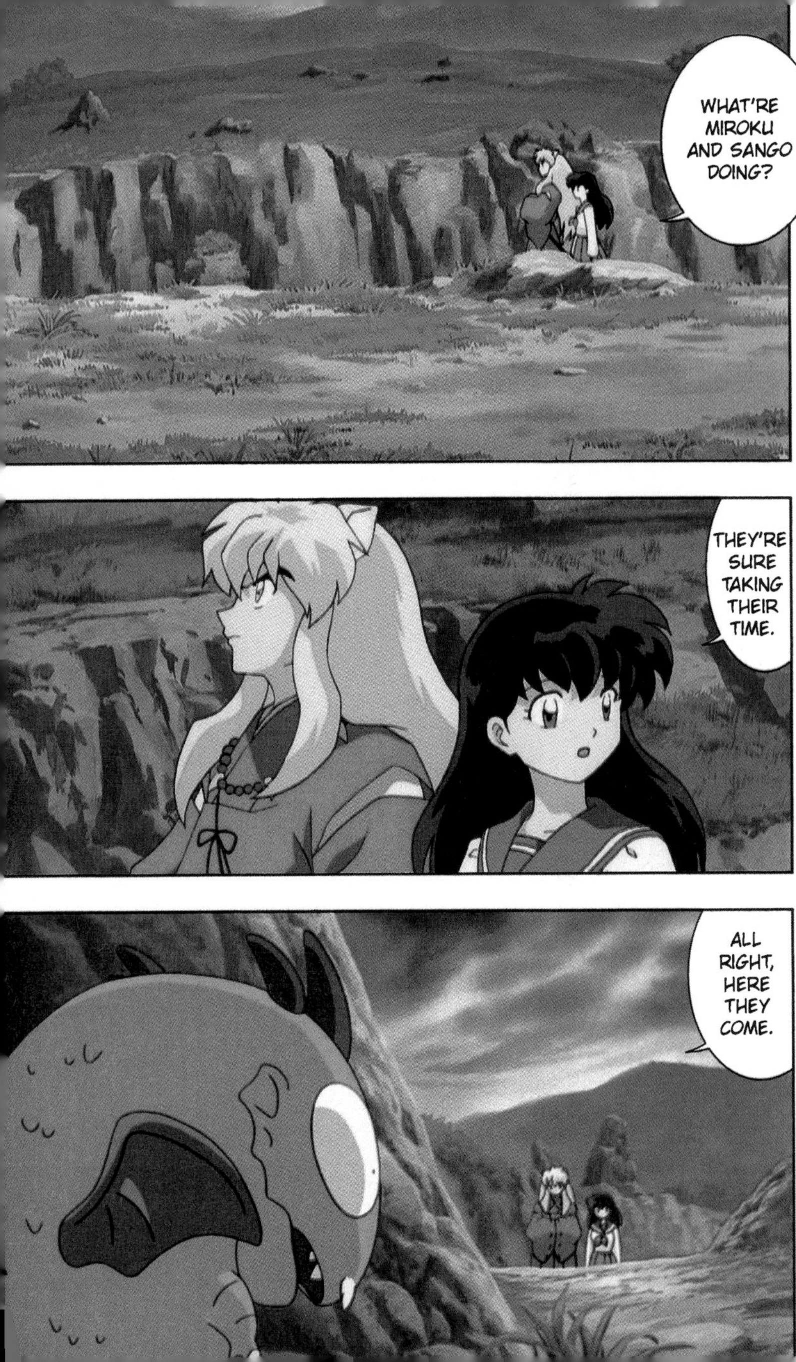
WHAT'RE MIROKU AND SANGO DOING?
THEY'RE SURE TAKING THEIR TIME.
ALL RIGHT, HERE THEY COME.

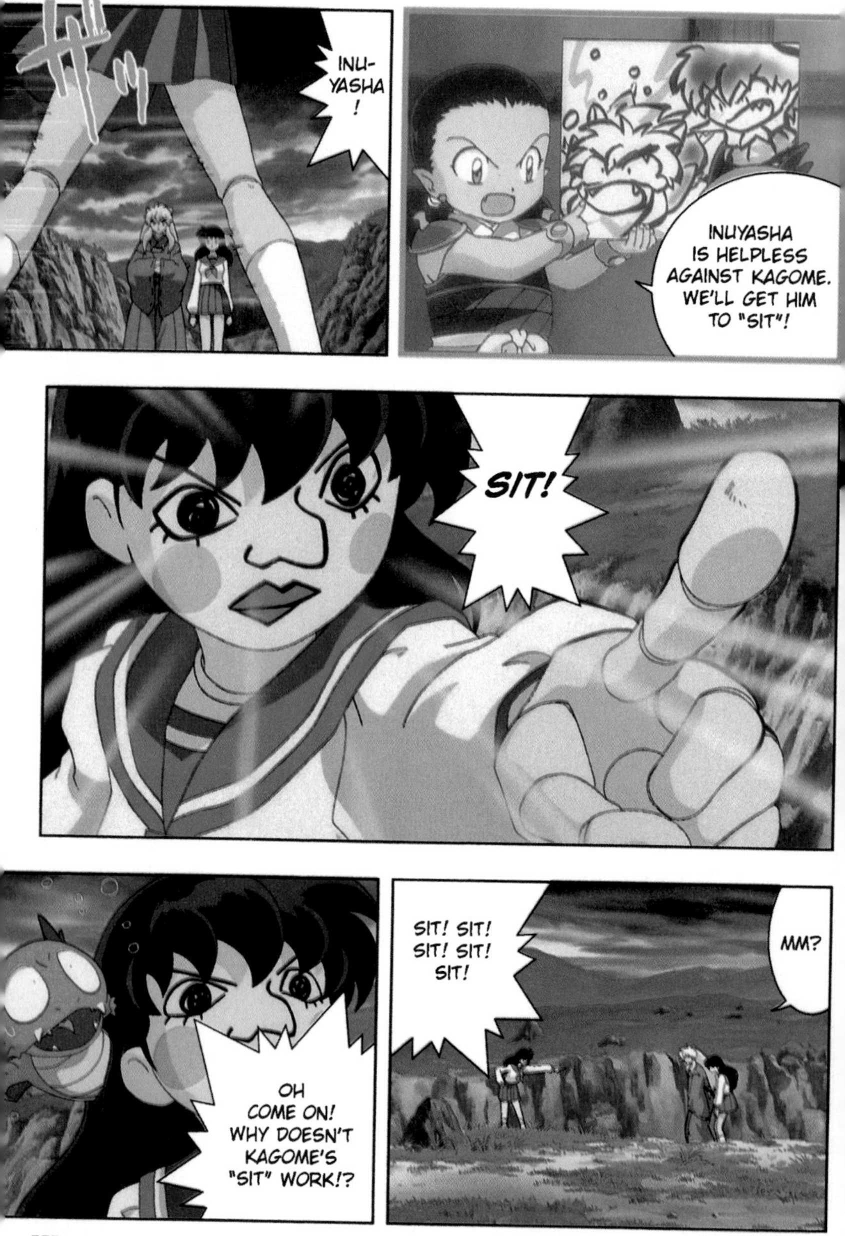
INUYASHA IS HELPLESS AGAINST KAGOME. WE'LL GET HIM TO "SIT"!
INU-YASHA!
SIT!
MM?
SIT! SIT! SIT! SIT! SIT!
OH COME ON! WHY DOESN'T KAGOME'S "SIT" WORK!?

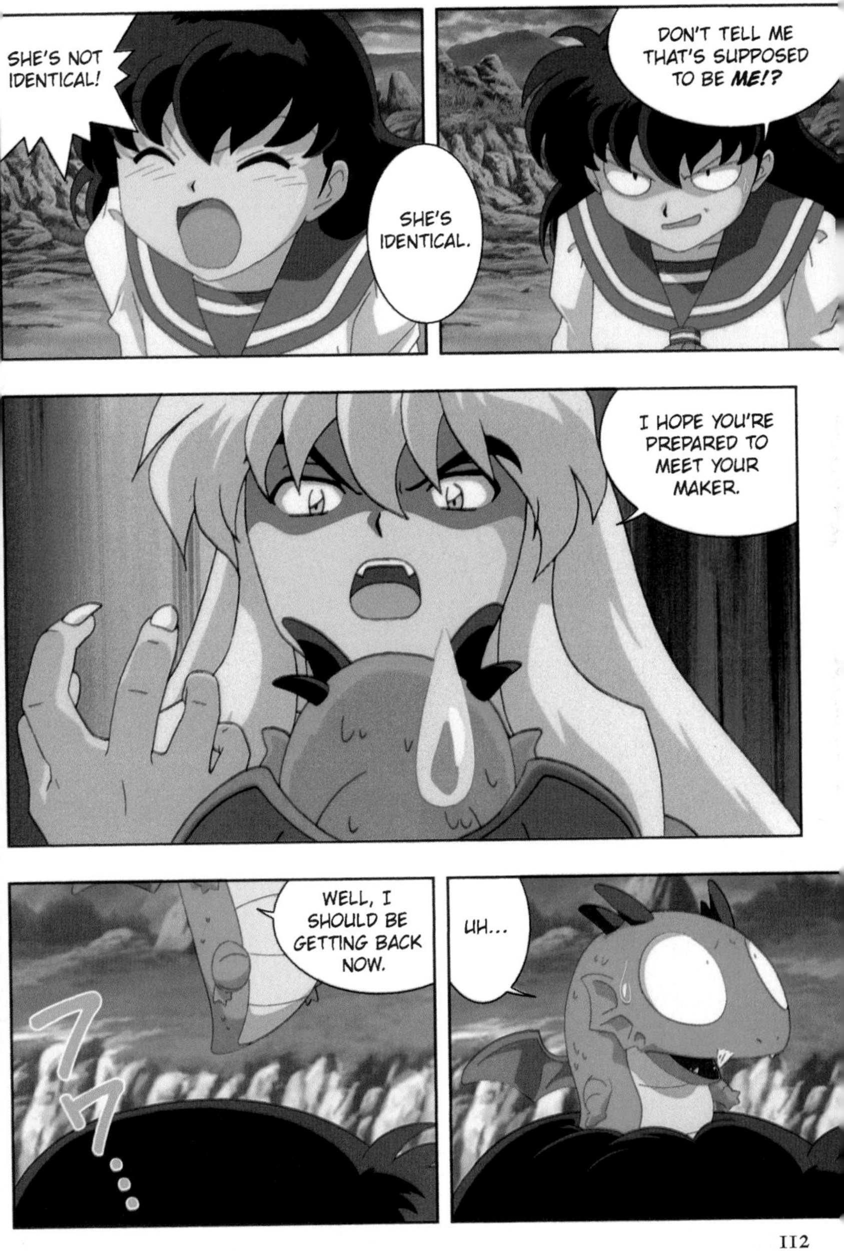
DON'T TELL ME THAT'S SUPPOSED TO BE ME!?
SHE'S IDENTICAL.
SHE'S NOT IDENTICAL!
I HOPE YOU'RE PREPARED TO MEET YOUR MAKER.
UH...
WELL, I SHOULD BE GETTING BACK NOW.

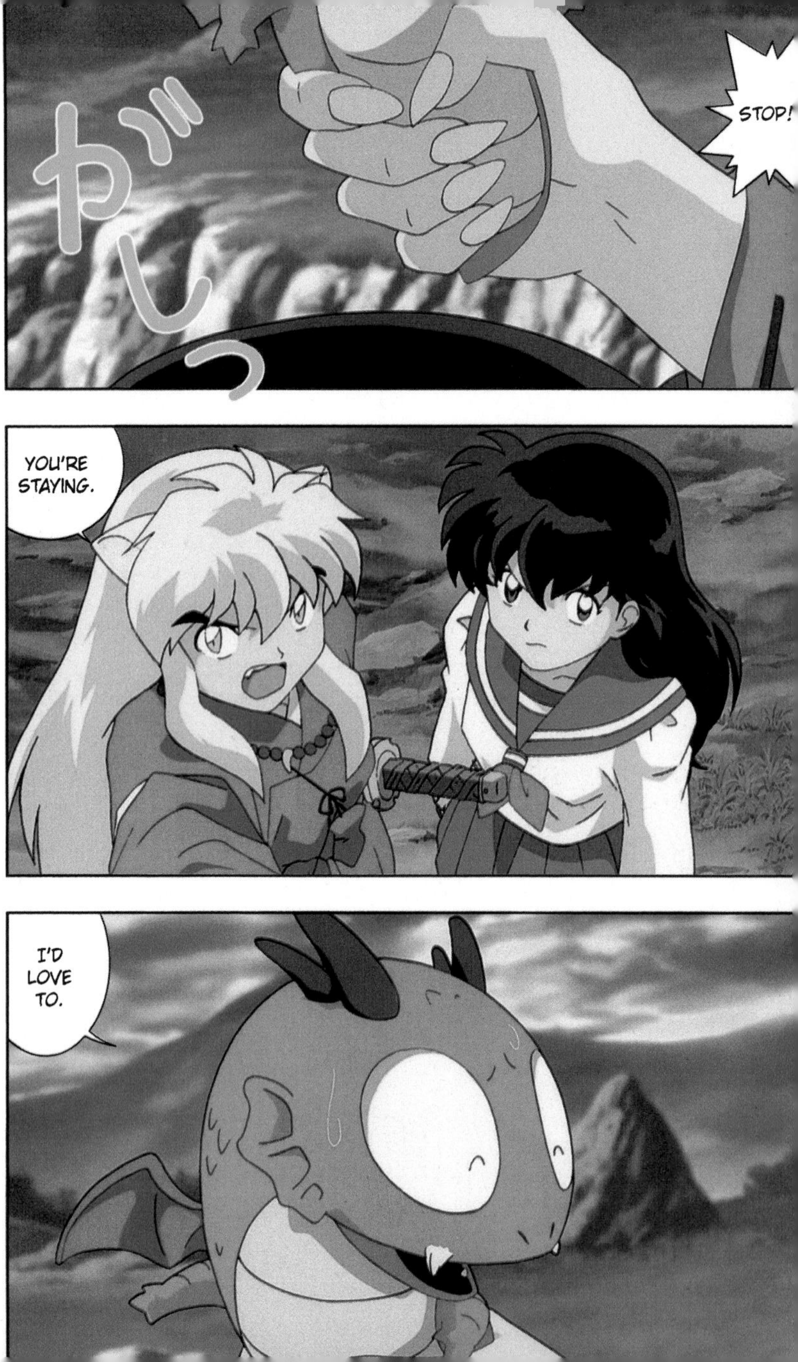
STOP!
がしっ
YOU'RE STAYING.
I'D LOVE TO.

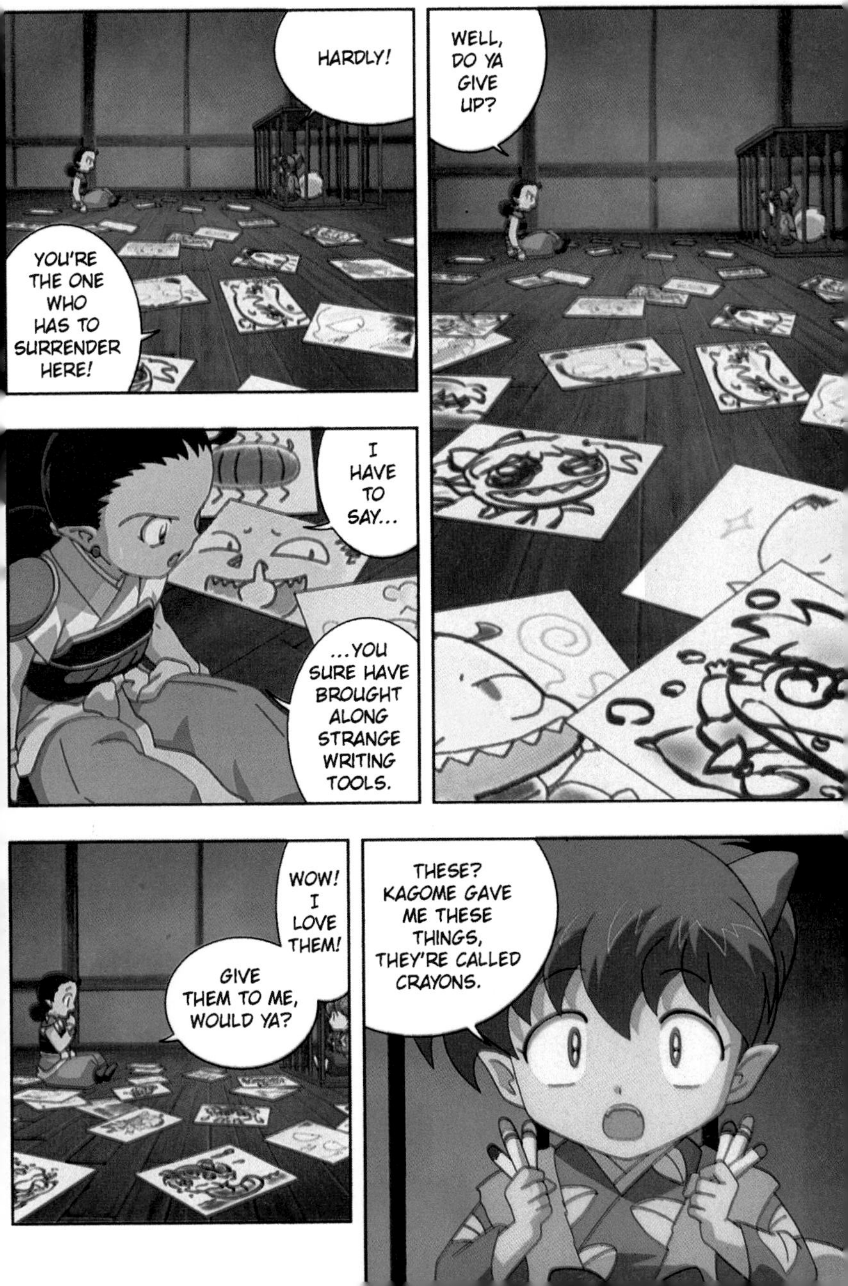
WELL, DO YA GIVE UP?
HARDLY!
YOU'RE THE ONE WHO HAS TO SURRENDER HERE!
I HAVE TO SAY...
...YOU SURE HAVE BROUGHT ALONG STRANGE WRITING TOOLS.
THESE? KAGOME GAVE ME THESE THINGS, THEY'RE CALLED CRAYONS.
WOW! I LOVE THEM!
GIVE THEM TO ME, WOULD YA?

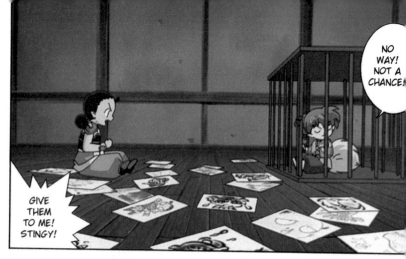

NO WAY! NOT A CHANCE!

GIVE THEM TO ME! STINGY!

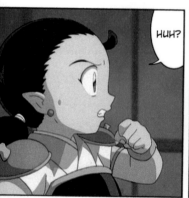

HUH?

LET'S SEE...IF YOU LET ME OUT OF THIS PLACE, I MIGHT RECONSIDER.

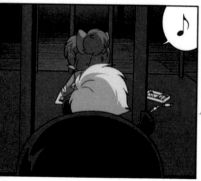

♪

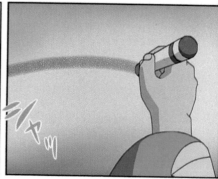

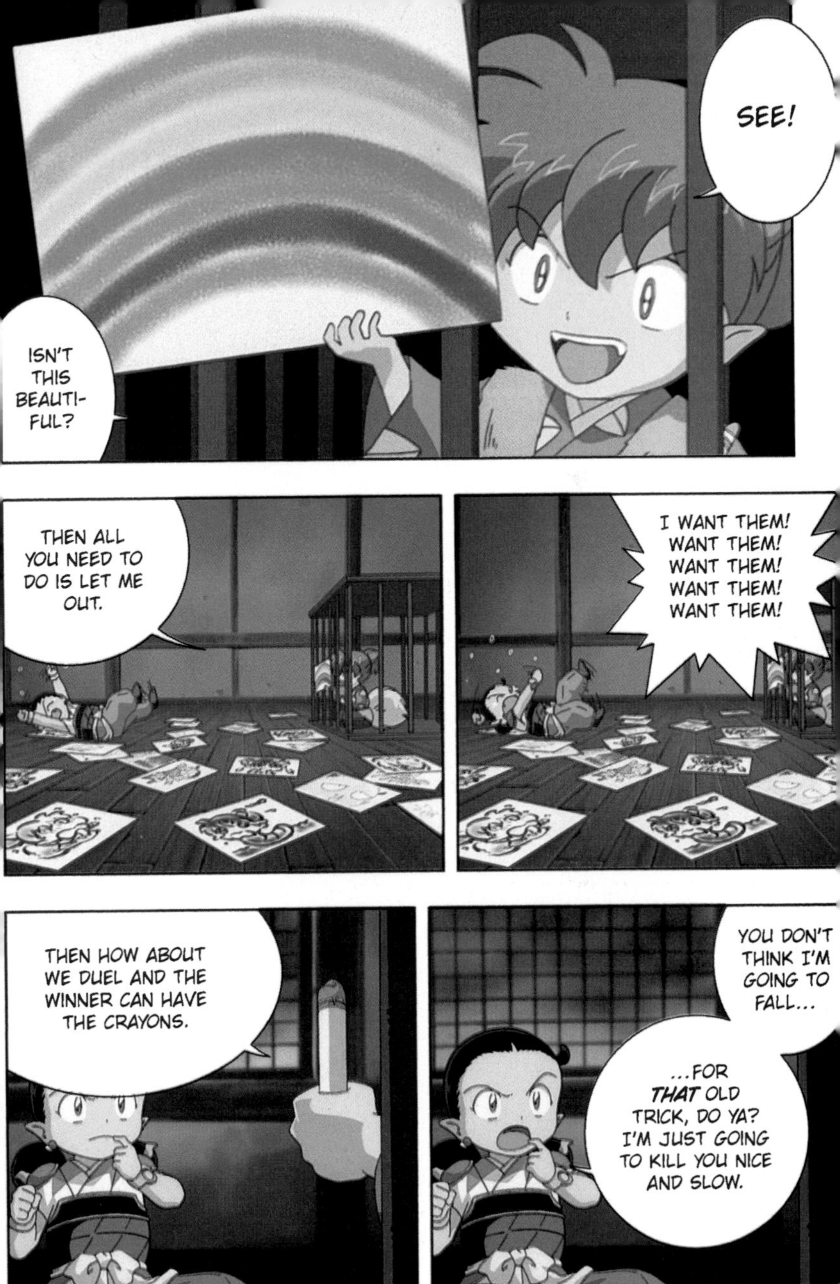
SEE!
ISN'T THIS BEAUTI-FUL?
THEN ALL YOU NEED TO DO IS LET ME OUT.
I WANT THEM! WANT THEM! WANT THEM! WANT THEM! WANT THEM!
THEN HOW ABOUT WE DUEL AND THE WINNER CAN HAVE THE CRAYONS.
YOU DON'T THINK I'M GOING TO FALL...
...FOR *THAT* OLD TRICK, DO YA? I'M JUST GOING TO KILL YOU NICE AND SLOW.

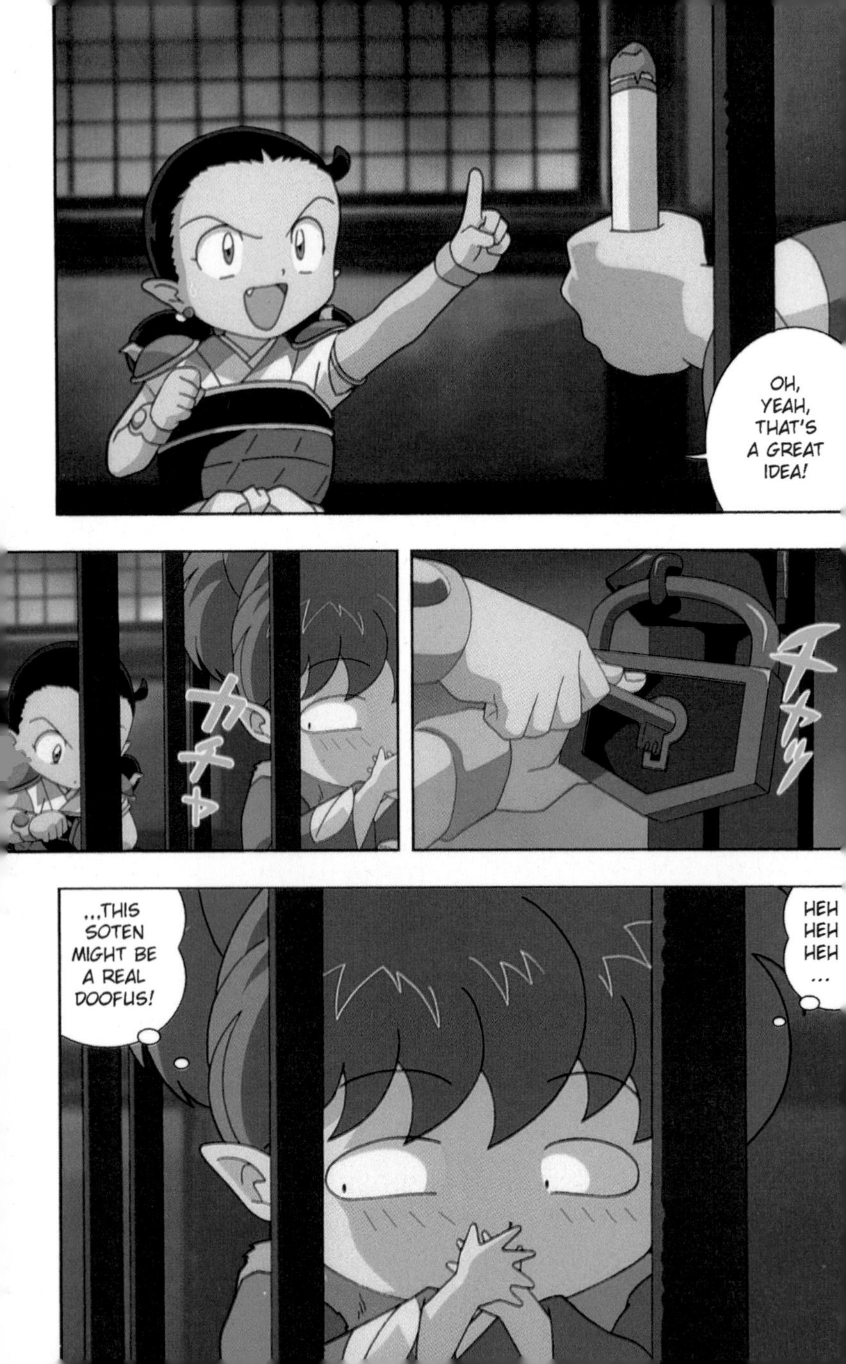
OH, YEAH, THAT'S A GREAT IDEA!
...THIS SOTEN MIGHT BE A REAL DOOFUS!
HEH HEH HEH ...

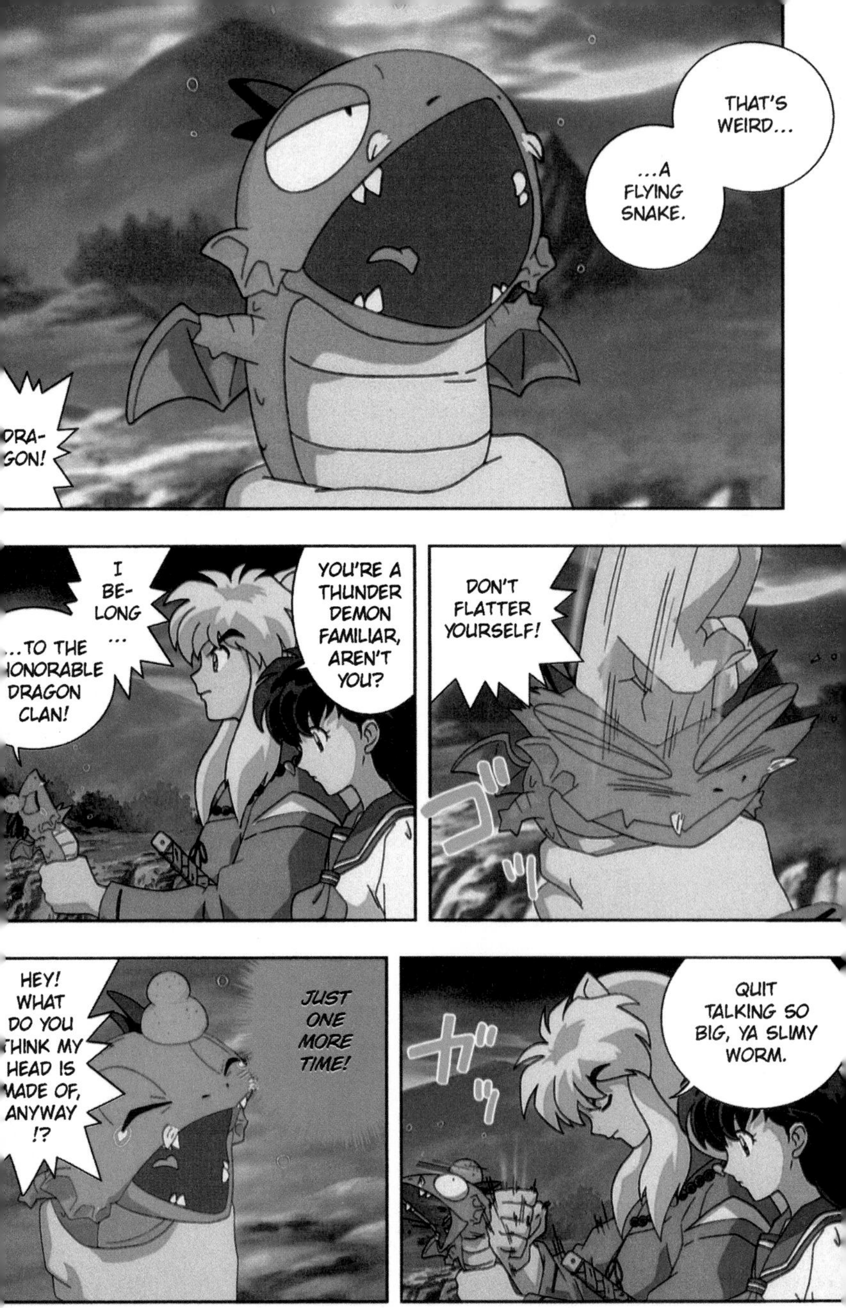
THAT'S WEIRD...
...A FLYING SNAKE.
DRA-GON!
DON'T FLATTER YOURSELF!
YOU'RE A THUNDER DEMON FAMILIAR, AREN'T YOU?
I BE-LONG...
...TO THE HONORABLE DRAGON CLAN!
QUIT TALKING SO BIG, YA SLIMY WORM.
JUST ONE MORE TIME!
HEY! WHAT DO YOU THINK MY HEAD IS MADE OF, ANYWAY!?

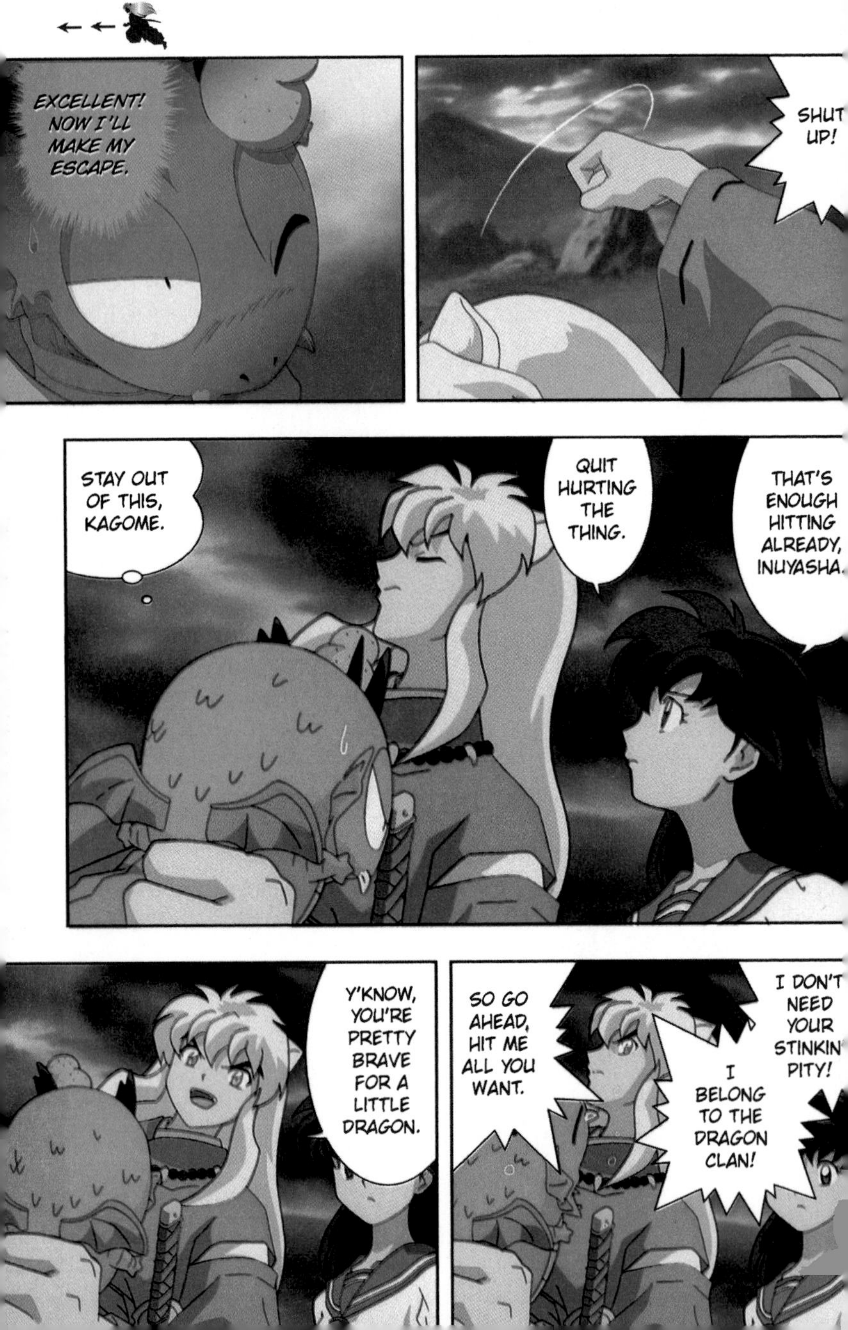
SHUT UP!
EXCELLENT! NOW I'LL MAKE MY ESCAPE.
THAT'S ENOUGH HITTING ALREADY, INUYASHA.
QUIT HURTING THE THING.
STAY OUT OF THIS, KAGOME.
I DON'T NEED YOUR STINKIN' PITY!
I BELONG TO THE DRAGON CLAN!
SO GO AHEAD, HIT ME ALL YOU WANT.
Y'KNOW, YOU'RE PRETTY BRAVE FOR A LITTLE DRAGON.

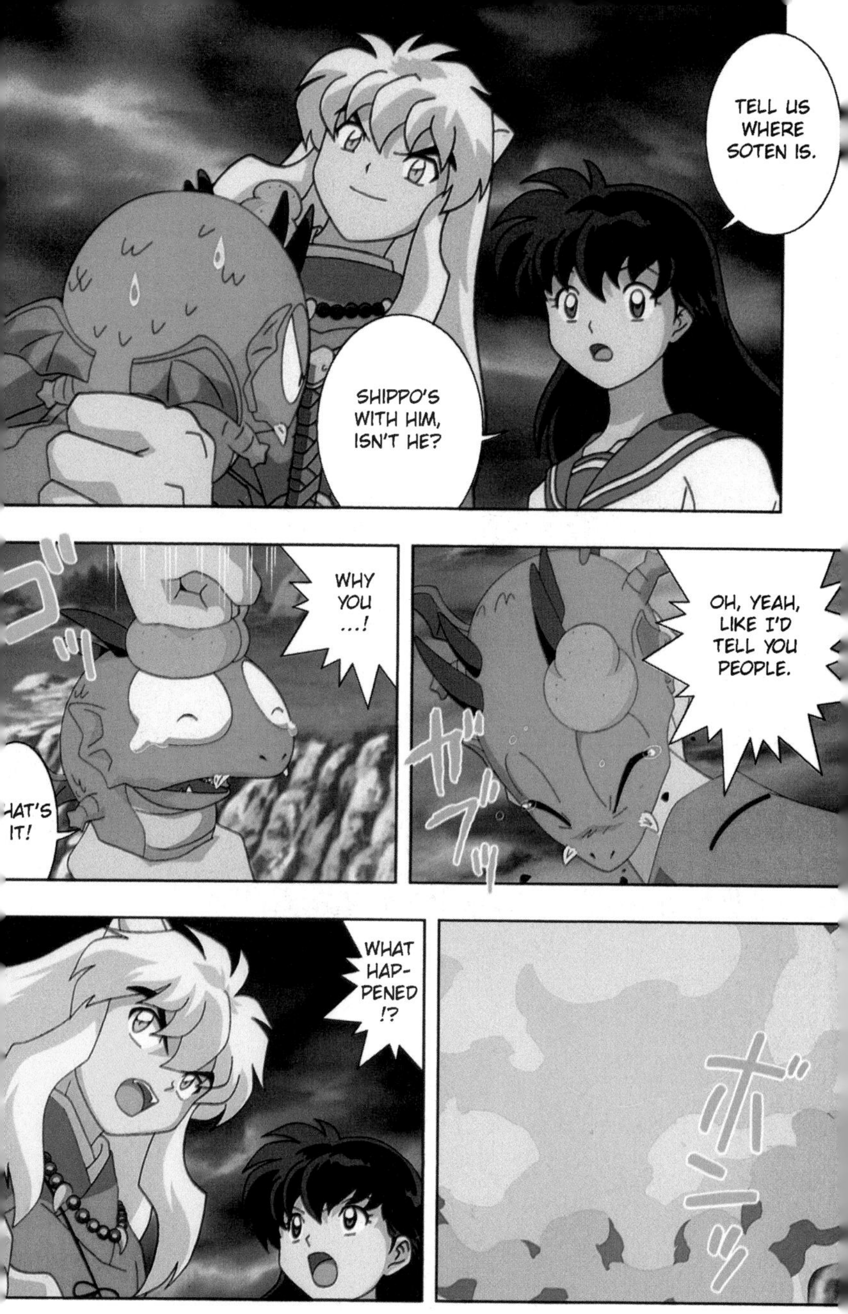
TELL US WHERE SOTEN IS.
SHIPPO'S WITH HIM, ISN'T HE?
OH, YEAH, LIKE I'D TELL YOU PEOPLE.
WHY YOU ...!
HAT'S IT!
WHAT HAP-PENED !?

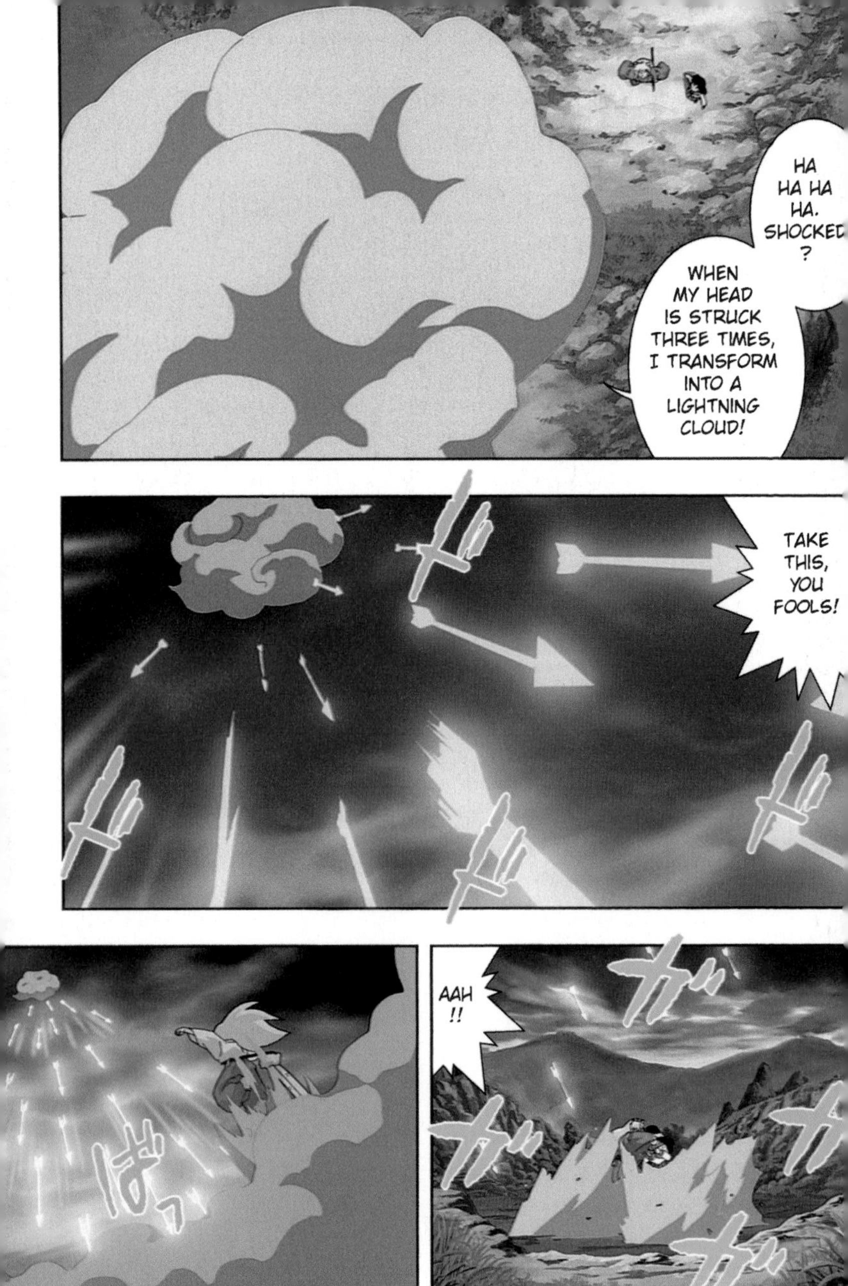
HA HA HA HA. SHOCKED?
WHEN MY HEAD IS STRUCK THREE TIMES, I TRANSFORM INTO A LIGHTNING CLOUD!
TAKE THIS, YOU FOOLS!
AAH!!
ばっ

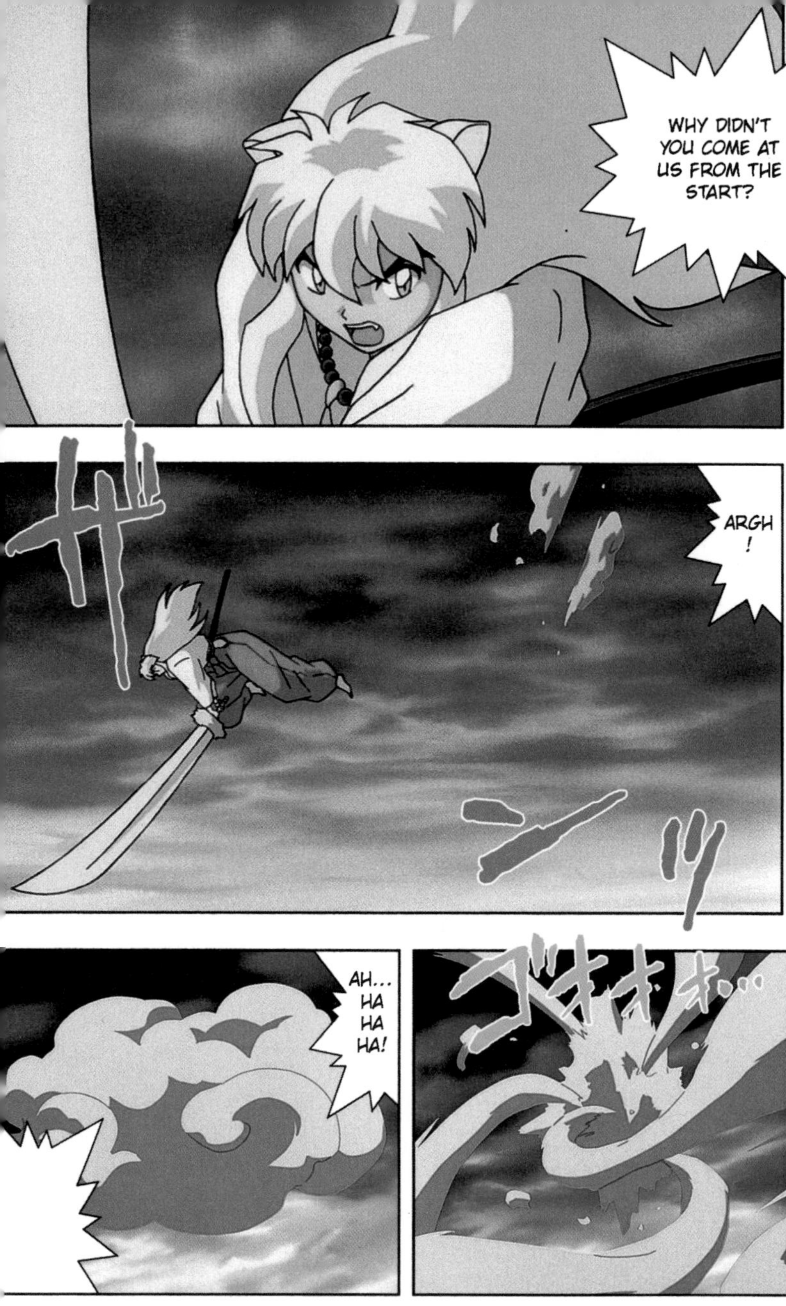
WHY DIDN'T YOU COME AT US FROM THE START?
ARGH!
AH... HA HA HA!

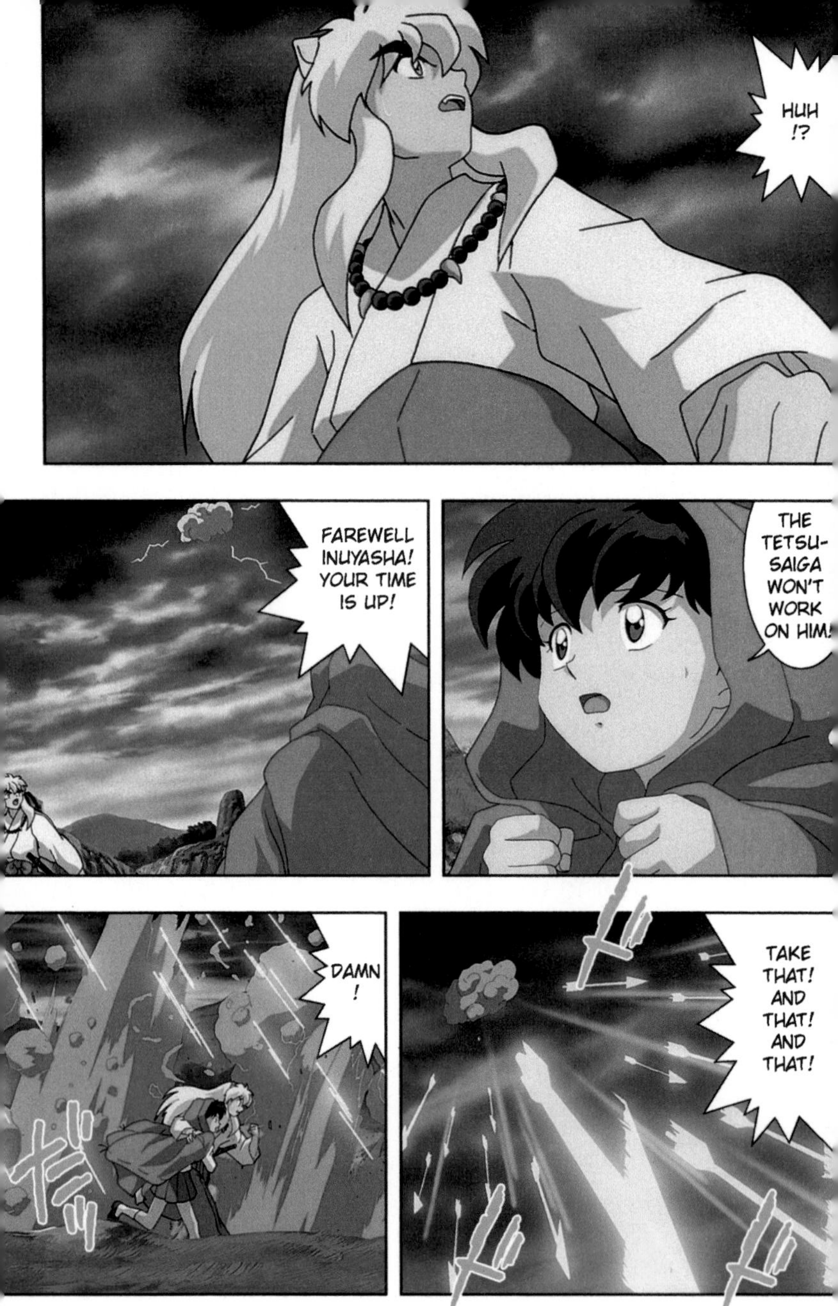
HUH !?
THE TETSU-SAIGA WON'T WORK ON HIM!
FAREWELL INUYASHA! YOUR TIME IS UP!
TAKE THAT! AND THAT! AND THAT!
DAMN !

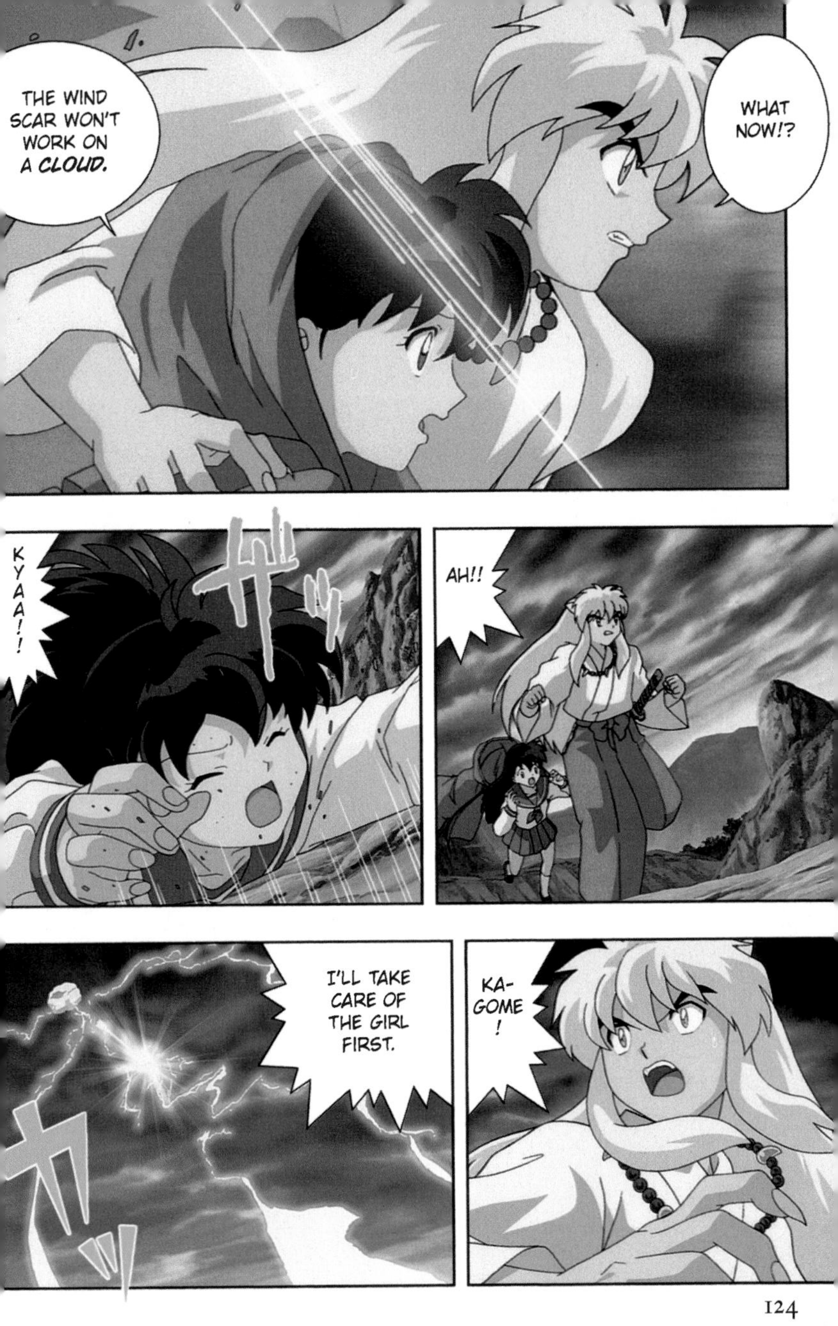
WHAT NOW!?
THE WIND SCAR WON'T WORK ON A *CLOUD.*
AH!!
KYAA!!
KA-GOME!
I'LL TAKE CARE OF THE GIRL FIRST.

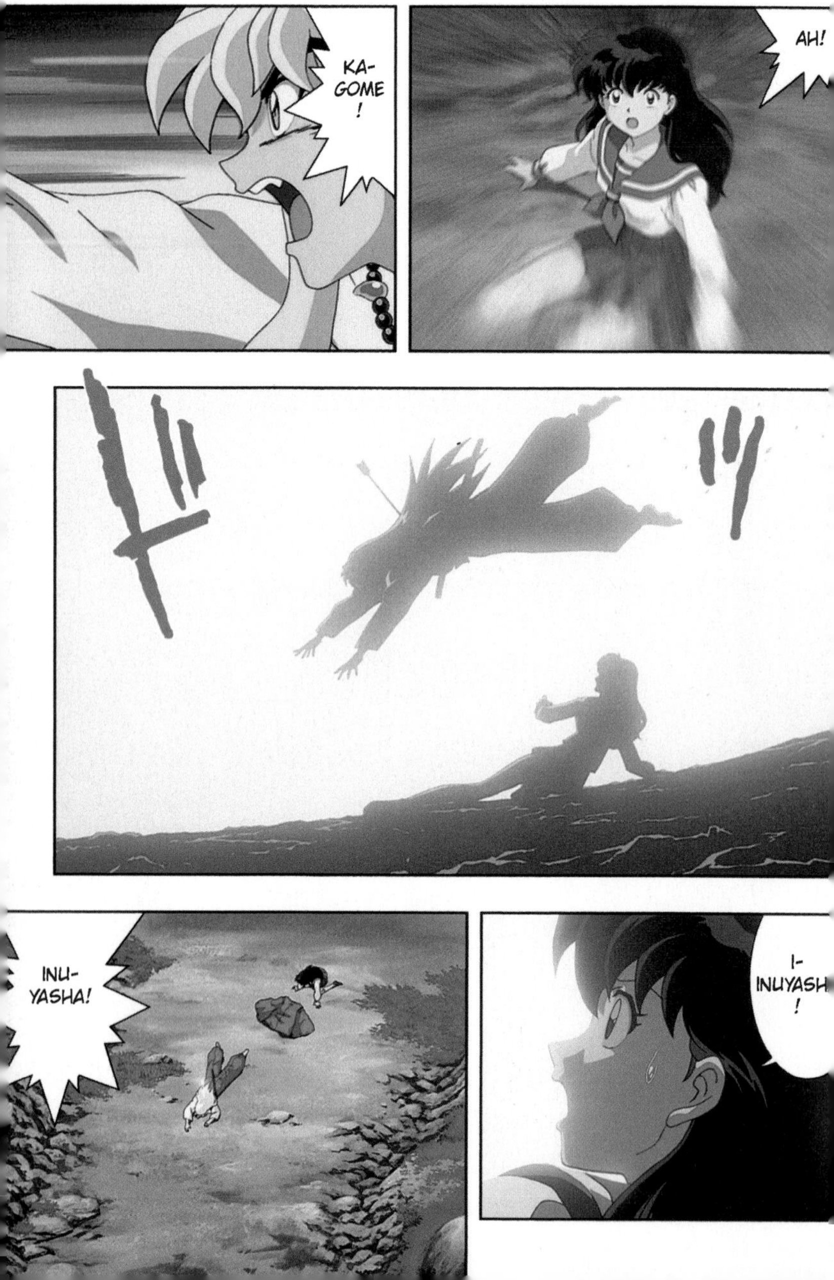
AH!
KA- GOME !
I- INUYASH !
INU- YASHA!

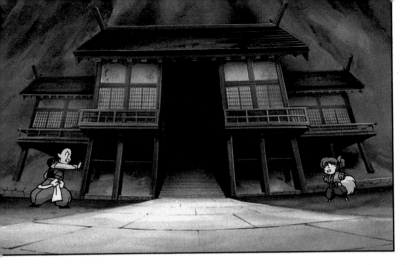

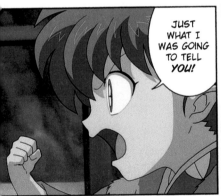

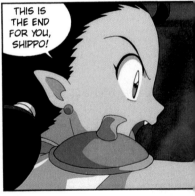

THIS IS THE END FOR YOU, SHIPPO!
JUST WHAT I WAS GOING TO TELL *YOU!*
HAH!!
タッ
TAKE THIS! FOX FIRE!
ゴオッ

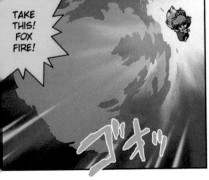

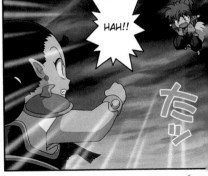

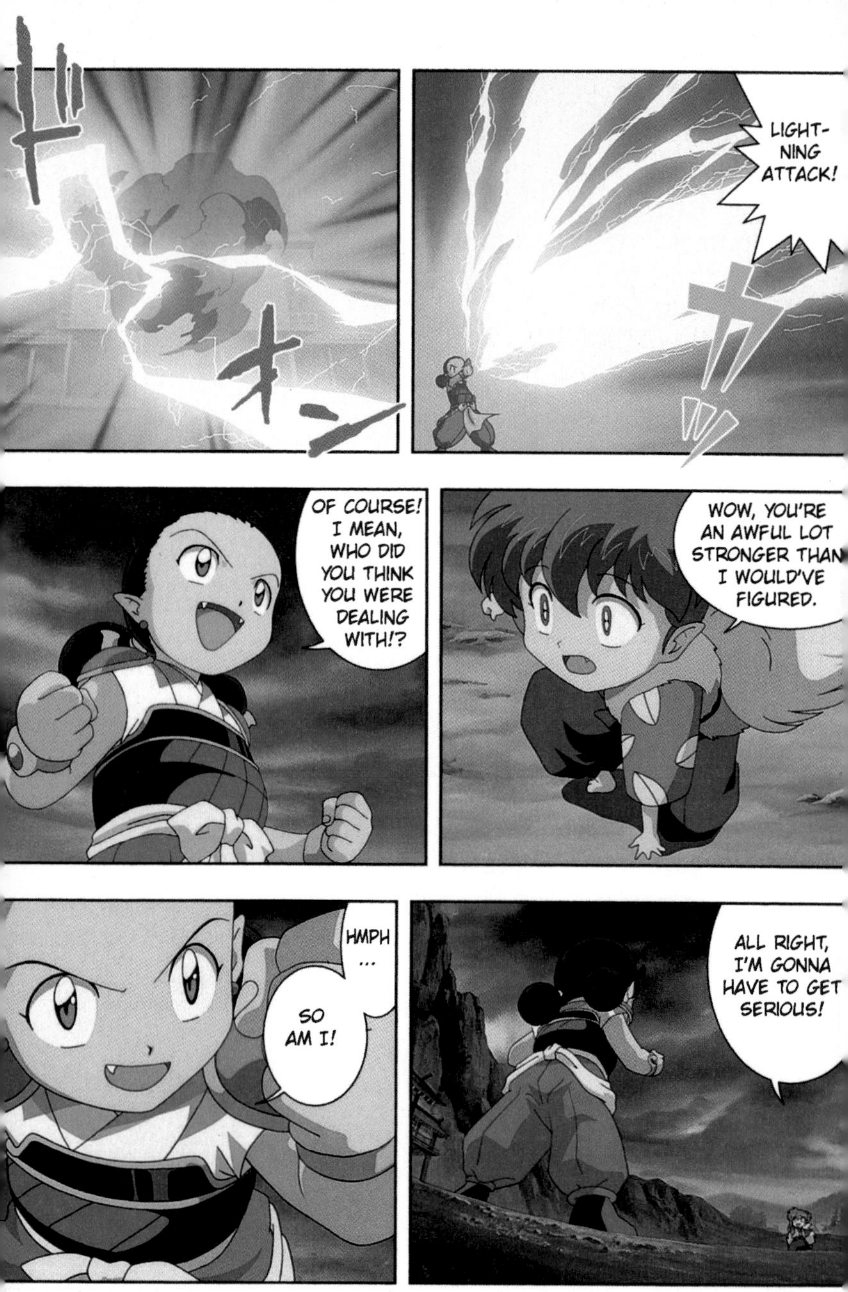
LIGHT-NING ATTACK!
カッ
ドオン
WOW, YOU'RE AN AWFUL LOT STRONGER THAN I WOULD'VE FIGURED.
OF COURSE! I MEAN, WHO DID YOU THINK YOU WERE DEALING WITH!?
ALL RIGHT, I'M GONNA HAVE TO GET SERIOUS!
HMPH ...
SO AM I!

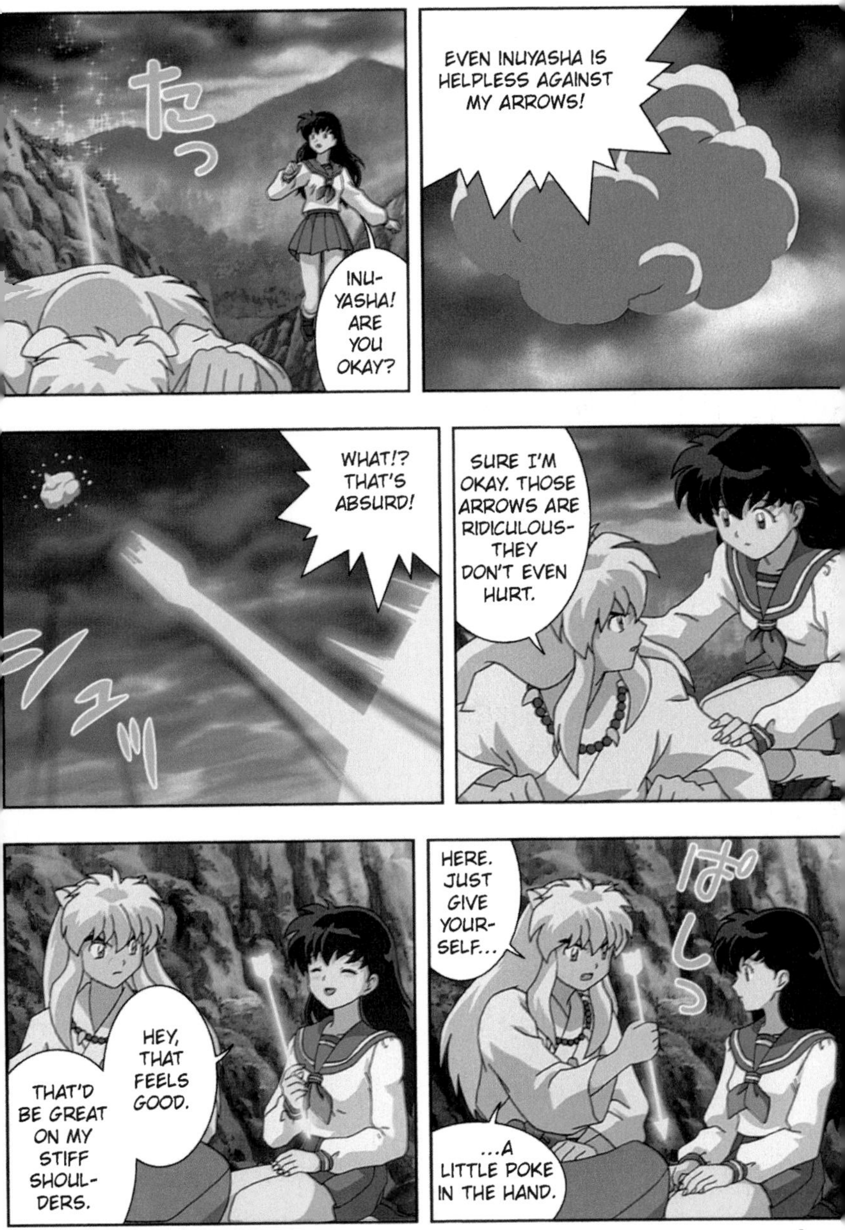
EVEN INUYASHA IS HELPLESS AGAINST MY ARROWS!
たっ
INU-YASHA! ARE YOU OKAY?
SURE I'M OKAY. THOSE ARROWS ARE RIDICULOUS-THEY DON'T EVEN HURT.
WHAT!? THAT'S ABSURD!
シュッ
はしっ
HERE. JUST GIVE YOUR-SELF...
...A LITTLE POKE IN THE HAND.
HEY, THAT FEELS GOOD.
THAT'D BE GREAT ON MY STIFF SHOUL-DERS.

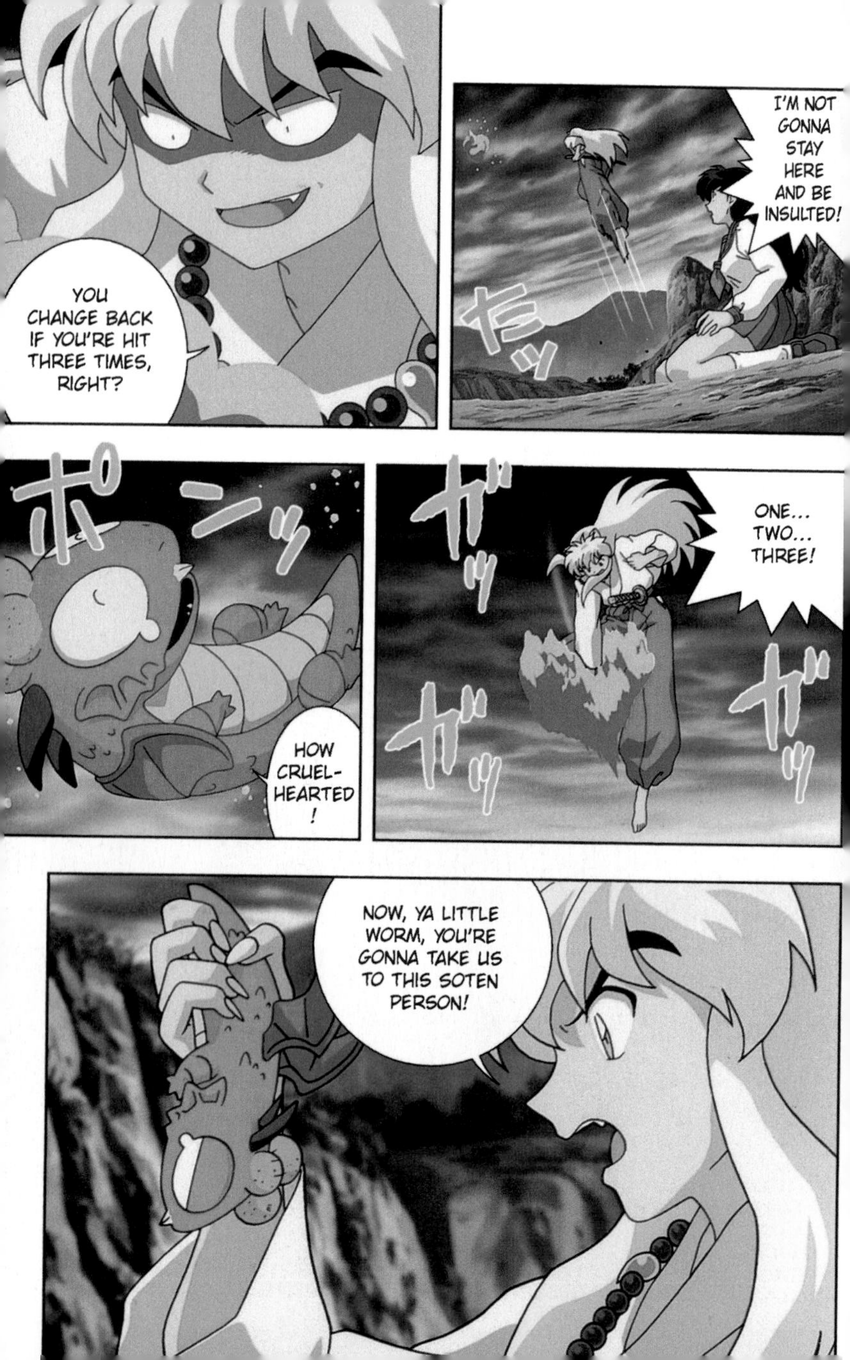

I'M NOT GONNA STAY HERE AND BE INSULTED!
たッ
YOU CHANGE BACK IF YOU'RE HIT THREE TIMES, RIGHT?
ガッ
ONE... TWO... THREE!
ガッ
ガッ
ポンッ
HOW CRUEL-HEARTED!
NOW, YA LITTLE WORM, YOU'RE GONNA TAKE US TO THIS SOTEN PERSON!

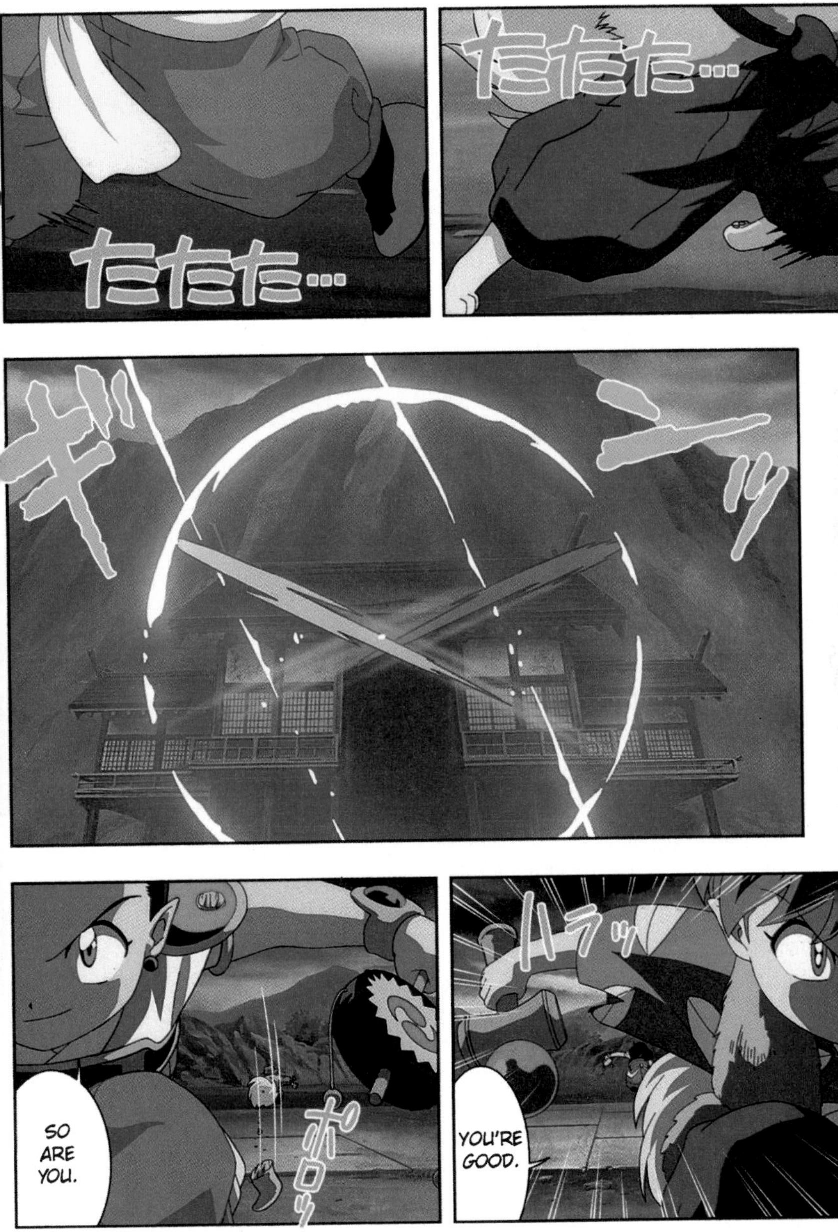
たたた…
たたた…
ギーッ
ハラッ
YOU'RE GOOD.
SO ARE YOU.
ポロッ

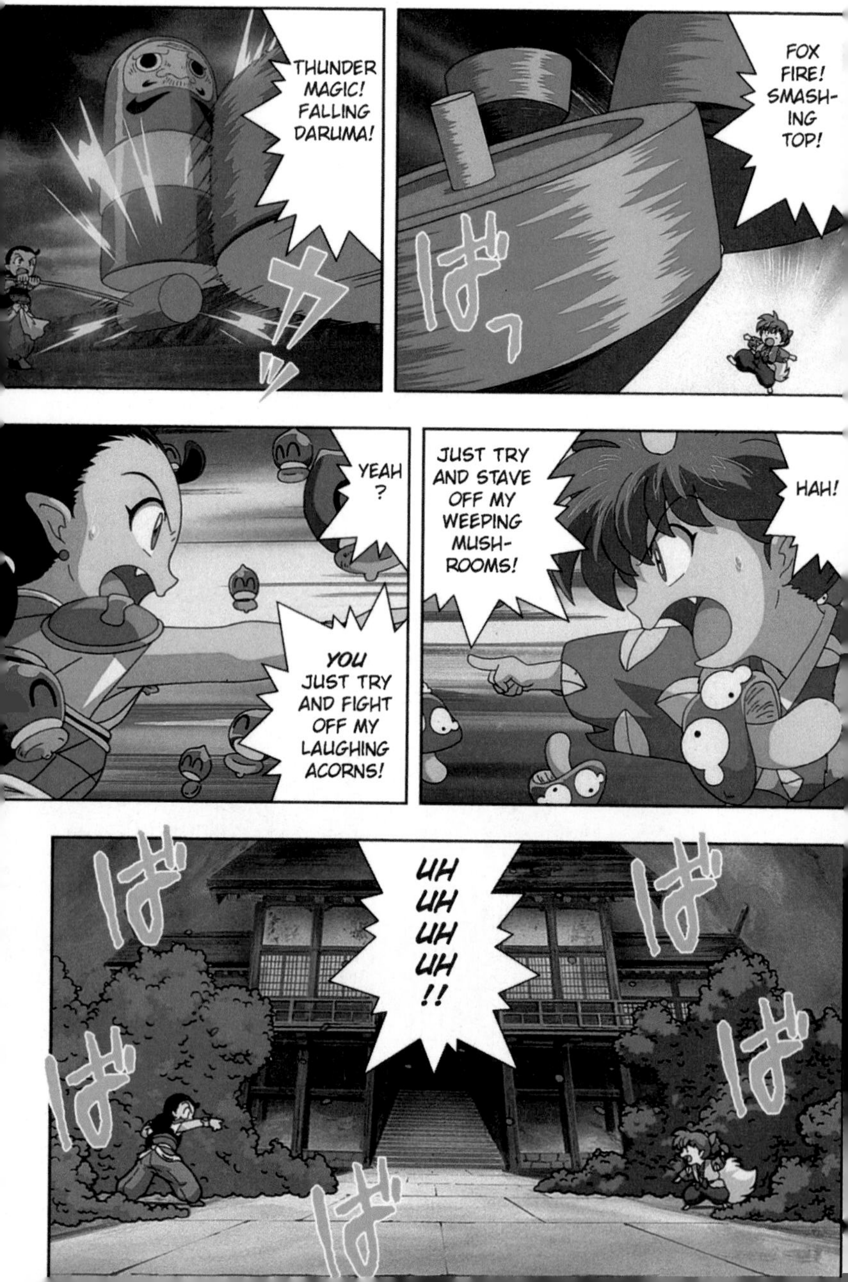
FOX FIRE! SMASHING TOP!
ばっ
THUNDER MAGIC! FALLING DARUMA!
カッ
HAH!
JUST TRY AND STAVE OFF MY WEEPING MUSHROOMS!
YEAH?
YOU JUST TRY AND FIGHT OFF MY LAUGHING ACORNS!
ば
ば
UH UH UH UH!!
ば
ば
ば

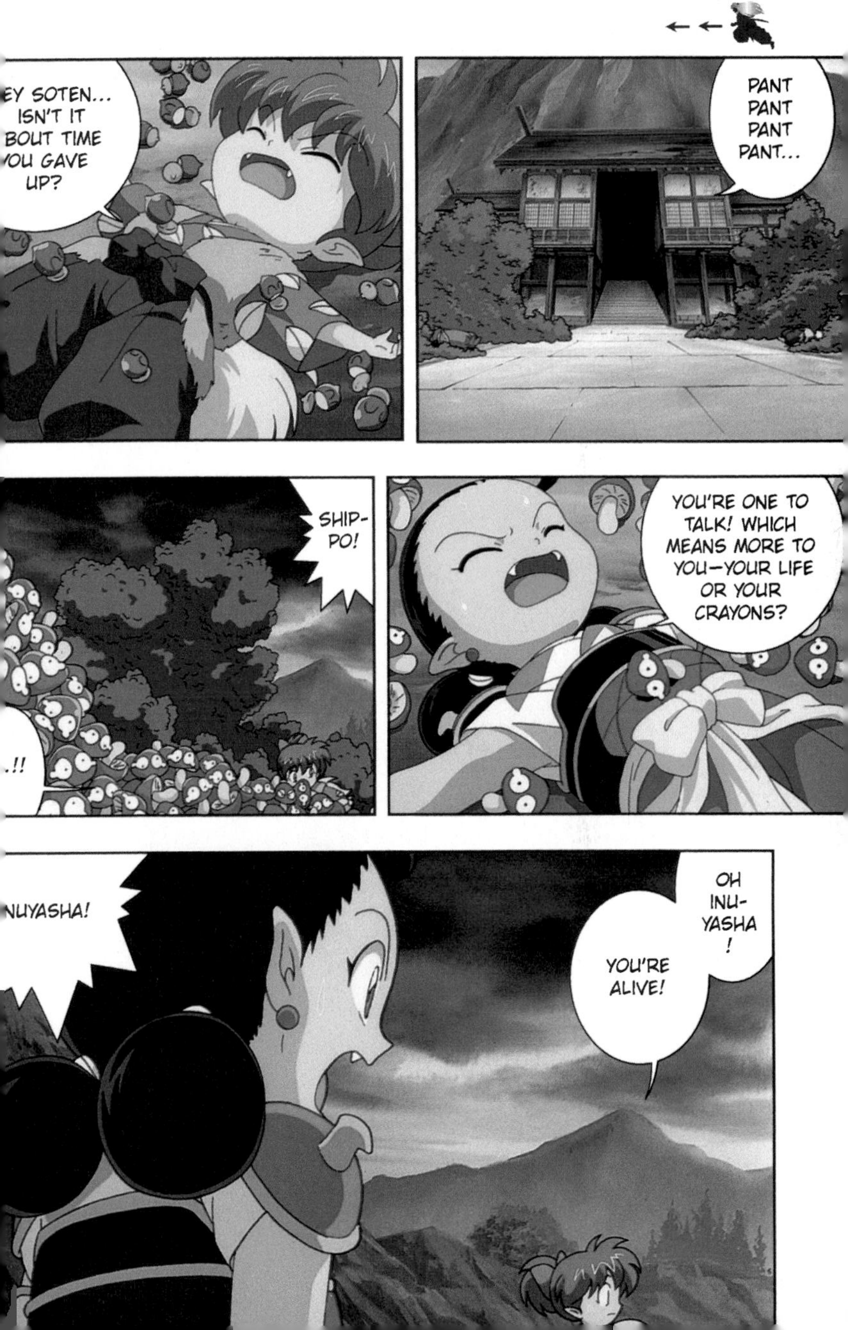

PANT PANT PANT PANT...
EY SOTEN... ISN'T IT BOUT TIME OU GAVE UP?
YOU'RE ONE TO TALK! WHICH MEANS MORE TO YOU—YOUR LIFE OR YOUR CRAYONS?
SHIP-PO!
.!!
OH INU-YASHA!
YOU'RE ALIVE!
NUYASHA!

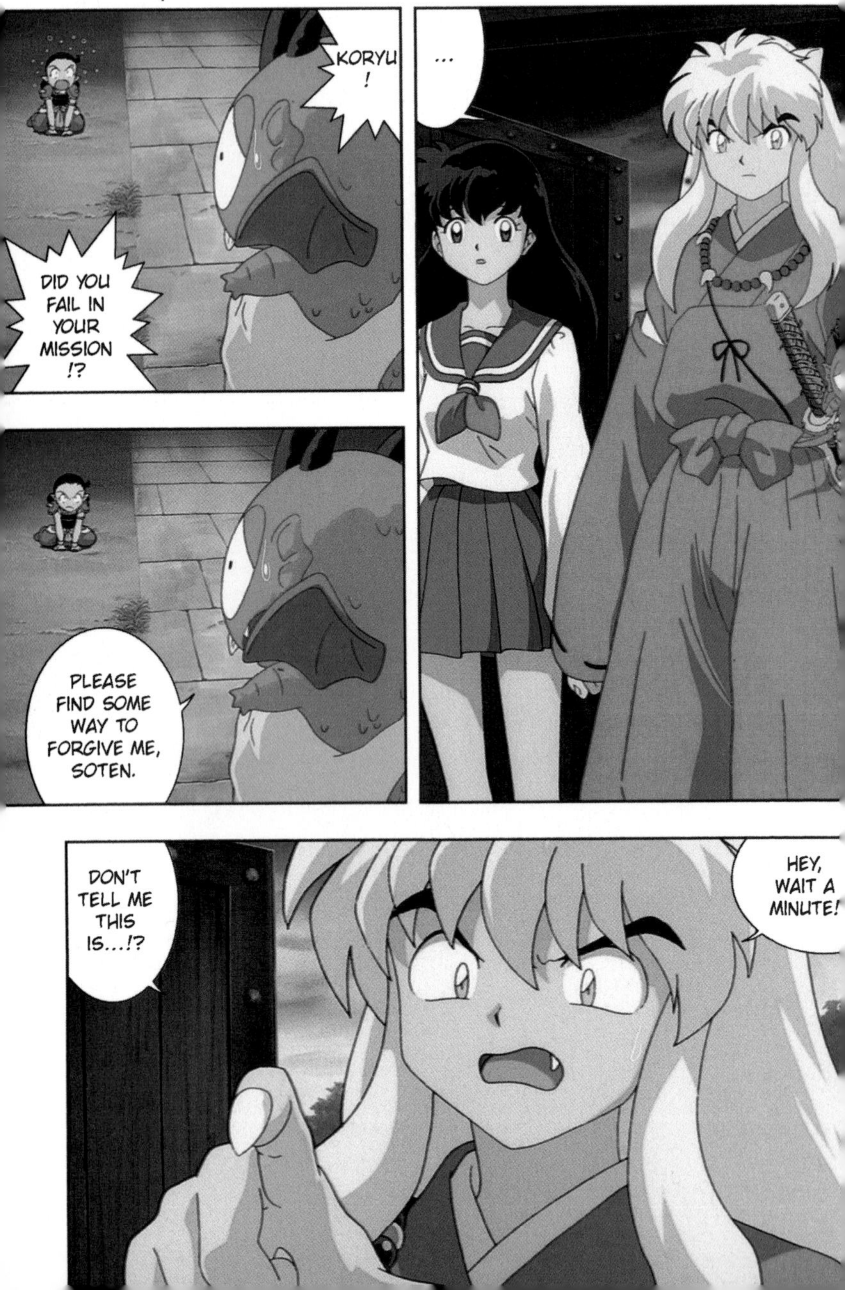
...
KORYU!
DID YOU FAIL IN YOUR MISSION!?
PLEASE FIND SOME WAY TO FORGIVE ME, SOTEN.
HEY, WAIT A MINUTE!
DON'T TELL ME THIS IS...!?

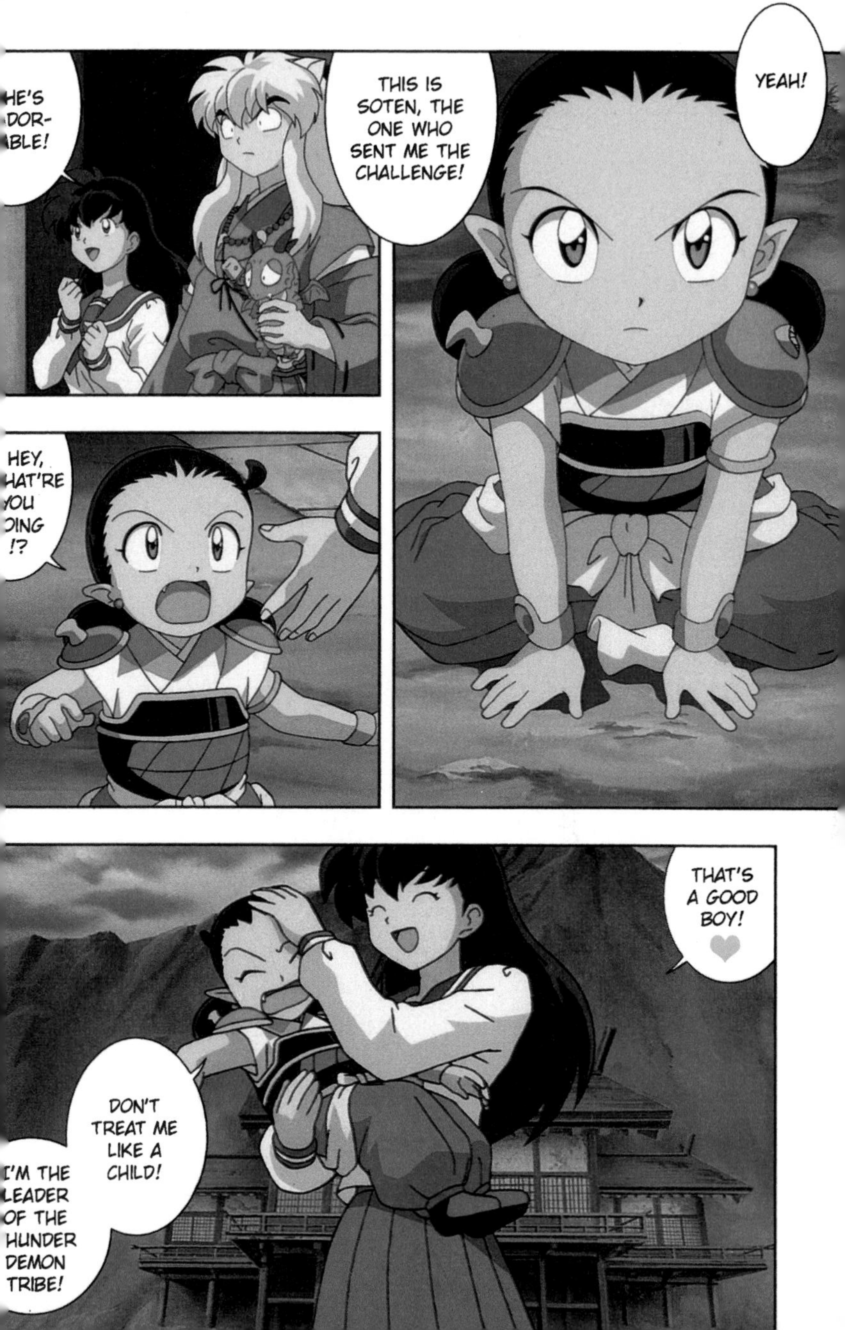
THIS IS SOTEN, THE ONE WHO SENT ME THE CHALLENGE!
YEAH!
HE'S DOR- BLE!
HEY, HAT'RE YOU OING !?
THAT'S A GOOD BOY! ♥
DON'T TREAT ME LIKE A CHILD!
I'M THE LEADER OF THE HUNDER DEMON TRIBE!

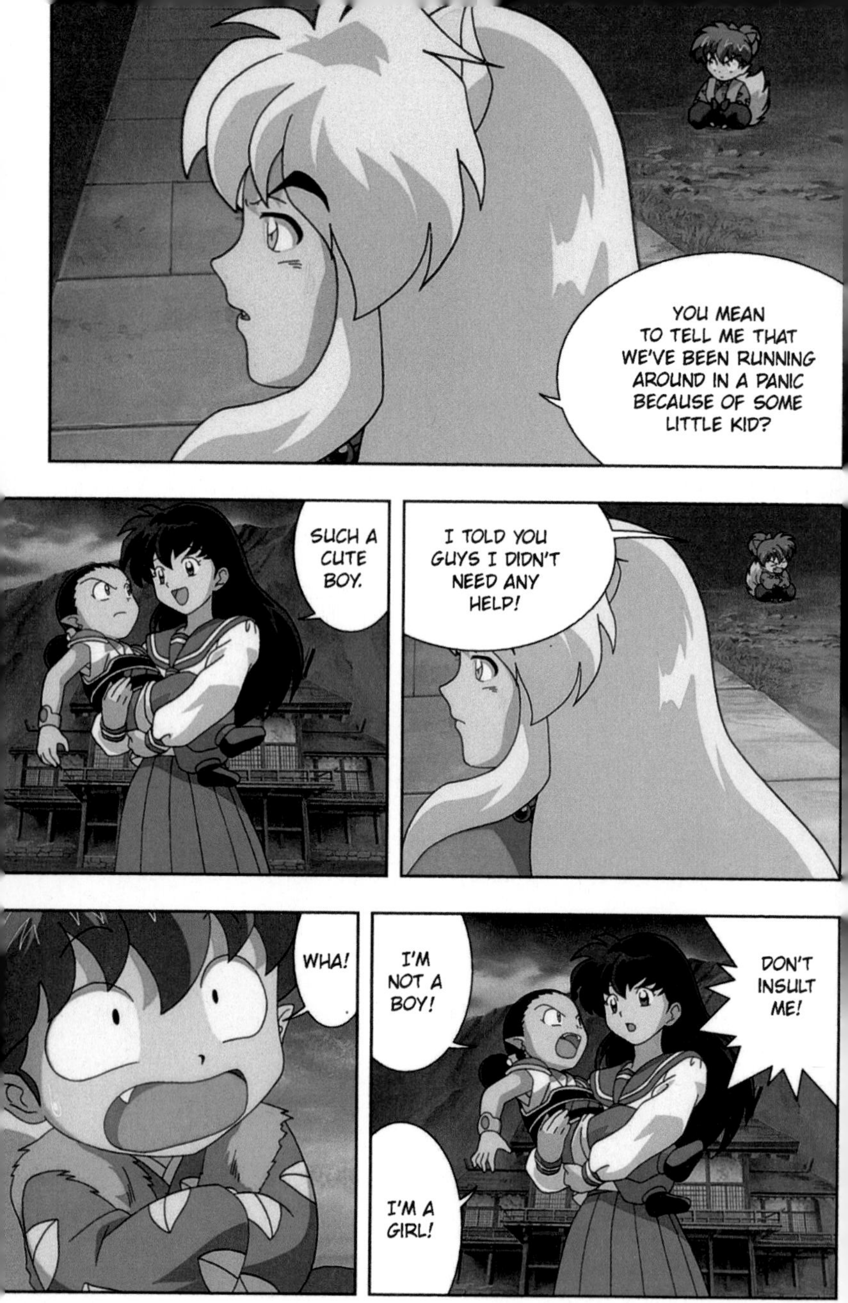
YOU MEAN TO TELL ME THAT WE'VE BEEN RUNNING AROUND IN A PANIC BECAUSE OF SOME LITTLE KID?
I TOLD YOU GUYS I DIDN'T NEED ANY HELP!
SUCH A CUTE BOY.
DON'T INSULT ME!
I'M NOT A BOY!
I'M A GIRL!
WHA!

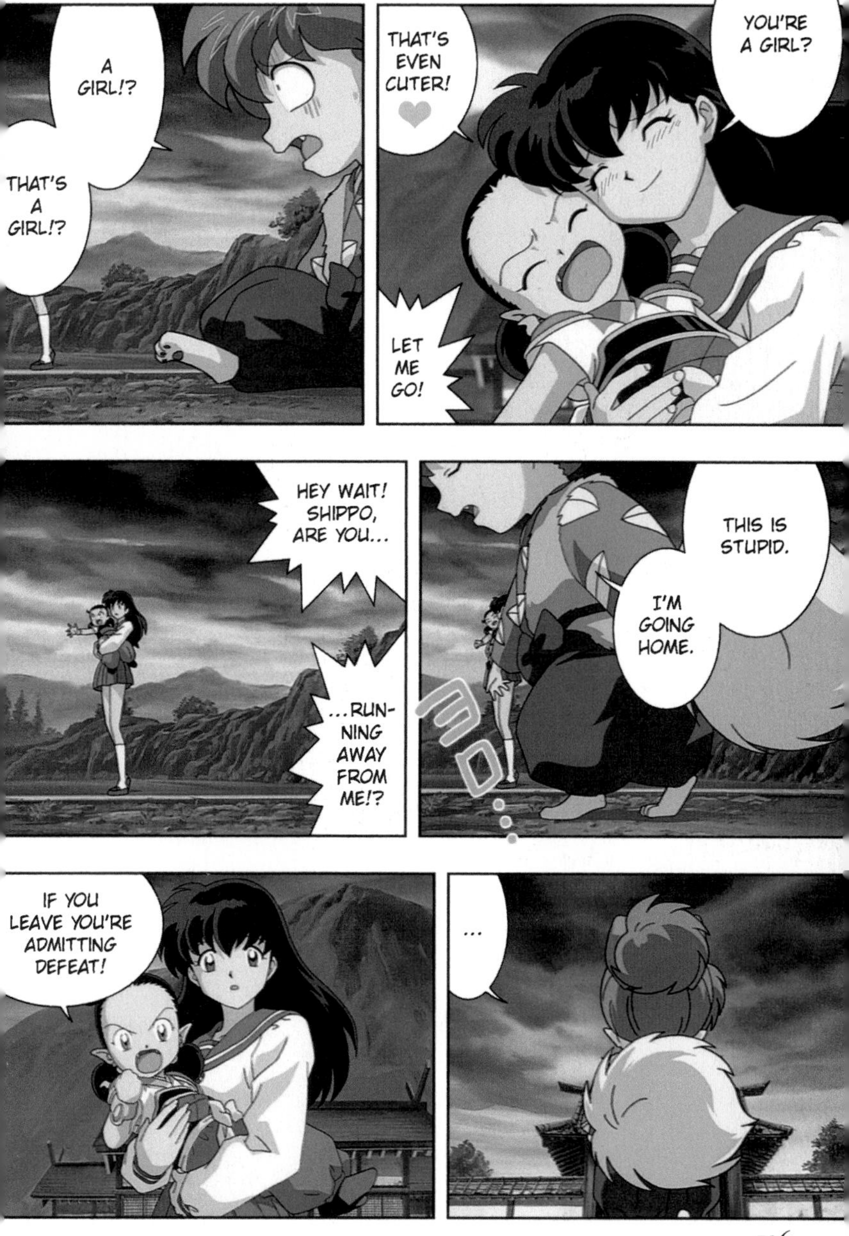
YOU'RE A GIRL?
THAT'S EVEN CUTER! ♥
LET ME GO!
A GIRL!?
THAT'S A GIRL!?
THIS IS STUPID.
I'M GOING HOME.
HEY WAIT! SHIPPO, ARE YOU...
...RUN-NING AWAY FROM ME!?
...
IF YOU LEAVE YOU'RE ADMITTING DEFEAT!

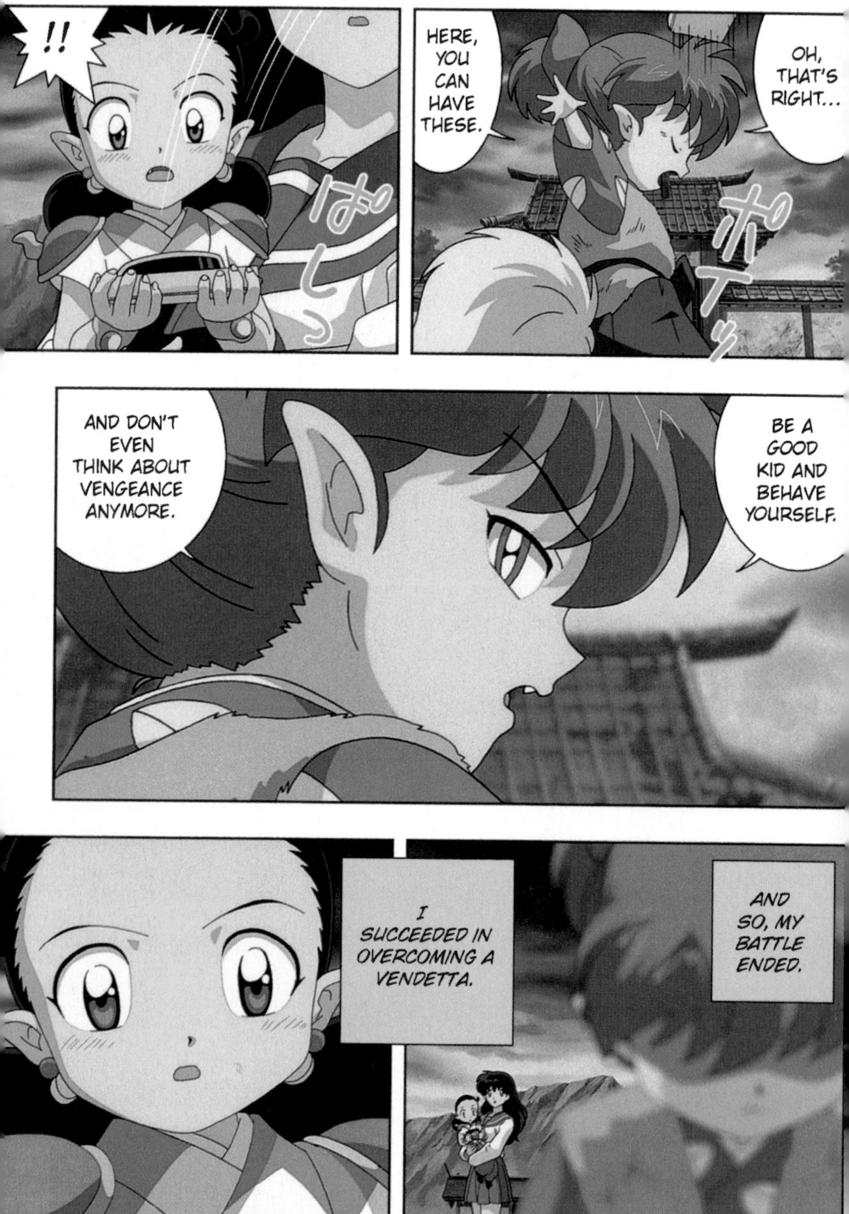
OH, THAT'S RIGHT...
HERE, YOU CAN HAVE THESE.
ポテッ
!!
ぱしっ
BE A GOOD KID AND BEHAVE YOURSELF.
AND DON'T EVEN THINK ABOUT VENGEANCE ANYMORE.
AND SO, MY BATTLE ENDED.
I SUCCEEDED IN OVERCOMING A VENDETTA.

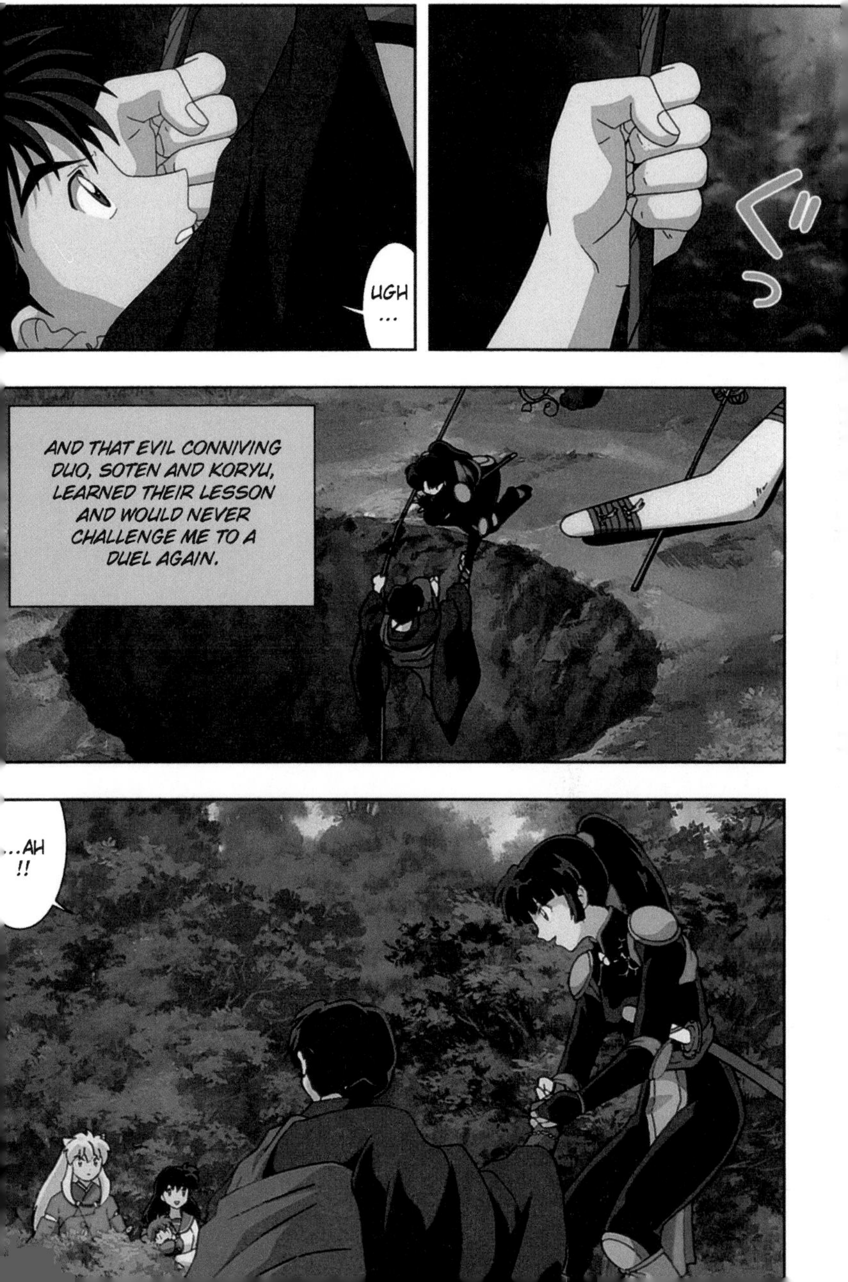
ぐっ
UGH...
AND THAT EVIL CONNIVING DUO, SOTEN AND KORYU, LEARNED THEIR LESSON AND WOULD NEVER CHALLENGE ME TO A DUEL AGAIN.
...AH !!

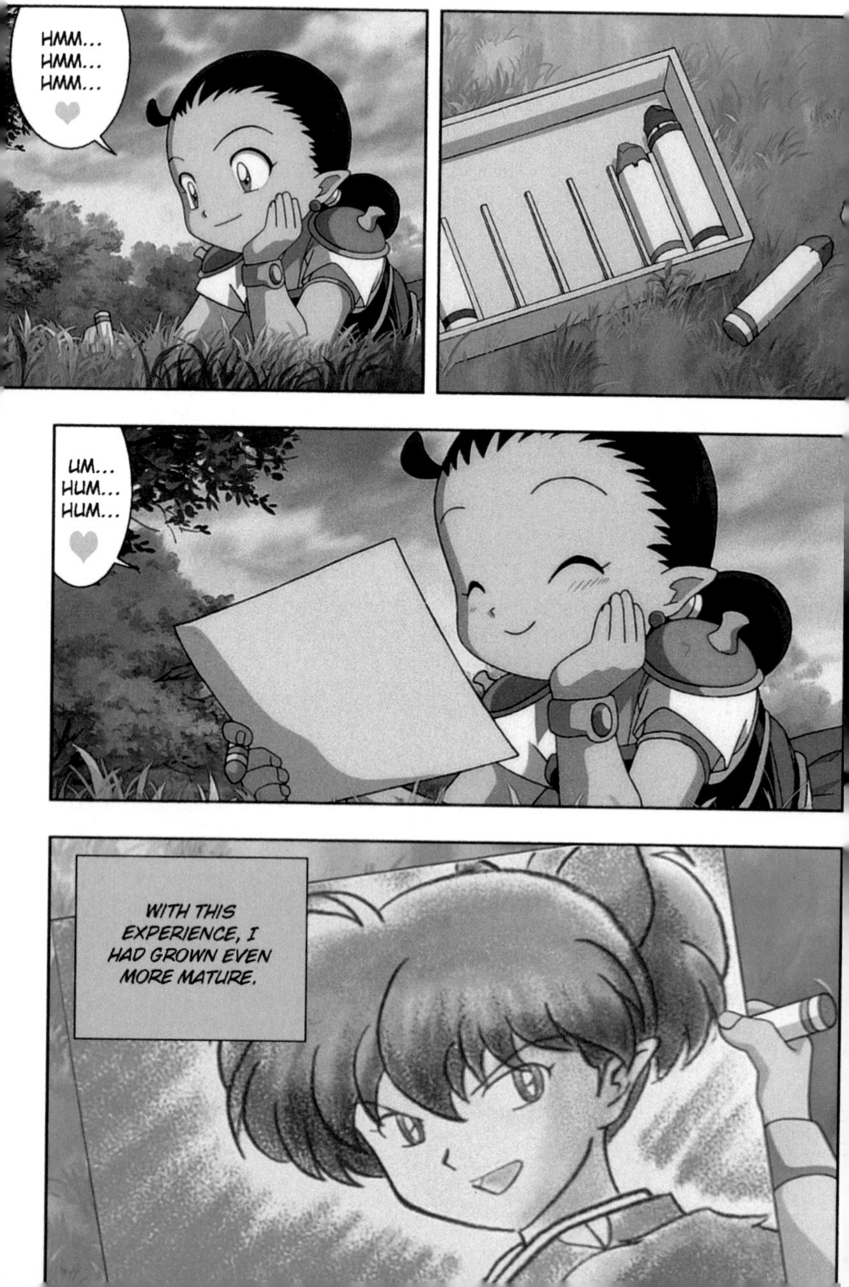
HMM... HMM... HMM... ♥
UM... HUM... HUM... ♥
WITH THIS EXPERIENCE, I HAD GROWN EVEN MORE MATURE.

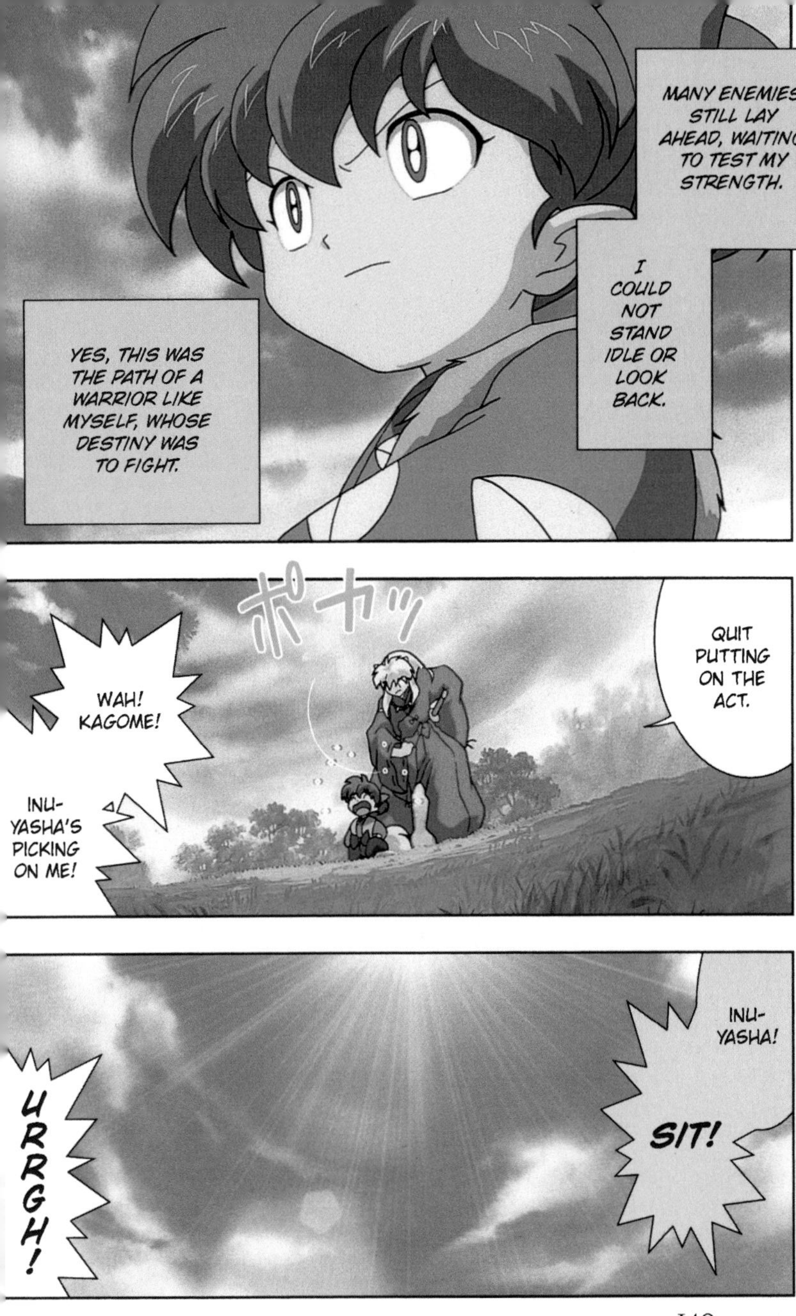
MANY ENEMIES STILL LAY AHEAD, WAITING TO TEST MY STRENGTH.
I COULD NOT STAND IDLE OR LOOK BACK.
YES, THIS WAS THE PATH OF A WARRIOR LIKE MYSELF, WHOSE DESTINY WAS TO FIGHT.
QUIT PUTTING ON THE ACT.
ポカッ
WAH! KAGOME!
INU-YASHA'S PICKING ON ME!
INU-YASHA!
SIT!
URRGH!

69
Terror of the Faceless Man!

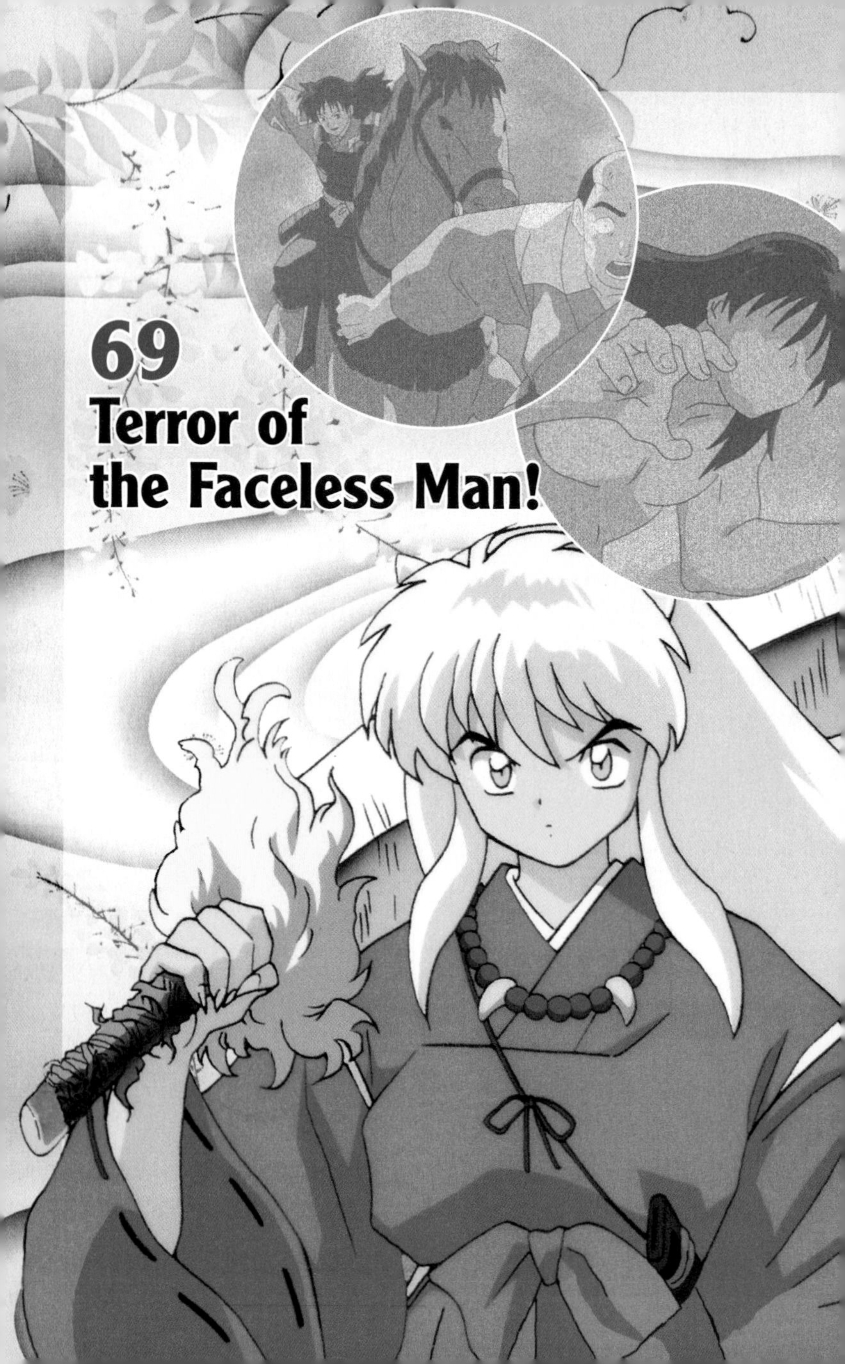

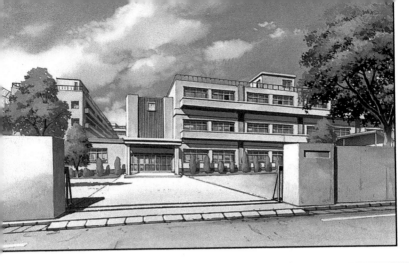

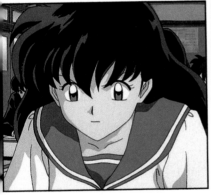

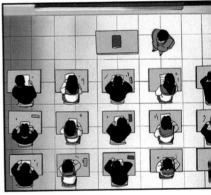

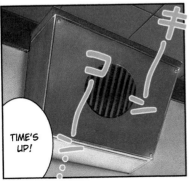

キーン

コーン

...

TIME'S
UP!

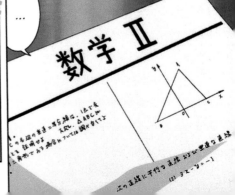

数学 II

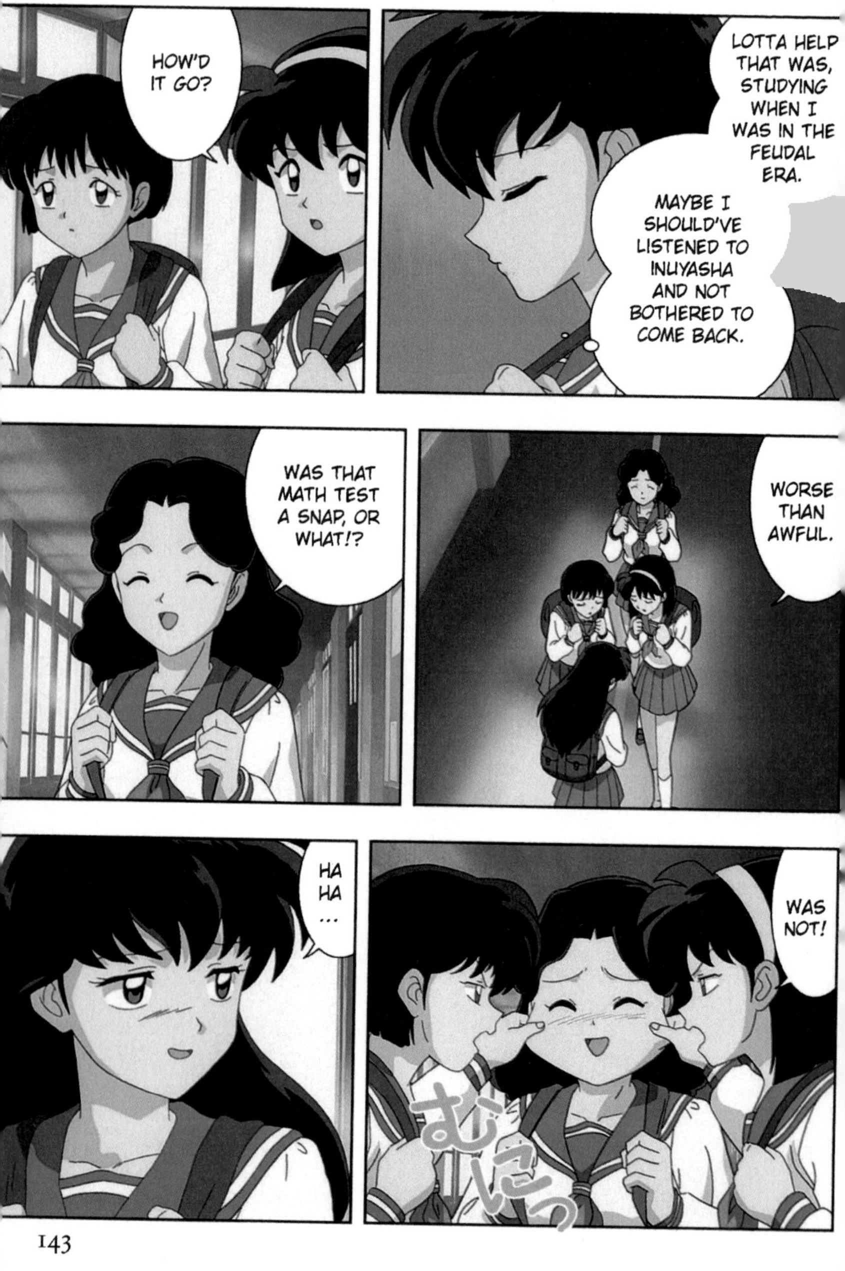
HOW'D IT GO?
LOTTA HELP THAT WAS, STUDYING WHEN I WAS IN THE FEUDAL ERA.
MAYBE I SHOULD'VE LISTENED TO INUYASHA AND NOT BOTHERED TO COME BACK.
WAS THAT MATH TEST A SNAP, OR WHAT!?
WORSE THAN AWFUL.
HA HA ...
WAS NOT!
むにっ

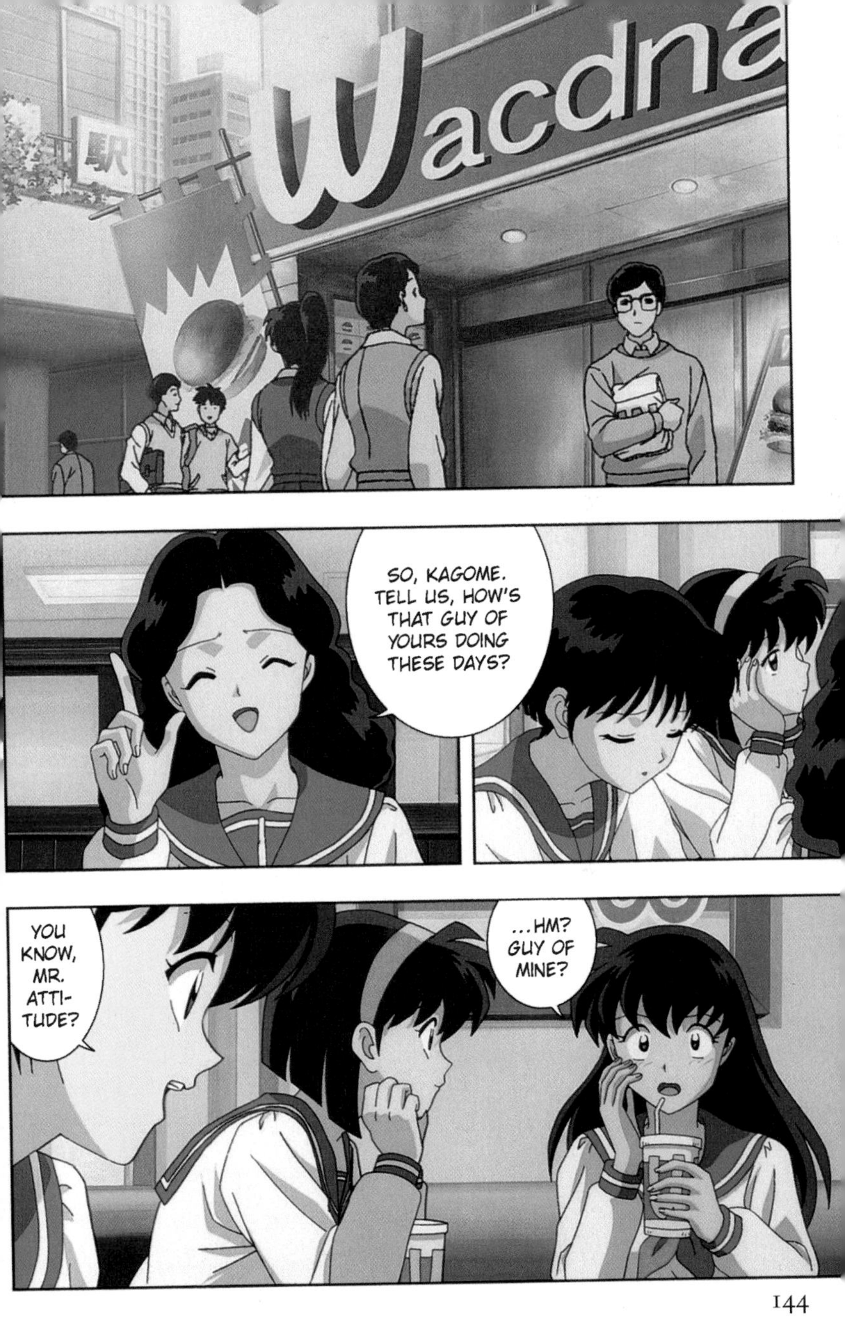
Wacdna
駅
SO, KAGOME. TELL US, HOW'S THAT GUY OF YOURS DOING THESE DAYS?
...HM? GUY OF MINE?
YOU KNOW, MR. ATTI-TUDE?

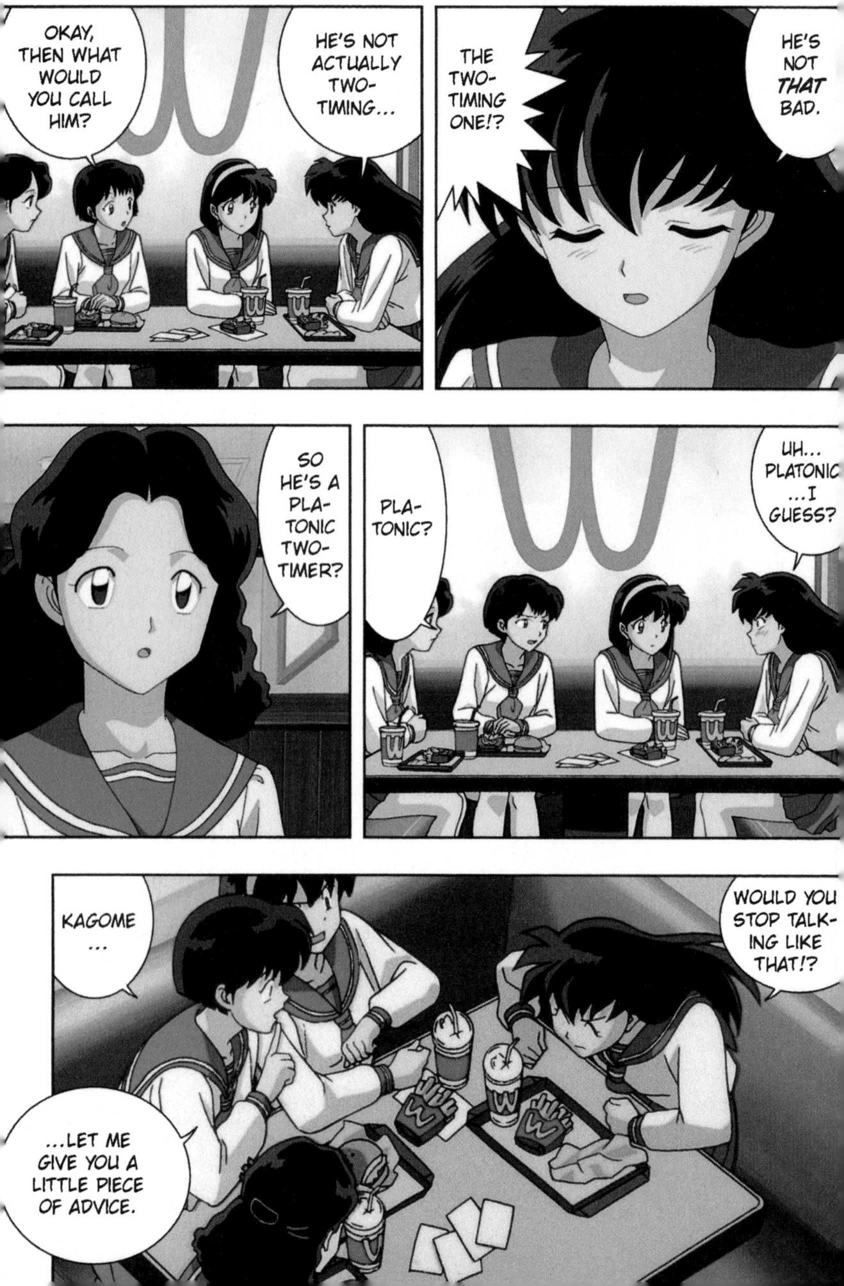
HE'S NOT THAT BAD.
THE TWO-TIMING ONE!?
HE'S NOT ACTUALLY TWO-TIMING...
OKAY, THEN WHAT WOULD YOU CALL HIM?
UH... PLATONIC ...I GUESS?
PLA-TONIC?
SO HE'S A PLA-TONIC TWO-TIMER?
WOULD YOU STOP TALKING LIKE THAT!?
KAGOME...
...LET ME GIVE YOU A LITTLE PIECE OF ADVICE.

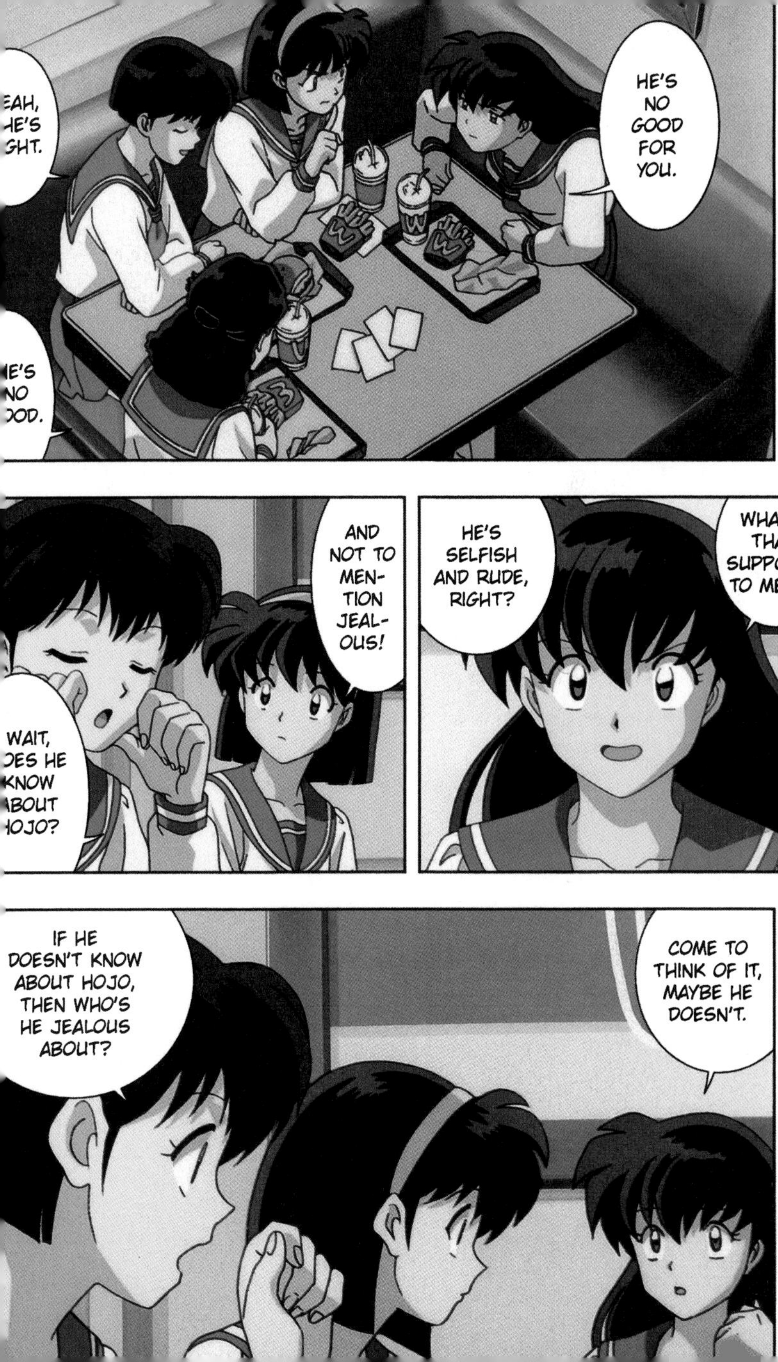
HE'S NO GOOD FOR YOU.
EAH, HE'S GHT.
E'S NO OOD.
WHAT'S THAT SUPPOSED TO MEAN?
HE'S SELFISH AND RUDE, RIGHT?
AND NOT TO MEN-TION JEAL-OUS!
WAIT, ES HE KNOW BOUT OJO?
COME TO THINK OF IT, MAYBE HE DOESN'T.
IF HE DOESN'T KNOW ABOUT HOJO, THEN WHO'S HE JEALOUS ABOUT?

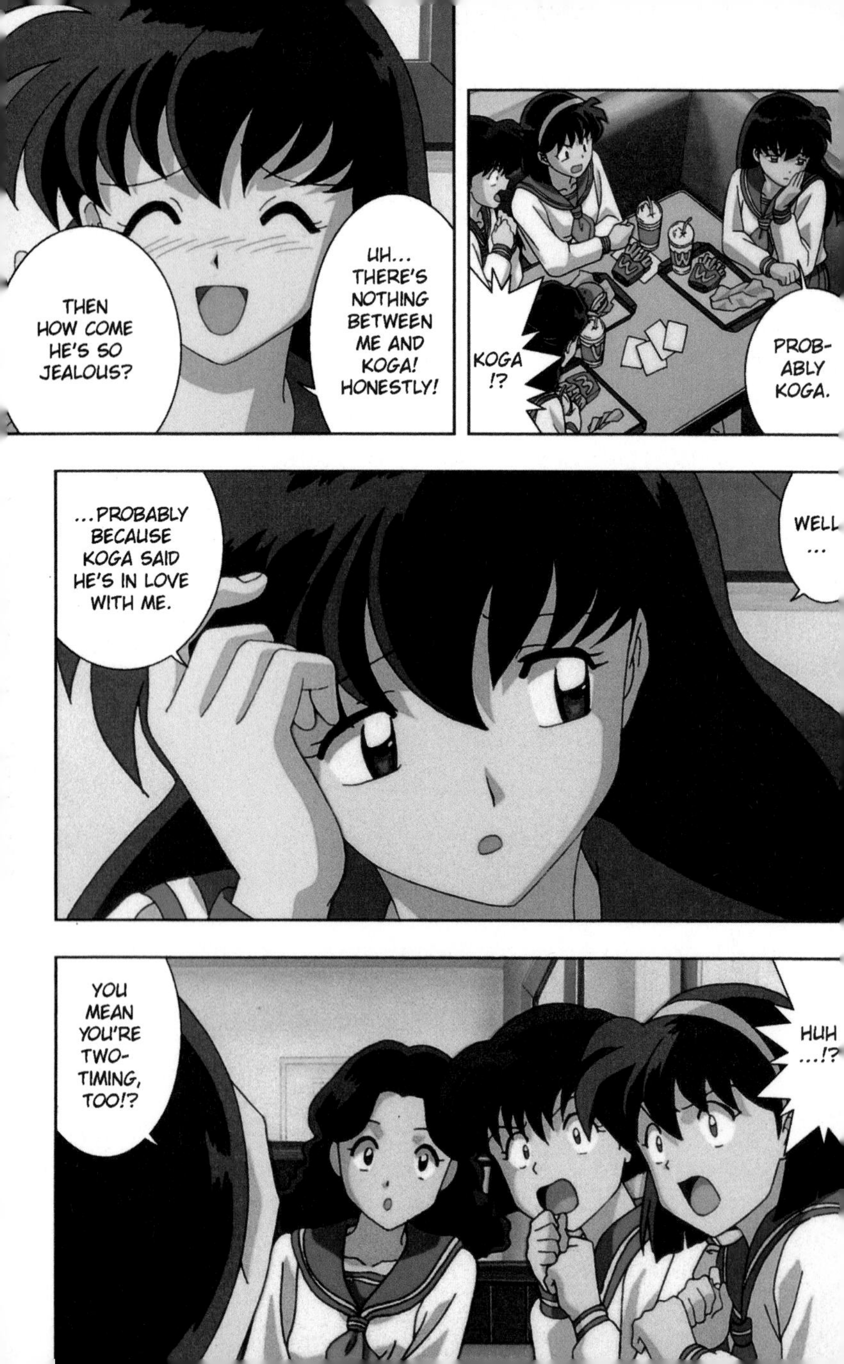
PROBABLY KOGA.
KOGA!?
UH... THERE'S NOTHING BETWEEN ME AND KOGA! HONESTLY!
THEN HOW COME HE'S SO JEALOUS?
WELL...
...PROBABLY BECAUSE KOGA SAID HE'S IN LOVE WITH ME.
HUH...!?
YOU MEAN YOU'RE TWO-TIMING, TOO!?

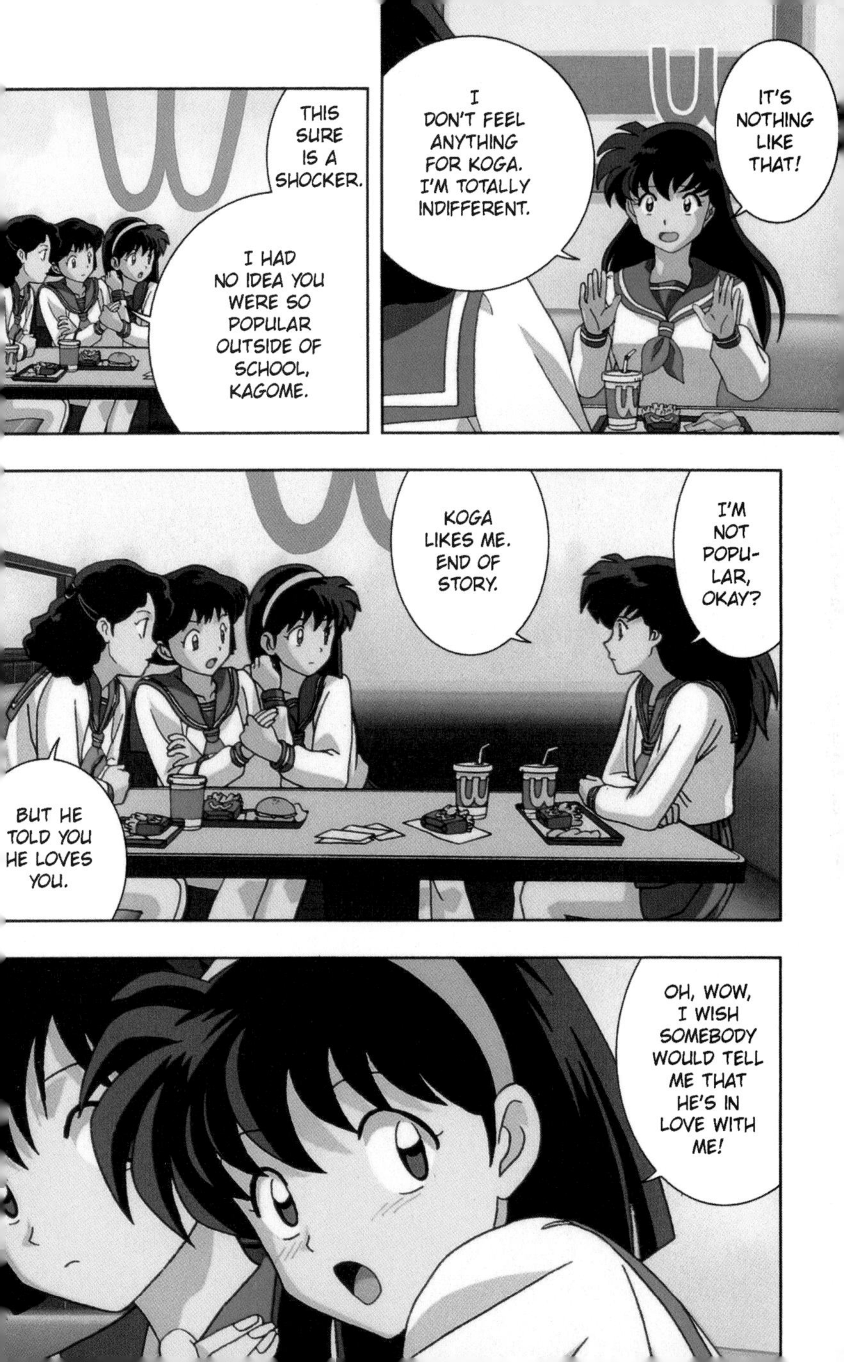
IT'S NOTHING LIKE THAT!
I DON'T FEEL ANYTHING FOR KOGA. I'M TOTALLY INDIFFERENT.
THIS SURE IS A SHOCKER.
I HAD NO IDEA YOU WERE SO POPULAR OUTSIDE OF SCHOOL, KAGOME.
I'M NOT POPU-LAR, OKAY?
KOGA LIKES ME. END OF STORY.
BUT HE TOLD YOU HE LOVES YOU.
OH, WOW, I WISH SOMEBODY WOULD TELL ME THAT HE'S IN LOVE WITH ME!

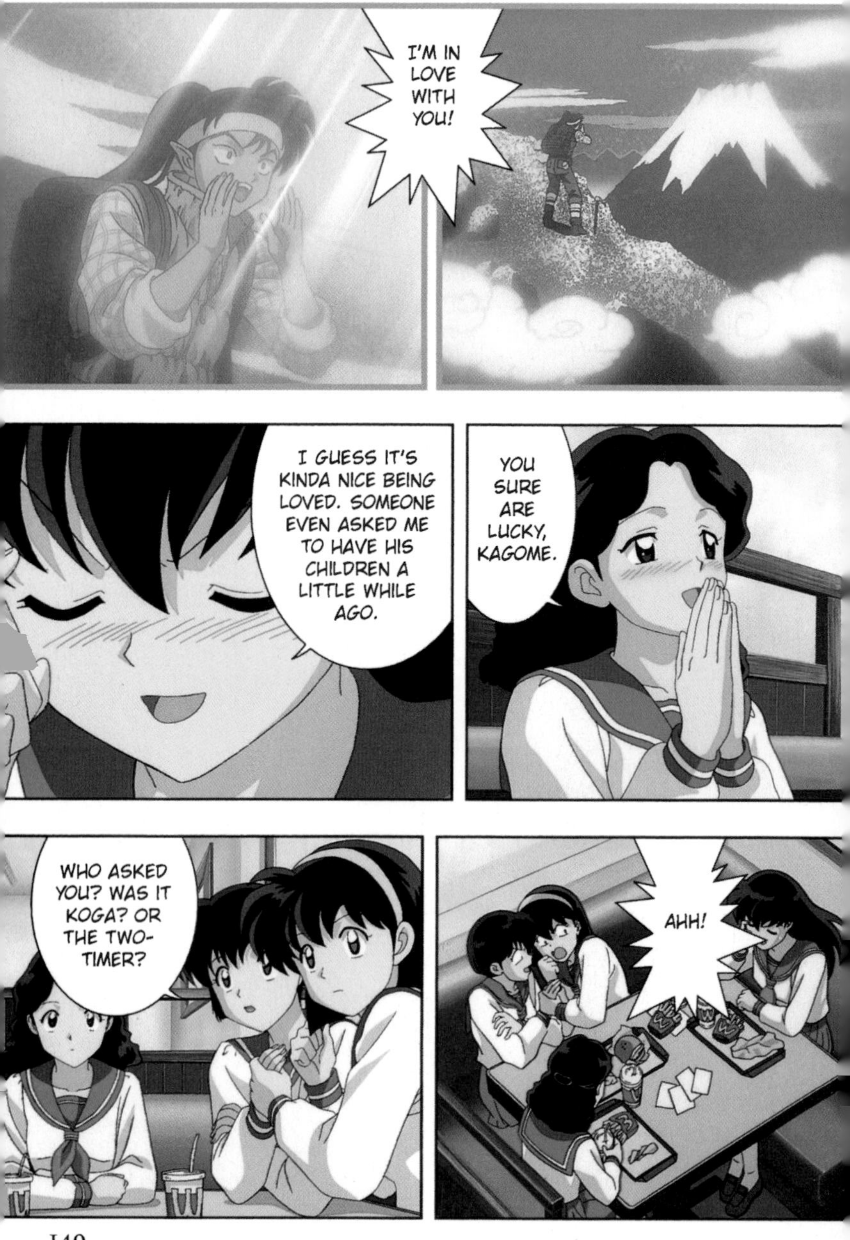
I'M IN LOVE WITH YOU!
YOU SURE ARE LUCKY, KAGOME.
I GUESS IT'S KINDA NICE BEING LOVED. SOMEONE EVEN ASKED ME TO HAVE HIS CHILDREN A LITTLE WHILE AGO.
AHH!
WHO ASKED YOU? WAS IT KOGA? OR THE TWO-TIMER?

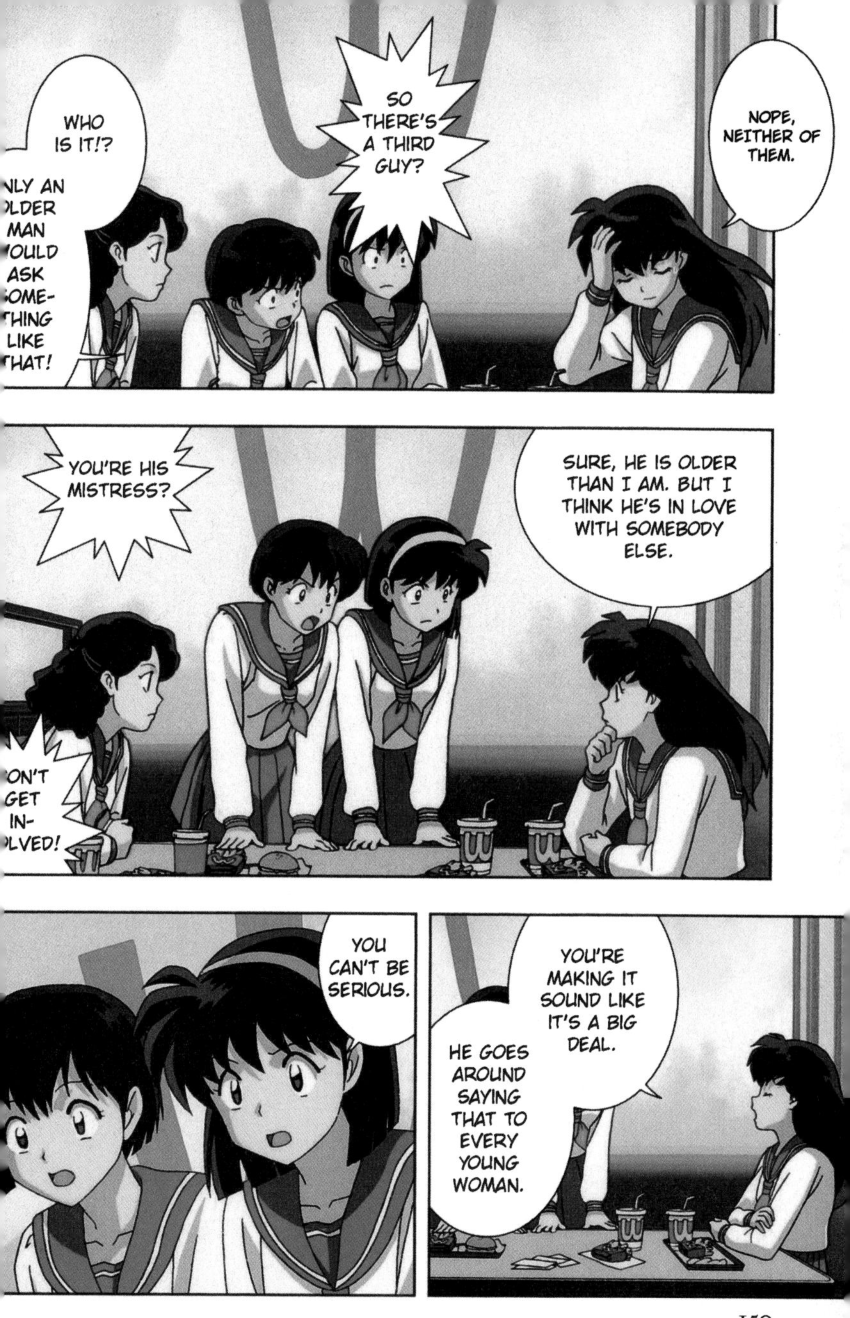
NOPE, NEITHER OF THEM.
SO THERE'S A THIRD GUY?
WHO IS IT!?
NLY AN LDER MAN OULD ASK OME- THING LIKE HAT!
SURE, HE IS OLDER THAN I AM. BUT I THINK HE'S IN LOVE WITH SOMEBODY ELSE.
YOU'RE HIS MISTRESS?
ON'T GET IN- LVED!
YOU'RE MAKING IT SOUND LIKE IT'S A BIG DEAL.
HE GOES AROUND SAYING THAT TO EVERY YOUNG WOMAN.
YOU CAN'T BE SERIOUS.

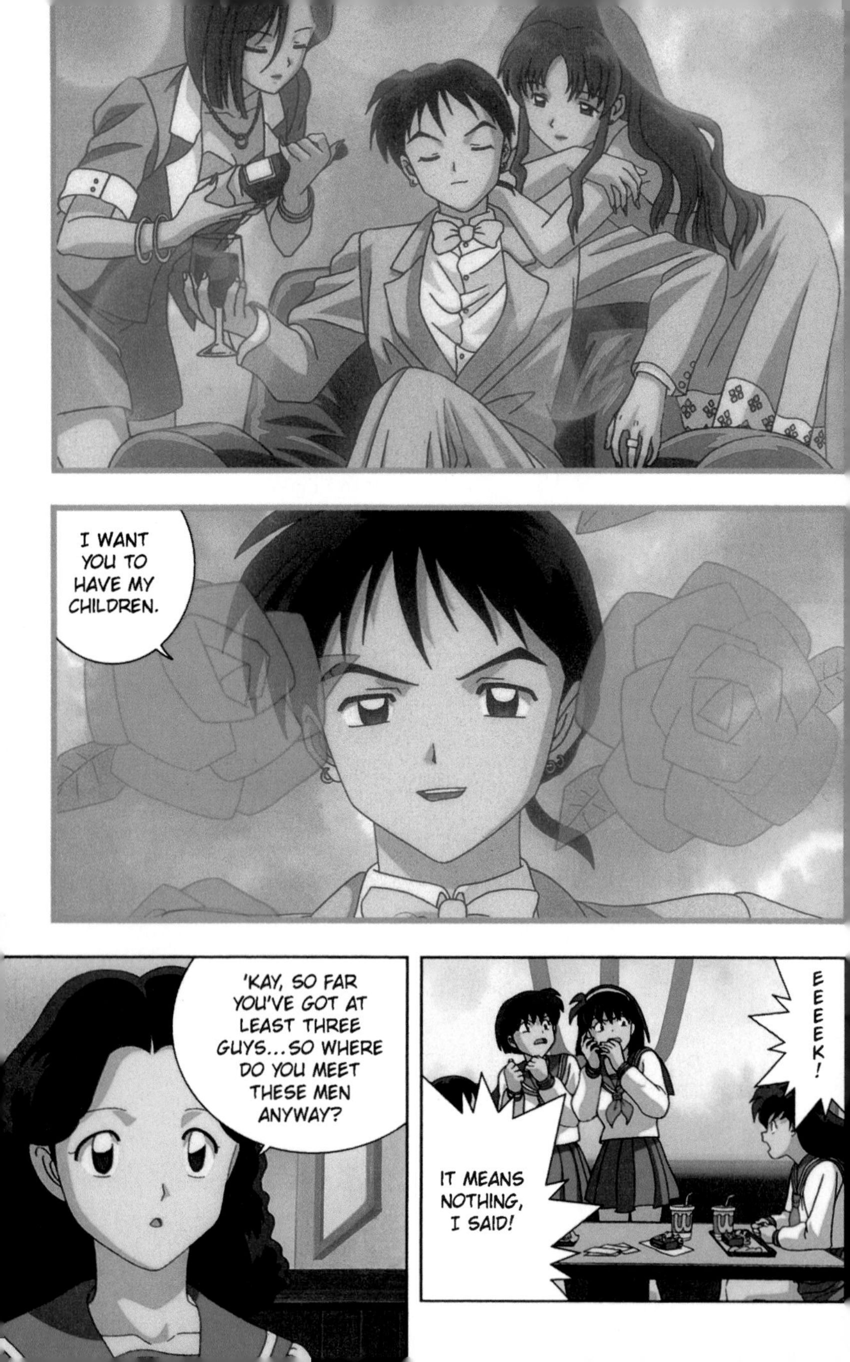
I WANT YOU TO HAVE MY CHILDREN.
EEEEEK!
IT MEANS NOTHING, I SAID!
'KAY, SO FAR YOU'VE GOT AT LEAST THREE GUYS...SO WHERE DO YOU MEET THESE MEN ANYWAY?

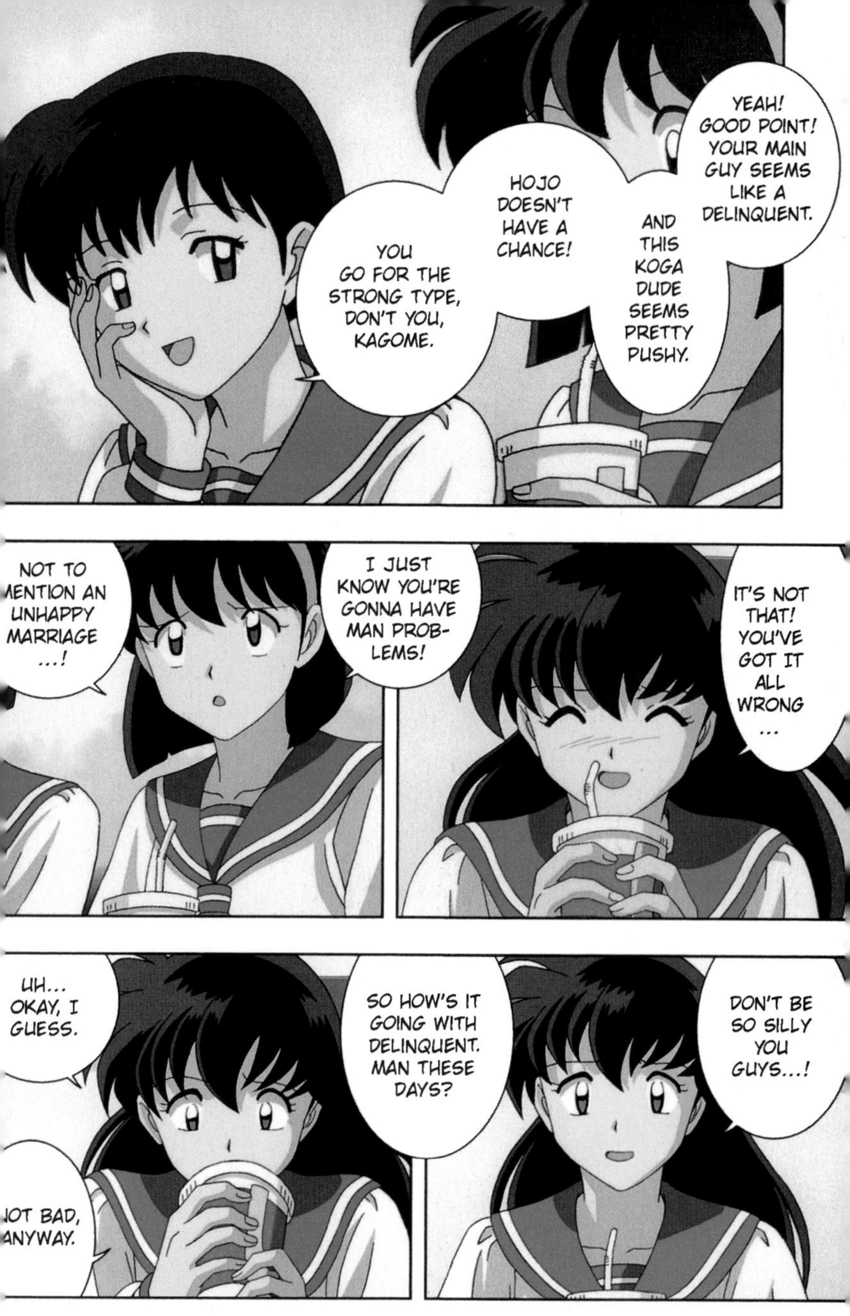
YEAH! GOOD POINT! YOUR MAIN GUY SEEMS LIKE A DELINQUENT.
AND THIS KOGA DUDE SEEMS PRETTY PUSHY.
HOJO DOESN'T HAVE A CHANCE!
YOU GO FOR THE STRONG TYPE, DON'T YOU, KAGOME.
IT'S NOT THAT! YOU'VE GOT IT ALL WRONG ...
I JUST KNOW YOU'RE GONNA HAVE MAN PROB-LEMS!
NOT TO MENTION AN UNHAPPY MARRIAGE ...!
DON'T BE SO SILLY YOU GUYS...!
SO HOW'S IT GOING WITH DELINQUENT. MAN THESE DAYS?
UH... OKAY, I GUESS.
NOT BAD, ANYWAY.

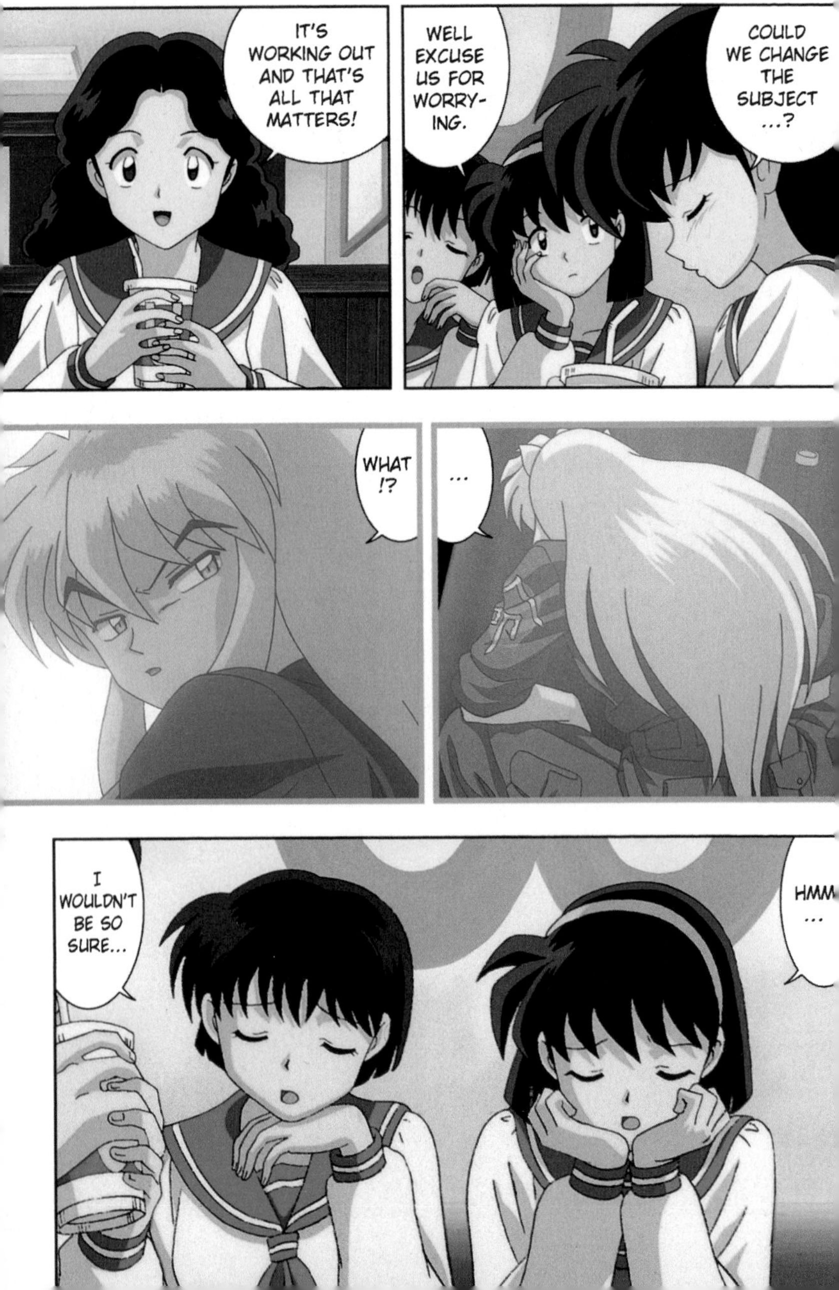
COULD WE CHANGE THE SUBJECT ...?
WELL EXCUSE US FOR WORRYING.
IT'S WORKING OUT AND THAT'S ALL THAT MATTERS!
...
WHAT!?
HMM ...
I WOULDN'T BE SO SURE...

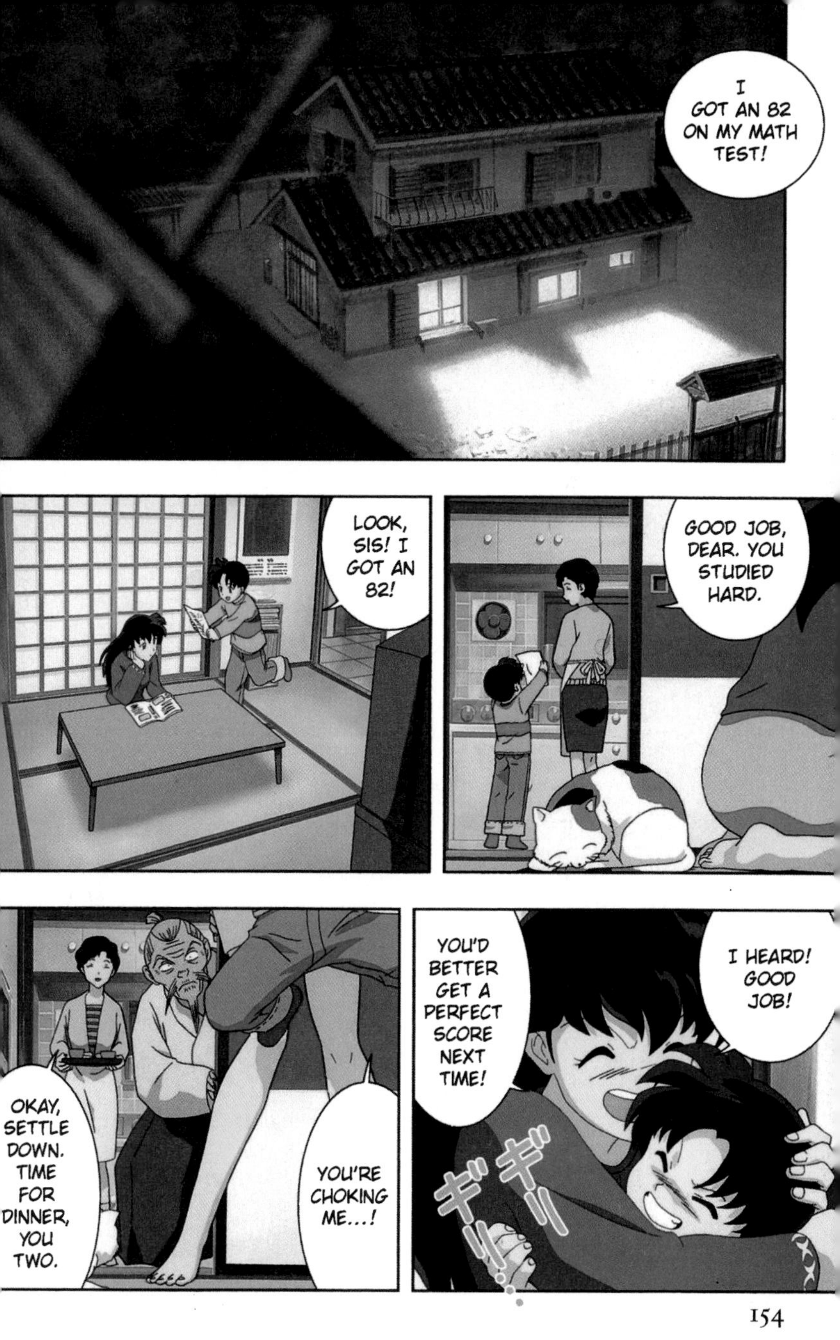
I GOT AN 82 ON MY MATH TEST!
GOOD JOB, DEAR. YOU STUDIED HARD.
LOOK, SIS! I GOT AN 82!
I HEARD! GOOD JOB!
YOU'D BETTER GET A PERFECT SCORE NEXT TIME!
ギリ
ギリ…
YOU'RE CHOKING ME...!
OKAY, SETTLE DOWN. TIME FOR DINNER, YOU TWO.

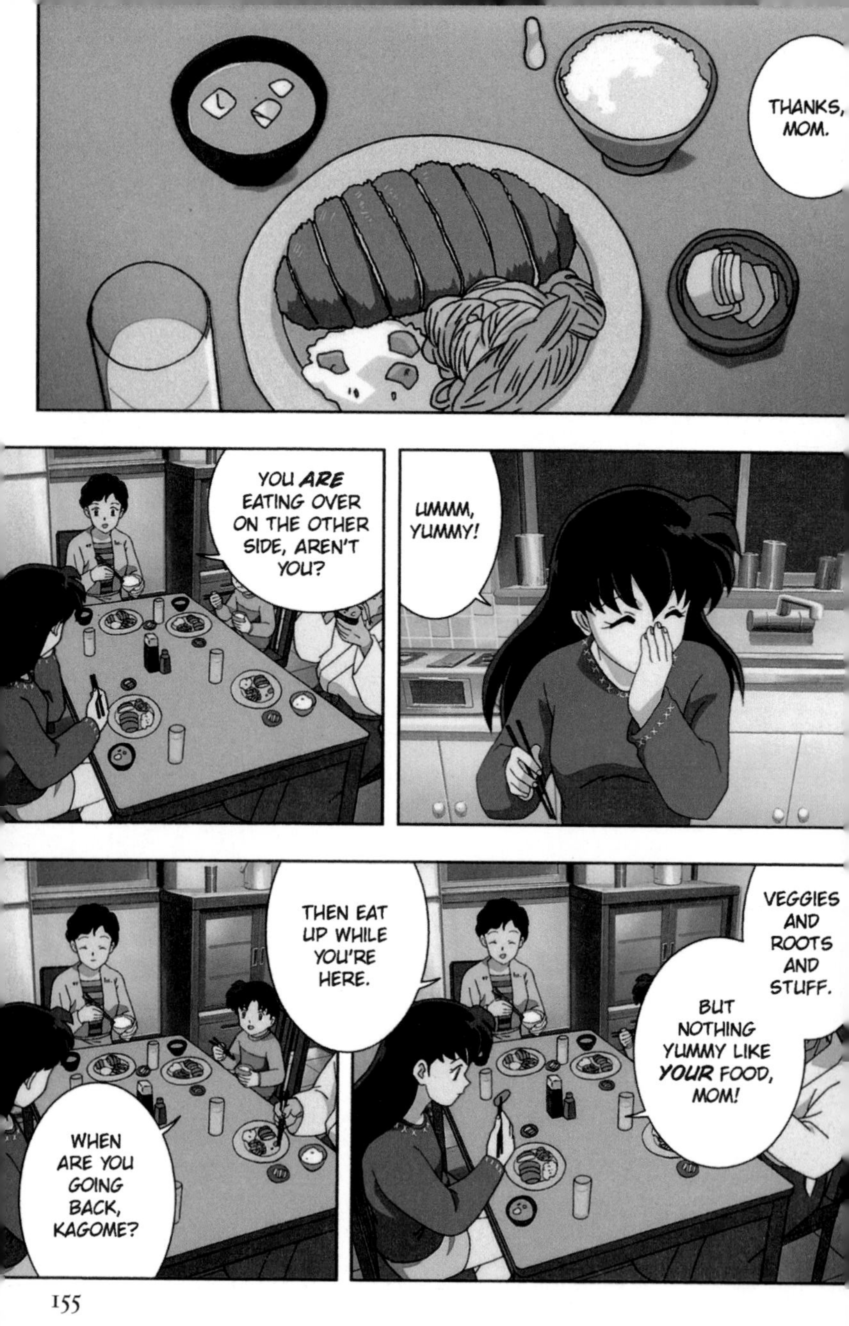
THANKS, MOM.
UMMM, YUMMY!
YOU ARE EATING OVER ON THE OTHER SIDE, AREN'T YOU?
VEGGIES AND ROOTS AND STUFF.
BUT NOTHING YUMMY LIKE YOUR FOOD, MOM!
THEN EAT UP WHILE YOU'RE HERE.
WHEN ARE YOU GOING BACK, KAGOME?

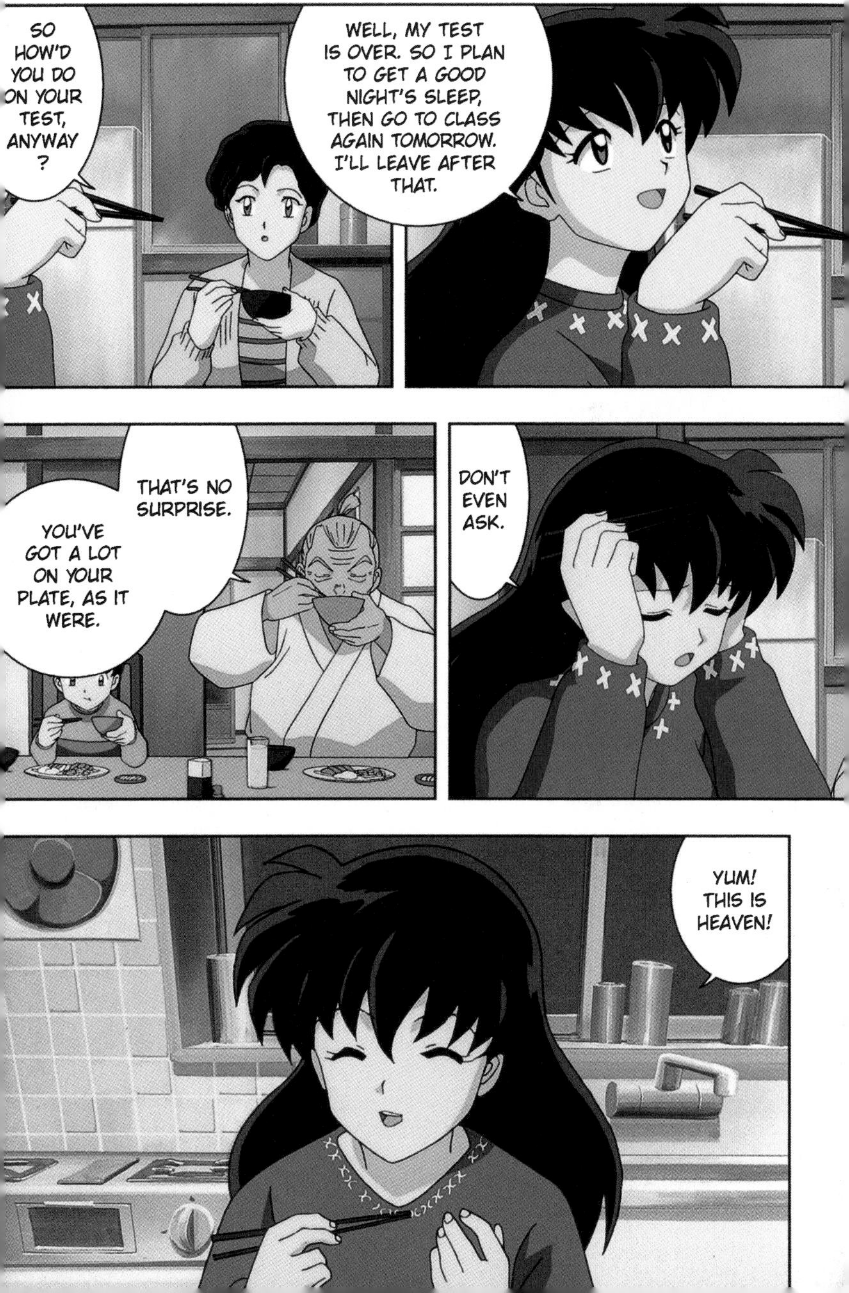
WELL, MY TEST IS OVER. SO I PLAN TO GET A GOOD NIGHT'S SLEEP, THEN GO TO CLASS AGAIN TOMORROW. I'LL LEAVE AFTER THAT.
SO HOW'D YOU DO ON YOUR TEST, ANYWAY?
DON'T EVEN ASK.
THAT'S NO SURPRISE.
YOU'VE GOT A LOT ON YOUR PLATE, AS IT WERE.
YUM! THIS IS HEAVEN!

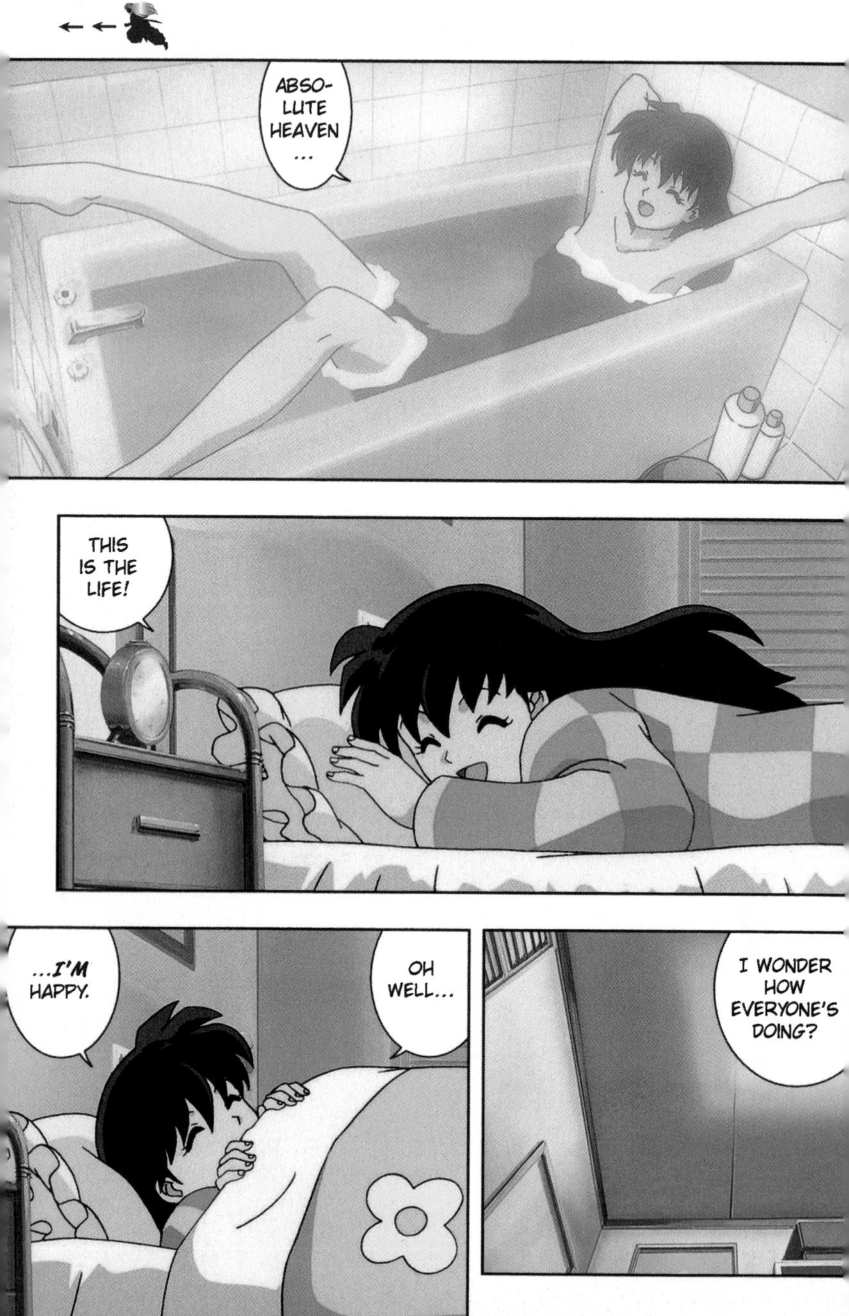
ABSO-LUTE HEAVEN ...
THIS IS THE LIFE!
I WONDER HOW EVERYONE'S DOING?
OH WELL...
...I'M HAPPY.

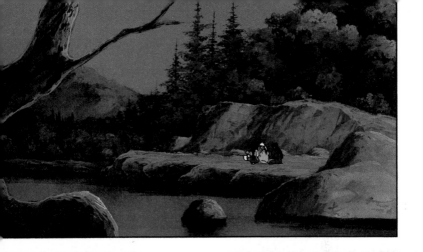

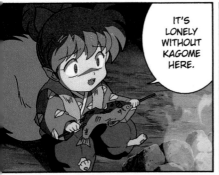

IT'S LONELY WITHOUT KAGOME HERE.

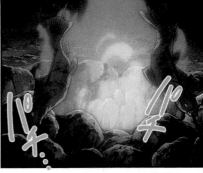

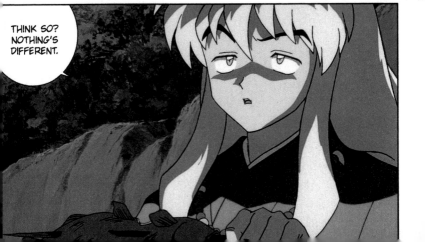

THINK SO? NOTHING'S DIFFERENT.

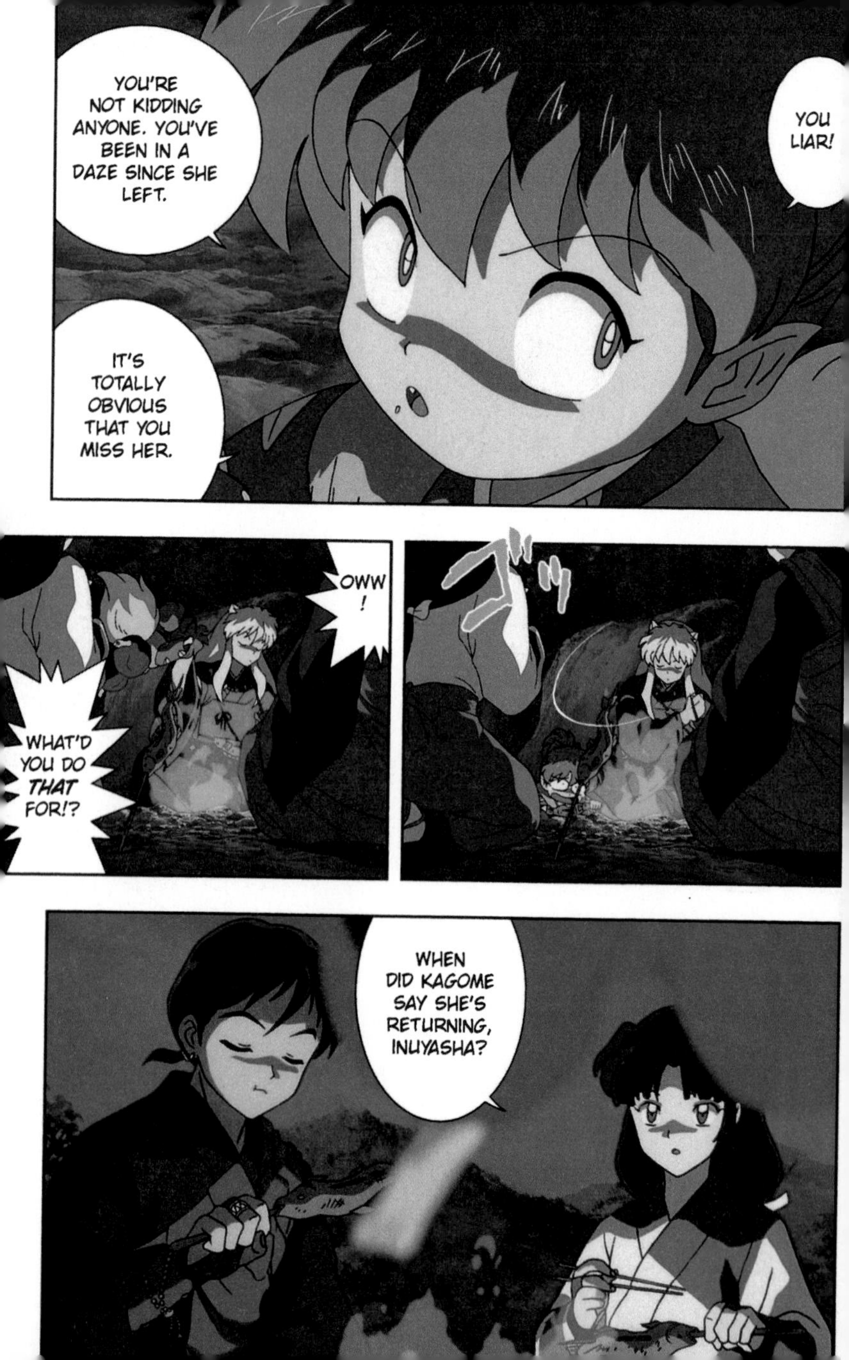
YOU LIAR!
YOU'RE NOT KIDDING ANYONE. YOU'VE BEEN IN A DAZE SINCE SHE LEFT.
IT'S TOTALLY OBVIOUS THAT YOU MISS HER.
ゴッ
OWW!
WHAT'D YOU DO *THAT* FOR!?
WHEN DID KAGOME SAY SHE'S RETURNING, INUYASHA?

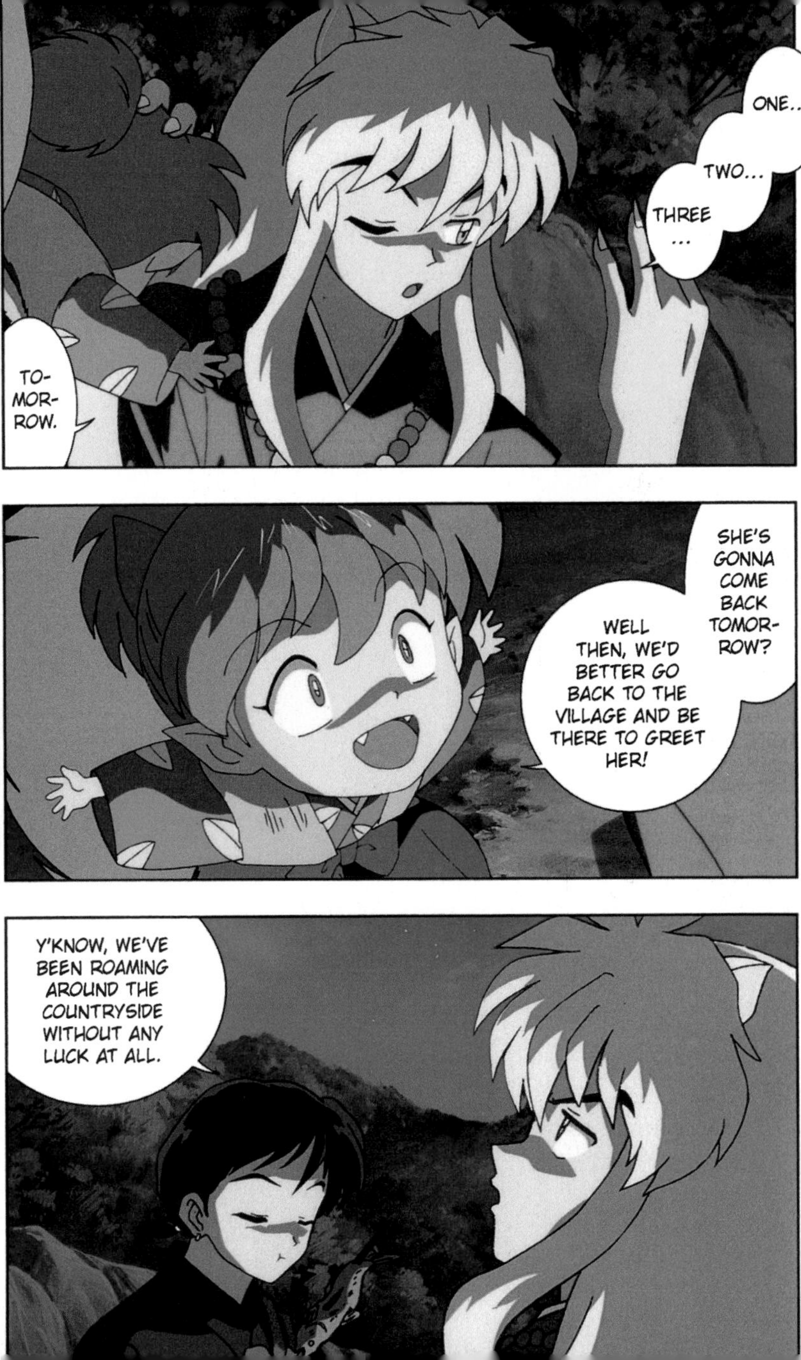
ONE...
TWO...
THREE ...
TO-MOR-ROW.
SHE'S GONNA COME BACK TOMOR-ROW?
WELL THEN, WE'D BETTER GO BACK TO THE VILLAGE AND BE THERE TO GREET HER!
Y'KNOW, WE'VE BEEN ROAMING AROUND THE COUNTRYSIDE WITHOUT ANY LUCK AT ALL.

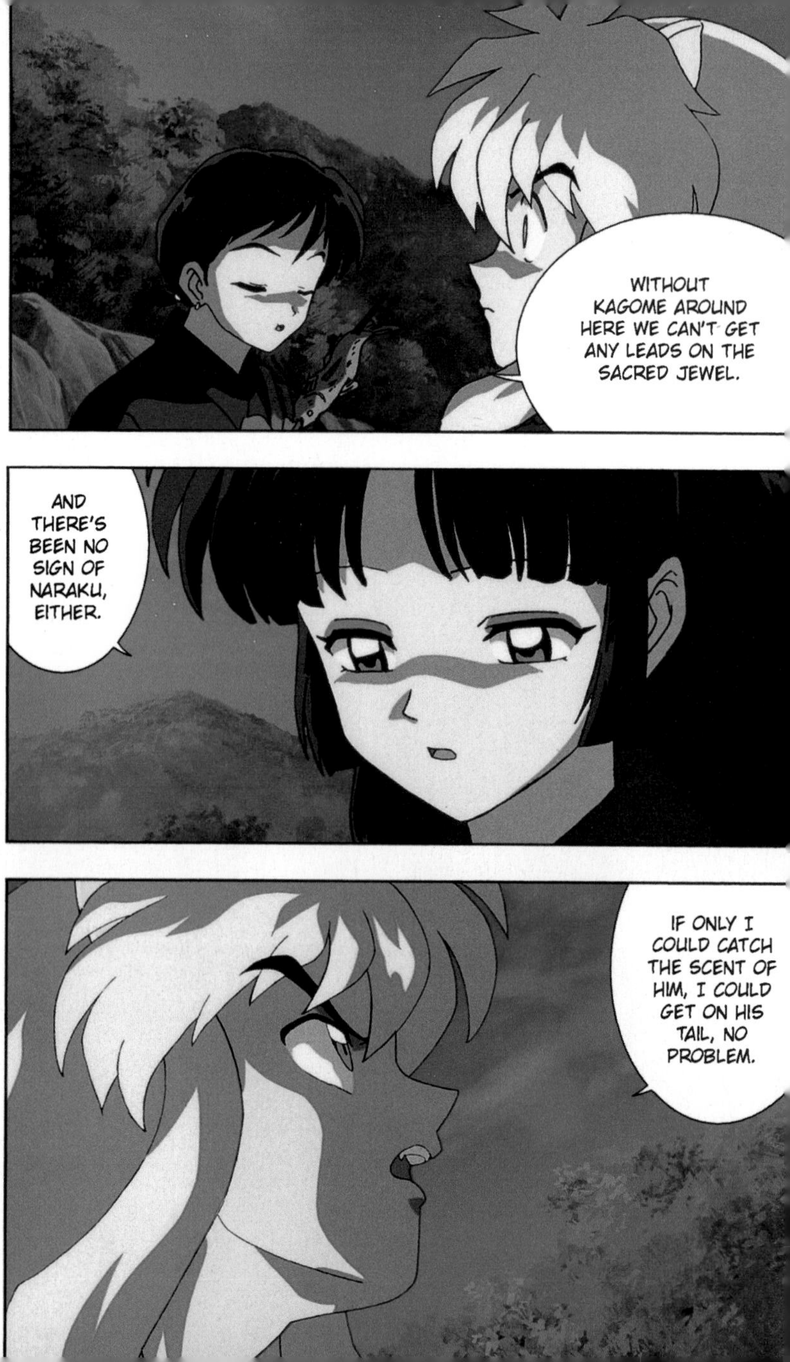
WITHOUT KAGOME AROUND HERE WE CAN'T GET ANY LEADS ON THE SACRED JEWEL.
AND THERE'S BEEN NO SIGN OF NARAKU, EITHER.
IF ONLY I COULD CATCH THE SCENT OF HIM, I COULD GET ON HIS TAIL, NO PROBLEM.

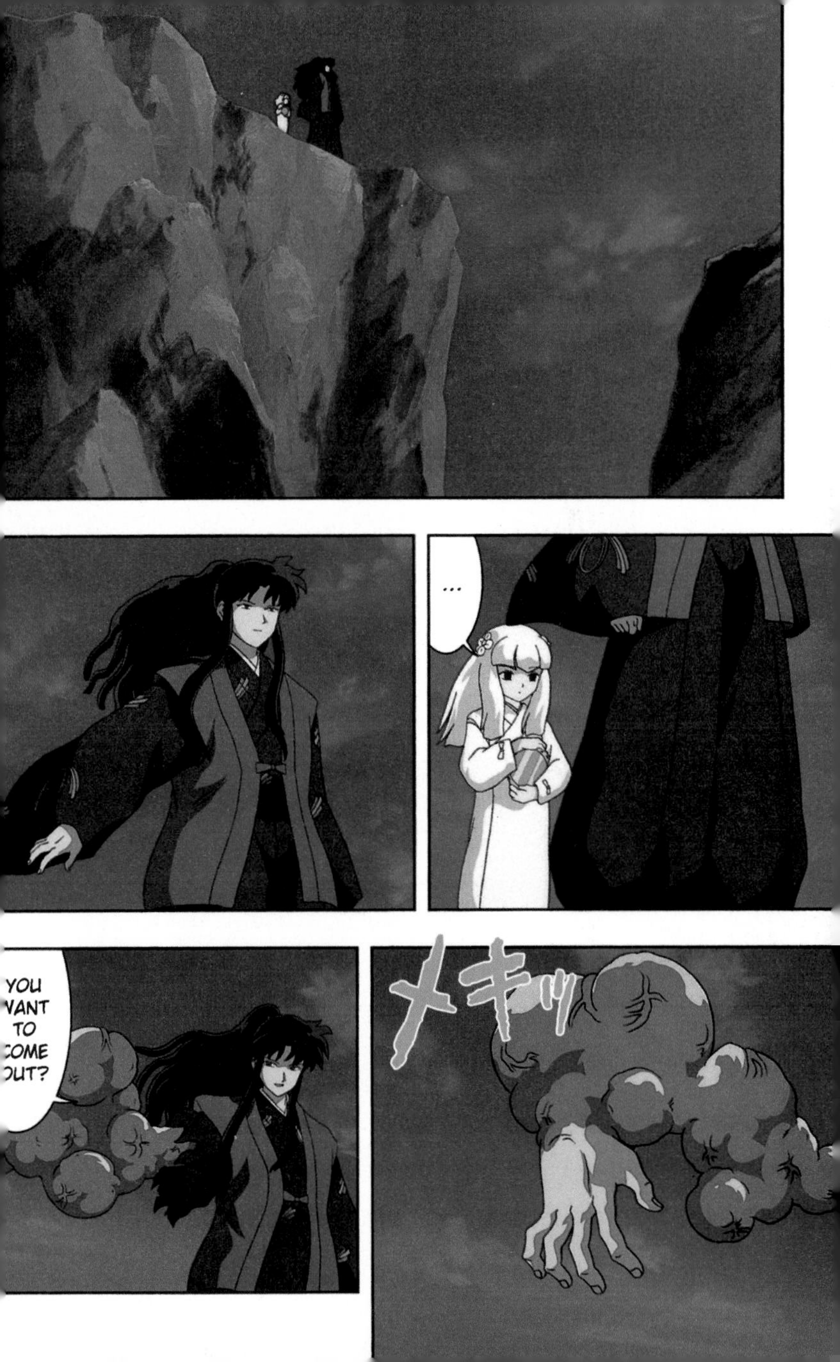
...
メキッ
YOU
VANT
TO
COME
OUT?

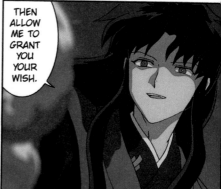

THEN ALLOW ME TO GRANT YOU YOUR WISH.

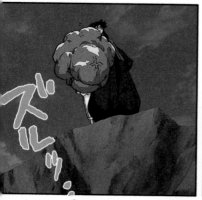

WHO WAS THAT? MY BROTH-ER?

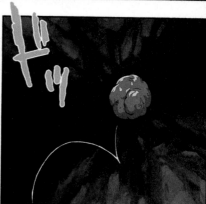

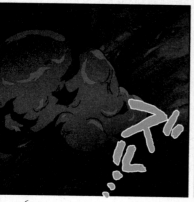

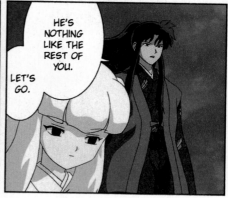

HE'S NOTHING LIKE THE REST OF YOU.

LET'S GO.

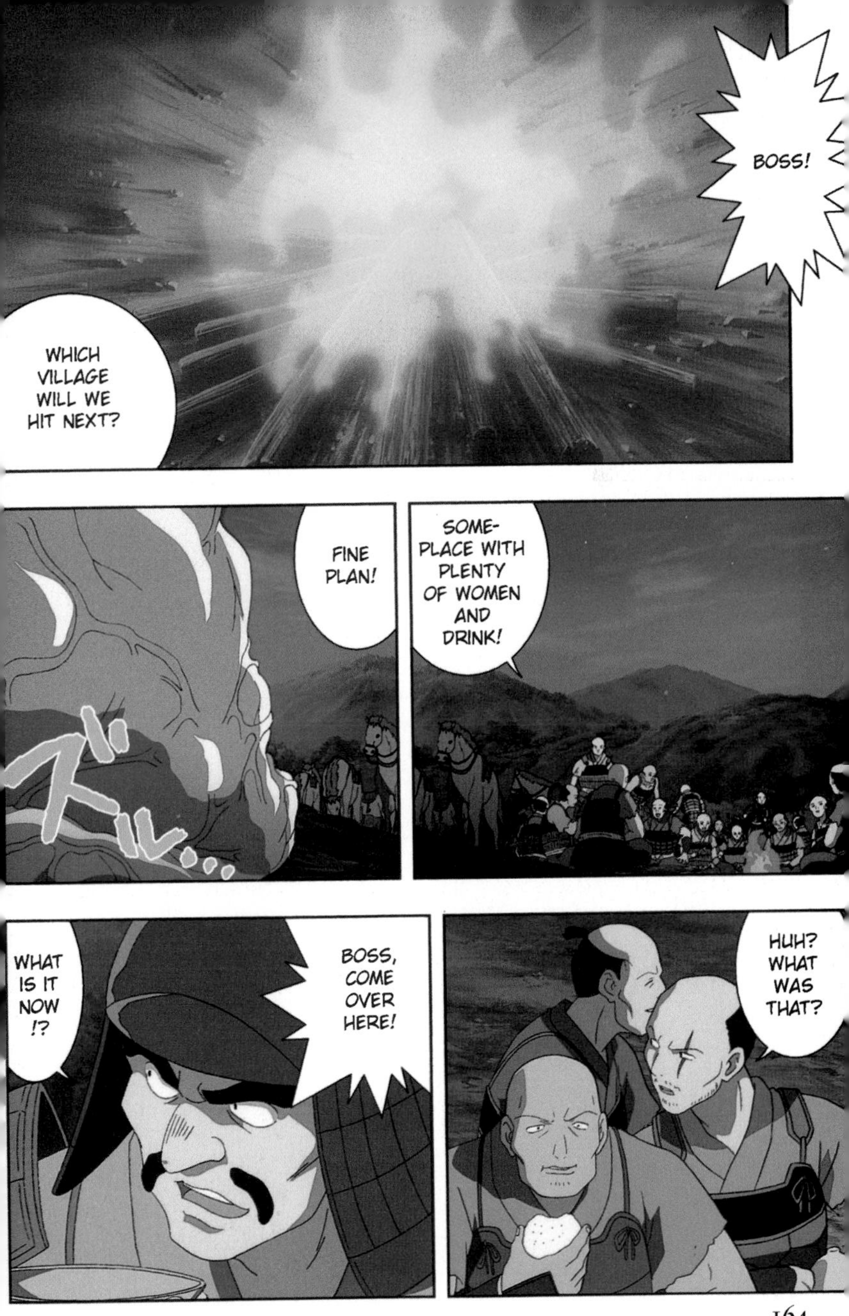
BOSS!
WHICH VILLAGE WILL WE HIT NEXT?
SOME-PLACE WITH PLENTY OF WOMEN AND DRINK!
FINE PLAN!
ズル…
HUH? WHAT WAS THAT?
BOSS, COME OVER HERE!
WHAT IS IT NOW!?

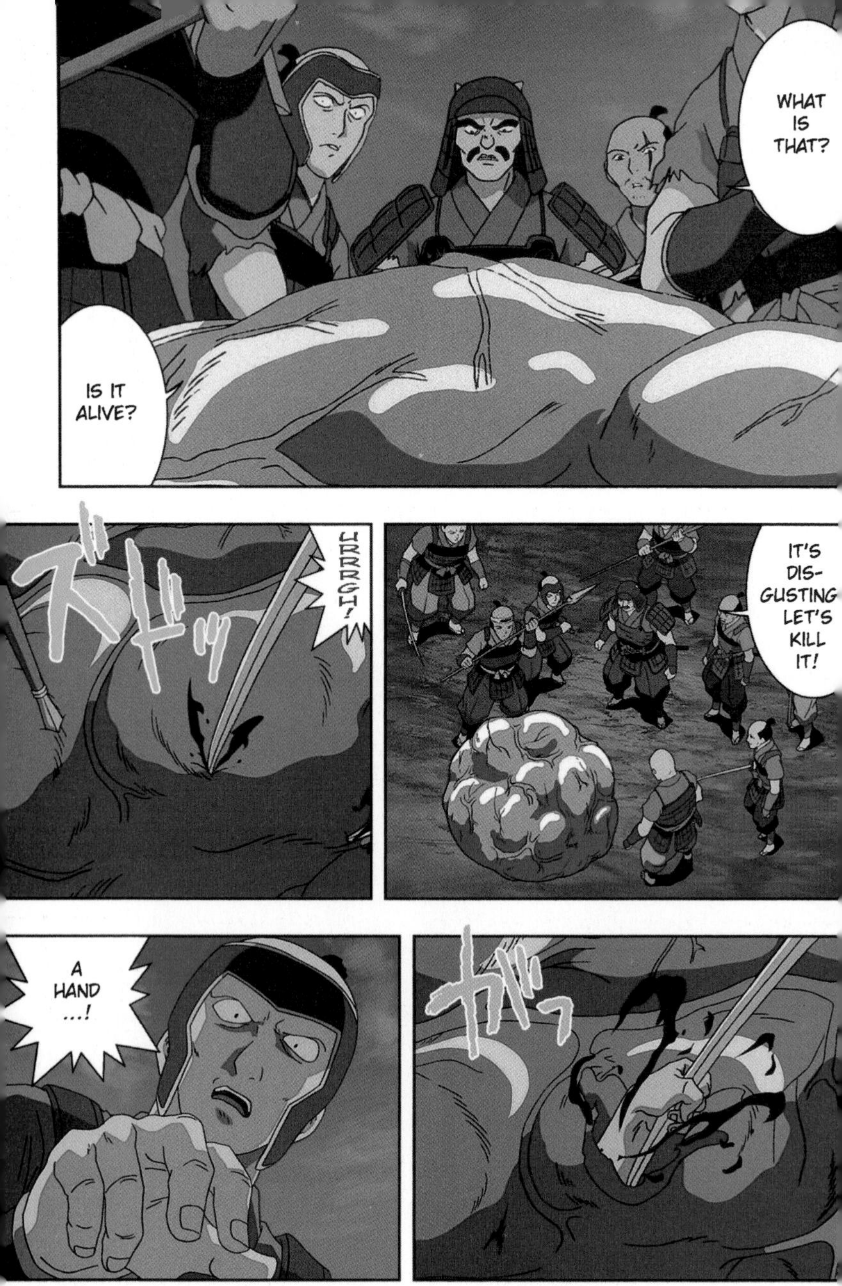
WHAT IS THAT?
IS IT ALIVE?
IT'S DIS-GUSTING LET'S KILL IT!
URRRGH!
ズドッ
ガッ
A HAND ...!

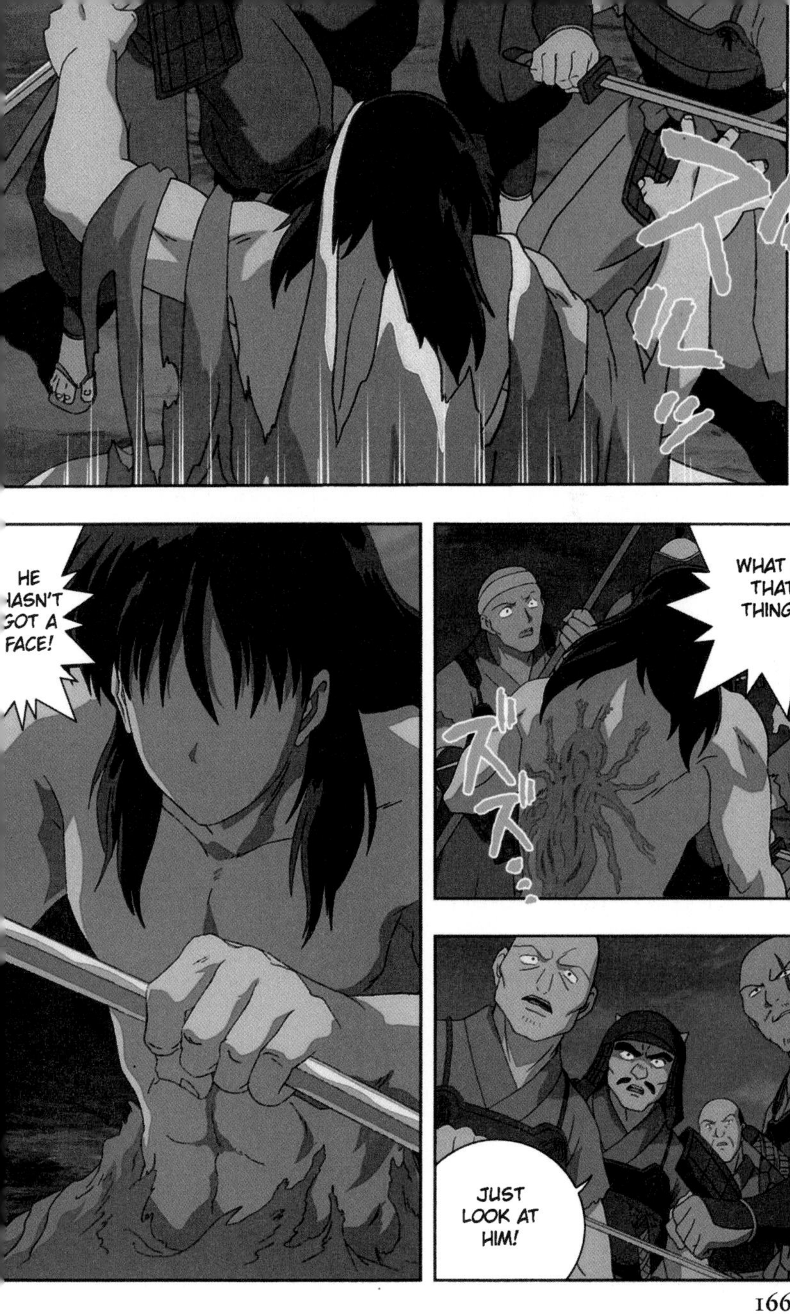
ズルッ
WHAT IS THAT THING?
JUST LOOK AT HIM!
HE HASN'T GOT A FACE!

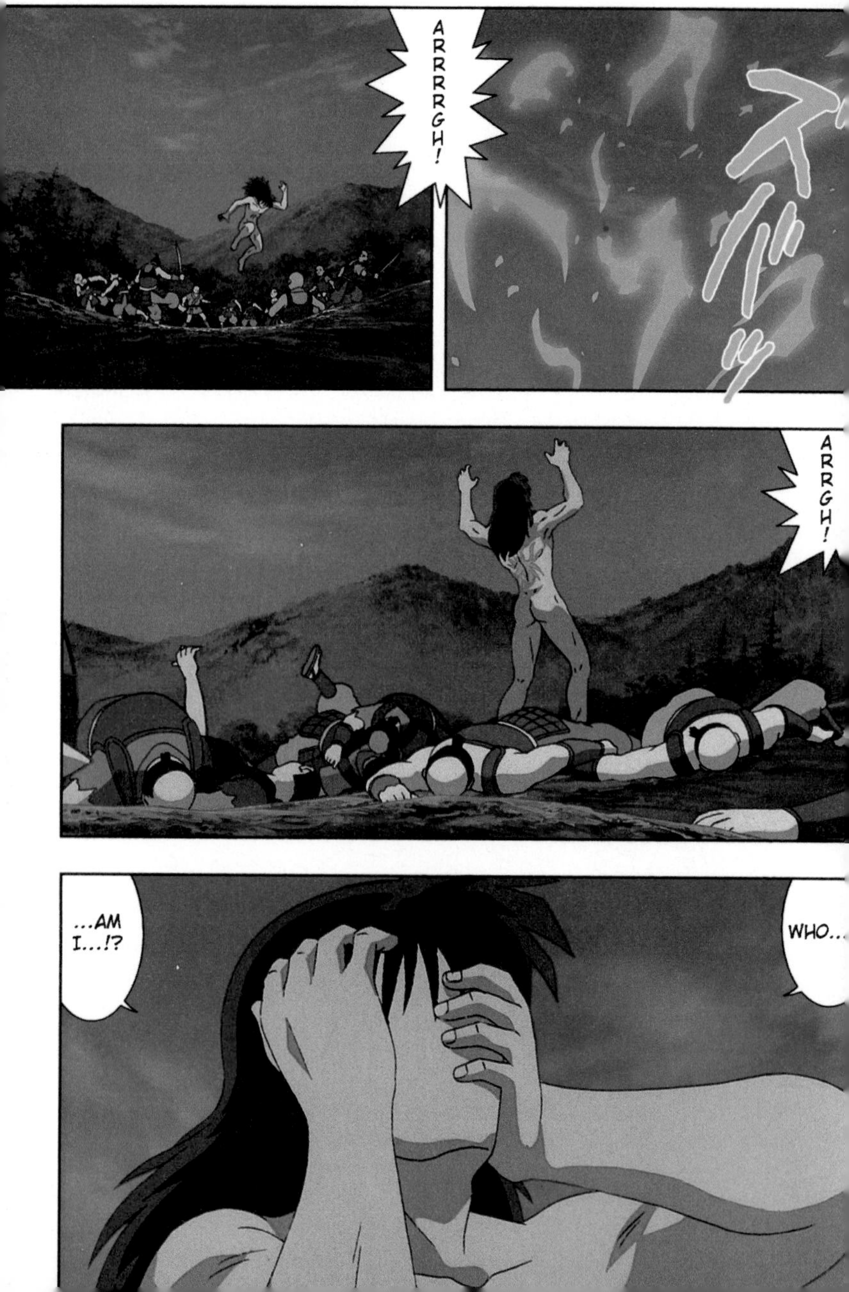
ARRRRGH!
ARRGH!
WHO...
...AM I...!?

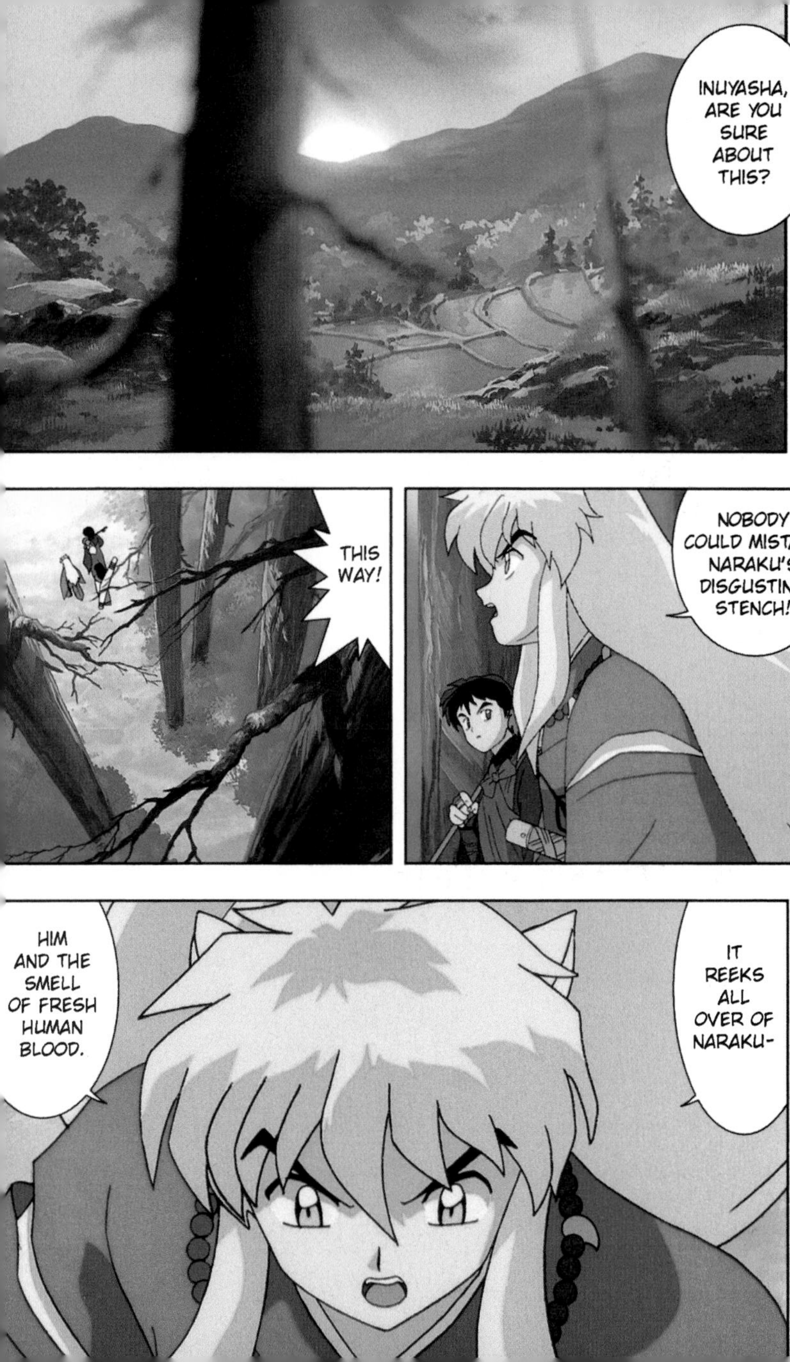
INUYASHA, ARE YOU SURE ABOUT THIS?
NOBODY COULD MISTAKE NARAKU'S DISGUSTING STENCH!
THIS WAY!
IT REEKS ALL OVER OF NARAKU-
HIM AND THE SMELL OF FRESH HUMAN BLOOD.

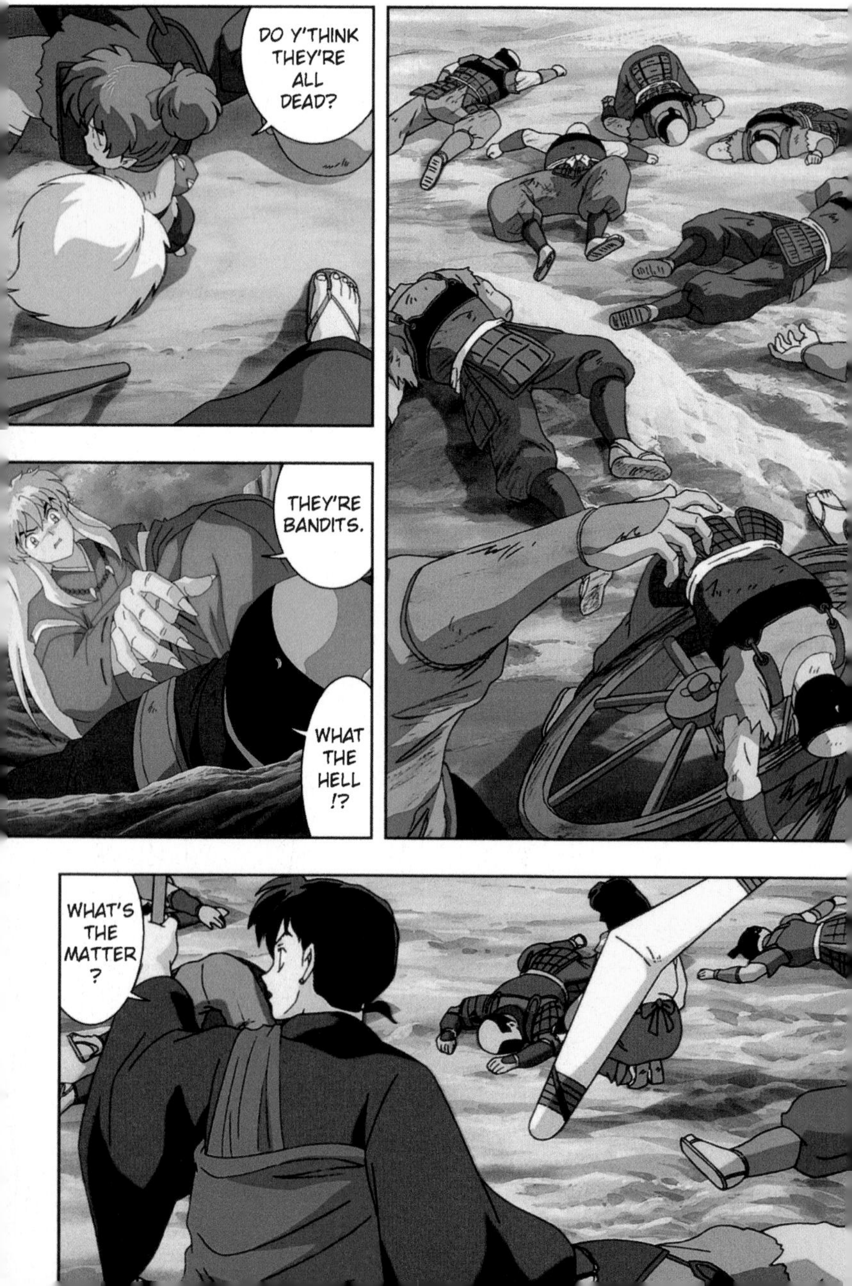
DO Y'THINK THEY'RE ALL DEAD?
THEY'RE BANDITS.
WHAT THE HELL !?
WHAT'S THE MATTER ?

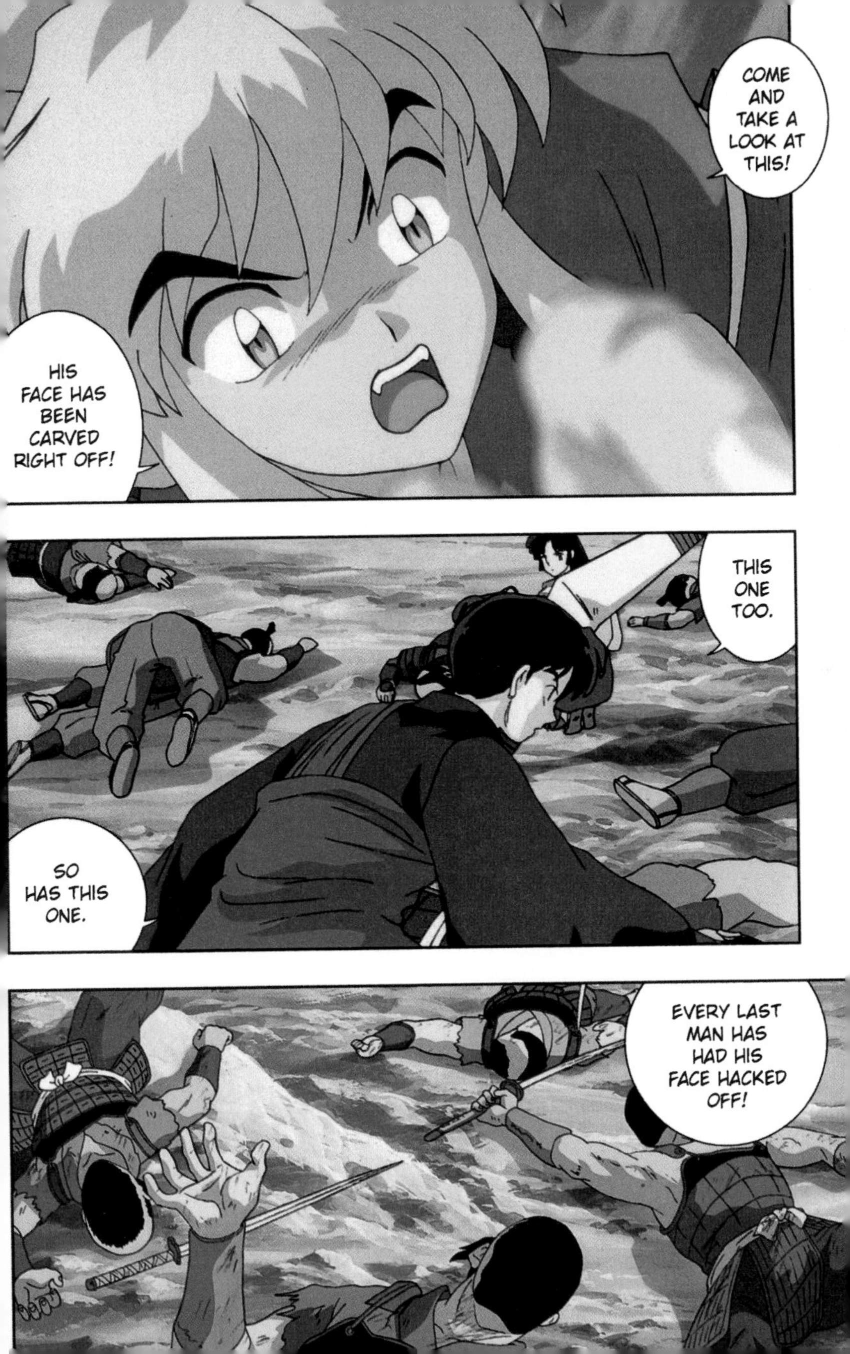
COME AND TAKE A LOOK AT THIS!
HIS FACE HAS BEEN CARVED RIGHT OFF!
THIS ONE TOO.
SO HAS THIS ONE.
EVERY LAST MAN HAS HAD HIS FACE HACKED OFF!

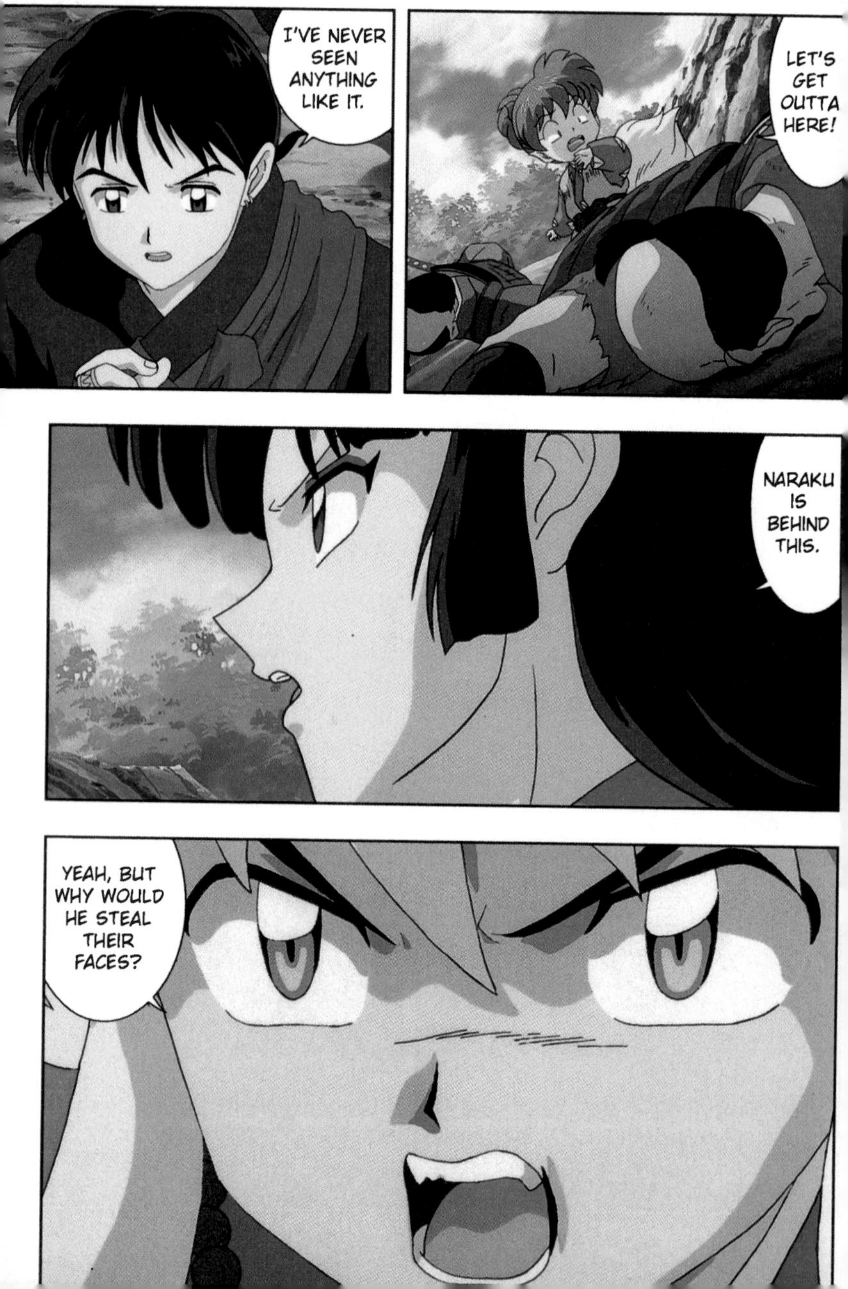

LET'S GET OUTTA HERE!
I'VE NEVER SEEN ANYTHING LIKE IT.
NARAKU IS BEHIND THIS.
YEAH, BUT WHY WOULD HE STEAL THEIR FACES?

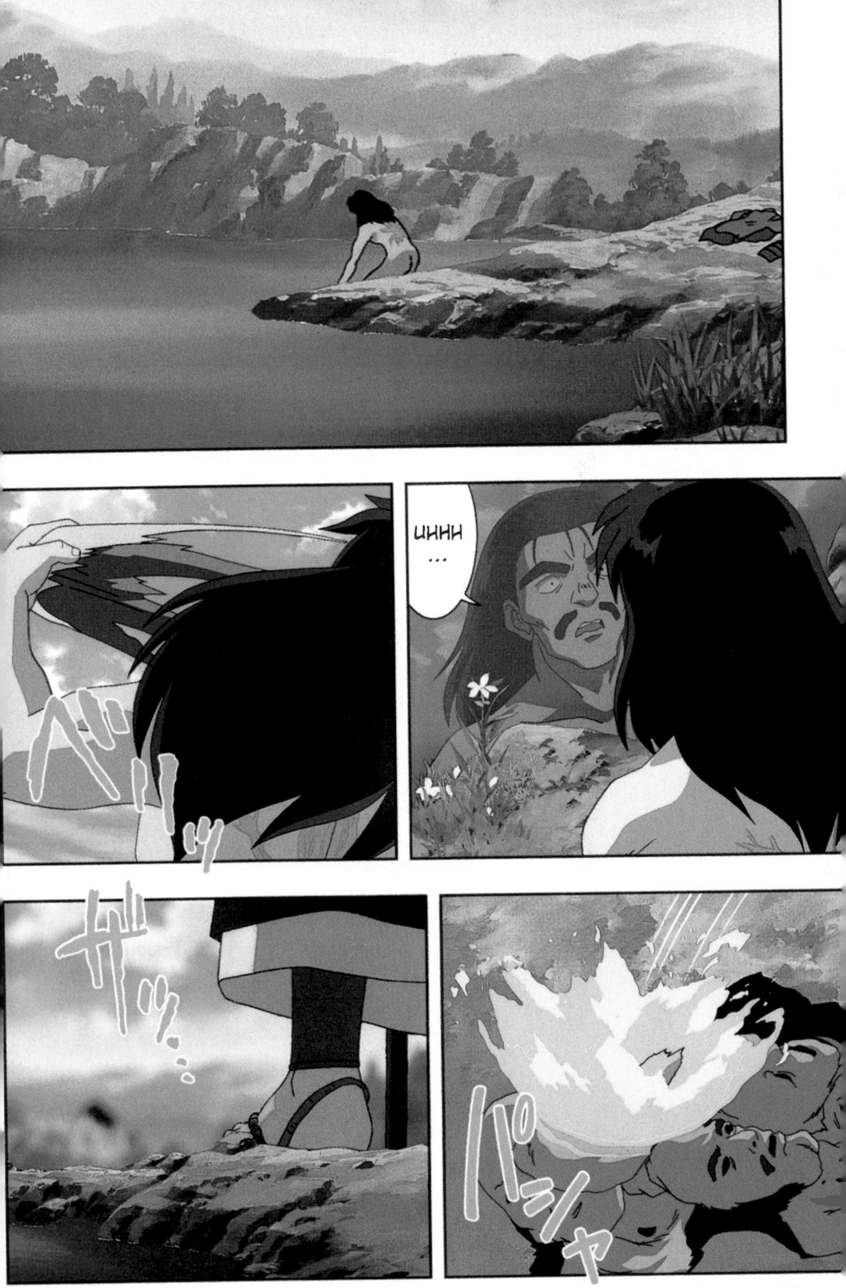
UHHH
...
ベリッ
パシャ
ザッ

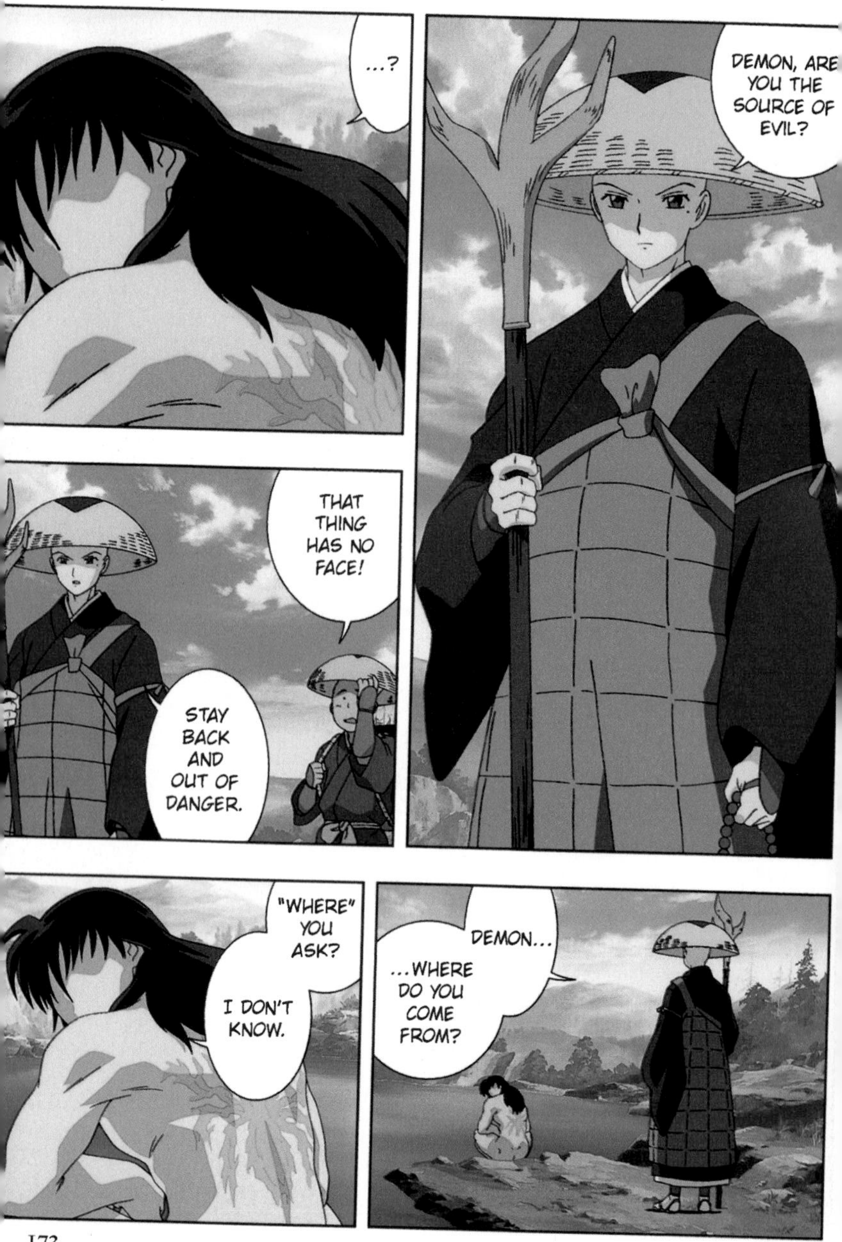
DEMON, ARE YOU THE SOURCE OF EVIL?
...?
THAT THING HAS NO FACE!
STAY BACK AND OUT OF DANGER.
DEMON...
...WHERE DO YOU COME FROM?
"WHERE" YOU ASK?
I DON'T KNOW.

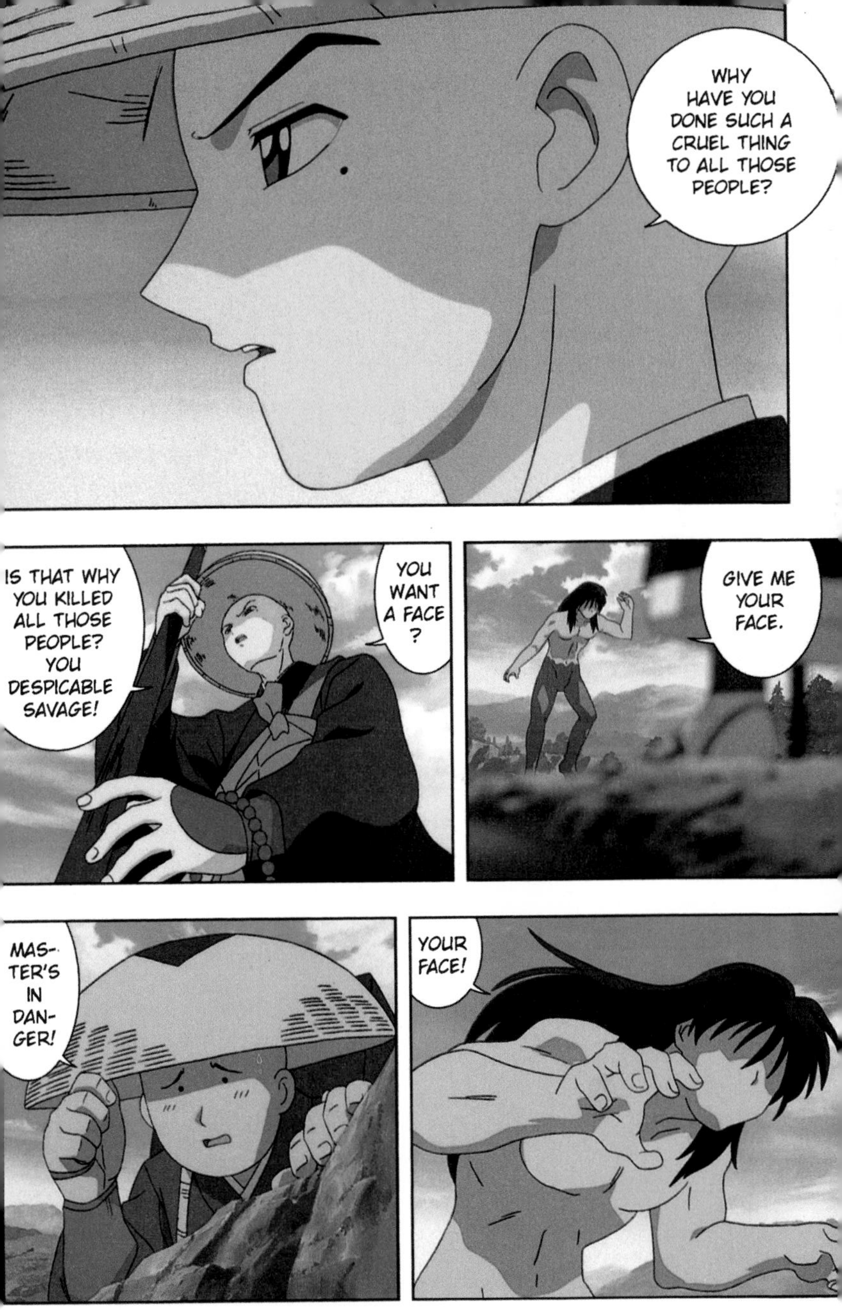
WHY HAVE YOU DONE SUCH A CRUEL THING TO ALL THOSE PEOPLE?
GIVE ME YOUR FACE.
YOU WANT A FACE?
IS THAT WHY YOU KILLED ALL THOSE PEOPLE? YOU DESPICABLE SAVAGE!
YOUR FACE!
MASTER'S IN DANGER!

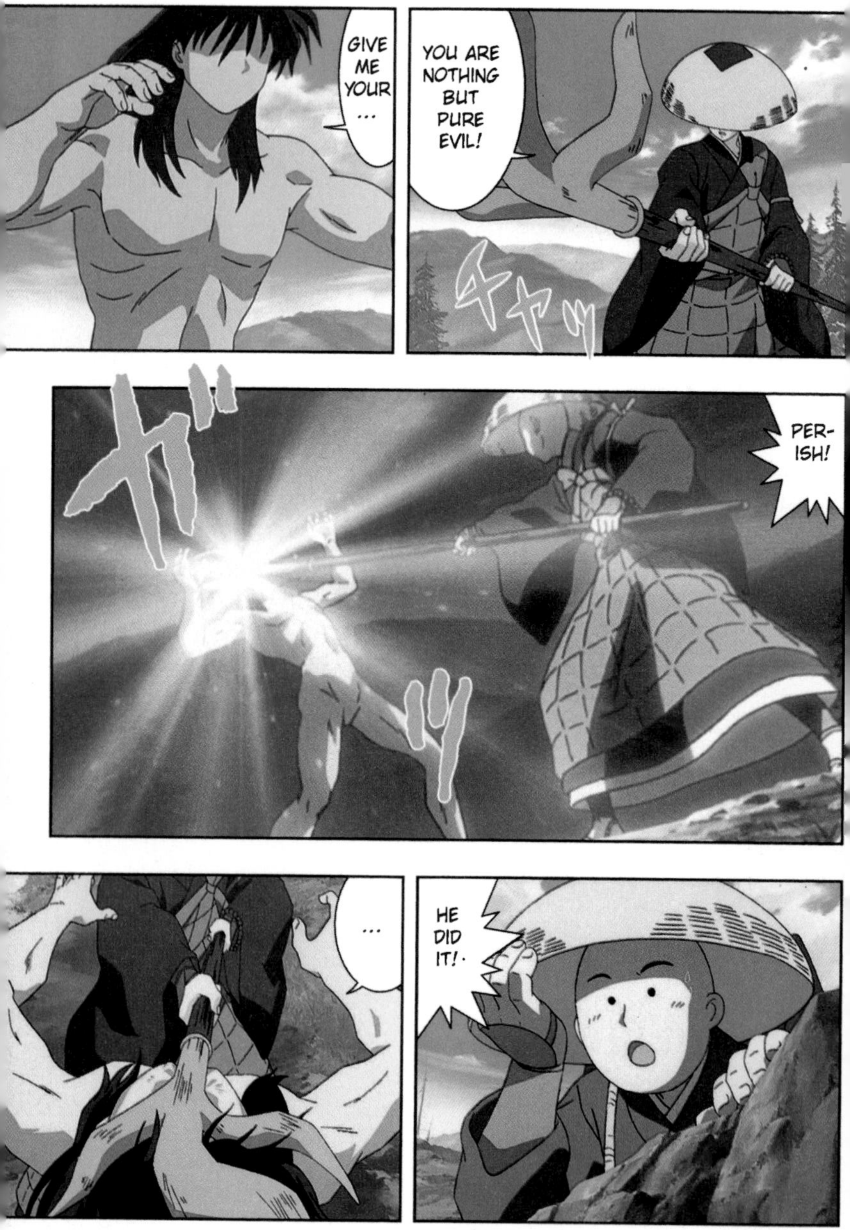

YOU ARE NOTHING BUT PURE EVIL!
GIVE ME YOUR ...
PER-ISH!
HE DID IT!
...

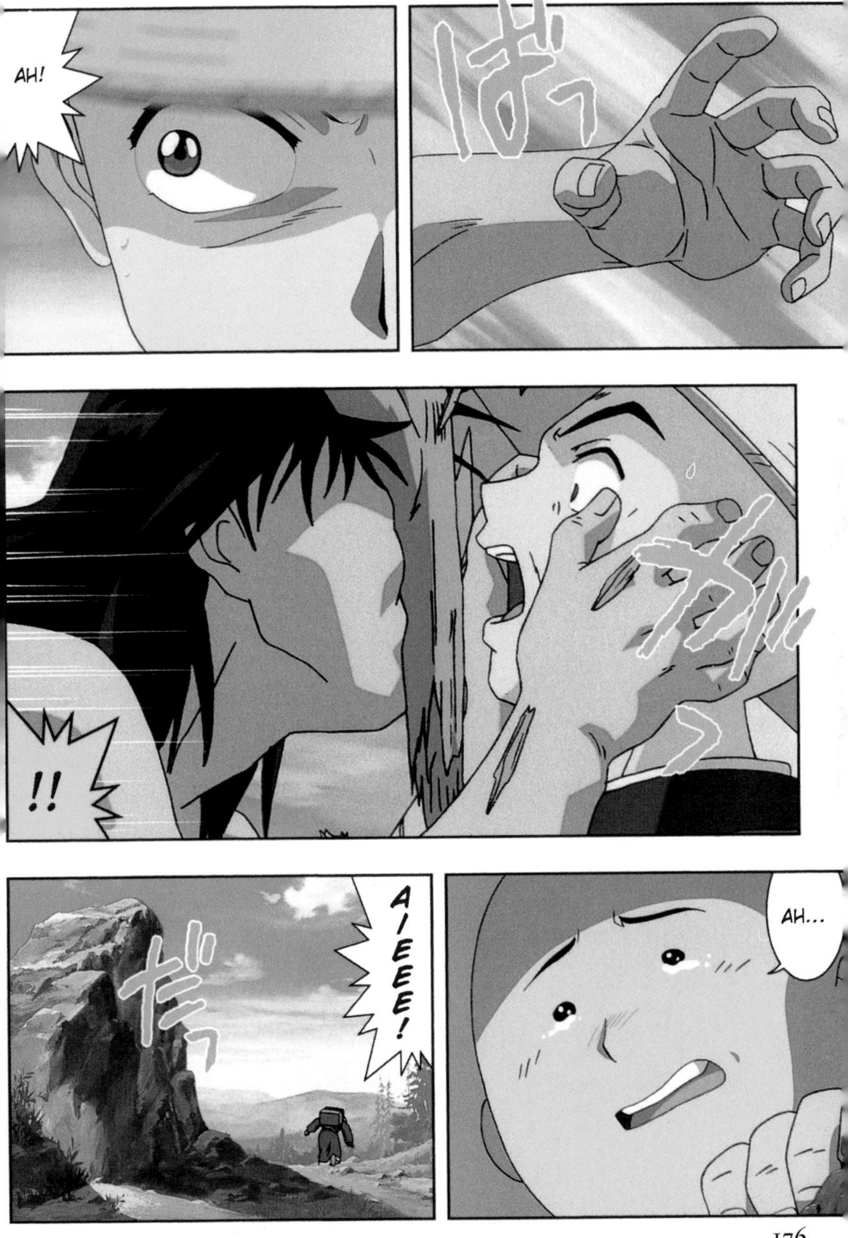
ぱっ
AH!
ガッ
!!
AH...
ダッ
AIEEE!

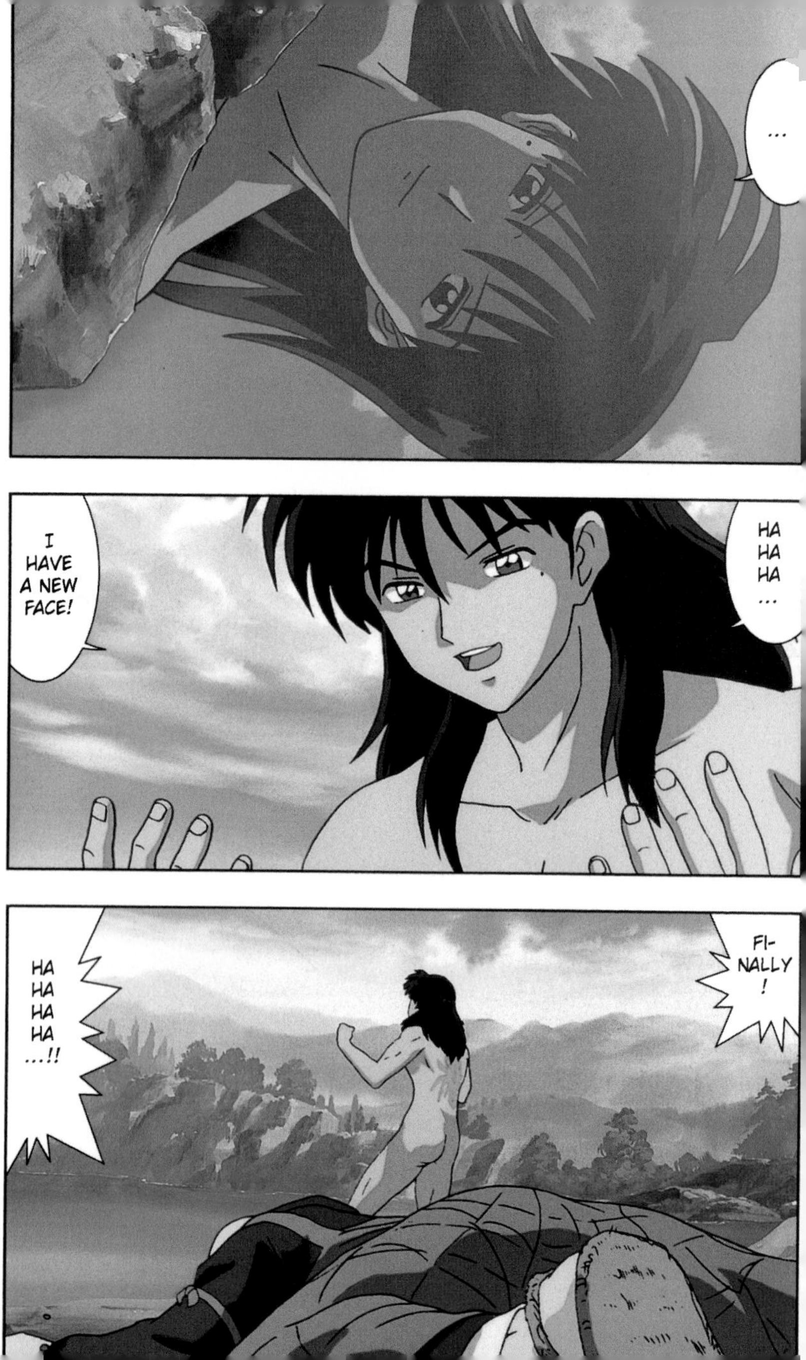
...
HA HA HA ...
I HAVE A NEW FACE!
FI-NALLY!
HA HA HA HA ...!!

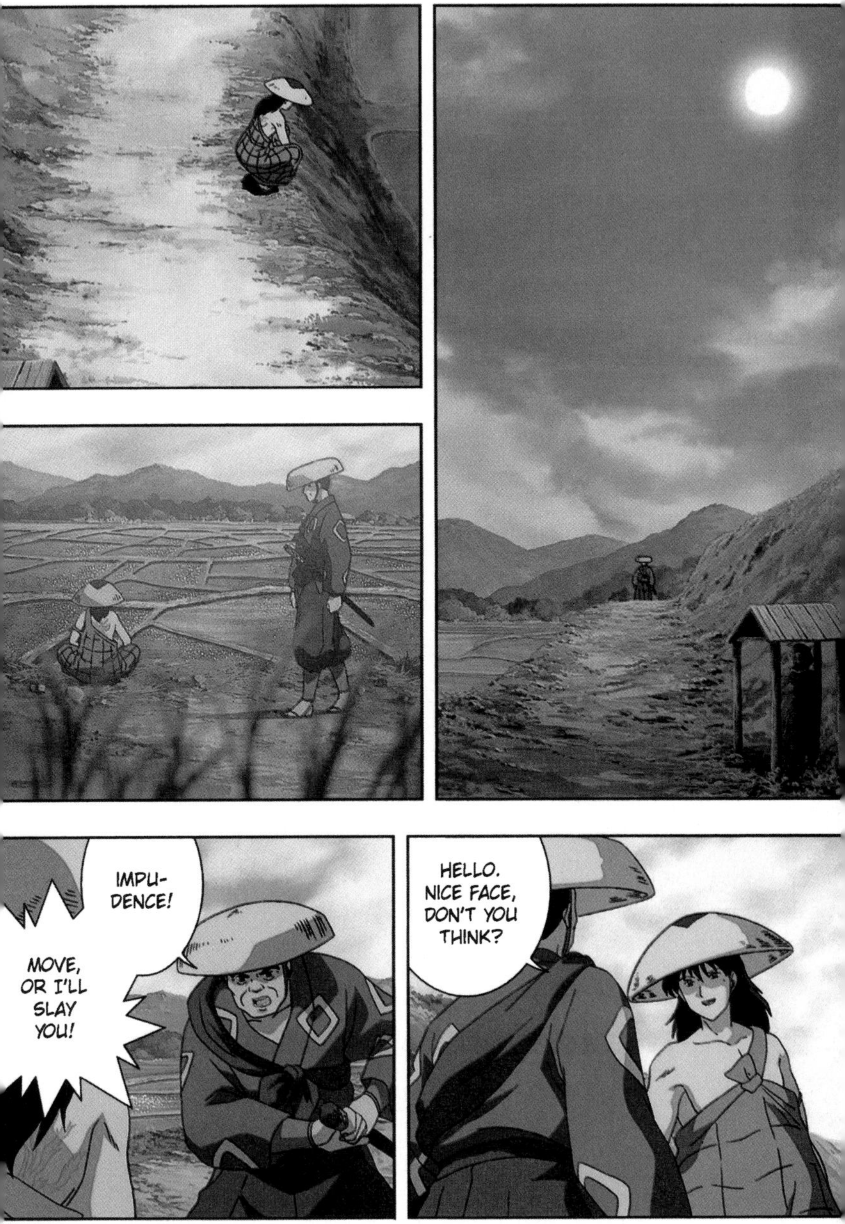
HELLO. NICE FACE, DON'T YOU THINK?
IMPU-DENCE!
MOVE, OR I'LL SLAY YOU!

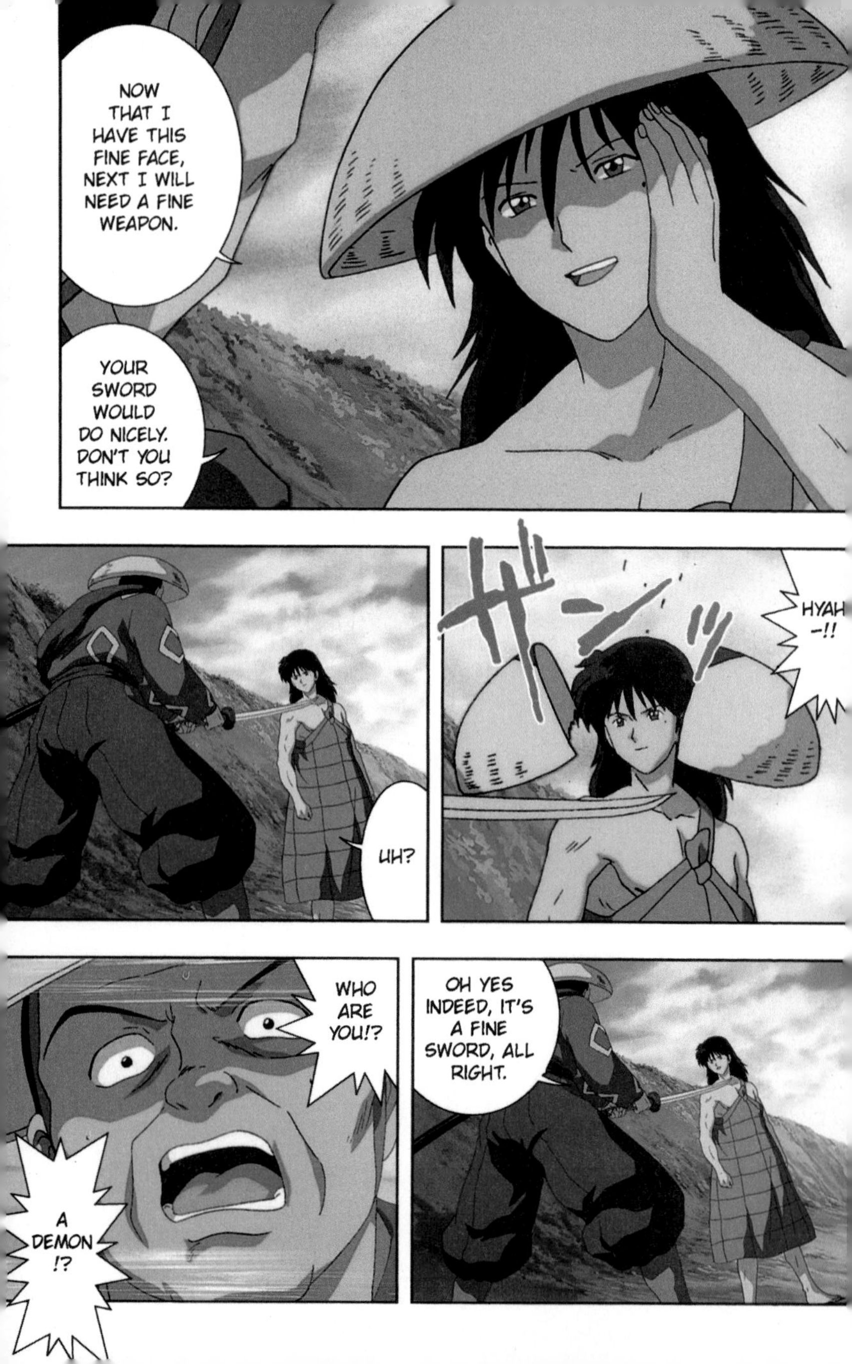
NOW THAT I HAVE THIS FINE FACE, NEXT I WILL NEED A FINE WEAPON.
YOUR SWORD WOULD DO NICELY. DON'T YOU THINK SO?
ザンッ
HYAH—!!
UH?
OH YES INDEED, IT'S A FINE SWORD, ALL RIGHT.
WHO ARE YOU!?
A DEMON!?

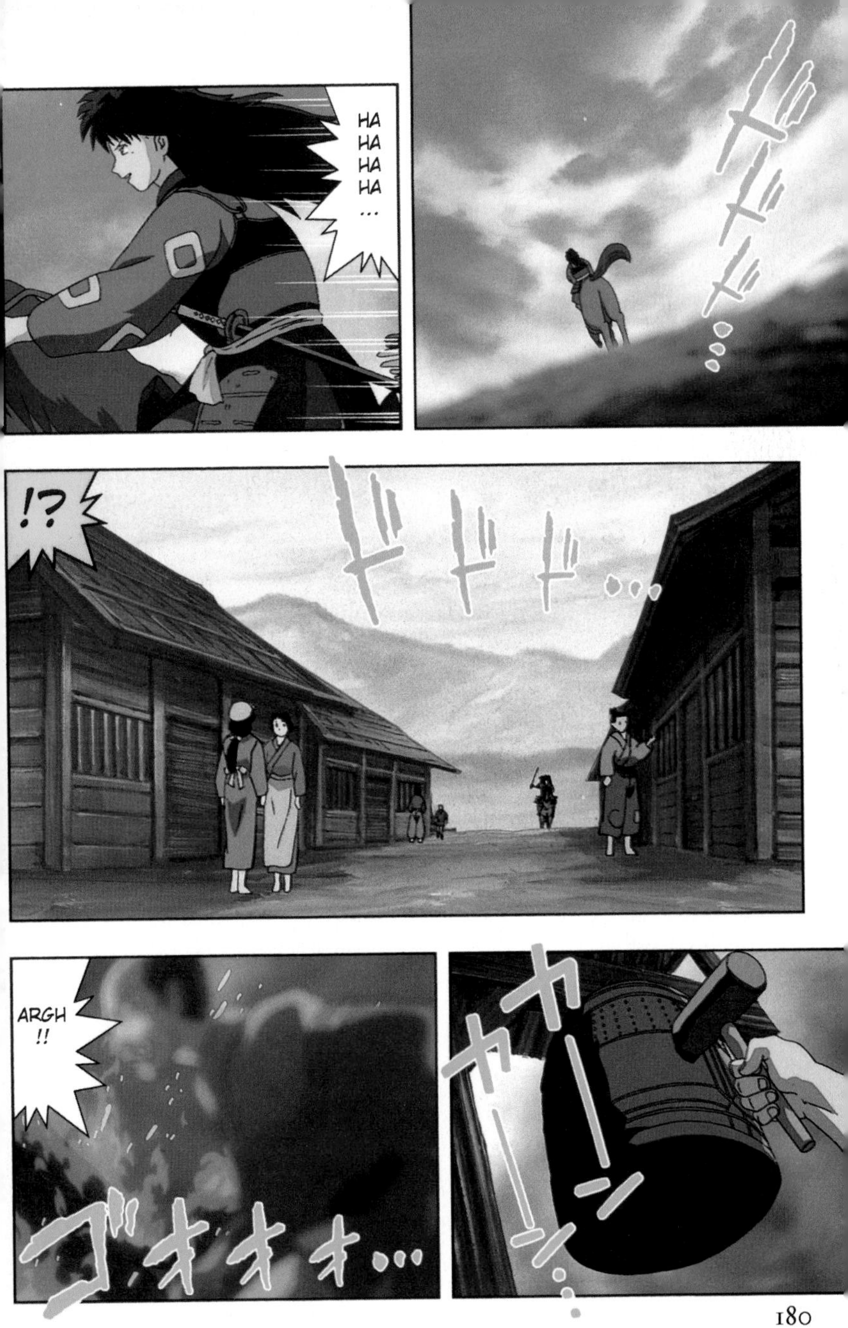
ドドドド…
HA HA HA HA ...
ドドド…
!?
ヤーン ヤーン…
ARGH !!
ゴオオオ…

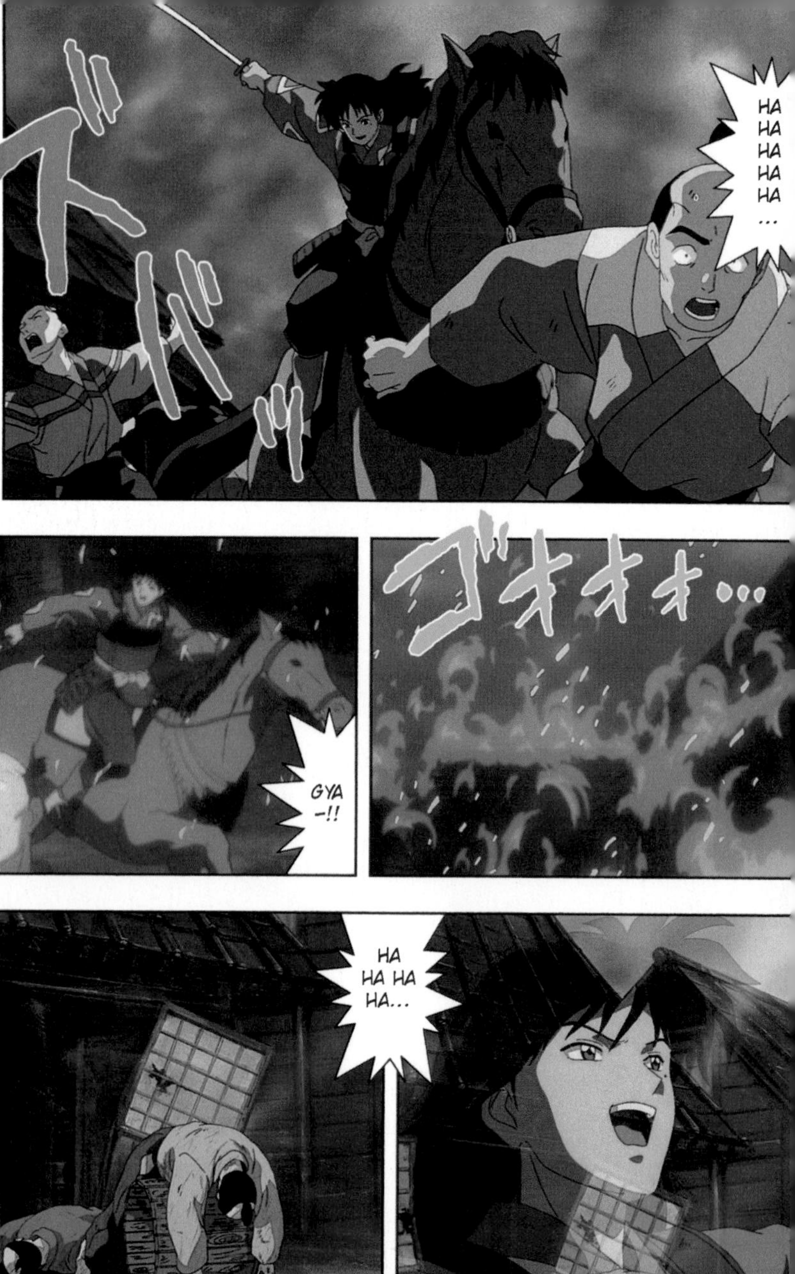
ズドッ
HA HA HA HA HA ...
ゴオオオ…
GYA —!!
HA HA HA HA...

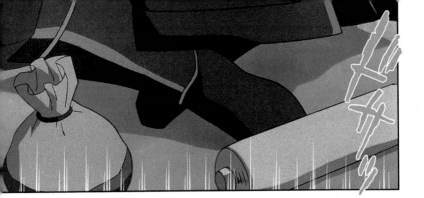

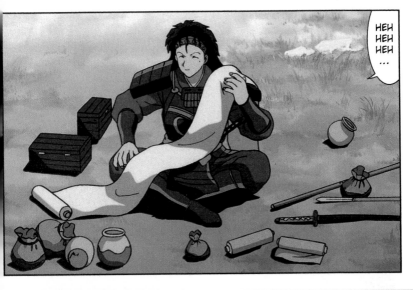

HEH
HEH
HEH
...

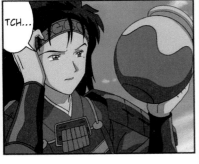

TCH...

HM...

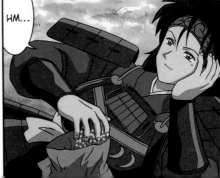

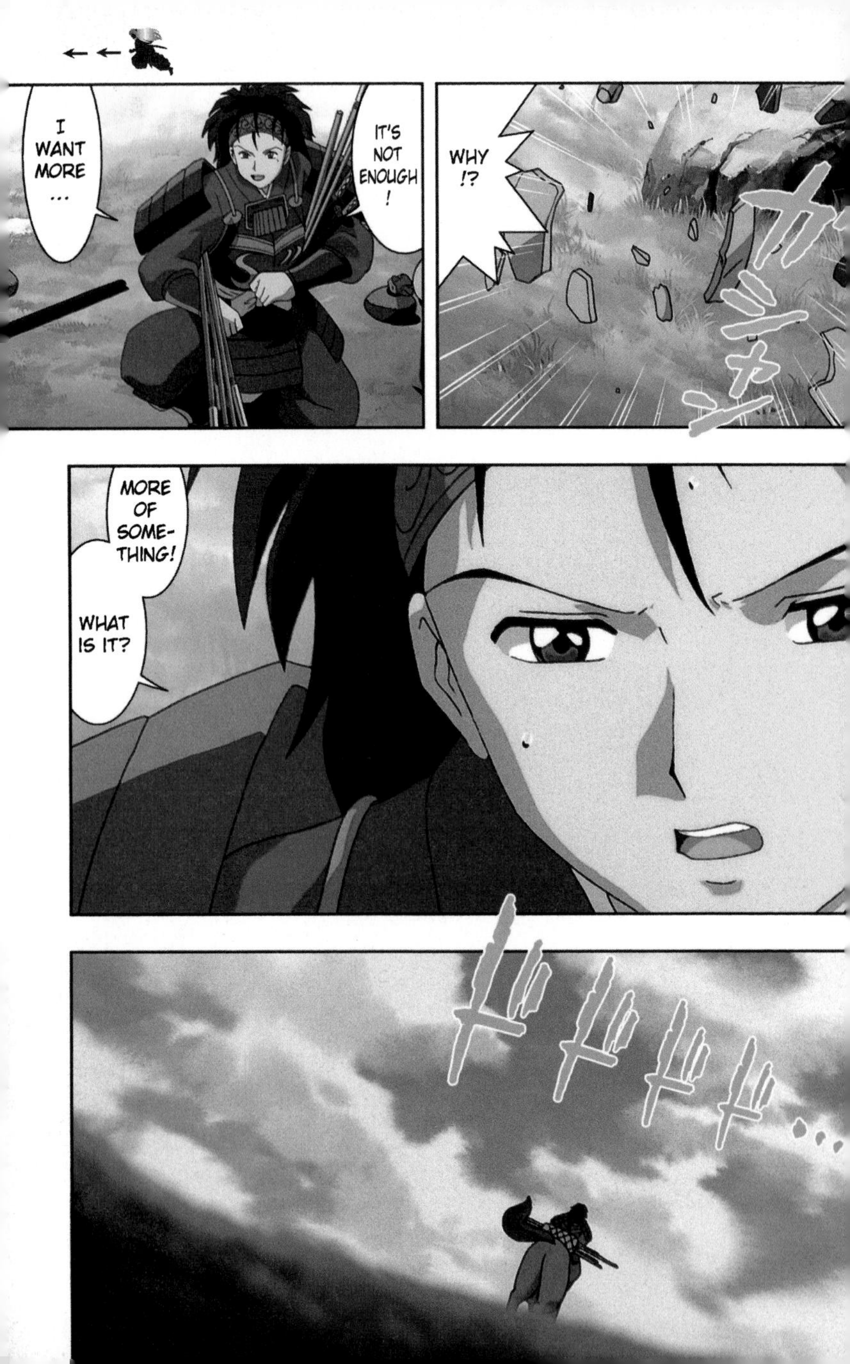
WHY!?
IT'S NOT ENOUGH!
I WANT MORE ...
MORE OF SOMETHING!
WHAT IS IT?

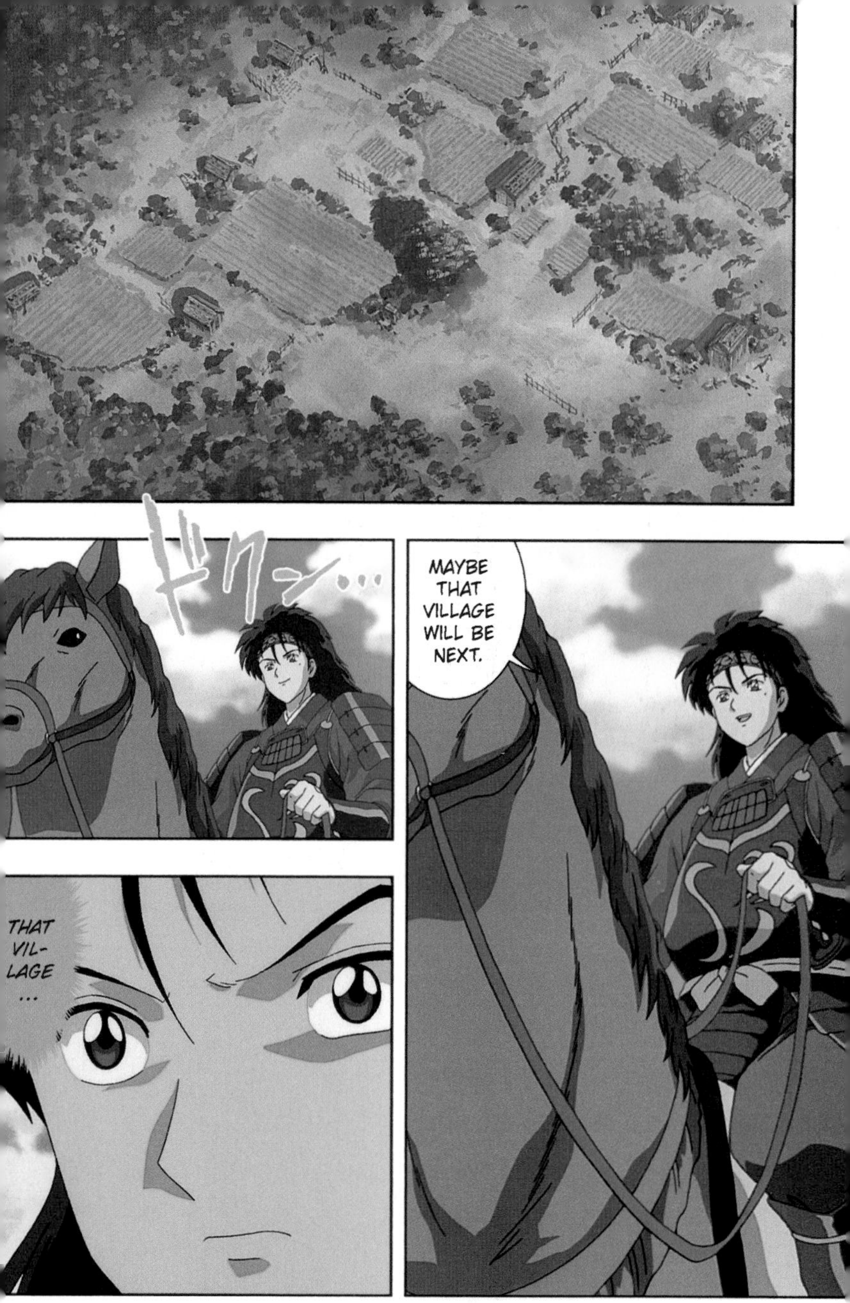
MAYBE THAT VILLAGE WILL BE NEXT.
ドクン…
THAT VIL-LAGE …

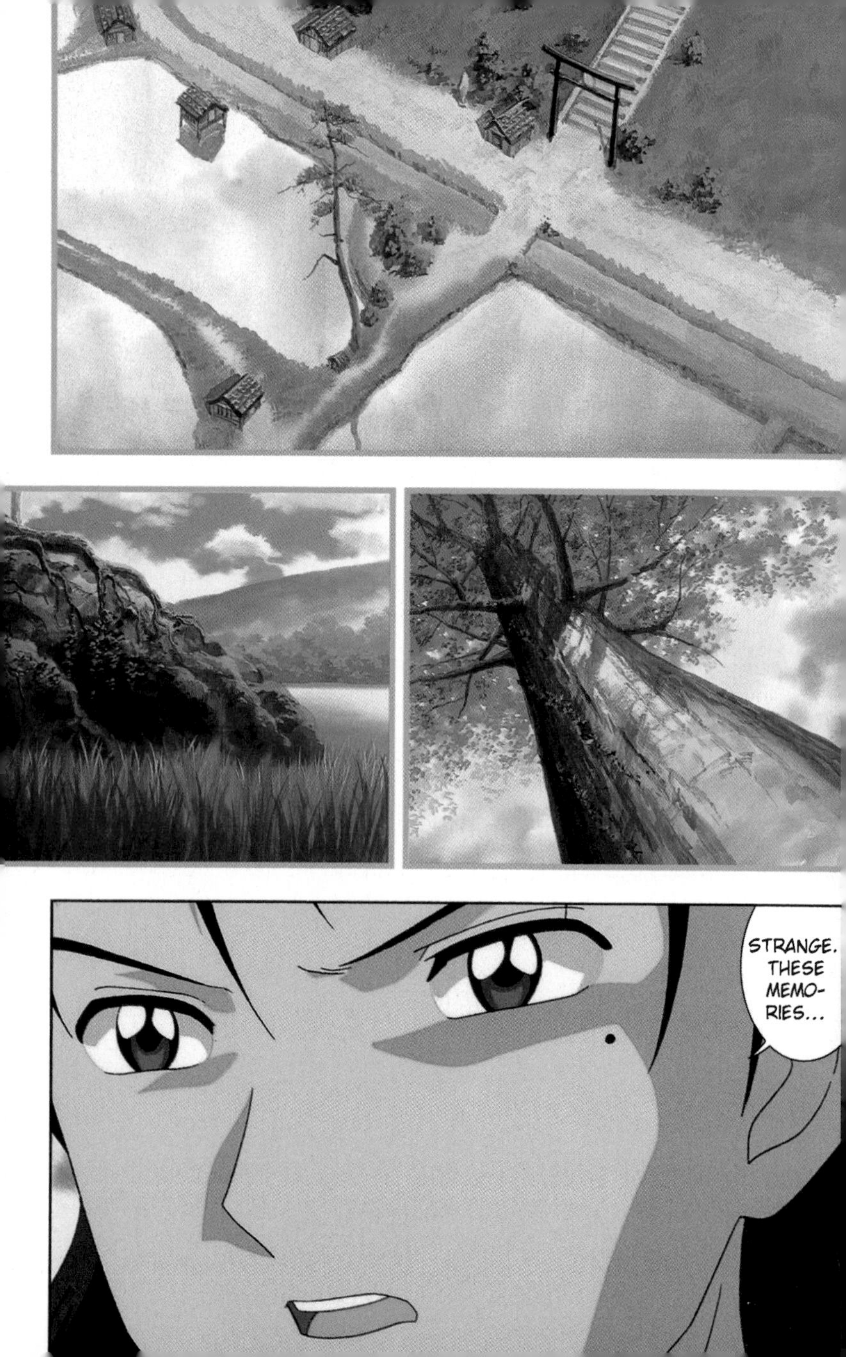
STRANGE. THESE MEMO-RIES...

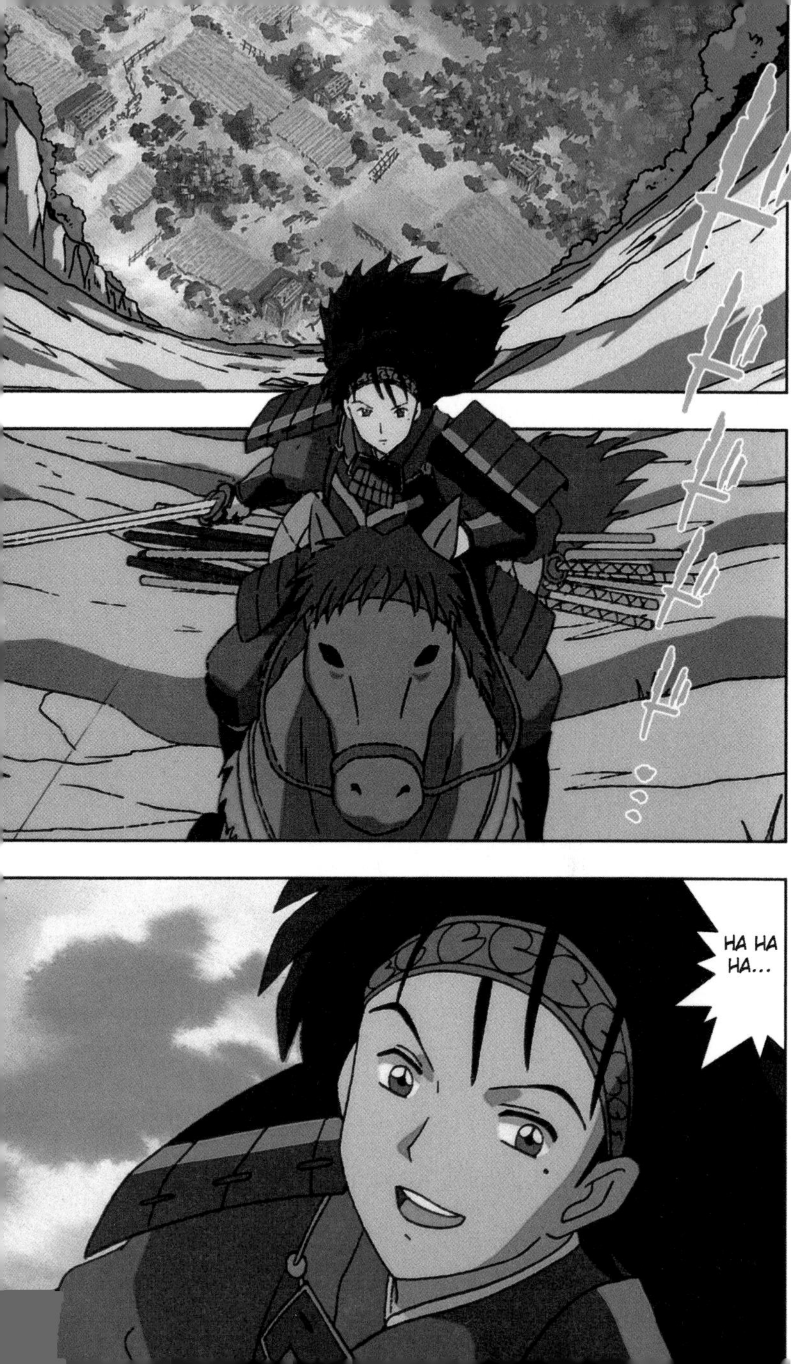
HA HA HA...

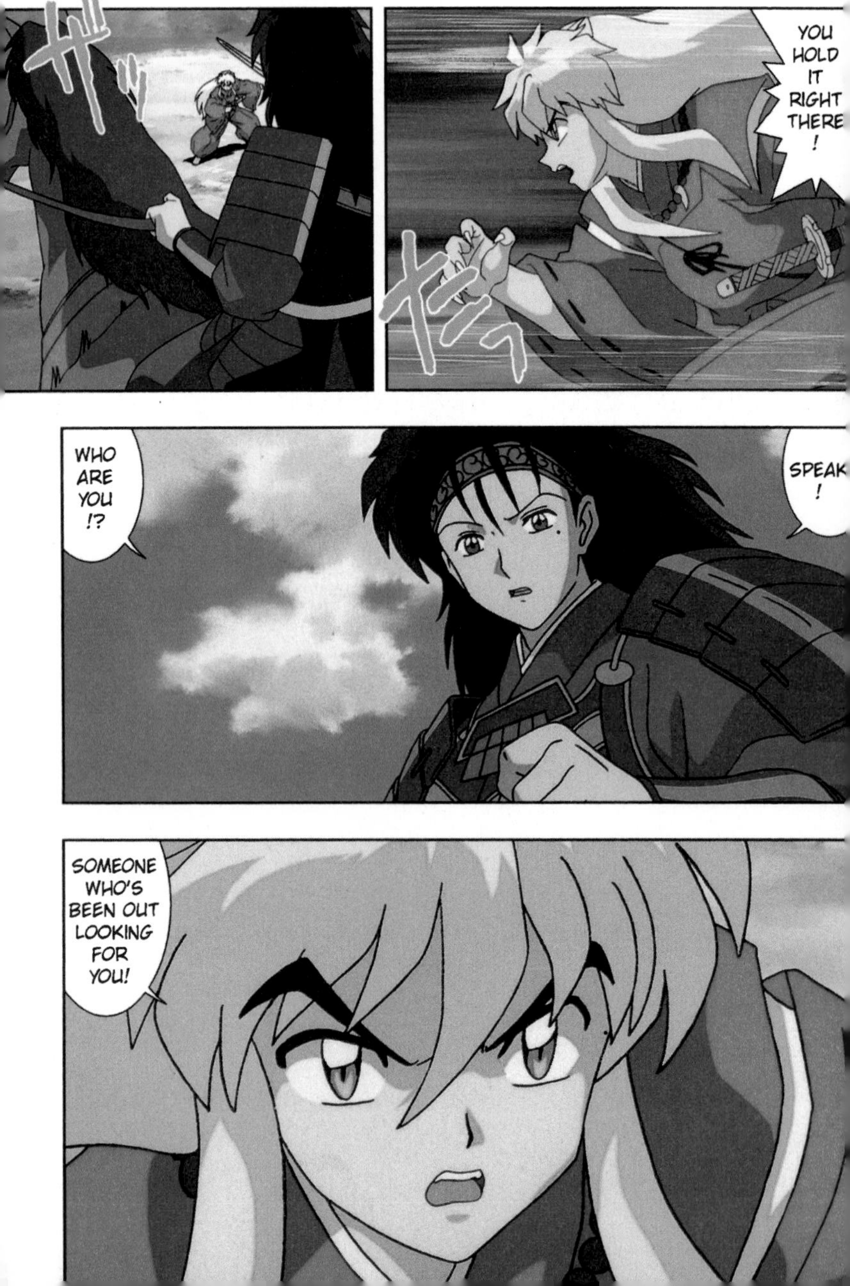

YOU HOLD IT RIGHT THERE!
SPEAK!
WHO ARE YOU!?
SOMEONE WHO'S BEEN OUT LOOKING FOR YOU!

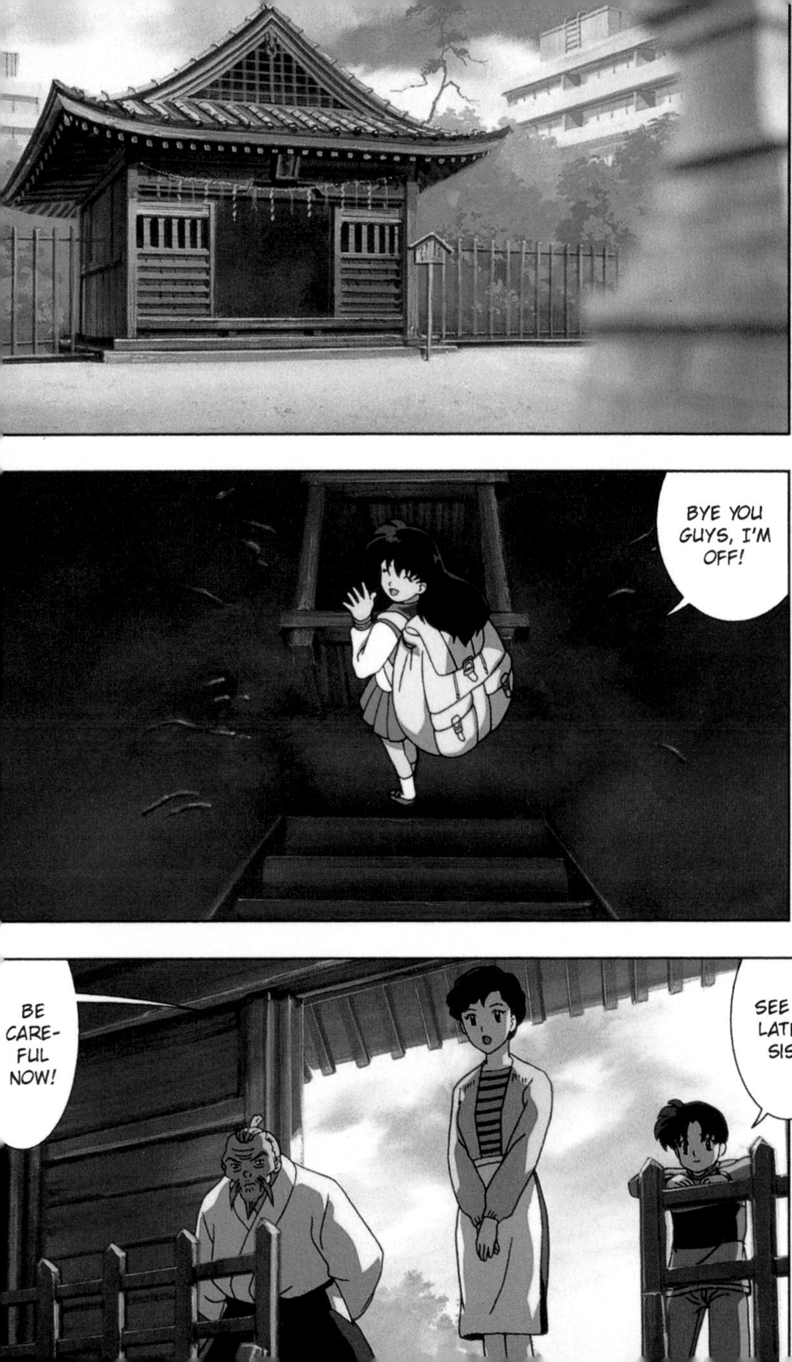
BYE YOU GUYS, I'M OFF!
SEE YA LATER, SIS!
BE CARE-FUL NOW!

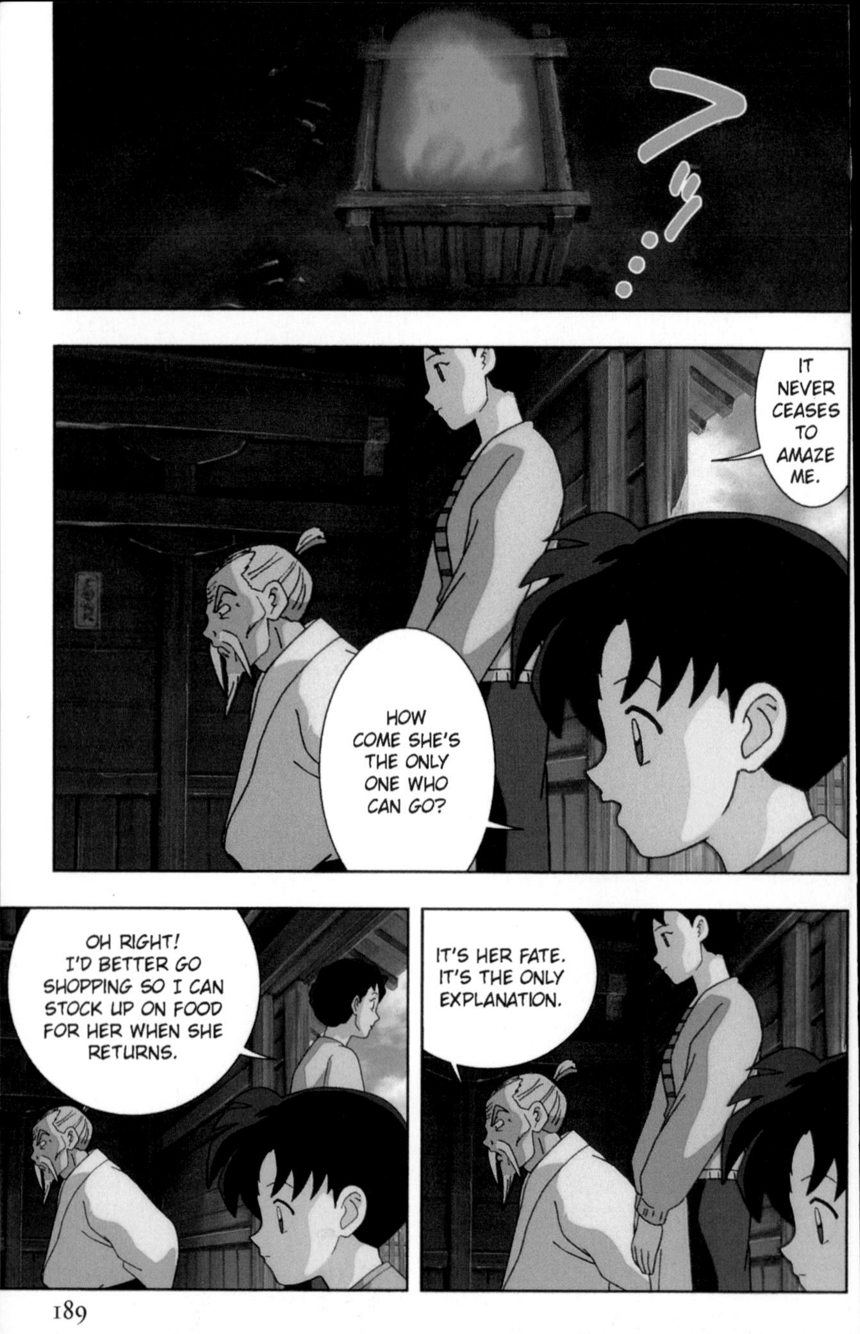
IT NEVER CEASES TO AMAZE ME.
HOW COME SHE'S THE ONLY ONE WHO CAN GO?
IT'S HER FATE. IT'S THE ONLY EXPLANATION.
OH RIGHT! I'D BETTER GO SHOPPING SO I CAN STOCK UP ON FOOD FOR HER WHEN SHE RETURNS.

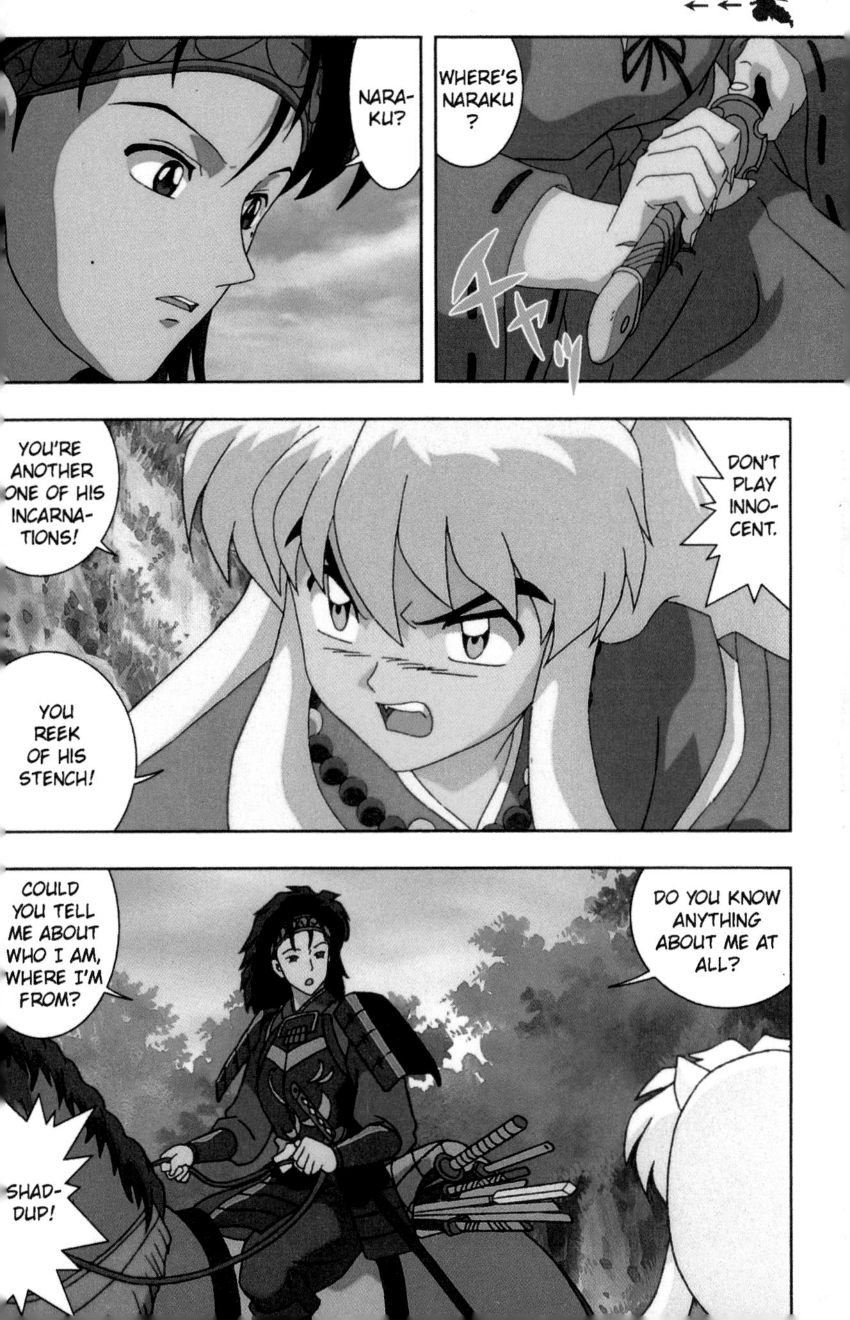
WHERE'S NARAKU?
チャッ
NARA-KU?
DON'T PLAY INNO-CENT.
YOU'RE ANOTHER ONE OF HIS INCARNA-TIONS!
YOU REEK OF HIS STENCH!
DO YOU KNOW ANYTHING ABOUT ME AT ALL?
COULD YOU TELL ME ABOUT WHO I AM, WHERE I'M FROM?
SHAD-DUP!

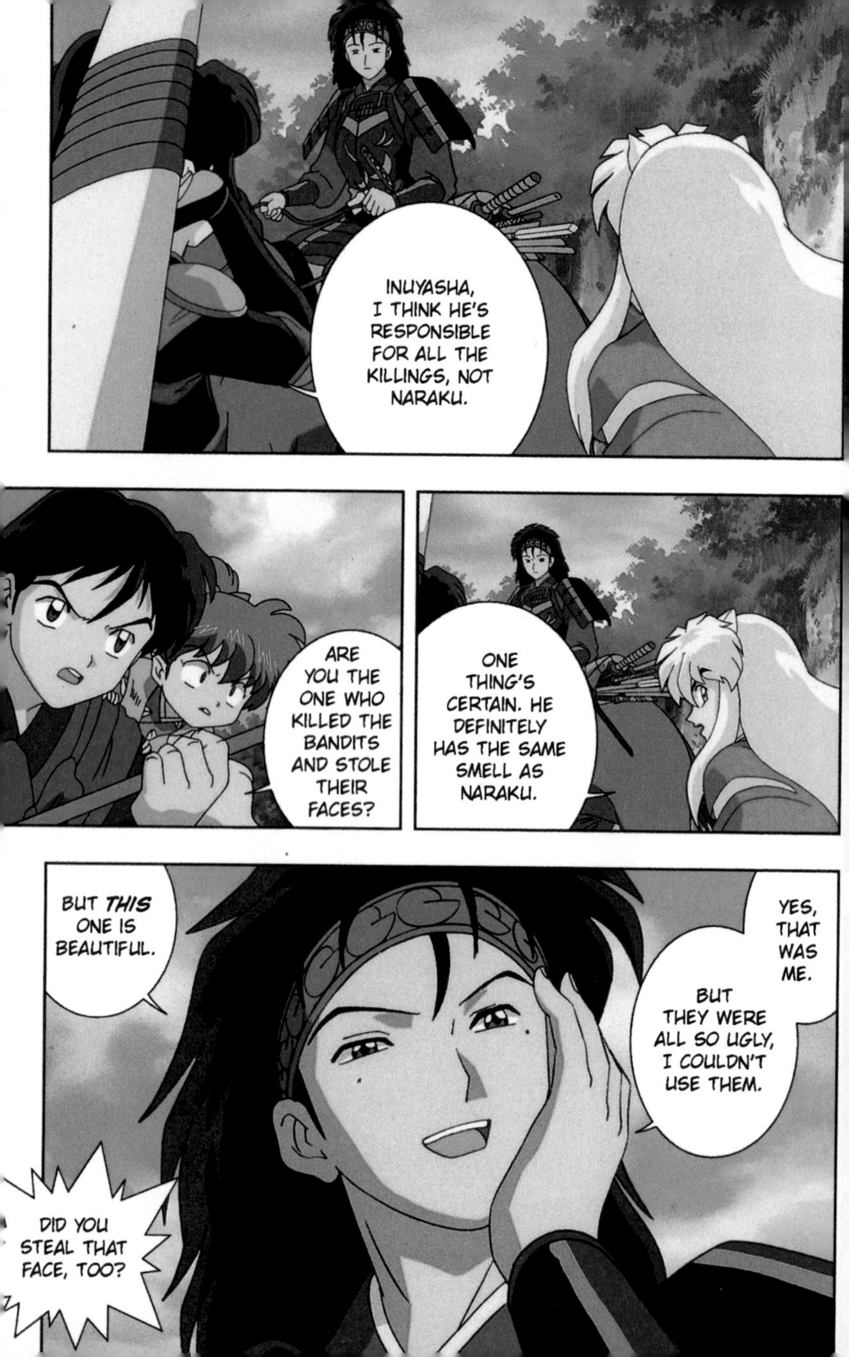
INUYASHA, I THINK HE'S RESPONSIBLE FOR ALL THE KILLINGS, NOT NARAKU.
ONE THING'S CERTAIN. HE DEFINITELY HAS THE SAME SMELL AS NARAKU.
ARE YOU THE ONE WHO KILLED THE BANDITS AND STOLE THEIR FACES?
YES, THAT WAS ME.
BUT THEY WERE ALL SO UGLY, I COULDN'T USE THEM.
BUT *THIS* ONE IS BEAUTIFUL.
DID YOU STEAL THAT FACE, TOO?

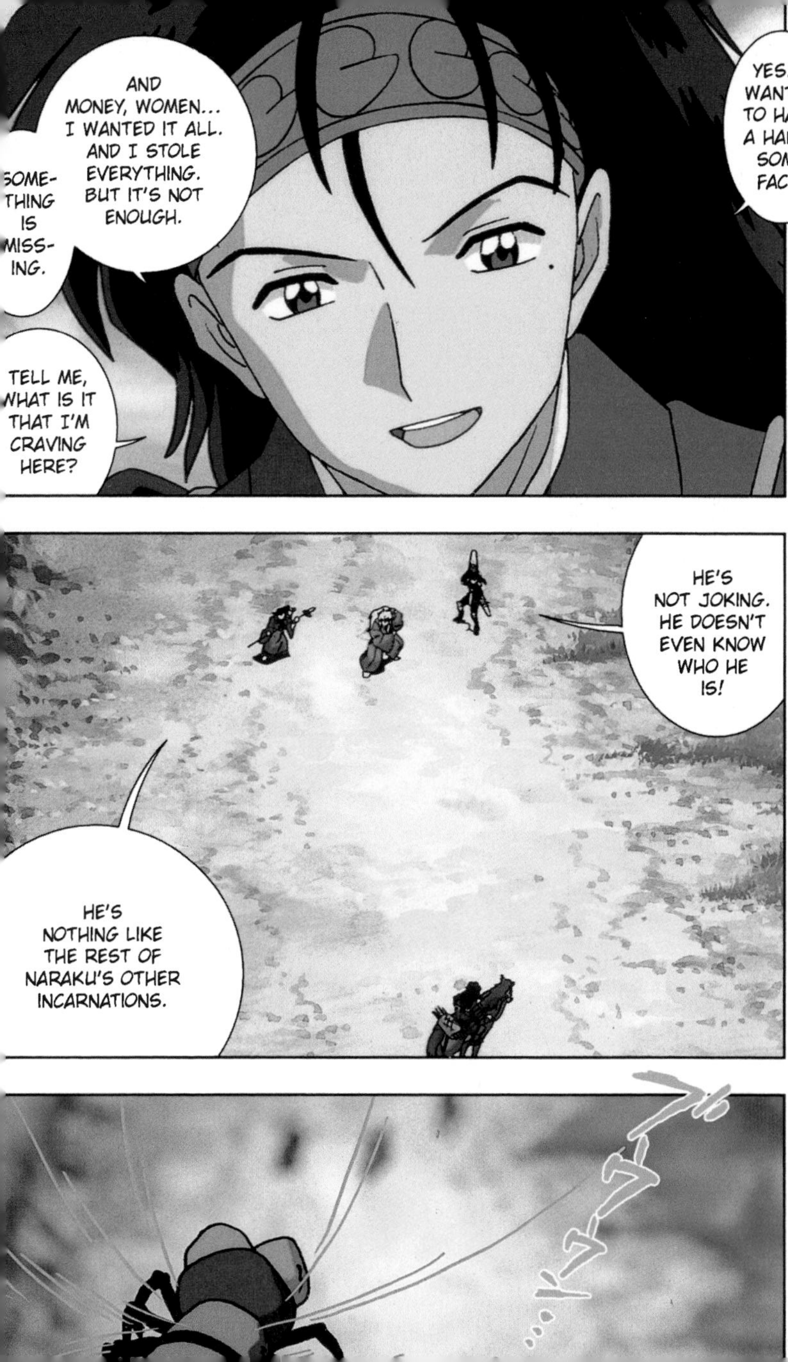
YES. I WANTED TO HAVE A HANDSOME FACE.
AND MONEY, WOMEN... I WANTED IT ALL. AND I STOLE EVERYTHING. BUT IT'S NOT ENOUGH.
SOMETHING IS MISSING.
TELL ME, WHAT IS IT THAT I'M CRAVING HERE?
HE'S NOT JOKING. HE DOESN'T EVEN KNOW WHO HE IS!
HE'S NOTHING LIKE THE REST OF NARAKU'S OTHER INCARNATIONS.

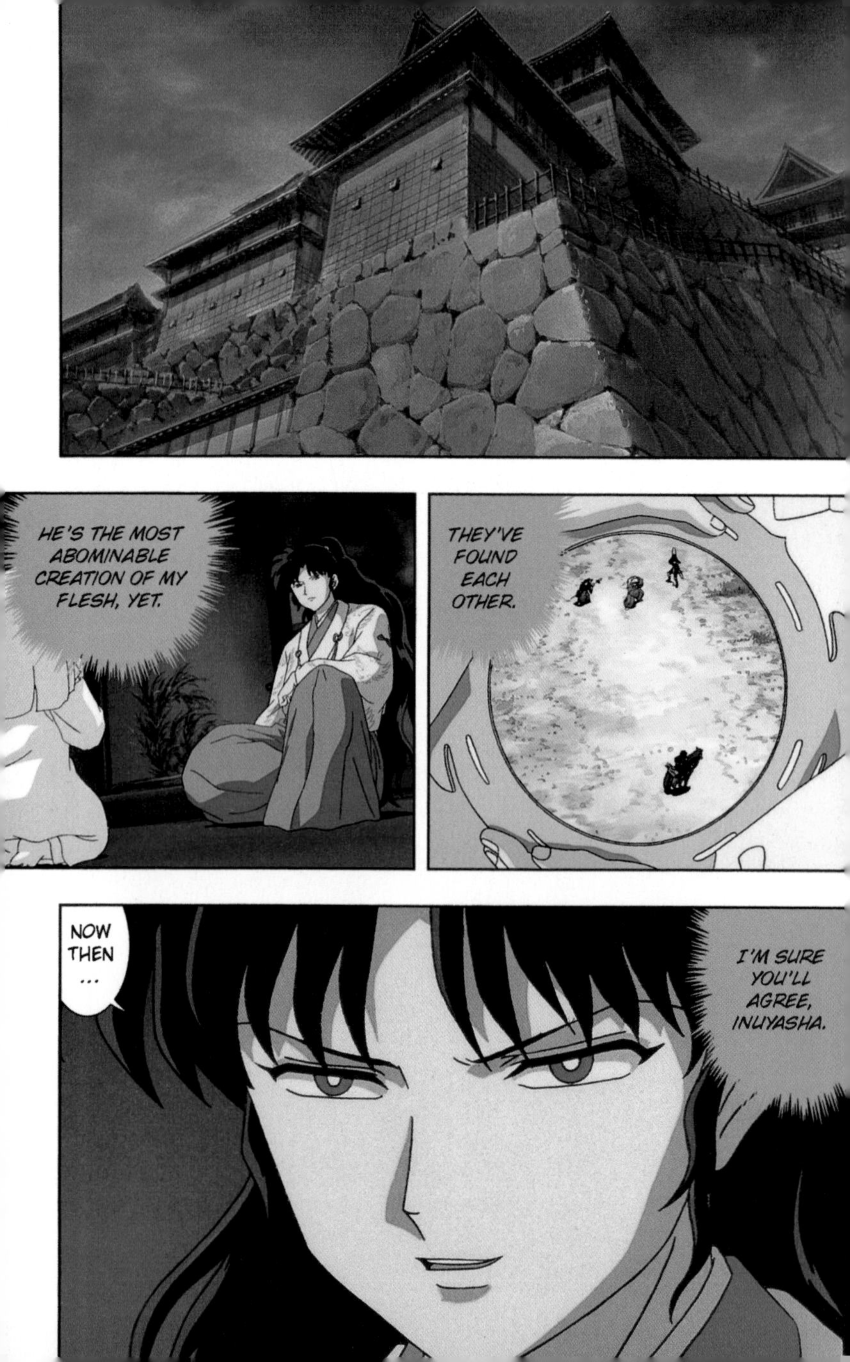
THEY'VE FOUND EACH OTHER.
HE'S THE MOST ABOMINABLE CREATION OF MY FLESH, YET.
I'M SURE YOU'LL AGREE, INUYASHA.
NOW THEN ...

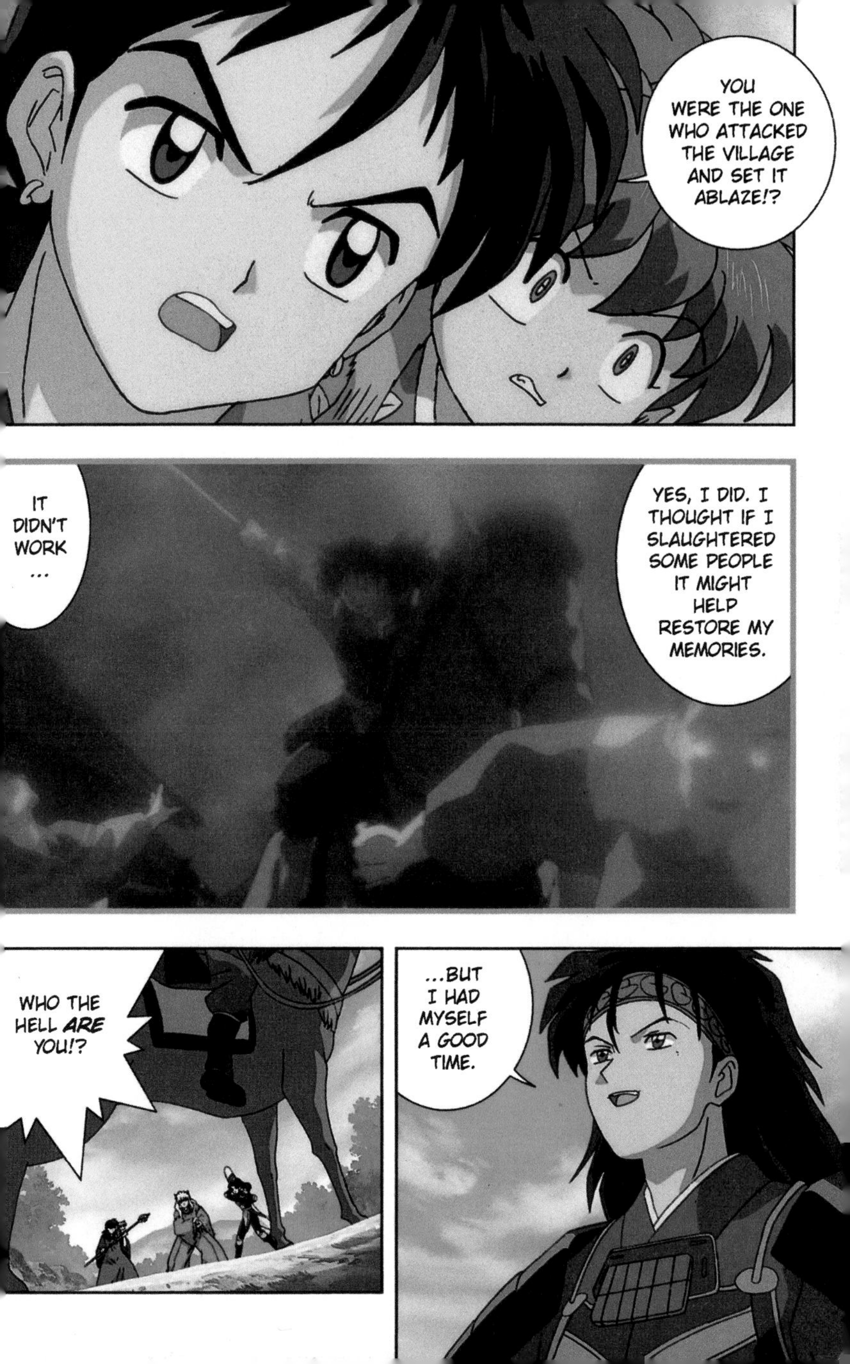
YOU WERE THE ONE WHO ATTACKED THE VILLAGE AND SET IT ABLAZE!?
YES, I DID. I THOUGHT IF I SLAUGHTERED SOME PEOPLE IT MIGHT HELP RESTORE MY MEMORIES.
IT DIDN'T WORK ...
...BUT I HAD MYSELF A GOOD TIME.
WHO THE HELL *ARE* YOU!?

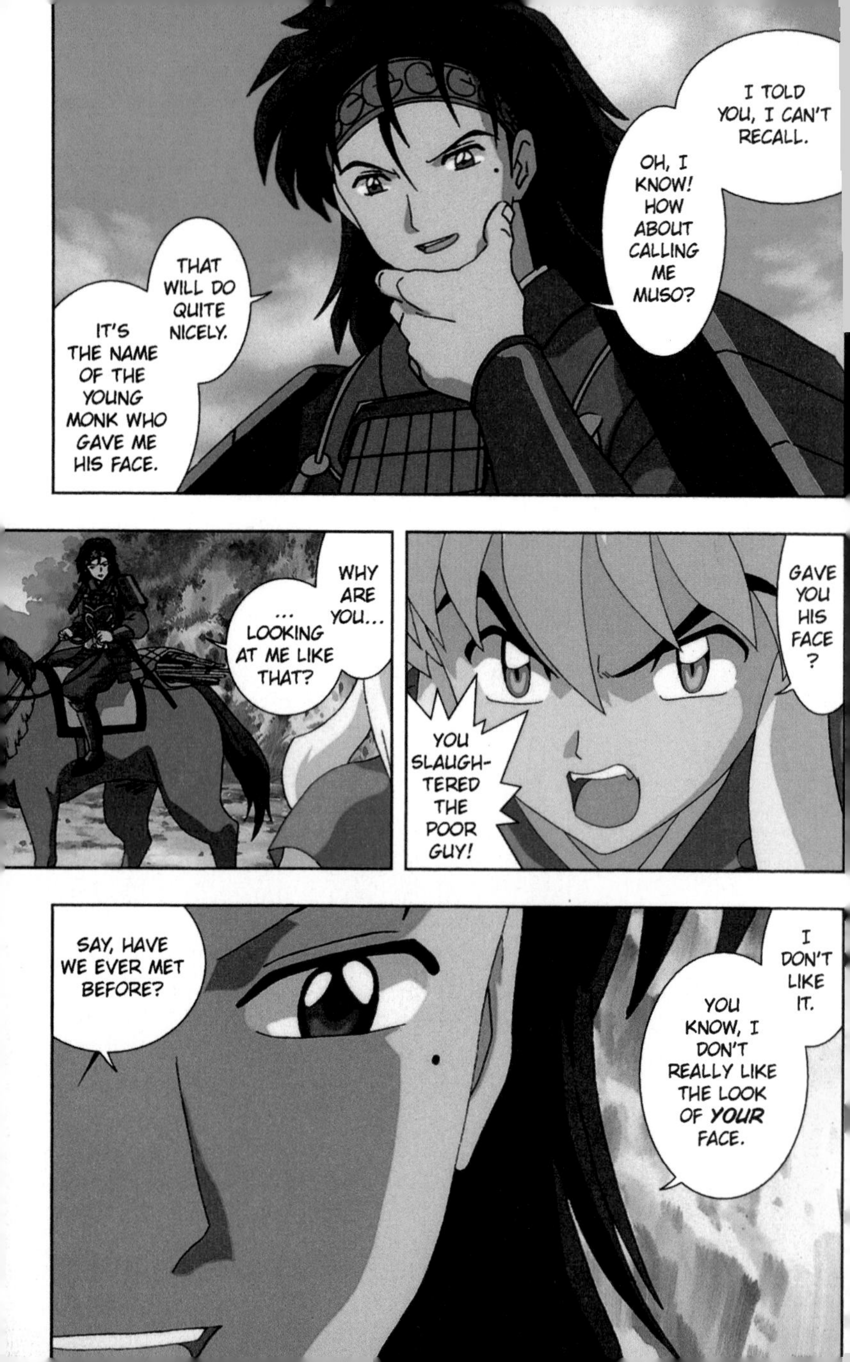

I TOLD YOU, I CAN'T RECALL.
OH, I KNOW! HOW ABOUT CALLING ME MUSO?
THAT WILL DO QUITE NICELY.
IT'S THE NAME OF THE YOUNG MONK WHO GAVE ME HIS FACE.
GAVE YOU HIS FACE?
YOU SLAUGHTERED THE POOR GUY!
WHY ARE YOU...
...LOOKING AT ME LIKE THAT?
I DON'T LIKE IT.
YOU KNOW, I DON'T REALLY LIKE THE LOOK OF *YOUR* FACE.
SAY, HAVE WE EVER MET BEFORE?

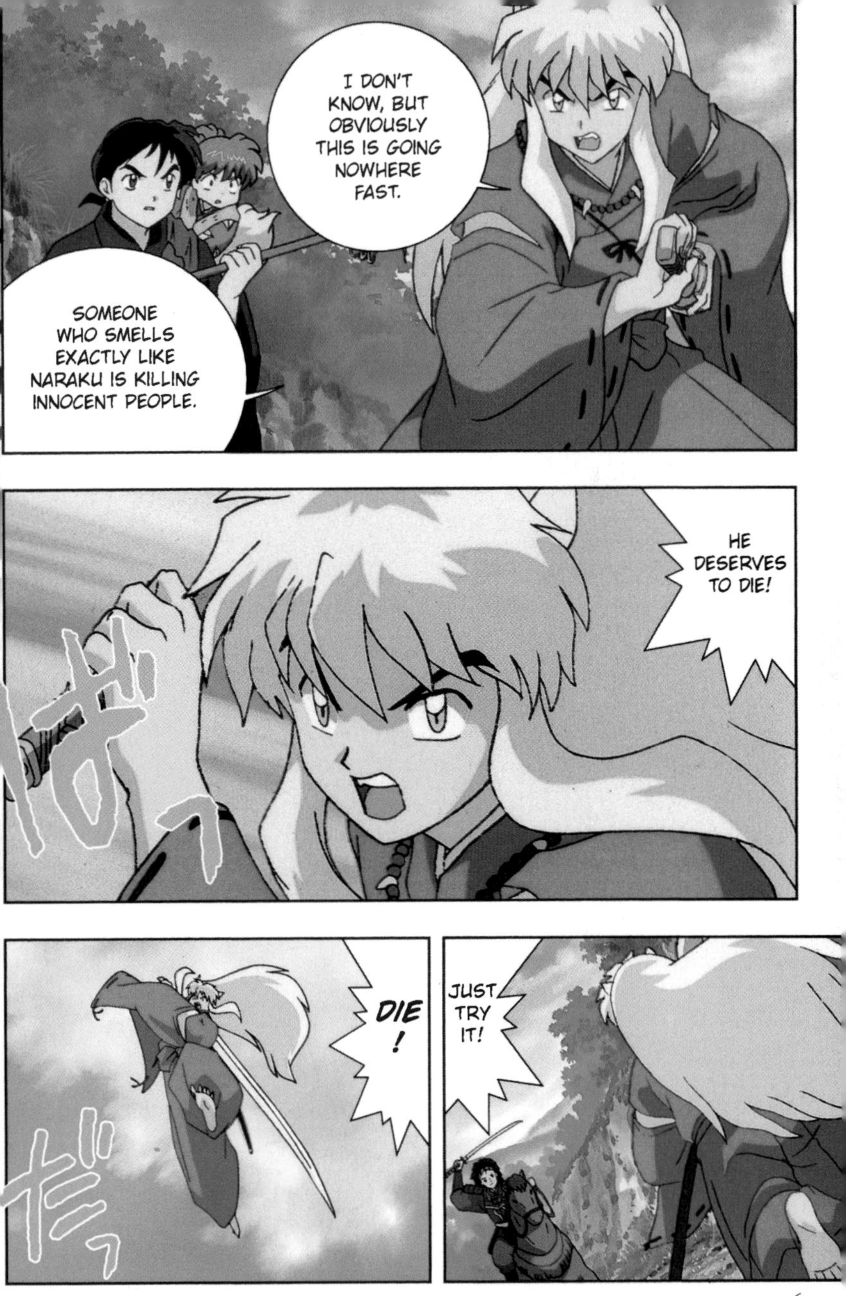

I DON'T KNOW, BUT OBVIOUSLY THIS IS GOING NOWHERE FAST.
SOMEONE WHO SMELLS EXACTLY LIKE NARAKU IS KILLING INNOCENT PEOPLE.
HE DESERVES TO DIE!
ばっ
JUST TRY IT!
DIE!
だっ

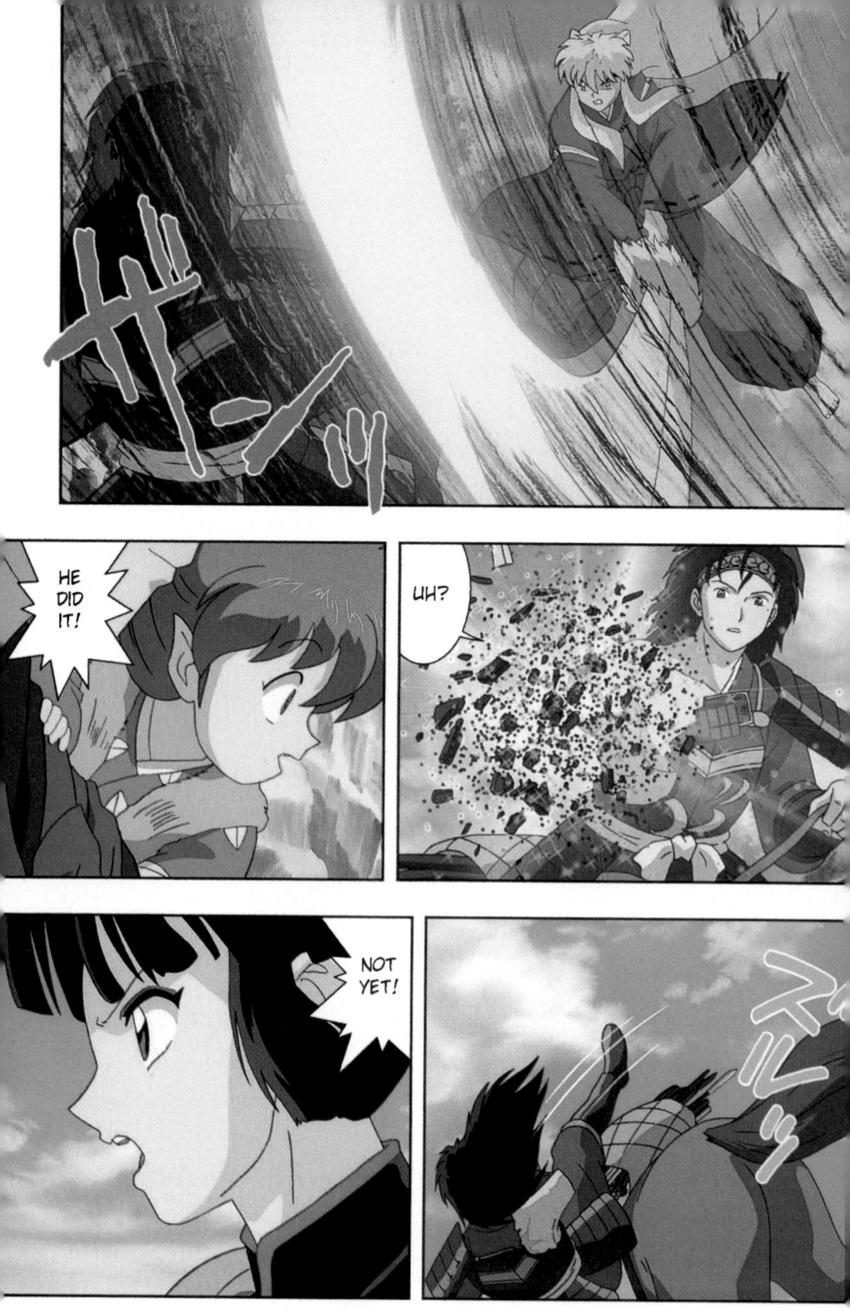
ザーッ
UH?
HE DID IT!
NOT YET!

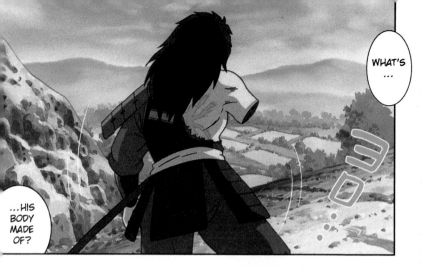

WHAT'S
...

...HIS BODY MADE OF?

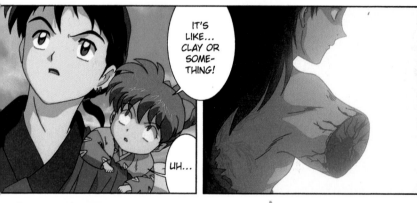

IT'S LIKE... CLAY OR SOMETHING!

UH...

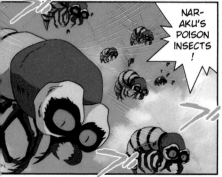

NAR-AKU'S POISON INSECTS!

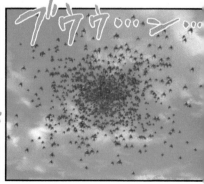

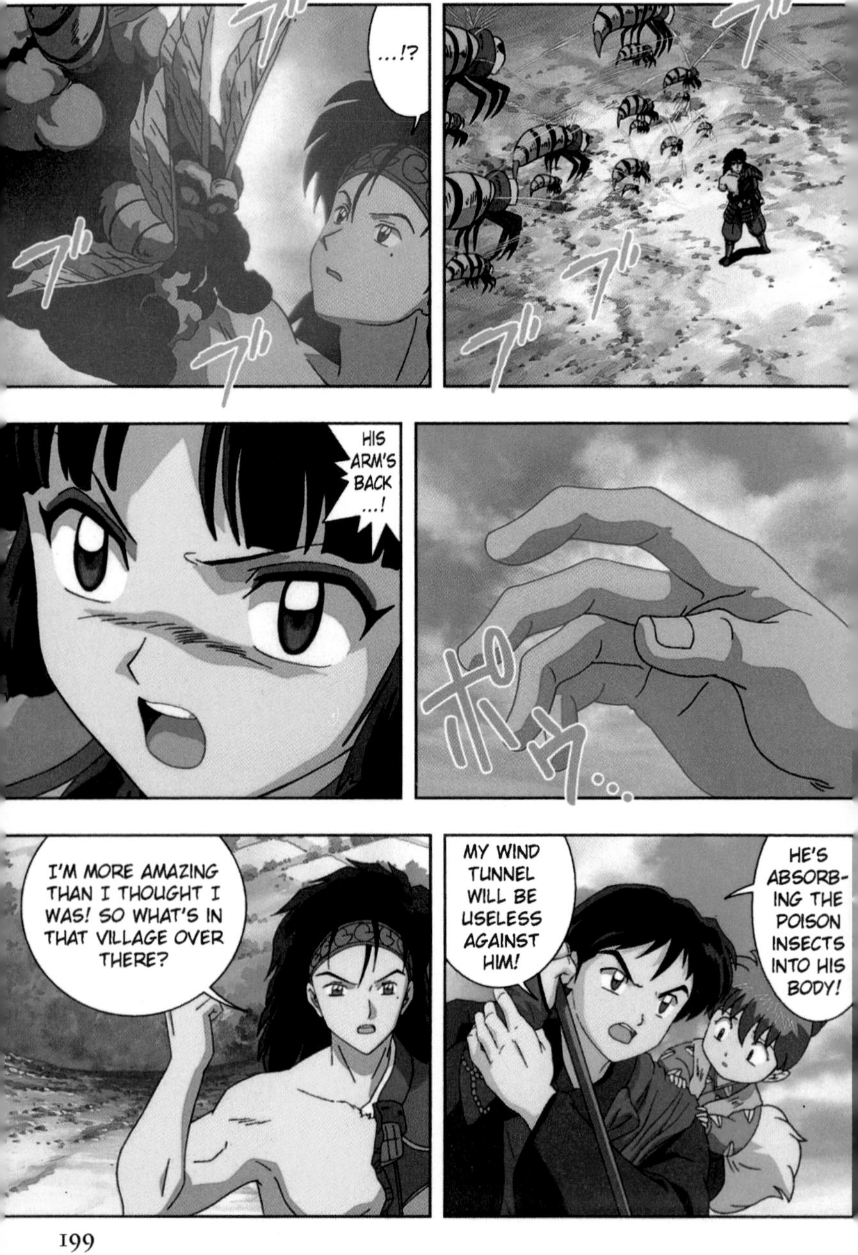
ブ
ブ
ブ
ブ
ブ
...!?
ブ
ブ
ポゥ...
HIS ARM'S BACK ...!
HE'S ABSORB-ING THE POISON INSECTS INTO HIS BODY!
MY WIND TUNNEL WILL BE USELESS AGAINST HIM!
I'M MORE AMAZING THAN I THOUGHT I WAS! SO WHAT'S IN THAT VILLAGE OVER THERE?

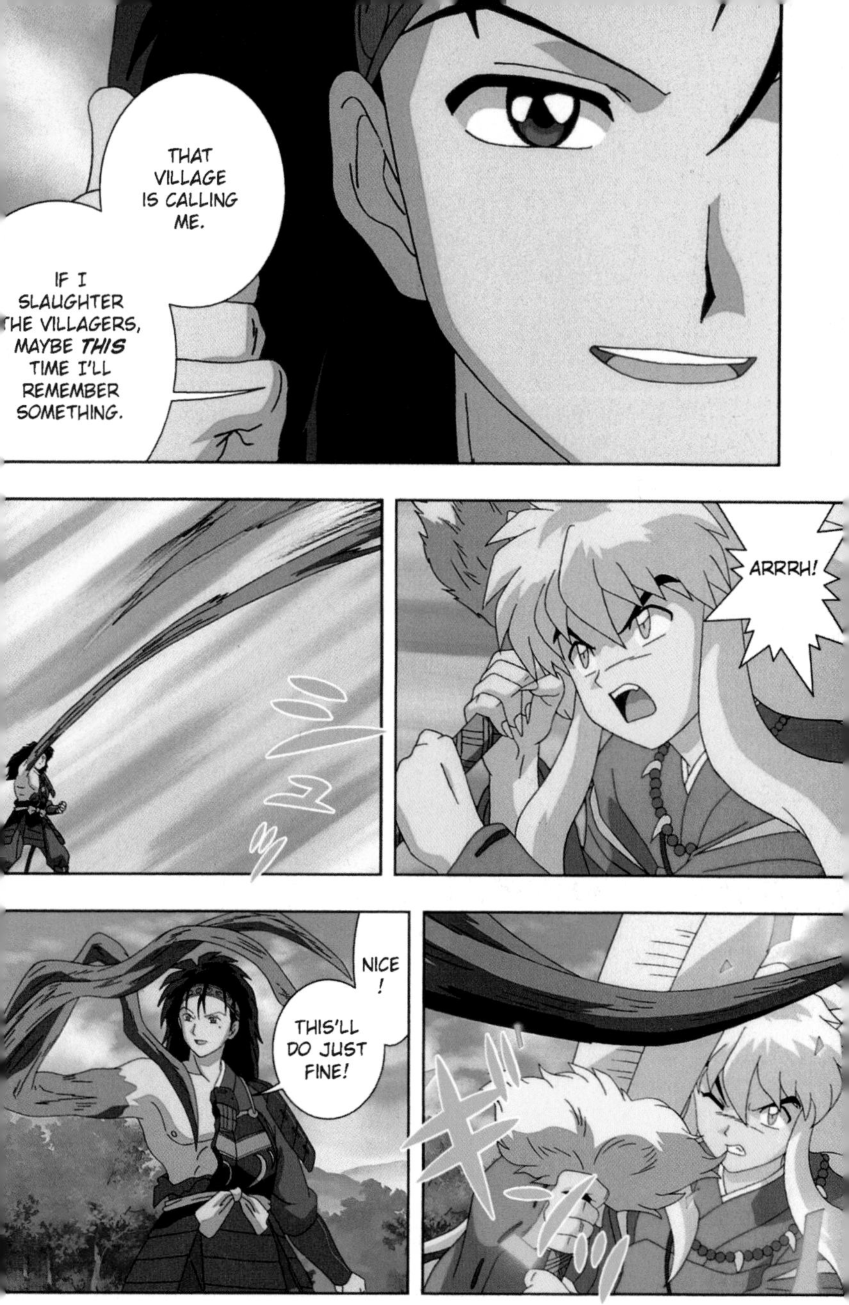
THAT VILLAGE IS CALLING ME.
IF I SLAUGHTER THE VILLAGERS, MAYBE *THIS* TIME I'LL REMEMBER SOMETHING.
ARRRH!
NICE!
THIS'LL DO JUST FINE!

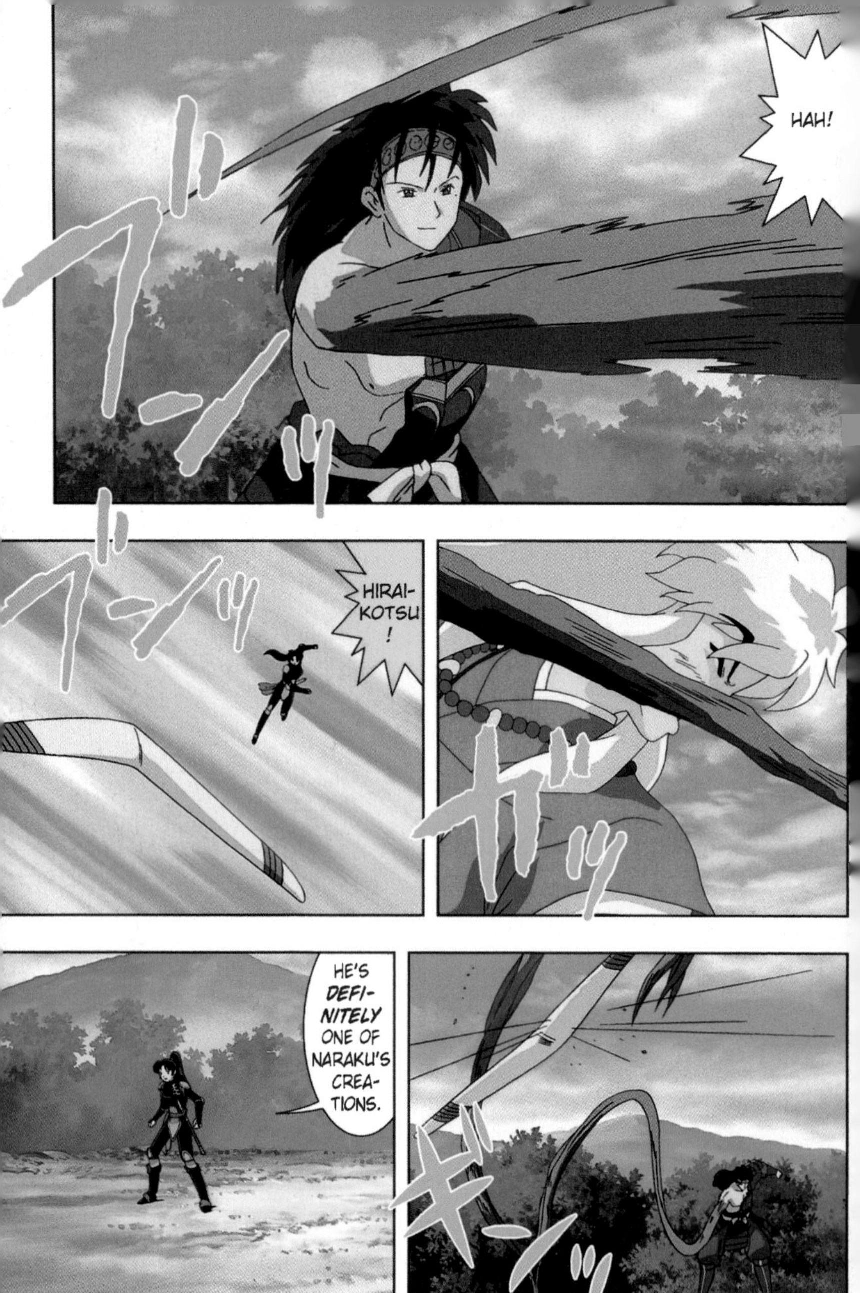
HAH!
ブーンッ
ガッ
HIRAI-KOTSU!
ブーンッ
ギーンッ
HE'S *DEFINITELY* ONE OF NARAKU'S CREATIONS.

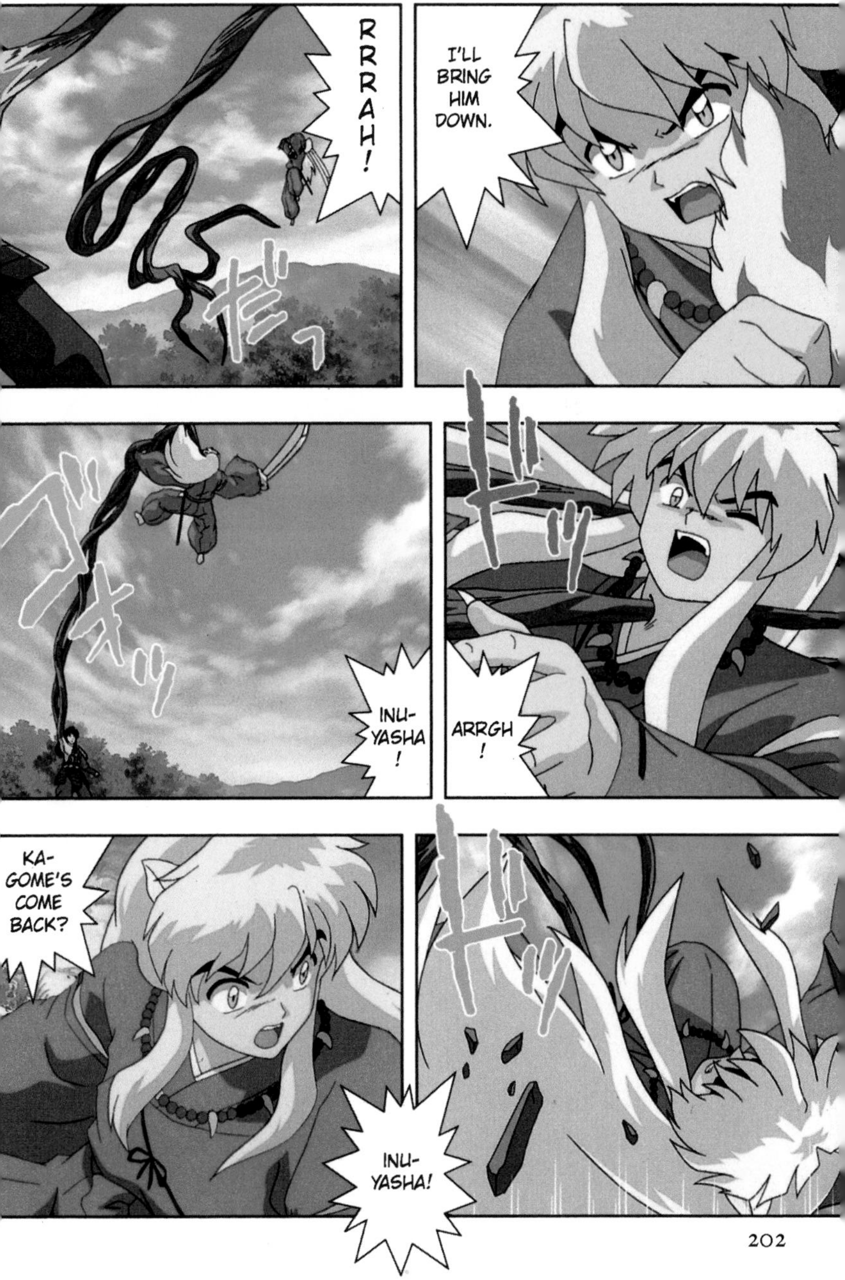
I'LL BRING HIM DOWN.
RRRAH!
ARRGH!
INU-YASHA!
KA-GOME'S COME BACK?
INU-YASHA!

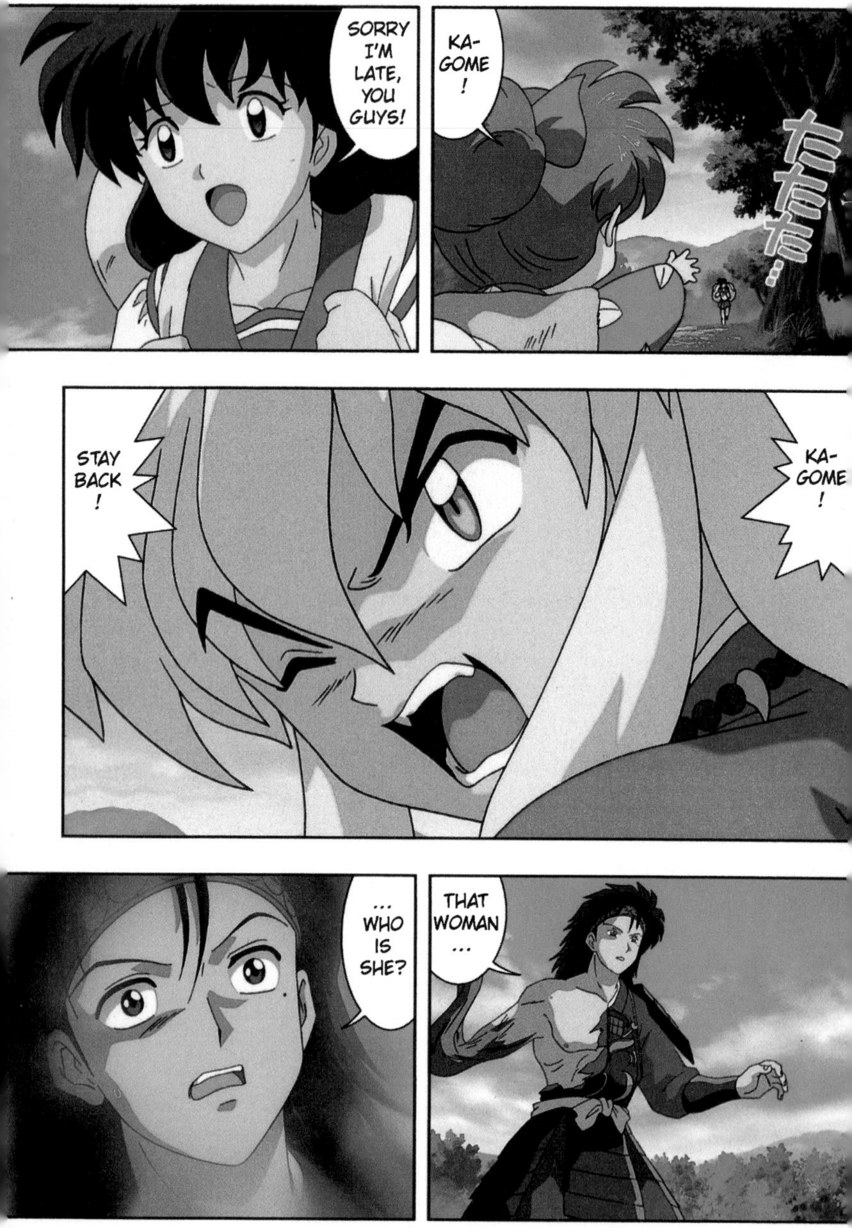
KA-GOME!
たたた…
SORRY I'M LATE, YOU GUYS!
KA-GOME!
STAY BACK!
THAT WOMAN…
…WHO IS SHE?

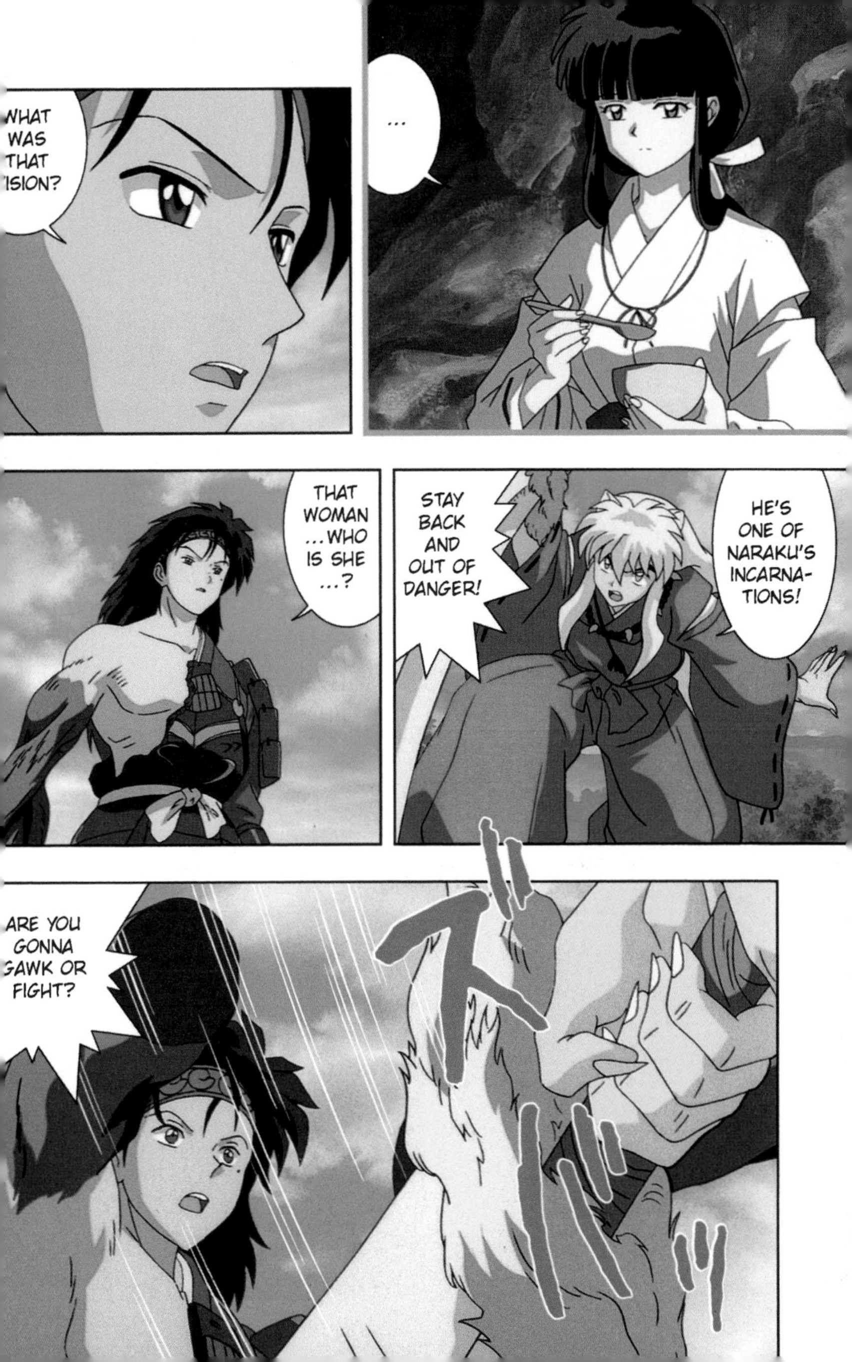
...
WHAT WAS THAT ISION?
HE'S ONE OF NARAKU'S INCARNATIONS!
STAY BACK AND OUT OF DANGER!
THAT WOMAN ...WHO IS SHE ...?
ズ
ARE YOU GONNA AWK OR FIGHT?

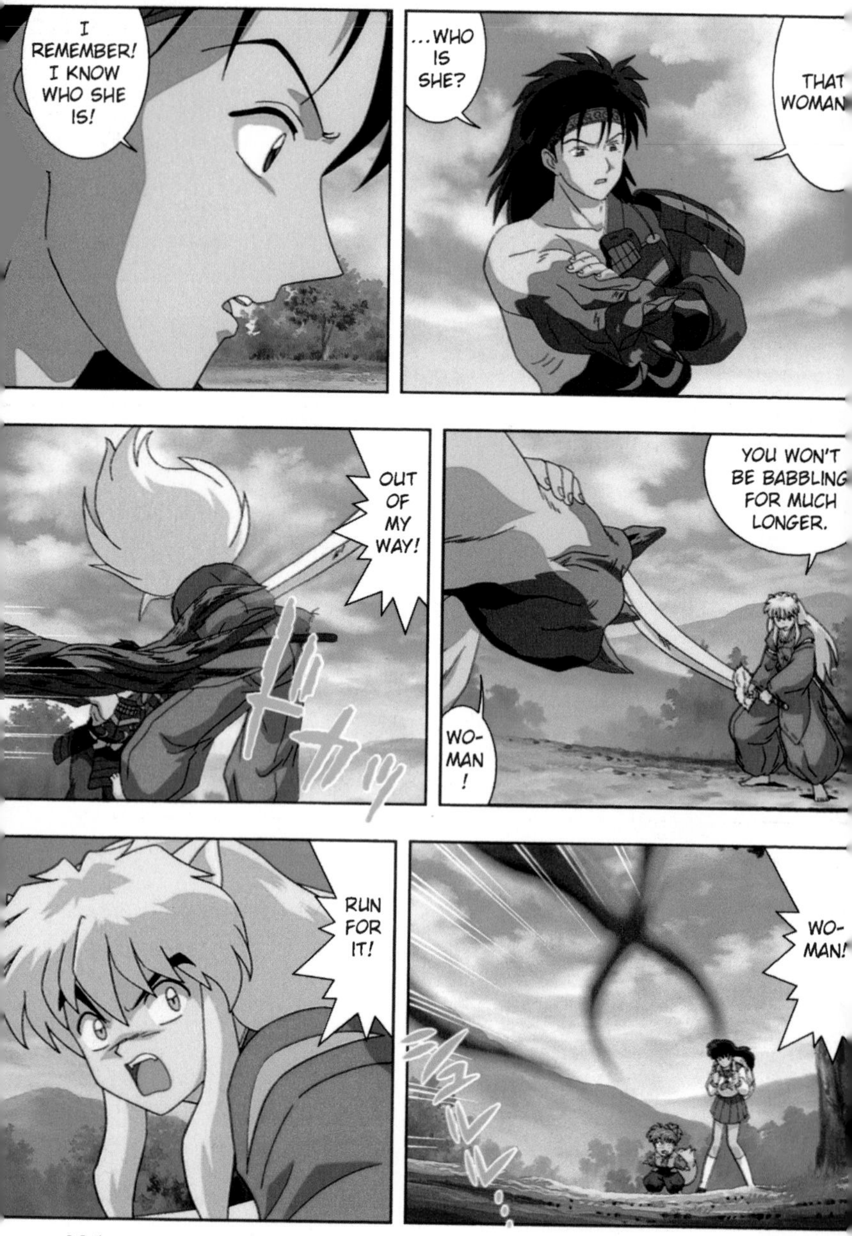
THAT WOMAN
...WHO IS SHE?
I REMEMBER! I KNOW WHO SHE IS!
YOU WON'T BE BABBLING FOR MUCH LONGER.
WO-MAN!
OUT OF MY WAY!
ドカッ
WO-MAN!
RUN FOR IT!

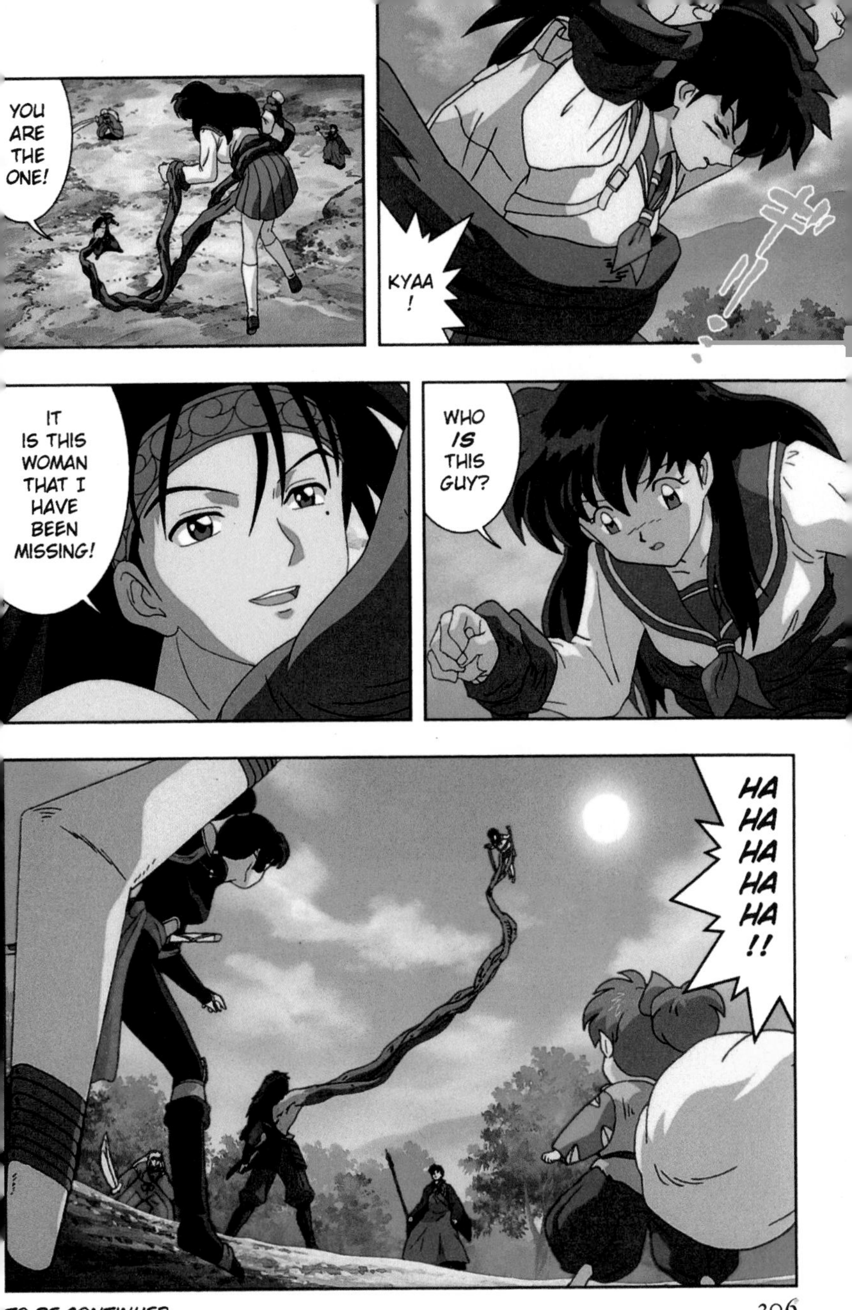
KYAA!
YOU ARE THE ONE!
WHO *IS* THIS GUY?
IT IS THIS WOMAN THAT I HAVE BEEN MISSING!
HA HA HA HA HA!!

TO BE CONTINUED

Glossary of Sound Effects

Each entry includes: the location, indicated by page number and panel number (so 3.1 means page 3, panel number 1); the phonetic romanization of the original Japanese; and our English "translation"—we offer as close an English equivalent as we can.

29.4 FX: Dosa (Kirara dumps her passengers, who fall on ground)

30.3 FX: Gan (clunk as Inuyasha is hit in the head with staff)

31.1 FX: Buuuuu…n… (insects buzzing)
31.2 FX: Bu bu bu (buzzing)

32.5 FX: Za (Kagura lands on her feet)

34.2 FX: Ba (Kagura brandishes fan)
34.3 FX: Goh (blades whoosh)
34.3 FX: Ta (Koga leaps)
34.4 FX: Ga ga ga (blades strike)
34.5 FX: Ga (blade strikes ground)

35.1 FX: Goh (whooshing)
35.2 FX: Dohn (Koga thrown by impact of blade)
35.5 FX: Ga ga ga ga (blades strike ground near Koga)

36.2 FX: Dohn (Koga gets thrown by impact of a blade)
36.4 FX: Ga (really big blade hits)

38.3 FX: Bu bu bu (insects buzzing)
38.5 FX: Bun (Sango's hiraikotsu flies)

39.1 FX: Zan (Sango throws her weapon)
39.2 FX: Pashi (demon sashimi)
39.4 FX: Da (Koga goes in for attack)

Chapter 67
The Howling Wind of Betrayal

6.1 FX: Doh (skull army comes for Koga)
6.4 FX: Goh (wind blades whoosh)
6.5 FX: Gyun (blades fly)

7.1 FX: Zan (blades strike)
7.2 FX: Kiin (shard flies off)

9.1 FX: Su (a shooting star)
9.2 FX: Sura (star turns into a vision of Sesshomaru)

10.1 FX: Goh (Kagura whooshes up to Sesshomaru on her feather)

11.2 FX: Cha (little metal clink as Sesshomaru puts his hand on his sword hilt)

15.2 FX: Goh (Kagura whooshes up)
15.5 FX: Goh (Kagura whooshes away)

16.3 FX: Su (Sesshomaru abruptly turns and walks off)

24.5 FX: Dokun dokun… (pulsating)

28.2 FX: Ta (Koga's footfall)

29.1 FX: Ta ta ta… (running)

53.4 FX: Zan (demon split into pieces)

54.1 FX: Go (demons split into chunks)
54.3 FX: Dosa (demon falls)

56.3 FX: Ba (Inuyasha lunges for jewel shards)
56.4 FX: Toh (Koga flips and lands)
56.5 FX: Pohh… (Koga rises to his feet)

57.3 FX: Ta (Koga runs off)

58.2 FX: Goh (Koga whooshes off)

60.1 FX: Su… (Kagura flies into courtyard on her feather)

61.4 FX: Gishi… (door to secret room creaks open)
61.6 FX: Kata… (Kagura follows)

62.3 FX: Gii… (creaking)
62.4 FX: Shurururu… (Naraku's tentacle snakes out at Kagura)

63.1 FX: Zuru (Kagura gets pulled in)

65.3 FX: Shuru (tentacle reaches for Kagura)
65.4 FX: Gishi… (tentacle squeezes)

Chapter 68
Shippo Gets an Angry Challenge

72.3 FX: Gorogoro… (cloud covers sun)

73.1 FX: Ka (lightning strikes)
73.2 FX: Doh (arrow lands)

78.1 FX: Bun (Inuyasha throws his blade)
78.2 FX: Zudo (Thunder Brother stabbed through the back)

40.1 FX: Baki (Koga's fist connects with Kagura's face)
40.3 FX: Kin… (shards get knocked loose)
40.6 FX: Ba (Koga lunges for jewel shards)

41.1 FX: Goh (whoosh)
41.3 FX: Go go (Koga knocked around by whirlwind)
41.5 FX: Go go go (Koga rolls over, still getting knocked around)

42.2 FX: Gohhhh… (whooshing)

43.2 FX: Da (Inuyasha dashes in)

44.1 FX: Kaaa… (dawn breaks)

45.1 FX: Gohhh… (whooshing)
45.2 FX: Dosa (Koga collapes)
45.4 FX: Goh (whoosh of whirlwind)
45.5 FX: Doh (a new whirlwind strikes Koga)

46.1 FX: Gohh… (whooshing)

47.1 FX: Suuu… (Inuyasha changes back into a demon)
47.5 FX: Ba (Inuyasha brandishes Tetsusaiga at Kagura)

51.1 FX: Da (Inuyasha lunges for Kagura)
51.2 FX: Gohh… (whoosh)
51.4 FX: Goh (whoosh)
51.5 FX: Doga (Inuyasha strikes with sword)

52.1 FX: Zan (Tetsusaiga cuts through whirlwind)
52.3 FX: Gohh… (whirlwind whooshes out of existence)

53.1 FX: Goh (demons whoosh in)
53.3 FX: Ba (demons hit)

78.3 FX: Zan (Inuyasha slashes through staff)

79.2 FX: Go (smack)

81.3 FX: Ka (lightning)
81.4 FX: Buru buru… (Shippo trembling)

84.3 FX: Poka poka poka (Koryu bops himself or herself three times on the head)
84.4 FX: Pon (pop!)

88.1 FX: Buru buru (trembling)

90.1 FX: Noro noro (Shippo walking on shaky legs)
90.2 FX: Ba (Inuyasha gestures with his sword)

91.2 FX: Zuzu… (Shippo skids along)

92.4 FX: Gara… (boulder teeters)

93.1 FX: Goro goro (boulder rolls down hill)
93.3 FX: Ta (Inuyasha leaps)
93.5 FX: Oro oro (Shippo freaking out)
93.6 FX: Dohn (boulder thunders down hill)

94.1 FX: Doh doh doh doh (boulder chases Shippo)
94.4 FX: Pon (Shippo turns into a ball)
94.5 FX: Basa (net captures Shippo]

98.2 FX: Tohn (Shippo takes out his secret weapon)
98.3 FX: Tohn tohn (Shippo plays with ball toy)
99.3 FX: Basa (Soten smacks Koryu on the head with scroll)

100.1 FX: Gohh… (whooshing as Kirara flies)

100.4 FX: Pata pata (catnip burning merrily)

101.5 FX: Goh (whoosh as Kirara falls)

105.1 FX: Boh (cover over hidden pit collapses)

111.2 FX: Za (disguised Koryu appears)

112.5 FX: Fuwa… (Koryu flies up)

113.1 FX: Gashi (Inuyasha gets a grip on Koryu)

115.4 FX: Sha (sound of crayon moving across paper)

117.2 FX: Cha (Soten unlocks Shippo's cage)
117.3 FX: Kacha (Soten opens door to cage)

118.2 FX: Go (Inuyasha bops Koryu on head)
118.4 FX: Ga (whack)

120.2 FX: Gabu (Koryu chomps on Inuyasha's hand)
120.3 FX: Go (pound on the noggin from Inuyasha)
120.4 FX: Bon (hissing smoke)

121.2 FX: Doh doh doh doh (Koryu shoots out arrows)
121.3 FX: Ga ga ga ga (arrows strike)
121.4 FX: Ba (Inuyasha attacks)

122.2 FX: Zan (Inuyasha attacks)
122.3 FX: Gohh… (whooshing)

123.4 FX: Doh doh doh (Koryu shoots arrows)
123.5 FX: Da (Inuyasha runs with Kagome)

140.2 FX: Poka (Shippo gets bopped on the head)

Chapter 69
Terror of the Faceless Man!

142.5 FX: Ki—n Ko—n… (the bell rings)

143.5 FX: Muni (Eria and Yuka pull Aumi's cheeks)

154.4 FX: Giri giri… (Kagome squeezes Sota super tight, maybe gives him a noogie)

158.2 FX: Pachi pachi (flames crackle)

159.22 FX: Goh (smack!)

162.4 FX: Meki (Naraku's arm changes shape)

163.2 FX: Zuru… (something pops out of Naraku's body)
163.3 FX: Doh (…and bounces to the ground)
163.6 FX: Zuru… (blob lurks and moves around)

164.1 FX: Ga hahaha---… [scripted: rowdy ad libs after a successful raid]
164.3 FX: Zuru… (something wicked this way comes)

165.3 FX: Zudo (bandits stabs at thing)
165.4 FX: Ga (hand from thing grabs sword)

166.1 FX: Zuru (the blob urns into a man)
166.2 FX: Zuzu… (rustling)

167.1 FX: Zuba (slash sound)

172. 3 FX: Beri (sticky sound as the Faceless Man pulls the face off)

124.3 FX: Za (Kagome falls)
124.5 FX: Ka (lightning)

125.3 FX: Doh (Inuyasha struck by lightning arrow)

126.4 FX: Ta (Soten attacks)
126.5 FX: Goh (whooshing)

127.1 FX: Ka (lightning shines)
127.2 FX: Dohn (lightning strikes)

128.2 FX: Ta (Kagome runs up to Inuyasha)
128.4 FX: Shu (here comes an arrow)
128.5 FX: Pashi (Inuyasha pulls out arrow)

129.1 FX: Ta (Inuyasha takes off after Koryu)
129.3 FX: Ga ga ga (punch punch punch)
129.4 FX: Pon (pop)

130.1 FX: Ta ta ta… (running)
130.2 FX: Ta ta ta…. (running)
130.3 FX: Gin (Shippo and Soten's magic attacks collide)
130.4 FX: Hara (Shippo winds up for a throw)
130.5 FX: Poro (something drops)

131.1 FX: Ba (here comes the giant top)
131.2 FX: Ka (sparks fly from daruma)
131.5 FX: Ba ba ba ba ba (mushrooms and acorns everywhere)

136.3 FX: Yoro (Shippo starts to walk off)

137.1 FX: Poi (Shippo throws box of crayons)
137.2 FX: Pashi (Soten catches box)

138.1 FX: Gu (someone makes a fist)

172.4 FX: Pasha (splash)
172.5 FX: Za (foot step)

175.1 FX: Cha
(Muso brandishes fighting staff)
175.3 FX: Ga (Muso strikes)

176.1 FX: Ba (Faceless Man reaches for Muso)
176.3 FX: Ga (Faceless Man grabs Muso)
176.5 FX: Da (something gruesome happens to Muso)

179.2 FX: Zan (slice)

180.1 FX: Doh doh doh (horse galloping)
180.3 FX: Doh doh doh… (galloping)
180.4 FX: Ka—n ka—n
(village bell rung in warning)

181.1 FX: Zuba (slash)
181.1 FX: Gohhh (whooshing)

182.1 FX: Dosa
(loot gets tossed to the ground)

183.1 FX: Gashan (pot thingy breaks as Faceless Man tosses it away)
183.4 FX: Doh doh doh… (galloping)

184.2 FX: Dokun… (pulsation)

186.1 & 2 FX: Doh doh doh doh doh…
(galloping)

187.1 FX: Da (running)
187.2 FX: Za (Inuyasha plants himself in the faceless man's path)

189.1 FX: Fu… (Kagome falls down well)

190.1 FX: Cha (Inuyasha puts his hand on his sword)

192.3 FX: Buu… (buzzing)

196.2 FX: Ba
(Inuyasha brandishes Tetsusaiga)
196.4 FX: Da (Inuyasha rushes Faceless Man)

197.1 FX: Zan (slash)
197.4 FX: Zuru… (the faceless man falls off his horse)

198.1 FX: Yoro… (the faceless man staggers as his arm is cut off)
198.4 FX: Buuu…n (poison wasps buzzing)
198.5 FX: Bu bu bu (buzzing)

199.1 FX: Bu bu bu (more buzzing)
199.2 FX: Bu bu bu (buzzing)
199.3 FX: Poh…
(the Faceless Man has a new arm)

200.3 FX: Shu
(Faceless Man shoots his arm out)
200.4 FX: Gin (tentacle arm clangs off sword)

202.2 FX: Da (Inuyasha leaps)
202.3 FX: Doh (Inuyasha is stabbed)
202.4 FX: Goh (the faceless man's arm grabs Inuyasha)
202.5 FX: Doh
(Inuyasha slammed to ground)

203.1 FX: Ta ta ta… (running)

204.5 FX: Zuba (big slash)

205.4 FX: Doka (Inuyasha is knocked aside)
205.5 FX: Shururu…
(tentacle arm snakes out)

206.1 FX: Giri (Kagome gets grabbed)

INUYASHA

The Ultimate Source for Fans!
Based on the best-selling manga series

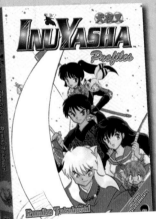

- Stunning, full color series artwork
- Historical feudal fairy tale facts
- Comments from Rumiko Takahashi on every aspect of her creative process
- Eight-page *Inuyasha* interview with Takahashi

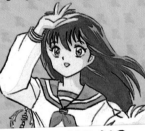

Complete
collection
at **store.**

inuyasha.viz.com

www.viz.com